Sustainable Entrepreneurship and Investments in the Green Economy

Andrei Jean Vasile
Petroleum-Gas University of Ploiesti, Romania

Domenico Nicolò
University Mediterranea of Reggio Calabria, Italy

A volume in the Advances in Business Strategy and Competitive Advantage (ABSCA) Book Series

IGI GLOBAL
DISSEMINATOR OF KNOWLEDGE
www.igi-global.com

Published in the United States of America by
IGI Global
Business Science Reference (an imprint of IGI Global)
701 E. Chocolate Avenue
Hershey PA 17033
Tel: 717-533-8845
Fax: 717-533-8661
E-mail: cust@igi-global.com
Web site: http://www.igi-global.com

Library of Congress Cataloging-in-Publication Data

Names: Jean-Vasile, Andrei, 1982- editor. | Nicolò, Domenico, 1966- editor.
Title: Sustainable entrepreneurship and investments in the green economy / Andrei Jean Vasile and Domenico Nicolò, editors.
Description: Hershey, PA : Business Science Reference, [2017]
Identifiers: LCCN 2016052951| ISBN 9781522520757 (hardcover) | ISBN 9781522520764 (ebook)
Subjects: LCSH: Sustainable development. | Entrepreneurship--Environmental aspects. | Investments--Environmental aspects.
Classification: LCC HC79.E5 S86862 2017 | DDC 658.4/083--dc23 LC record available at https://lccn.loc.gov/2016052951

This book is published in the IGI Global book series Advances in Business Strategy and Competitive Advantage (ABSCA) (ISSN: 2327-3429; eISSN: 2327-3437)

British Cataloguing in Publication Data
A Cataloguing in Publication record for this book is available from the British Library.

Advances in Business Strategy and Competitive Advantage (ABSCA) Book Series

ISSN:2327-3429
EISSN:2327-3437

Mission

Business entities are constantly seeking new ways through which to gain advantage over their competitors and strengthen their position within the business environment. With competition at an all-time high due to technological advancements allowing for competition on a global scale, firms continue to seek new ways through which to improve and strengthen their business processes, procedures, and profitability.

The **Advances in Business Strategy and Competitive Advantage (ABSCA) Book Series** is a timely series responding to the high demand for state-of-the-art research on how business strategies are created, implemented and re-designed to meet the demands of globalized competitive markets. With a focus on local and global challenges, business opportunities and the needs of society, the **ABSCA** encourages scientific discourse on doing business and managing information technologies for the creation of sustainable competitive advantage.

Coverage

- Value Chain
- Innovation Strategy
- Value Creation
- Business Models
- Ethics and Business Strategy
- Strategic management
- Core Competencies
- Strategy Performance Management
- Co-operative Strategies
- Small and Medium Enterprises

IGI Global is currently accepting manuscripts for publication within this series. To submit a proposal for a volume in this series, please contact our Acquisition Editors at Acquisitions@igi-global.com or visit: http://www.igi-global.com/publish/.

The Advances in Business Strategy and Competitive Advantage (ABSCA) Book Series (ISSN 2327-3429) is published by IGI Global, 701 E. Chocolate Avenue, Hershey, PA 17033-1240, USA, www.igi-global.com. This series is composed of titles available for purchase individually; each title is edited to be contextually exclusive from any other title within the series. For pricing and ordering information please visit http://www.igi-global.com/book-series/advances-business-strategy-competitive-advantage/73672. Postmaster: Send all address changes to above address.

Titles in this Series

For a list of additional titles in this series, please visit: www.igi-global.com

Managerial Strategies and Solutions for Business Success in Asia
Patricia Ordóñez de Pablos (University of Oviedo, Spain)
Business Science Reference • copyright 2017 • 376pp • H/C (ISBN: 9781522518860) • US $195.00 (our price)

Collective Creativity for Responsible and Sustainable Business Practice
Ziska Fields (University of KwaZulu-Natal, South Africa)
Business Science Reference • copyright 2017 • 385pp • H/C (ISBN: 9781522518235) • US $200.00 (our price)

Applying Neuroscience to Business Practice
Manuel Alonso Dos Santos (Universidad Católica de la Santísima Concepción, Chile)
Business Science Reference • copyright 2017 • 332pp • H/C (ISBN: 9781522510284) • US $200.00 (our price)

Handbook of Research on Fuzzy and Rough Set Theory in Organizational Decision Making
Arun Kumar Sangaiah (VIT University, India) Xiao-Zhi Gao (Aalto University, Finland) and Ajith Abraham (Machine Intelligence Research Labs, USA)
Business Science Reference • copyright 2017 • 474pp • H/C (ISBN: 9781522510086) • US $275.00 (our price)

Strategic Policy-Based Network Management in Contemporary Organizations
Kazuya Odagiri (Sugiyama Jogakuen University, Japan)
Business Science Reference • copyright 2017 • 186pp • H/C (ISBN: 9781683180036) • US $170.00 (our price)

Digital Entrepreneurship and Global Innovation
Ioan Hosu (Babeş-Bolyai University, Romania) and Ioana Iancu (Babeş-Bolyai University, Romania)
Business Science Reference • copyright 2017 • 301pp • H/C (ISBN: 9781522509530) • US $195.00 (our price)

IGI GLOBAL
DISSEMINATOR OF KNOWLEDGE
www.igi-global.com

701 E. Chocolate Ave., Hershey, PA 17033
Order online at www.igi-global.com or call 717-533-8845 x100
To place a standing order for titles released in this series,
contact: cust@igi-global.com
Mon-Fri 8:00 am - 5:00 pm (est) or fax 24 hours a day 717-533-8661

Editorial Advisory Board

Table of Contents

Detailed Table of Contents

Although young firms are very vulnerable, significant differences emerge by comparing the survival rates of the companies in the first stage of life in different countries and industries, of different sizes, and with different characteristics of the leader (team of co-founders): education, previous entrepreneurial experience, reputation, etc. Many variables influence the performance of the companies and their chances of survival. Each enterprise is a singularity. Thus, it is methodologically wrong and naive any attempt to define ideal models and general "recipes" to reduce the vulnerability of the young firms. This hypothesis is confirmed by the analysis of the survival rates of the young firms born in the USA and in EU. The variance of the five-year survival rate is very high by comparing companies from different nations, of different size classes, those operating in different industries, and those whose leaders have or not have any previous entrepreneurial experience. The lack of corporate reputation is the only weakness common to the young firms. Since these companies do not have a history that can prove their ability to satisfy their commitments toward the stakeholder, they haven't a reputation and therefore are very weak their bonds of trust with stakeholders. The first difficulty, these weak bonds of trust are broken and young businesses collapse in on themselves. To achieve sustainability, young firms must quickly build a corporate reputation to strengthen the bonds of trust with the stakeholders. By this way, they will be more resistant to the difficulties. This is the only effective general "recipes".

Enterprise sustainability depends on the economic performance. Achieving the economic performance is the main goal of every company since the beginnings. The instability of the economic environment imposes finding new paradigms in valuing the business opportunities. In this context, analyzing the influences of cost productivity profit trinomial in the contemporary enterprises represents an important step in identifying the potential growth avenues of the financial results. From this perspective, the chapter contains along the theoretical approaches regarding the sustainable entrepreneurship and investments paradigm in the green economy, an economic analysis of the main economic outcomes, in order to revile, both the competitive factors and risks assumptions for modern companies in the larger context of market globalization and integration. Also, this chapter aims to revile the evolution of the main factors which influences the economic performances in case of a real Romanian company during and post crisis period.

Disclosure of corporate social and environmental sustainability, resumed in ‘sustainability reports’, have occupied most of the attention of accounting thought and practice over the last few decades. Evaluation of ecological footprint and social sensitiveness is becoming relevant also for the investors. The chapter presents institutional disclosure concerning social, environmental, and integrated (financial, social and environmental) issues in a threefold perspective. The first is a historical one: after some definitions the birth and development of sustainability reports are presented to the reader. The second is a theoretical one: a paradigm or framework is developed for including what various experiences and literature have supplied until nowadays. The third is an empirical one presenting the main sustainability scoring criteria mostly used today, and an empirical survey on the car industry. Some concluding notes follow from the comparison of the aforementioned perspectives.

Green economy has become highly relevant over the last years. We are currently experiencing pollution issue and environmental decay that had its origin, however, in the previous centuries. The development of industrial economy inevitably entails the production of waste, in such a quantity that the environment is incapable of assimilating and transforming it naturally. Therefore, it is believed that one of the main green economy sectors is the waste retrieval and recycling, that means waste management. In the existing literature, this sector has not been deeply analyzed from a viewpoint of performance business analysis. Although a European legislation exists, every country manages this business by itself. After a historical introduction, this study, using the regression model, analyses the variables that influence the Italian business of waste retrieval and recycling, in the process establishing which of them has a deeper impact on performance.

This chapter proposes an important study of the cosmetics industry in relation to green marketing and sustainability concerns from the historical context and its evolution to the present day. The aim of this chapter is to explain the significant impact of green marketing on the cosmetics industry as a new future prospect that benefits all parties and what can be learned from history. This chapter intends to address the existence of sustainability concepts through history, which have become an interesting phenomenon in the present day. The aspects to be discussed include (1) new prospects and opportunities from green marketing for the cosmetics industry; (2) the evolution of the cosmetics industry; and (3) green marketing and green concepts in the cosmetics industry.

Transport systems are important pollution sources, mainly in terms of greenhouse gases, noise and land consumption. To mitigate the problem and safeguard airport development at the same time, the involved stakeholders are fixing goals, priorities

Preface

Sustainable development is increasingly relying on generation of economic growth whilst still protecting the environment. Such a growth is driven by green entrepreneurs who are utilizing green factors as their competitive advantage in competitive markets. They not only consider the lack of economic resources, or the optimal combination in production process and sustainable consumption, but also provide innovative entrepreneurial solutions in achieving a sustainable economic model in changing world.

The international market of green products is booming. Over the last decades it developed into the popular alternative to consumption of harmful products. Moreover, awareness of green production and interest to consumption of green products are growing internationally. In this context, the green entrepreneurship and sustainable investments on competitive markets are the valuable research fields, and the need for finding proper solutions and rich to pertinent conclusions is more than necessary.

However, research on green entrepreneurship to date has been upon entrepreneurial ventures, neglecting wider economic and social contexts within which they operate. The book addresses these wider networks of support and answers to such concerning subjects as how to ensure sustainable development of green entrepreneurship, attract investments, succeed on high-competitive markets and consider climate changes, resource paradigms, sustainable consumption, rural communities and environmental constrains for more environmentally friendly products and services.

The book main was to provide relevant theoretical frameworks and the latest empirical research findings in area of green entrepreneurship and its impacts into sustainable development of investment activity on competitive markets. The book was also designed to become a reference for practitioners, students, professors in field of green entrepreneurship research and investments by presenting the newest findings in the field and developing the theoretical framework. In this context the main objectives of the book were:

- To create a reference for practitioners, students, professors in field of green entrepreneurship research;

- To present the newest findings in the field of green entrepreneurship;
- To provide a platform for green entrepreneurship debate.

The theme is definitely impact editors' fields of research, since its major part is related to sustainable development of agricultural production through a range of activities, including green entrepreneurship. The publication is intended to become a continuation of editors' research of green economic structures in modern business and society.

The target audience of this book will be composed of professionals and researchers working in the field of green economics, investments and entrepreneurship. The book outcome is intended to be shared with an international network of stakeholders, including research institutions, universities, and individual researches in such spheres as: green development strategies, economic models and patterns, market economy, investments portfolio, administrative sciences and management, managerial techniques, sociology, business theory. Moreover, the book provides useful insights and support executives for policy makers and investors. The book contains nine chapters which offer an integrative approach regarding the research on sustainable entrepreneurship and investments.

In this context, Chapter 1 deals with the young firm's sustainability and corporate reputation: a comparison of the survival rates in the US and EU and it is written by prof. PhD Domenico Nicolò from the University Mediterranea of Reggio Calabria, Italy. The hypothesis of this chapter is based on the results of the analysis of the survival rates for young firms born in the USA and in EU. The author argues that the variance of the five-year survival rate is very high by comparing companies from different nations, of different size classes, those operating in different industries, and those whose leaders have or not have any previous entrepreneurial experience. Also, he argues that the lack of corporate reputation is the only weakness common to the young firms.

Chapter 2 presents theoretical and practical approaches in understanding the influences of cost-productivity-profit trinomial in contemporary enterprises development. The chapter is jointly written by PhD Andrei Jean-Vasile and Mrs. Alexandra Alecu, MA student at Petroleum-Gas University of Ploiesti, Romania. The instability of the economic environment imposes the analysis of the cost productivity profit trinomial influences in identifying the potential growth revenues of the financial results. The chapter contains along the theoretical approaches regarding the sustainable entrepreneurship and investments paradigm in green economy, an economic analysis of the main economic outcomes. Also, the chapter aims to revile the evolution of the main factors which influences the economic performances in case of a real Romanian company during and post crisis period.

Chapter 3 called "Integrated Sustainability Reports: Historical Survey, Theoretical Proposals, and Best Practices" presents institutional disclosure concerning social issues, environmental issues, and integrated (financial, social and environmental) issues under a threefold perspective. The first one is historical: after some definitions, the birth and development of sustainability reports is presented to the reader. The second one is theoretical: a paradigm or framework is attempted for including what various experiences and literature have supplied until nowadays. The third one is empirical, presenting the main using scoring criteria, about sustainability, and an empirical survey on the car industry. The chapter is designed by two Italian researchers Giuseppe Valenza from University of Reggio Calabria and Massimo Costa from University of Palermo.

Chapter 4 is concerning the "Game Theory Coopetitive Perspective for Sustainability of Global Feeding: Agreements Among Vegan and Non-Vegan Food Firms," and it is written by David Carfi (University of California Riverside, USA), Alessia Donato, (University of Messina, Italy) and Dania Panuccio, (University of Messina, Italy). In this study, the authors propose possible agreements among different food producers, in order to develop a new better conceived diet for the future generations, by using a competitive approach and game theory. Specifically, the authors shall consider food producers and sellers of vegan (respectively, vegetarian) and non-vegan (or non-vegetarian) food. The competitive approach used by the authors provides a mathematical game theory model, which could help producers of vegan food a simpler entry in the market and free significant publicity.

Meanwhile, the model could allow producers of non-vegetarian food a smooth transaction to vegetarian and vegan production. In particular, authors propose an agreement setting among McDonald's and Muscle of Wheat, because they think that Muscle of Wheat cannot enter a global market without the help of a large food producer already in the market. The game theory model represents an asymmetric R&D alliance between McDonald's and Muscle of Wheat.

Chapter 5 is called "Green Information System for a Sustainable Enterprise," written by Laura-Diana Radu (Alexandru Ioan Cuza University of Iasi, Romania), explores the necessity and applicability of green IS. Organizations are interested in adopting green technologies regardless if they refer to production processes, parts design or other activities that just secure the proper organization's functioning, as it results from recent studies. Considering these results, it is demanded that the green concept is assimilated in both the development and usage phase. As the author argues the literature has made it clear that this leads to environmental benefits, but it cannot guarantee that these initiatives will also benefit the organizations that implement green concepts. The criteria proposed by the author for early evaluation of the conditions needed to for green IS implementation can be used in the selection and approval phase of the agile life-cycle project model, in order to identify the organization's ability to adapt to these changes.

Chapter 6 is dedicated to the role of waste management in the green economy, an empirical analysis of economic data of the business. Massimo Saita and Maria Vittoria Franceschelli from the University of Milano Bicocca, Italy. This chapter contains an analysis conducted on a representative sample of the Italian retrieval and recycling sector, a sector of undoubtedly high relevance and importance within the green economy context. Authors argue that the analyzed companies record positive results altogether. The authors present also a few limitations of the study as: 1) the analysis has been conducted by analyzing solely the Italian retrieval and recycling companies which have lodged their financial statements in the last year; 2) reliance was placed exclusively on results from one year, the 2014 financial year; 3) The current market crisis, which has been already going on for several years, has undoubtedly impacted on company performances in general, hence those of the analyzed companies as well; 4) exclusive reliance was placed on the data available from the Aida database; 5) since any reference to other studies in the recycling sector was lacking, studies from different sectors were taken into account.

Chapter 7 is written by Suhaili Ramli form the University of York, United Kingdom and it is dealing with the green marketing form the prospect in the cosmetics industry. As the author argues this chapter proposes an important study of the cosmetics industry in relation to green marketing and sustainability concerns from the historical context and its evolution to the present day. The aim of this chapter is to explain the significant impact of green marketing on the cosmetics industry as a new future prospect that benefits all parties and what can be learned from history. This chapter intends to address the existence of sustainability concepts through history, which have become an interesting phenomenon in the present day. The aspects discussed include new prospects and opportunities from green marketing for the cosmetics industry, the evolution of the cosmetics industry and green marketing and green concepts in the cosmetics industry.

The Chapter 8 is dealing with the green airport investments to mitigate externalities - procedural and technological strategies and it is written by Maria Nadia Postorino from the Mediterranea University of Reggio Calabria, Italy and Luca Mantecchini and Filippo Paganelli from the University of Bologna, Italy. As the authors argue to mitigate the problem and safeguard airport development at the same time, the involved stakeholders are fixing goals, priorities and duties in order to promote the sustainable development of the air transport industry at global level and the wellness of local communities. It is desirable to estimate airport noise and carbon impacts in order to suitably manage them and identify strategies in line with the concept of green economy. In this chapter, a general framework to identify optimal procedures and methods to evaluate the effectiveness of policies addressed to reduce airport impacts on the airport surrounding is proposed. The case study of the airport of Bologna is presented as an example of Transport Company that effectively operates to minimize its noise and carbon impacts. According to the proposed general framework, impacts and estimated costs to achieve the status of green company have been computed

The final chapter of the book is addressed to the cover crops in the process of achievement of sustainability in the ecological systems of agriculture and it is written by Vladan Ugrenović, from the Institute "Tamiš" Pančevo, Serbia and Vladimir Filipović, Institute for Medicinal Plants Research "Dr Josif Pančić", Belgrade, Serbia. The authors start from the premise that the use of cover crops is widespread practice in organic farming systems. Cover crops can be defined as crops that are usually not grown commercially, and can have a multiple role in crop rotations. The benefit of cover crops has been known since long. Legumes are used as biological fixer of nitrogen for the next crop, and are established during periods when the soil is without major crops in order to reduce erosion. In recent years, the role of cover crops has been extended to the biocontrol of weeds, pests and diseases, as well as to the overall improvement of soil quality by increasing organic matter, encouraging the circulation of nutrients and reducing soil compaction.

In this context *Sustainable Entrepreneurship and Investments in the Green Economy* chapters presents specific aspects regarding the actual researches on sustainable entrepreneurship, business practices, resources usage aspects and investments in highly competitive and functional economies. The main topics of book addresses to the following aspects, but not limited to:

- Green marketing;
- Productivity and efficiency analysis;
- Contemporary enterprises functional paradigms;
- Best practices in refrigeration;
- Business investments strategies;
- Sustainable investments;
- Integrated sustainability reports;
- Ecological systems of agriculture;
- Externalities;
- Procedural and technological strategies for enterprises;
- Green airports;
- Cosmetics industry;
- Waste management;
- Green information system for a sustainable enterprise;
- Game theory;
- Global feeding;

- Vegan and non-vegan food firms.

The editors hope that this book will be a basically reference in the research field and it will bring new paradigm understandings in evolution of the environment and new business ideas, start-ups sustainability, clean tech start-ups, green incubators, accelerators and young firms sustainability, green spin off, knowledge and technological transfer, logistics, operation and production, green marketing, corporate organization, green districts, clusters, and networks, and other complementary research topics.

All submitted chapters were double-blind reviewed. There are no submission or acceptance fees for manuscripts submitted to the *Sustainable Entrepreneuship and Investments in the Green Economy* and all the manuscripts were accepted based on a double-blind peer review editorial process.

The editors of *Sustainable Entrepreneurship and Investments in the Green Economy* hope that this book provides a good framework for future researches and provides interesting readings for all those interested.

Andrei Jean-Vasile
Petroleum-Gas University of Ploiesti, Romania

Domenico Nicolò
University Mediterranea of Reggio Calabria, Italy

Acknowledgment

The editors wish to thank to all the contributors of this book for their interest and quality works and to all the anonymous referees for their help in improving the quality of the chapters submitted and accepted. Also, the editors are deeply thankfully to Mrs. Alexandra Alecu for her help in drafting and editing the manuscripts and to the IGI Global editorial staff involved in developing the current book project for their warm support and recommendations.

Chapter 1
Young Firms Sustainability and Corporate Reputation:
A Comparison of the Survival Rates in the US and EU

Domenico Nicolò
University Mediterranea of Reggio Calabria, Italy

ABSTRACT

Although young firms are very vulnerable, significant differences emerge by comparing the survival rates of the companies in the first stage of life in different countries and industries, of different sizes, and with different characteristics of the leader (team of co-founders): education, previous entrepreneurial experience, reputation, etc. Many variables influence the performance of the companies and their chances of survival. Each enterprise is a singularity. Thus, it is methodologically wrong and naive any attempt to define ideal models and general "recipes" to reduce the vulnerability of the young firms. This hypothesis is confirmed by the analysis of the survival rates of the young firms born in the USA and in EU. The variance of the five-year survival rate is very high by comparing companies from different nations, of different size classes, those operating in different industries, and those whose leaders have or not have any previous entrepreneurial experience.

DOI: 10.4018/978-1-5225-2075-7.ch001

The lack of corporate reputation is the only weakness common to the young firms. Since these companies do not have a history that can prove their ability to satisfy their commitments toward the stakeholder, they haven't a reputation and therefore are very weak their bonds of trust with stakeholders. The first difficulty, these weak bonds of trust are broken and young businesses collapse in on themselves. To achieve sustainability, young firms must quickly build a corporate reputation to strengthen the bonds of trust with the stakeholders. By this way, they will be more resistant to the difficulties. This is the only effective general "recipes". (Nicolò 2015; Nicolò & Ferrara 2015).

BACKGROUND

Companies are very fallible in their first stage of life (Reynolds & Miller, 1992; Van de Ven, 1992; Van de Ven et al., 1989; Venkataraman et al., 1990; Knaup, 2005; Knaup & Piazza, 2005). High vulnerability is a distinctive feature (general trait) of young companies (Nicolò 2015; Nicolò and Ferrara 2015).

According to the literature, the principal causes of weakness of young firms are:

1. Context variables (Mintzberg, 1973; Dubini & Schillaci, 1988; Buttà, 2003; Moore, 2006; Adner & Kapoor, 2010; Moss Kanter, 2012);
2. Strategic choices and the suitability of those choices to meet the characteristics of the industry (Biggadike, 1976; Miller & Camp, 1985; Cooper et al. 1986; Sandberg, 1986; McDougall et al. 1992);
3. Activities of the founder to give life to the company by spending the appropriate amount of time on essential processes before and after its foundation (Gartner, 1988; Bygrave, 1989; Timmons, 1990; Vesper, 1990; Longsworth, 1991; Cooper, 1993);
4. The sequence in which key start up processes are performed (Gartner, 1985; Van de Ven, 1992; Van de Ven & Poole, 1995; Van de Ven & Engleman, 2004; Carter et al., 1996; Aldrich, 1999; Delmar & Shane, 2002; Liao et al., 2005);
5. Characteristics of the founder/s (Child, 1972; Kirzner, 1979; Carland et al., 1984; Gartner, 1985; Katz & Gartner, 1988; Storer, 1988; Miles et al., 1988; Shaver & Scott, 1991). Background of the start up founders: social aspects of gender (Birley, 1989; Brush, 1992), tolerance to risk (Brockhaus, 1980), persistence (Brockhaus & Horwitz, 1986; Gatewood et al., 1995), education, expertise and entrepreneurial experience (Weick, 1972; Sandberg, 1986; Bird, 1993; Chandler & Hanks, 1994), and reputation (Nicolò 2015, Nicolò & Ferrara 2015).

Although scholars have emphasized the influence of some variables than the other, the analysis conducted in this paper sheds light on how many variables affect the chances of survival of enterprises during the first stage of life. As shown in the following sections, relevant differences can be observed by comparing survival rates of the young US and European companies in different countries and industries, by different sizes, with different characteristics of the leader (s), etc. Each enterprise is a singularity and no general "recipe" can be effective to lead young companies to overcome the first stage of life. This is because there are so many potentially critical factors and can be combined in so many different ways over time.

Variance of the Survival Rates of Young Firms in Different Cohorts and in Different Countries and Industries

This research examines the survival rates of young firms from USA (data set from Bureau of Labour Statistic) and EU countries (data set from Eurostat).

The following Table 1 shows a very low variance of the survival rates in US companies from 1994 to 2013. A naive observer would infer from US survival rates a stable rate of survival in 20 years, despite the volatility of the economic cycle. This wrong conclusion depends from the very high level of aggregation of the data. In the average rates there is homogeneous data created by phenomenon that is not linearly related.

The average of survival rates erases the differences from comparisons between countries and industries. These differences are evident observing the fifth year survival rates by country (Table 2) and industry (Table 3).

Table 1. Variance analysis of survival rates of new establishments in USA (Bureau of Labour Statistics, US Department of Labour)

Year	Variance 1994-2013
1st year survival rate	1.77
2nd year survival rate	3.10
3rd year survival rate	3.48
4th year survival rate	4.38
5th year survival rate	2.78
10th year survival rate	0.32
15th year survival rate	0.11

For the examined cohorts (from 2006-11 to 2010-15), variance analysis of the fifth year survival rate shows no linear trend: it is low for some nations and high for other (Table 2).

A no-linear trend also emerges by comparing the fifth year survival rates of different countries and cohorts. Variance analysis shows a relevant variance (from a minimum of 9.16 to a maximum of 17.36). It follows that the chances of survival are different depending on the country in which the companies are established and the year in which they were born (Table 2).

Relevant differences emerge also by comparing the fifth year survival rates of different industries and different cohorts (Table 3).

Variance analysis shows that in USA it is relevant for the survival chances the country where a company is established, the industry in which it operates and the year of birth (cohorts).

Even in Europe the survival rates of the enterprises show a low variance in time, for the cohorts from 2004/09 to 2008/13. This is the result of relying on the average trend, regardless of nation or industry. When focusing on segmented data by nation (Table 4):

Table 2. 5th year survival rates of private sector by country (Bureau of Labour Statistics, US Department of Labour)

Country	Cohorts					Variance (A)
	2010_15	2009_14	2008_13	2007_12	2006_11	
Alabama	50.10	48.80	46.30	42.30	42.10	**13.40**
Alaska	49.80	49.20	49.10	49.90	47.30	**1.09**
Arizona	48.50	45.10	42.10	40.40	41.10	**11.22**
Arkansas	47.20	43.50	44.70	46.60	44.30	**2.47**
California	55.80	53.00	53.00	48.70	45.40	**16.88**
Colorado	48.30	47.50	44.60	44.20	43.90	**4.17**
Connecticut	54.60	46.70	44.20	45.40	43.90	**19.46**
Delaware	45.50	50.20	46.90	45.00	39.00	**16.60**
Columbia	47.70	50.20	43.30	43.40	42.20	**11.74**
Florida	47.00	45.40	39.50	38.40	35.90	**22.52**
Georgia	50.40	49.60	47.20	45.70	45.60	**4.89**
Hawaii	53.70	57.30	52.50	50.20	49.40	**9.83**
Idaho	48.80	45.80	42.00	37.50	39.80	**20.68**
Illinois	50.80	50.20	47.90	47.80	47.40	**2.43**

continued on following page

Table 2. Continued

Country	Cohorts					Variance (A)
	2010_15	2009_14	2008_13	2007_12	2006_11	
Indiana	50.60	51.30	49.10	47.10	48.00	**3.06**
Iowa	54.00	52.30	50.90	51.80	51.90	**1.30**
Kansas	49.20	48.90	49.10	49.50	50.10	**0.22**
Kentucky	49.60	50.20	50.40	48.80	46.40	**2.63**
Louisiana	51.30	50.00	49.10	47.60	46.80	**3.27**
Maine	52.10	53.70	49.10	49.40	49.60	**4.10**
Maryland	49.80	48.40	44.50	44.10	44.80	**6.75**
Massachusetts	60.10	58.40	57.40	54.60	52.80	**8.64**
Michigan	54.00	52.80	50.40	46.60	45.60	**13.71**
Minnesota	54.10	55.00	49.20	48.60	44.40	**18.86**
Mississippi	48.30	48.70	45.30	46.30	45.10	**2.81**
Missouri	52.00	52.70	47.90	48.70	49.40	**4.41**
Montana	54.00	51.90	48.00	46.10	46.10	**12.75**
Nebraska	55.40	53.70	53.00	52.40	50.90	**2.75**
Nevada	48.30	47.90	45.40	43.10	41.80	**8.21**
New Hampshire	48.60	46.90	44.60	42.60	43.00	**6.60**
New Jersey	47.00	46.90	44.10	44.60	43.50	**2.65**
New Mexico	46.20	44.50	43.50	43.40	45.50	**1.51**
New York	51.20	51.00	49.60	49.80	49.80	**0.57**
North Carolina	51.40	50.20	47.30	47.20	48.40	**3.41**
North Dakota	57.40	57.20	55.30	56.20	57.90	**1.09**
Ohio	52.10	50.20	49.10	48.00	47.70	**3.22**
Oklahoma	51.20	49.40	48.20	49.50	46.70	**2.80**
Oregon	50.10	48.20	44.80	42.10	42.90	**11.80**
Pennsylvania	49.40	50.00	50.40	51.80	53.20	**2.35**
Puerto Rico	49.70	49.90	46.00	46.10	44.00	**6.60**
Rhode Island	49.00	46.70	44.50	45.60	45.00	**3.19**
South Carolina	49.40	46.10	42.90	41.20	43.60	**10.18**
South Dakota	56.20	53.30	53.10	55.10	55.50	**1.89**
Tennessee	47.30	46.80	43.70	43.20	43.80	**3.72**
Texas	52.10	52.20	50.10	49.20	49.60	**2.00**
Utah	50.70	48.60	42.40	40.90	43.00	**18.24**

continued on following page

Table 2. Continued

Country	Cohorts					Variance (A)
	2010_15	2009_14	2008_13	2007_12	2006_11	
Vermont	51.20	52.30	47.00	46.60	44.90	**10.13**
Virginia	48.90	48.10	45.70	45.60	44.60	**3.34**
Virgin Islands	51.10	46.30	43.20	50.20	40.10	**21.56**
Washington	49.20	47.90	41.30	40.30	42.50	**16.30**
West Virginia	51.50	48.80	49.40	47.70	46.60	**3.43**
Wisconsin	56.40	55.60	53.40	51.50	51.80	**4.86**
Wyoming	50.40	48.80	46.20	45.30	48.20	**4.18**
Variance (B)	**9.16**	**10.89**	**14.35**	**16.46**	**17.36**	

Table 3. 5th year survival rates of private sector by industry (Bureau of Labour Statistics, US Department of Labour)

Industries	2010_15	2009_14	2008_13	2007_12	2006_11	Var.
Agriculture, forestry, fishing, and hunting	66.40	64.00	60.90	60.10	57.40	**12.26**
Mining, quarrying,and oil and gas extraction	49.00	51.10	49.10	49.70	51.10	**1.08**
Utilities	50.20	56.10	51.70	57.50	56.60	**10.57**
Construction	47.80	42.50	36.10	33.80	33.20	**39.57**
Manufacturing	54.00	50.50	48.10	48.80	49.40	**5.38**
Wholesale trade	46.40	46.30	43.90	43.70	43.80	**1.96**
Retail trade	56.90	58.20	54.00	52.90	52.10	**6.88**
Transportation and warehousing	50.30	47.80	44.20	41.80	41.10	**15.50**
Information	43.00	40.90	40.10	42.90	41.90	**1.59**
Finance and insurance	52.00	49.50	46.60	43.80	43.40	**13.65**
Real estate and rental and leasing	54.60	54.50	47.10	42.80	40.10	**43.98**
Professional, scientific, and technical services	46.00	45.00	43.50	44.50	44.50	**0.82**
Management of companies and enterprises	53.00	53.80	51.40	51.80	53.30	**1.04**
Administrative and waste services	47.90	46.10	44.10	44.50	44.10	**2.73**
Educational services	54.00	54.00	51.70	51.70	53.60	**1.43**
Health care and social assistance	60.80	59.40	62.30	60.10	55.90	**5.66**
Arts, entertainment, and recreation	52.90	47.50	45.50	43.40	41.80	**18.57**
Accommodation and food services	52.80	52.90	51.50	50.30	50.30	**1.63**
Other services (except public administration)	54.60	54.30	52.70	51.60	51.20	**2.37**
Var.	**29.42**	**35.60**	**41.83**	**46.18**	**44.24**	
Total private	51.40	50.10	47.80	46.40	45.40	

Table 4. Survival rates variance - cohorts 2009/13 (Eurostat)

Countries	1st year survival rate	2nd year survival rate	3rd year survival rate	4th year survival rate	5th year survival rate
Austria	2.86	12.91	9.50	4.70	4.13
Belgium	0.60	8.04	5.42	2.49	0.85
Denmark	4.09	6.58	3.94	3.61	0.39
Germany	1.00	1.40	0.97	0.67	0.71
Luxembourg	0.03	0.70	1.47	1.55	3.12
Netherland	33.17	31.96	30.96	36.41	14.23
Norway	2.73	3.50	5.50	2.94	2.68
Sweden	0.36	0.89	5.38	4.48	1.99
UK (Eurostat)	20.93	22.01	22.03	14.12	6.30
Ireland	3.16	4.49	27.39	32.57	4.84
Bulgaria	3.30	4.97	4.98	3.40	3.48
Czech Rep.	4.26	2.22	3.52	6.72	4.78
Estonia	6.84	19.56	17.38	60.18	1.99
Hungary	5.08	8.21	8.30	2.86	5.17
Latvia	10.14	16.32	2.52	22.56	20.16
Poland	1.45	5.97	4.94	4.02	2.29
Slovenia	0.88	7.08	28.56	37.58	29.15
Slovakia	17.22	36.74	21.96	10.79	12.83
Spain	4.41	3.84	2.45	6.86	14.20
France	28.21	51.12	47.66	21.48	0.64
Italy	16.01	17.82	7.85	3.16	2.17
Cyprus	3.04	7.48	19.61	33.54	-
Portugal	0.63	4.33	15.04	20.28	17.40

1. Netherland, France, Slovenia, UK, Estonia, and Slovakia show a very high variance of the business survival rates in time;
2. on the contrary, the variance is low in East Europe, moreover in Bulgaria, Czech Rep., Hungary, and Poland;
3. in the Mediterranean countries the variance analysis of the survival rates for the above mentioned cohorts reveal that some countries a low variance in time (Spain and Italy) and for others a high variance (Cyprus, France, and Portugal).

Young firms performance, then survive or death, depend from the economic cycle. But, why survival rates in time see almost unchanging (in the examined cohorts 2009-13)? For example, the consolidation of established firms may statistically result in a growth cycle. But this shows well established companies growing as a whole. Also when the economic cycle is rescinding it implies well established firms are primarily the cause for these downward trends. This trend can be noticed in employment and other statistical indicators. But for the young companies, the economic cycle does not significantly affect their vulnerability nor do young firms affect these statistics with respect to the volume of start up failing in the first 5 years. The ability to measure survival rates also requires more distinctive factors best explained by reputation. The factors affecting start ups are not related to economic factors but unique factors to their young age. The factors resulting from companies being young is invariant with respect to statistics, which effectively measure the trends of well established firms.

By comparing the average survival rates of different countries, a high variance emerges (Table 5). European Union is not homogeneous ecosystem. Developing countries coexist with advanced economies with numerous degrees of hierarchy for established firms and young firms. This creates a complex ecosystem where the startups are greatly at the mercy of factors unrecorded by the data agencies. The survival rate is much more significant comparing nation by nation to determine which countries are fostering survival chances for start up ecosystems. The ability to foster start up survival requires a focus on the ability to distinguish by national context.

The heterogeneous nature of the nations and industries make survival data generic with respect to specific causes. The ability to compare this data requires significant experience with being able to interpret contextual factors not shown in the data. The company birth rate in some countries may be be due to low barriers of entry, while low survival rates may be due to regulatory factors. So the ability to determine the context of data is often not related to the data itself.

In the all the nations, first stage of life is very hard for enterprises. In the statistics it appears relative to only year or nation. Nevertheless, by comparing survival rates nation by nation and industries there are wide differences in interpretation. But the data only shows central tendencies of aggregated variables in homogenous models. The differences show the diversity of factors related to startup ecosystems. This ability to aggregate data defines a context unable to account for specific variables. Experience with a specific country and its environment profiles the qualitative aspects not inherent in statistical data.

The more wide the phenomenon investigated and the longer a period of observation, the more it appears regular and constant in time. If the details are segmented into 'space', country and sector; then the trend is irregular (nonlinear) as a result of differences between national ecosystems. A comparison of models derived from logical assumptions reveals specific constraints but not the possible factors weight

Table 5. Average Survival Rates by country - cohorts 2009/13 (Eurostat)

Countries	1th year survival rate	2th year survival rate	3th year survival rate	4th year survival rate	5th year survival rate
Austria	88.74	78.54	70.71	66.38	62.00
Belgium	90.33	71.19	62.24	56.06	59.44
Germany	76.97	61.62	51.75	44.84	39.86
Luxembourg	89.43	78.23	68.82	61.15	54.63
Netherland	-	74.17	62.12	54.10	47.83
Var. Centre Europe	**39.70**	**47.98**	**55.27**	**65.34**	**81.05**
Denmark	73.45	60.53	53.13	47.18	42.56
Norway	82.56	66.59	55.66	47.52	40.91
Sweden	96.39	85.94	75.94	67.97	61.74
Finland	74.85	66.65	63.43	54.30	53.27
Var. North Europe	**110.52**	**122.27**	**105.09**	**94.49**	**95.26**
UK (Eurostat)	88.62	72.63	56.12	46.63	38.39
Ireland	83.64	73.24	65.77	57.21	49.94
Var. Islands	**12.43**	**0.19**	**46.57**	**56.02**	**66.67**
Bulgaria	81.27	67.15	57.63	50.76	45.14
Czech Rep.	79.41	66.58	58.64	50.91	45.90
Estonia	84.11	69.28	59.49	50.81	45.48
Hungary	74.30	59.10	49.79	43.05	37.75
Latvia	79.53	63.23	50.88	44.60	40.25
Poland	87.41	70.80	56.15	48.54	43.54
Var. Est Europe	**20.10**	**18.15**	**16.93**	**12.07**	**10.91**
France	81.77	70.28	61.99	56.30	51.94
Spain	77.27	63.66	53.97	47.81	43.40
Italy	82.36	70.78	61.51	54.05	48.65
Slovenia	89.82	76.98	66.82	60.26	56.68
Var. Mediterranean Europe	**27.04**	**29.59**	**28.17**	**27.13**	**31.21**
Total Var.	**37.00**	**42.33**	**45.20**	**46.19**	**54.86**

affecting an individual startup during its ecological relationship to the market. Observing the trend of survival rate at 5 years with reference to the United States or Europe reveals a high consistency over time. If, however, we observe the trend of the survival rate in the different countries, there emerge variations in 'time', with reference to the same country. The meaning of those rates is much more significant to the experts of the national regions and industries even though the macro trend remains aggregated.

When considering individual countries, we realize that there is a certain variability that makes it very influential country in which the companies were born about their chances of survival. There are, in fact, countries in which the 5-year survival is particularly low, as survival rates have values of around 40% (Hungary, UK, Germany, Norway, Latvia), and countries where rates have values instead close to 60% (Austria, Sweden and Belgium). The common element is that these survival rates are lower than those of mature companies, however, the rates are far from similar.

Undoubtedly firms undergo a tough selection and only fifty percent of them, on average, survives the fifth year. This selection was harder in the first 2 years, especially in the first. In subsequent years, however, the survival rate of businesses survivors grows. High vulnerability, therefore, a characteristic inherent to young enterprises, which distinguishes them from those that are in development stages subsequent to the first. Many companies are extinguished shortly after birth because run out of money before achieving their market targets (Damodaran 2009)

Table 6. Average 5th year survival rates by industry - cohorts 2009/13 (Eurostat)

Industry	Var.
Mining and quarrying	241.19
Manufacturing	108.72
Electricity Gas, Steam, air conditioning supply	180.32
Water supply, severage, waste management, remediation activity	106.30
Construction	122.09
Wholesale, retail. trade repair of motor vehicles and motorcycles	68.18
Transportation and storage	86.24
Accommodation and food services activities	39.26
Information and communication	88.46
Real estate activities	253.34
Professional, scientific and technical activities	75.58
Administrative and support service activities	111.22
Education	138.73
Human health and social work activities	114.40
Arts, entertainment and recreation	95.50
Other services activities	221.73
ICT	96.49

The same conclusion is reached by examining the survival rates of companies operating in different industries. For the 2009-2013 cohorts, in different industries, there was a high variability in survival rates five years in different countries.

Other Factor Influencing Survival of Young Firms: Birth Rate, Size (in Terms of Number of Employees), Experience of the Founder/s

Enterprises birth rates, size of the companies, entrepreneurial experience of the founders, and survival rates of European companies are shown in the following sections.

Birth Rates and Survival Rates an Inverse Relationship

A higher birth rate of business should result in a more hard selection of the newly established companies. Higher birth rates also characterize the areas where there is a low selection because there are low barriers to entry. As a consequence people start weak companies with low chance to survive.

For these reasons, in industries and countries with high birth rates it is obvious to expect lower survival rates. To test this hypothesis, a correlation between birth rates and survival rates at 5 years in different European countries is proposed.

For the European nations, the survival rates at 5 years, reported aggregate statistical data based on industries. The so-called 'Business Economy' has been whether there is a correlation with birth rates and survival rates. The calculation showed a significant inverse correlation, -0.6655889776: to higher birth rates, as had been supposed, are associated with lower survival.

Entrepreneurial Experience of Founder (s) and Survival of the Young Firms

From the logical point of view and theoretical, if the founder has had previous business experience, this should increase the chances of survival of the company. To test this hypothesis, the survival rates of businesses started by the founders with experience and with no previous experience were compared.

The low survival rates of young companies partly depends on the high percentage of the firms born on the initiative of a founder with no previous entrepreneurial experience. In Europe, for example, this percentage amounted on average to 77% (about 3 firms of 4).

To measure the influence of the experience of the founder (s) on survival rate of the newly made firms, the analysis of two samples was conducted. One sample results from entrepreneurs with experience. The other sample results from a dataset

Table 7. Birth rates and 5th year survival rates by country - years 2008/13 (Eurostat)

GEO/TIME	2008	2009	2010	2011	2012	2013	Average Birth rates	Average 5th year Survival rates
Belgium	5.41	4.58	5.23	5.25	5.01	3.59	4.85	60.04
Bulgaria	18.17	17.62	11.39	10.96	13.02	11.93	13.85	45.14
Czech Republic	3.81	10.93	11.43	10.55	8.66	8.02	8.90	45.90
Denmark	-	9.79	10.94	12.09	10.83	10.26	10.78	42.56
Germany	9.25	8.31	8.72	8.66	7.95	7.39	8.38	39.86
Estonia	18.20	9.94	11.09	11.87	12.17	-	12.65	45.48
Ireland	5.89	6.93	5.75	6.27	6.76	-	6.32	49.94
Spain	7.47	7.19	7.81	7.98	8.22	8.38	7.84	43.40
France	9.70	12.98	12.78	11.02	10.14	9.50	11.02	51.94
Croatia	-	-	-	-	8.20	10.13	9.17	-
Italy	7.06	7.22	6.65	6.67	6.97	7.08	6.94	48.65
Cyprus	3.27	3.04	3.91	4.52	5.45	6.15	4.39	48.91
Latvia	13.95	16.42	16.70	19.19	16.83	15.31	16.40	40.25
Lithuania	20.04	14.72	21.07	23.71	24.88	23.05	21.25	21.83
Luxembourg	9.92	9.27	9.52	9.70	9.52	9.78	9.62	54.63
Hungary	10.15	9.17	10.01	9.98	8.60	8.18	9.35	37.75
Malta	-	-	6.96	3.48	6.20	6.20	5.71	-
Netherlands	14.45	12.10	9.85	11.01	6.44	10.07	10.65	50.11
Austria	8.44	7.98	8.01	7.66	7.46	7.38	7.82	60.67
Poland	13.15	12.84	13.81	12.46	11.52	12.41	12.70	43.54
Portugal	14.62	12.13	11.85	12.39	12.47	14.53	13.00	30.24
Romania	14.66	9.48	8.71	13.00	12.26	22.18	13.38	43.01
Slovenia	11.72	11.33	10.33	10.16	10.09	13.25	11.15	56.68
Slovakia	15.51	16.34	13.19	14.39	10.58	9.95	13.33	40.79
Finland	10.20	8.98	9.92	9.78	8.90	6.14	8.99	47.44
Sweden	7.10	7.09	7.52	8.19	6.84	7.06	7.30	61.74
United Kingdom	12.99	10.09	10.48	11.57	11.80	14.66	11.93	39.54
Norway	9.58	8.68	7.72	8.17	8.70	9.21	8.68	40.91
Switzerland	-	-	-	-	-	-	-	-
Turkey	-	10.45	-	23.23	-	-	16.84	-

with entrepreneurs with no experience. This supposition without criticism would inevitably lead to wrong conclusions because the survival of businesses depends on numerous other variables. In this case this is important because this parameter of founder experience did not show significant correlation with survival rates. Thus the rate of survival is influenced by the experience of the founder, but this is not a justifiable claim from aggregate data.

For example, in the data for the European countries, there is no correlation between experience and survival at 3 and 5 years. The correlation index was very low: 0.04 for the survival rate at 5 years, and -0.04 for the survival rate at 3 years.

It is possible to suppose: young companies are very vulnerable because many of them are born on the initiative of entrepreneurs with no experience. The countries where the highest percentage of first-time entrepreneurs do not match those where survival is lowest. This result is only seemingly contradictory because it confirms the survival of businesses as a conglomerate of many variables.These differ from

Table 8. Entrepreneurial experience of the founder/s and the survival rates of young firms (2008/13) (Eurostat)

Country	Total (A)	No experiences (B)	% No experiences (B/A)	5th year survival rate (Business Economy 2010)	3rd year survival rate (Business Economy 2008)
Bulgaria	17.156	14.316	0.83	0.43	0.55
Czech Rep.	59.529	52.291	0.88	0.44	0.56
Denmark	7.709	5.785	0.75	0.42	
Estonia	1.968	1.099	0.56	0.46	0.63
France	24.736	17.740	0.72	0.51	0.66
Italy	143.004	102.200	0.71	0.50	0.65
Latvia	1.915	1.172	0.61	0.44	0.61
Lithuania	2.327	1.530	0.66	0.25	0.44
Luxembourg	1.294	620	0.48	0.54	0.69
Austria	13.463	11.182	0.83	0.62	0.73
Portugal	11.774	7.079	0.60	0.31	0.46
Romania	46.604	38.606	0.83	0.45	0.66
Slovenia	3.644	2.815	0.77	0.60	0.76
Slovakia	21.341	19.053	0.89	0.42	0.56
Sweden	12.203	7.548	0.62	0.62	0.77
Total	368.667	283.036	0.77	0.47	

sector to sector, from country to country, and depend on the characteristics of the firms and their founders. But these are not homogenous or continuous entities where aggregate data is accurate all the time. The importance is to find the capacity where aggregate data cannot be distinctly applied to specific variables without some form of considering a larger set of relevant variables.

Enterprises Size and Survival of Young Firms

The number of employees is a key indicator of the firm's size. To verify the existence of a correlation between the size, and the survival of young companies, we have used the data from Eurostat to the survival rate at 3 and 5 years of cohorts from 2008 to 2012, by country and by size, in terms of number of employees (1 to 4 employees 5 to 9 employees and with 10 and more employees).

The comparison reveals a strong correlation between the size and the survival of enterprises in all countries. Survival rates at 3 and 5 years far less for companies with a number of employees from 1 to 4 (micro-firms) than those with a workforce of between 5 to 9 and those with more than 10 employees. These last two classes have survival rates very similar to each other and much higher than those of micro companies. The exception can be observed in Estonia, Latvia and Lithuania, where the survival rates don't change.

The survival rates of companies that have more than 5 employees remain almost constant. Micro-enterprises weakness should depends by the inherent fragility of small businesses.

The number of employees and the survival of young companies are related, not only from a static point of view, in the sense that micro-enterprises are more vulnerable than those which have a greater number of employees, but also from a dynamic point of view: the average size of companies that survive will grow over time. The long series data of US firms that refers to the cohorts 1994-2015 (Table 9), confirm that the average size, in terms of number of employees, businesses survivors grows with the passage of time (http://www.bls.gov/bdm/us_age_naics_00_table7.txt). This demonstrates that companies that grow are those who can best overcome the difficulties and that, therefore, survive.

The data shown shed light on the European young companies, and those in the US. Undoubtedly undergo a tough selection and that, on average, only about fifty percent of them exceeds the fifth year. This selection was harder in the first two years, especially in the first. In subsequent years, however, the survival rate of businesses survivors grows (Table 9). High vulnerability, therefore, is a constant characteristic of the young companies that distinguishes them from the bigger ones.

Table 9. Number of employees and survival rates by country (2008/12) (Eurostat)

Countries	3rd survival rates by country (average years 2008-12)			5th years survival rates by country (average years 2008-12)		
	1 to 4 empl.	5 to 9 empl.	10 + empl.	1 to 4 empl.	5 to 9 empl.	10 + empl.
Czech Republic	54.94	72.29	74.15	43.29	60.85	63.93
Estonia	53.84	55.18	56.06	38.58	41.13	42.76
Spain	44.71	60.53	59.12	32.93	45.47	44.32
Italy	54.88	67.61	62.24	40.41	50.26	46.06
Latvia	58.73	63.80	67.16	44.81	45.68	48.15
Lithuania	82.27	83.68	84.73	-	-	-
Luxembourg	65.45	76.58	75.22	50.14	59.23	65.59
Hungary	41.94	51.51	48.46	28.61	37.82	34.41
Austria	68.42	79.06	77.44	58.57	70.59	69.38
Portugal	53.97	71.94	70.55	39.00	56.58	52.76
Romania	52.80	62.37	63.99	38.87	48.64	51.83
Slovenia	62.04	80.69	86.08	50.64	68.37	71.73

Sustainability of Young Firms and Corporate Reputation

The ability for these variables to be combined in various ways, exerts different effects when considering start ups as a whole. A focus on the founder may not consider properly the specific parameters in the environment of the start up. Thereby even finding the balance or equilibrium of these factors is not enough to resolving the issue of start up creation and survival.

Some particular cases can be stated to demonstrate the applicability of these models and the limitations. For example, a female entrepreneur with significant experience in her industry may have no expertise with startups and no reputation among her team, but a great reputation in her sector. There is an applicable model for studying gender based differences and expertise based differences but not one that is accurate for both. So a female entrepreneur may face significant challenges compared to a male colleague with similar expertise due to factors unseen with purely quantitative models. This is primarily due to the complex system surrounding startups, which prevents current models from holding outside the linear model. For example, the IT sector has different expertise required to interpret characteristics of startup founders from the commodity sector. And then these sectors have different properties in different regions of the country and in different countries. Each case is a singularity from these models because social systems are not homogenous spaces.

Table 10. Survival rates and average employment of survivors in USA (1994/2015) (Bureau of Labor Statistics, US Department of Labour)

Annual openings	Survival rates since birth	Survival rates of previous year's survivors	Average employment of survivors
March 1994	100.0	-	7.3
March 1995	79.6	79.6%	9.1
March 1996	68.1	85.6%	10.3
March 1997	60.6	89.0%	11.4
March 1998	54.3	89.6%	12.5
March 1999	49.6	91.3%	13.2
March 2000	45.2	91.1%	14.2
March 2001	41.5	91.8%	14.9
March 2002	38.3	92.3%	15.0
March 2003	35.7	93.2%	15.3
March 2004	33.6	94.1%	15.8
March 2005	31.8	94.6%	16.4
March 2006	30.3	95.3%	16.9
March 2007	28.7	94.7%	17.5
March 2008	27.2	94.8%	17.9
March 2009	25.5	93.8%	17.5
March 2010	24.1	94.5%	17.7
March 2011	23.0	95.4%	18.4
March 2012	22.0	95.7%	19.1
March 2013	21.2	96.4%	19.8
March 2014	20.3	95.8%	20.5
March 2015	19.5	96.1%	21.2

The interdependencies between variables influencing a company result in multiple possibilities changing over time, which often prevent the cause and effect from having a repeatable condition (Poole et al., 2000; Aldrich, 2001; Van de Ven, 2004; Nicolò, 2013). This is even more evident when one considers that each variable potentially influential on the survival of businesses presents a peculiar reaction time (Coda, 1983; Mouritsen & Bekke, 1999; Anderson-Gough et al., 2001; Nandhakumar & Jones, 2001) and a different degree sensitivity with respect to the stresses which it receives from the other. Over time also some variables influential lose relevance or leave the stage, others come into play (Nicolò, 2009, 2013).

As living organisms, therefore, companies can also cease to exist as a consequence of indefinite causes. Start ups are ecological components in a complex systems that evolve in a non-predictable way in a dynamic and turbulent environment (Mandelbrot, 2004). Every company constitutes a singularity, as has its structural characteristics and operational (genetic traits) that distinguish it from all others (Buttà, 2003), also with regard to the ability to overcome difficulties. It is therefore not possible to predict the outcome of the genetic process (Nicolò 2015; Nicolò & Ferrara 2015).

Therefore limited interpretations using statistical correlations often depend on the survival of young companies (effect) and on variable factors (causes). Companies, as parts of a complex system, have their operations influenced by various factors and the survival results (survival/failure) can not be interpreted by deterministic schemes (Morin, 1993).

Our research confirmed that business survival depends on many variables. It is impractical to build pathways to success of the genetic process of the enterprises on the basis of forced statistical correlations between some (necessarily few) variables (causes) and the survival of enterprises (effect). It is also impossible to identify all the remedies to the many causes that contribute to determining the crisis and the extinction of the newly established firms.

There is a general cause behind the characteristic weakness of young companies: the weakness of the bonds of trust with stakeholders which results from the lack of reputation. The lack of a history that can prove their ability to last over time, while remaining faithful to the commitments made to the stakeholders, in fact, gives rise to "weak links" with human resources, technical and financial they need to survive and develop. This trait makes these young firms very fragile compared to older companies. This source of weakness is inherent to all the companies in the first stage of life. The occurrence of the first difficulties, these bonds are severed and the company collapses on itself (Nicolò 2015; Nicolò & Ferrara 2015).

Building a reputation make companies more resistant than younger inevitable difficulties they face to establish itself in the market and achieve financial sustainability. The focus is on dynamic factors common to all young firms in the ability to have a resistance to the effects of failure. Much like how credit ratings protect established firms in macroeconomic models, the reputation can protect young firms in their daily operations with stakeholders.

Business survival requires the fulfillment of the expectations and interests of stakeholders (Pfeffer & Salancik, 1978). Otherwise lenders, suppliers, and investors will leave the company, and it will collapse on itself due lack of resources (Nicolò, 2001). Companies must also win the trust of customers. The ability to maintain these relationships is due to reputation.

The lack of reputation is also one of the fundamental causes of the frequent crises affecting small family business during generational chande of leadership.

Family business survival is affected from the lack of reputation of the successor to the leadership. Reputation of the family company is defined by its founder. When the transition to a new leader occurs, it causes a tremendous risk of failure due to the loss of reputation. The successor of the previous executive must win the trust of stakeholder, otherwise company will lose all the needed resources. The close identification that exists in these companies between the leader and the company, the successor puts a very difficult challenge: win the trust of customers and stakeholders. (Nicolò, 2001)

If the firm has a good reputation with stakeholders; then customers purchase their products because of the confidence in the expectations of the firm products. In these circumstances, even the investors and lenders consider the company worthy of trust. All other conditions being equal, investors will remain patient for longer term returns because they consider it low financial risk (Nicolò, 2015; Nicolò & Ferrara, 2015).

After the birth, firms deplete their cash supply more rapidly than their reputation is built. There is the high risk of running out of funds before winning the trust of customers. For this reason, companies must build a reputation expediently to strengthen ties with customers and stakeholders. This effort results in the company being more resistant to the difficulties of the startup stage (Nicolò, 2015; Nicolò & Ferrara, 2015).

The moment when companies decide to enter the market (Drucker, 1986) should follow encouraging signals from stakeholders through 'pilot-experiments'. The desire of many startups, as in software and fashion, to follow trends and ephemeral signs leads them to enter a market without preparation for risks and proper channels to sustain their operations. Gaining a reputation in the market is very important for the survival chances of the companies. This accumulated wealth of reputation starts a 'domino effect' spreading the confidence of stakeholders in the firm's ability to provide them appropriate rewards.

The reputation building process is fostered by strategic partnerships with suppliers, dealers, research centers, universities, etc. In this way, young companies can gain the confidence of other stakeholders through the building of trust networks. For example, if a young firm meets customers expectations, it can also gain the confidence of suppliers. This trust results in an effect of imitation, where the investors will now also trust the developing reputation of the start up. The 'domino effect' of these events to build reputation results in a model of trust (Nicolò, 2015; Nicolò & Ferrara, 2015).

This forms a fundamental characteristic of the relation of the market to young firms. Potential stakeholders trust the future expectations of the startup based on how active stakeholders maintain relations with the startup. This extends beyond investment equity and contracts with suppliers as is seen in national and industry data.

The characteristic of the founders and the company performance define a goodwill value deriving from a valuable intangible assets of the company: its reputation. The value of the brand is the fundamental driver of the company's value.

This reputation is built with patience and experience over time. It derives from trust of stakeholders and creates trust towards other stakeholders.

A short term orientation of companies is to sell in high volumes and develop market share to reach the IPO stage. A long term orientation of some companies based on providing long term value leads to the whole ecosystem developing a stable and long term reputation. This value driver to reputation is seen in established ecosystems but not so well in aggregated data.

The reputation building process must be started in the gestation stage also participating to business idea and business plan competitions. (Cannice, 2004; Wen & Chen, 2007; Russell et al., 2008; Bell, 2010; Ross & Byrd, 2011)

Young companies can take advantage from the reputation of the founder / s, if they have had previous business experience successful (Child, 1972; Chandler & Hanks, 1994; Buttà, 1995, 2003). On the contrary, the lack of experience of the founders is considered by the stakeholders a source of risk in itself. This has a negative impact on corporate reputation (Nicolò, 2015; Nicolò & Ferrara, 2015).

The ecosystem also can foster / hinder the process of building the company's reputation. Some ecosystems are highly specialized (for example, tourism, agro-industry, in research and in the high education, technology, fashion, etc.). Businesses can benefit from the brand of their ecosystem, since it attracts customers and human resources with high expertise and specialization. There are clear advantages for firms engaging in activities consistent with the specialization of the ecosystem in which they operate. The choice of the place in which to start the company, therefore, is crucial to mitigate the vulnerability.

Corporate reputation can be considered as a 'magnet' that attracts human, technical and financial resources. This attractive force changes in intensity due to interaction with the attractive forces exerted by other companies. The market entry of a competitor with a good reputation reduces the intensity of the attractive force exerted by other companies, which have to pay higher costs to maintain the bonds of trust with customers and stakeholders. (Nicolò, 2015; Nicolò & Ferrara, 2015)

From this perspective, it is easy to understand why young companies suffer the negative effects of the better reputation of businesses already established. They have no history that can testify to the company's ability to meet the expectations of stakeholders, the drafting of a strategic plan based on assumptions and estimates credibility plays a crucial role in accelerating the process of building a reputation. (Nicolò, 2015; Nicolò & Ferrara, 2015)

It is spreading more and more the conviction of data and big data to overshadow fundamental tools like the business plan. The business plan is useless only if it is a document of expectations and obligations to investors. This is because the assumptions in the business plan are often contradicted by reality. This reduces the trust in the business plan to convey a trustworthy reputation. And the focus on valuation on young firms causes the business plan to focus on gaining money before trust. Many business projects fail even if their implementation was planned in detail. In contrast, some companies achieve success even if they started without preparing a plan or even a product. This contradicts the data suggested by national and industry data because it demonstrate that start ups rely heavily on stakeholder trust to exist in the first years. The gestation stage focused on planning relationships with stakeholders is a method to overcome external and internal limits to their capacity.

This opinion is the result of a misunderstanding of the function of strategic planning. It must be regarded as a formal model and analytical by which:

1. Subject to criticism in a systematic way the assumptions underlying the strategy of starting and, in this way, correct errors and inconsistencies before giving life to the company;
2. Accelerate the process of building a company's reputation, which is the prerequisite for the realization of "strong ties" of trust with customers and stakeholders, thereby enhancing the company's ability to overcome the difficulties characteristic of the phase of startup;
3. Promptly perceive the need to modify the objectives and the strategic choices over the life of the company and, in this way, take an evolutionary process that preserves the consistency of their strategic approach with respect to changing conditions and variables of their the context of operation

Businesses may extinguish for many causes, within the company or arising from its environment, always different in each case. If a company ceases shortly after being established, errors of assessment in the design were committed, giving rise to a company with genetic defects (Nicolò 2015; Nicolò and Ferrara 2015).

CONCLUSION

Many studies and research have shown that a high percentage of businesses does not exceed the first stage of life. The high vulnerability is therefore a common feature of all the young firms. This trend is confirmed by our analysis of survival rates of European and US companies.

Businesses can cease to exist for many causes. Each company is a singularity, different from all the other, even for its ability to overcome the difficulties of the start up. Therefore, in order mitigate the vulnerability of young companies in their start-up, is naive any attempt to define principles and models based on statistical correlations between some variables, seen as causes, and the success / failure of the genetic process, seen as the effect.

This paper has highlighted the differences that emerge by comparing survival rates of companies operating in different countries and sectors, of different sizes (in terms of number of employees), and with characteristics of the startup leadership. (experienced startups and first time startups)

To counteract the high vulnerability of companies in the first stage of life it is effective to build a strong corporate reputation. By this way companies develop an immunological system to many categories of risk. This increases the ability to recover from the initial years of high risk. This is because a company with a strong reputation will be able to maintain the bond of trust with stakeholders even in periods of financial constraints.

The preparation of business plans increases the survival chances. This analytical model helps to build a strong reputation and to prevent errors and inconsistencies of the assumptions underlying the start up strategy.

REFERENCES

Adner, R., & Kapoor, R. (2010). Value creation in innovation ecosystems: How the structure of technological interdependence affects firm performance in new technology generations. *Strategic Management Journal, 31*(3), 306–333. doi:10.1002/smj.821

Aldrich, H. E. (1999). *Organizations evolving*. London: Sage Publications.

Aldrich, H. E. (2001). Who wants to be an evolutionary theorist: Remarks on the occasion of the Year 2000 OMT Distinguished Scholarly Career Award Presentation. *Journal of Management Inquiry, 10*(2), 115–127. doi:10.1177/1056492601102004

Anderson-Gough, F., Grey, C., & Robson, K. (2001). Tests of time: Organizational time-reckoning and the making of accountants in two multi-national accounting firms. *Accounting, Organizations and Society, 26*(2), 99–122. doi:10.1016/S0361-3682(00)00019-2

Australian Bureau of Statistics Business Register (ABSBR). (n.d.). *Counts of Australian Businesses, including Entries and Exit, Jun 2009 to Jun2013*. Retrieved from http://www.abs.gov.au/AUSSTATS/abs@.nsf/Lookup/8165.0Main+Features1Jun%202009%20to%20Jun%202013?OpenDocument

Bell, J. (2010). Student business plan competitions: who really does have access? *Small Business Institute National Conference Proceedings, 34*(1), 18-25.

Biggadike, R. C. (1976). *Corporate diversification: entry, strategy and performance*. Cambridge, MA: Harvard University Press.

Bird, B. J. (1993). Demographic approaches to entrepreneurship: The role of experience and background. *Advances in Entrepreneurship, Firm Emergence, and Growth, 1*, 11–48.

Birley, S. (1989). Female entrepreneurs: Are they really different? *Journal of Small Business Management, 27*(1), 32–37.

Brockhaus, R. H. (1980). Risk taking propensity of entrepreneurs. *Academy of Management Journal, 23*(3), 509–520. doi:10.2307/255515

Brockhaus, R. H., & Horwitz, P. S. (1986). The psicology of the entrepreneur. In D. L. Sexton & R. W. Smilor (Eds.), *The Art and the Science of Entrepreneurship* (pp. 25–48). Cambridge, MA: Ballinger.

Brush, C. G. (1992). Research of women business owners: Past trends, a new perspective and future directions. *Entrepreneurship: Theory and Practice, 16*(4), 5–30.

Buttà, C. (1995). *La genesi dell'impresa*. Milano: Franco Angeli.

Buttà, C. (2003). Elementi per una concettualizzazione del processo genetico. *Sinergie, 61-62*, 71–95.

Bygrave, W. D. (1989). The entrepreneurship paradigm (II): Chaos and catastrophes among quantum jump. *Entrepreneurship: Theory and Practice, 14*(2), 7–30.

Cannice, M. V. (2004). *Getting In on the University Business Plan Competition Circuit*. October 19. http://www.entrepreneur.com/article/73208

Carland, J. W., Hoy, F., Boulton, W. R., & Carland, J. A. (1984). Differentiating entrepreneurs from small business owners: A conceptualization. *Academy of Management Review, 9*(2), 354–359.

Carter, N., Gartner, B., & Reynolds, P. (1996). Exploring Start-up Event Sequences. *Journal of Business Venturing, 11*(3), 151–166. doi:10.1016/0883-9026(95)00129-8

CBS. (n.d.). *Statistical Abstract of Israel, 1014. Central Bureau of Statistics, Business Demography, A Collection of Statistical Data from the Business Register, 2003 – 2011*. Retrieved from http://www1.cbs.gov.il/webpub/pub/text_page_eng.html?publ=63andCYear=2011andCMonth=1

Chandler, G. N., & Hanks, S. H. (1994). Founder Competence, the environment and venture performance. *Entrepreneurship: Theory and Practice, 18*(3), 77–90.

Child, J. (1972). Organization structure, environment and performance: The role of strategic choice. *Sociology*, *6*(1), 2–22. doi:10.1177/003803857200600101

Coda, V. (1983). L'analisi delle relazioni di causa-effetto nel governo delle aziende. *Finanza Marketing e Produzione, 3*.

Cooper, A. C. (1993). Challenges in predicting new firm performance. *Journal of Business Venturing*, *8*(3), 241–254. doi:10.1016/0883-9026(93)90030-9

Cooper, A. C., Willard, G. E., & Woo, C. Y. (1986). Strategies of high-performing new and small firms: A reexamination of the niche concept. *Journal of Business Venturing*, *1*(3), 247–260. doi:10.1016/0883-9026(86)90003-0

Damodaran, A. (2009). *Valuing young start-up and growth companies estimation issues and valuation challenges*. Stern School of Business, New York University.

Davis, A., & Olson, E. M. (2008). Critical competitive strategy issues every entrepreneur should consider before going into business. *Business Horizons*, *51*(3), 211–221. doi:10.1016/j.bushor.2008.01.010

Delmar, F., & Shane, S. (2002). What firm founders do: A longitudinal study of the startup process. In W. D. Bygrave, C. G. Brush, P. Davidsson, & J. Fiet (Eds.), *Frontier of Entrepreneurship Research*. Babson College.

Drucker, P. F. (1986). *Innovazione e imprenditorialità, Etas, Milano*. Eurostat. Business Demography in Europe Statistics. Retrieved from http://ec.europa.eu/eurostat/web/structural-business-statistics/entrepreneurship/business-demograpy

Dubini, P., & Schillaci, C. E. (1988). L'influsso delle variabili ambientali nella decisione di avviare una nuova impresa. In G. Lorenzoni & A. Zenoni (Eds.), *Gli studi sull'imprenditorialità in Italia* (pp. 80–110). Roma: Bulzoni.

Gartner, W. B. (1985). A conceptual framework for describing the phenomenon of new venture creation. *Academy of Management Review*, *10*(4), 696–706.

Gartner, W. B. (1988). "Who is an entrepreneur?" is the wrong question. *American Journal of Small Business*, *12*(4), 11–32.

Gatewood, J., Shaver, K. S., & Gartner, W. B. (1995). A longitudinal cognitive factors influencing start-up behaviors and success at venture creation. *Journal of Business Venturing*, *10*(5), 371–391. doi:10.1016/0883-9026(95)00035-7

Government of Canada. (n.d.). *The state of entrepreneurship in Canada*. OECD-SDBS Business Demography Indicator. Retrieved from http://www.ic.gc.ca/eic/site/061.nsf/eng/rd02473.html

Katz, J. A., & Gartner, W. B. (1988). Properties of emerging organization. *Academy of Management Review*, *13*(3), 429–441.

Kirzner, I. M. (1979). *Percepition opportunity and profit*. Chicago: University of Chicago Press.

Knaup, A. E. (2005). Survival and longevity in the Business Employment Dynamics data. *Monthly Labor Review*, 50–56.

Knaup, A. E., & Piazza, M. C. (2007). Business Employment Dynamics Data: Survival and Longevity. *Monthly Labor Review*, 3–10.

Liao, J., Welsch, H., & Wee-Liang, T. (2005). Venture gestation paths of nascent entrepreneurs: Exploring the temporal patterns. *The Journal of High Technology Management Research*, *16*(1), 1–22. doi:10.1016/j.hitech.2005.06.001

Longsworth, E. K. (1991). *The Anatomy of a Start-Up*. Boston: Inc. Publishing.

Mandelbrot, B. (2004). *The (Mis)Behavior of Markets: A Fractal View of Risk, Ruin, and Reward*. Basic Books.

McDougall, P., Robinson, R. Jr, & DeNisi, A. (1992). Modeling new venture performance: An analysis of new venture strategy, industry structure, and venture origin. *Journal of Business Venturing*, *7*(4), 267–289. doi:10.1016/0883-9026(92)90002-9

Miles, R. E., Snow, C. C., Meyer, A. D., & Coleman, H. Jr. (1988). Organizational strategy, strutture and process. In *The strategy process*. Englewood Cliffs, NJ: Prentice-Hall Inc.

Miller, A., & Camp, B. (1985). Exploring determinants of success in corporate ventures. *Journal of Business Venturing*, *1*(1), 87–105. doi:10.1016/0883-9026(85)90009-6

Mintzberg, H. (1973). *The nature of managerial work*. New York: Harper & Row.

Moore, J. F. (2006). Business ecosystems and the view from the firm. *The Antitrust Bullettin*, *51*(1), 31–75.

Morin, E. (1993). *Introduzione al pensiero complesso*. Milano: Sperling & Kupfer.

Moss, K. R. (2012). Can America compete? Strategies for economic revival. *Harvard Magazine*. Retrieved from http://harvardmagazine.com/2012/09/the-business-ecosystem

Mouritsen, J., & Bekke, A. (1999). A space for time: Accounting and time based management in a high tecnology company. *Management Accounting Research*, *10*(2), 159–180. doi:10.1006/mare.1998.0092

Nandhakumar, J., & Jones, M. (2001). Accounting for time: Managing time in project-based teamworking. *Accounting, Organizations and Society*, *26*(3), 193–214. doi:10.1016/S0361-3682(99)00051-3

Nicolò. (2013). Monitoraggio delle sequenze e risultati aziendali *Management Control*, F. *Angeli, Milano*, *3*, 35–50.

Nicolò, D. (2001). *La transizione al vertice delle imprese familiari minori*. Torino: Giappichelli.

Nicolò, D. (2001). Il bilancio sociale come strumento di governo delle relazioni con gli stakeholder. In Atti del Seminario Internazionale: Nuovi strumenti di comunicazione aziendale. Confronto di esperienze in tema di bilancio sociale (pp. 431-447).

Nicolò, D. (2009). *Il reporting per segmenti e l'informativa settoriale secondo l'IFRS 8*. Milano: Giuffrè.

Nicolò, D. (2011). *Caratteristiche generali delle imprese e del vertice imprenditoriale, grado di evoluzione del sistema informativo e dissesto: evidenze di un'indagine empirica. In L'accertamento del passivo. Procedimento di verifica dei crediti, giudizi di impugnazione e questioni critiche: i risultati di una ricerca sui fallimenti italiani*. Milano: IPSOA, Gruppo Wolters Kluvers.

Nicolò, D. (2015), Towards a theory on corporate reputation and survival of young firms. *Procedia Economics and Finance*.

Nicolò, D., & Ferrara, N. (2015). Corporate reputation, business plan and start-up sustainability. In Startups and Start-up Ecosystems: Theories, Models and Successful Cases in the Mediterranean Area. ASERS Publishing, University of Craiova Printing House.

Normann, R. (1977). *Management for Growth*. New York: Wiley-Interscience.

Pfeffer, J., & Salancik, G. R. (1978). *The External Control of Organizations: A Resource Dependence Perspective*. New York: Harper & Row.

Poole, M. S., Van de Ven, A. H., Dooley, K., & Holmes, M. E. (2000). *Organizational Change and Innovation Process*. Oxford, UK: Oxford Univ. Press.

Porter, M. E. (2001). Strategy and the Internet. *Harvard Business Review*, (March): 62–78. PMID:11246925

Reynolds, P., & Miller, B. (1992). New firm gestation: Conception, birth, and implications for research. *Journal of Business Venturing*, *7*(5), 405–418. doi:10.1016/0883-9026(92)90016-K

Ross, L. W., & Byrd, K. A. (2011). Business Plan Competitions: Start-up "Idols" and Their Twenty-First Century Launch Pads. *Journal of Higher Education Theory and Practice*, *11*(4), 53–64.

Russell, R., Atchison, M., & Brooks, R. (2008). Business plan competitions in tertiary institutions: Encouraging entrepreneurship education. *Journal of Higher Education Policy and Management*, *30*(2), 123–138. doi:10.1080/13600800801938739

Sandberg, W. R. (1986). *New Venture Performance: The Role of Strategy and Industry Structure*. Lexington, MA: Lexington Books.

Shaver, K., & Scott, L. (1991). Person, process, choice: The psicology of new venture creation. Entrepreneurship. *Theory into Practice*, *16*(2), 23–45.

Storer, D. J. (1988). *Entrepreneurship and new firm*. Routledge.

Timmons, J. (1990). *New venture creation* (3rd ed.). Homewood, IL: R.D. Irwin.

United States Department of Labor, Bureau of Labor Statistics. (n.d.). *Business Employment Dynamics, Entrepreneurship and the U.S. Economy*. Author.

Van de Ven, A. H. (1992). Longitudinal Methods for studying the process of entrepreneurship. In D.L. Sexton & J.D. Kasarda (Eds.), The State of the Art of Entrepreneurship. Boston: PWS-Kent Publisher.

Van de Ven, A. H., & Engleman, R. M. (2004). Event- and outcome-driven explanations of entrepreneurship. *Journal of Business Venturing*, *19*(3), 343–358. doi:10.1016/S0883-9026(03)00035-1

Van de Ven, A. H., & Poole, M. S. (1995). Explaining development and change in organizations. *Academy of Management Review*, *20*(3), 510–540. doi:10.2307/258786

Venkataraman, S., Van de Ven, A. H., Buckeye, J., & Hudson, R. (1990). Starting up in turbulent environment: A process model of failure among firms wih high customer dependence. *Journal of Business Venturing*, *5*(5), 277–296. doi:10.1016/0883-9026(90)90006-F

Vesper, K. H. (1990). *New Venture Strategies* (2nd ed.). Englewood Cliffs, NJ: Prentice Hall.

Weick, K. E. (1972). *The social Psychology of Organizing* (2nd ed.). New York: Random House.

Wen, C. T., & Chen, Y. W. (2007). The innovation process of entrepreneurial teams in dynamic business plan competition: From sense-making perspective. *International Journal of Technology Management*, *39*(3/4), 346–363. doi:10.1504/IJTM.2007.013505

Chapter 2
Theoretical and Practical Approaches in Understanding the Influences of Cost–Productivity–Profit Trinomial in Contemporary Enterprises

Andrei Jean-Vasile
Petroleum-Gas University of Ploiesti, Romania

Alexandra Alecu
Petroleum-Gas University of Ploiesti, Romania

ABSTRACT

Enterprise sustainability depends on the economic performance. Achieving the economic performance is the main goal of every company since the beginnings. The instability of the economic environment imposes finding new paradigms in valuing the business opportunities. In this context, analyzing the influences of cost productivity profit trinomial in the contemporary enterprises represents an important step in identifying the potential growth avenues of the financial results. From

DOI: 10.4018/978-1-5225-2075-7.ch002

this perspective, the chapter contains along the theoretical approaches regarding the sustainable entrepreneurship and investments paradigm in the green economy, an economic analysis of the main economic outcomes, in order to revile, both the competitive factors and risks assumptions for modern companies in the larger context of market globalization and integration. Also, this chapter aims to revile the evolution of the main factors which influences the economic performances in case of a real Romanian company during and post crisis period.

INTRODUCTION

The business environment is vulnerable to global developments and the transformations of the economy, which is more interconnected than in the past, facilitates the spread of negative phenomena and events so much easier. Recent developments (Işfănescu et al., 2003; Folan, et al, 2006; Kato & Long, 2006; Gordon et al., 2009; Imbrescu et al., 2010; Iacovoiu et al., 2011; Teece, 2014; Turner et al., 2015; Shannak, 2015) have demonstrated the need for economy to use methods of identification and prevention of the risk of bankruptcy in the context of emphasizing the degree of economic instability, including at the level of the economies of the community space. From this perspective, the stability of businesses constitutes a fundamental objective in ensuring the promotion of the economic potential.

The instability of business' environment that characterizes recent developments in most contemporary economies requires a re-evaluation of the risk to which these companies are exposed. As it is already shown in numerous studies (Estrin and Bevan, 2003; Hu et al., 2004; Nicolaou, 2004), among the factors involving defining performance, the owner/manager's mentality is quite determinant in assuring company performance (Wijewardena et al., 2008; Burlton, 2015), also it is required an enterprise performance optimization strategy (George & Rodger, 2010) and measuring impact of enterprise information technology adoption on operational performance (McAfee, 2002; Schoar, 2002; Ştefănescu, 2005).

According to the numerous opinions expressed in literature (Andronic, 2000; Isfanescu, et al., 2002; Folan & Browne, 2005; Gunasekaran et al., 2005; Artene et al., 2009; Brunnert & Krcmar, 2015), and to the proposed models of use within them, to be able to preview the risk of insolvency and bankruptcy of a company can be used as both accounting procedures and banking methods, as experience has shown so far.

If we consider the first category, namely that of accounting methods, they call and apply particularly in the development of comparative analysis to determine the future trend in the evolution of the company's activity (Dinu, 2004; Helfert, 2006; Stratulat, 2009; Tabara and Dicu, 2011). Thus, these methods are considered issues such as the company's solvency analysis, achieving financial equilibrium based on revolving funds, financial security margin or solvency rates.

It should be noted that the use of these models is suitable only in achieving a temporary comparison in case of the same company or companies in similar sectors or which activities are identical, but are also able to give a relevant view on the security trends in the near future, with some certainty considering, however, the fact that the company's performance and the results are dependent on the evolution and instability of the economic environment in which the company operates as it is reviled in some studies like (Ţole, 2000; Ştefănescu, 2005; Robu & Sandu, 2006; Ciora, 2013; Grace et al., 2015).

The second category of methods used (Helfert, 2006; Bertoncelj & Kovac, 2008; Stratulat, 2009), namely banking methods consists of an early identification of vulnerabilities for the detection of the risk of insolvency and bankruptcy using as main tools of synthetic risk notes, as a result of the application of discriminant analysis statistical method, enabling certain functions-based score with which you can appreciate the company's vulnerability in terms of economic uncertainty.

The calculation of the function score is based on a series of financial indicators that determine the construction of a battery of financial rates obtained in the case of the premier groups which had different attitudes and behaviors in counteracting the risk of insolvency and bankruptcy.

When it comes to analyzing the risk of insolvency and bankruptcy, in the literature of specialty have been imposed, as methods-scoring two genuine evaluation models: model Altman and model Conan-Holder (Stănescu, 1996; Georgescu & Robu, 2001; Isfanescu, et al., 2002; Troie et al., 2003).

As it argues in the literature (Stratulat, 2009; Režnáková & Karas, 2015), the Altman Model or Model "Z" is the first statistical and mathematical model of forecasting of bankruptcy, initially developed by Professor Altman in 1968 and subsequently improved in 1977 and applied in the study of American firms. (Ţole, 2000; Stratulat, 2009).

Thus in the construction of the Model "Z"[1]'s score function are used five variables (rates) representative in understanding the evolution of the company's main financial status. The score obtained allows a selection and distribution of companies, as well as a rank of companies in state of bankruptcy or solvency, while allowing, at the same time, a quite eloquent estimation of the probability of insolvency and a possible risk of bankruptcy of the company. (Bamadio & Lebedev, 2015; Jan & Marimuthu, 2015) . Although this model has known improvements and subsequent development and applied in economic issues versions, the model is usually what

Altman applied in the case of private companies and it is of the form (Ţole, 2000; Režnáková & Karas, 2015):

$$Z = 1.2xr_1 + 1.4xr_2 + 3.3xr_3 + 0.6xr_4 + 1{,}0xr_5$$

Where,

$$r_1 = \frac{\text{Current assets}}{\text{Total assets}}.$$

$$r_2 = \frac{\text{Reinvested profit}}{\text{Total assets}}$$

$$r_3 = \frac{\text{Profit from exploitation}\left(\text{EBIT}\right)}{\text{Tottal assets}}$$

$$r_4 = \frac{\text{Market capitalization}}{\text{The book value of companies' debt relief}}.$$

$$r_5 = \frac{\text{Fiscal value}}{\text{Tottal assets}}.$$

In Table 1 is presented the value of Z-score distribution in the case of Model Altman in view of being aware of the risks of insolvency and bankruptcy of companies. The distribution and the allocation of companies depending on the value of the Z-score showshe three possible situations of company's status and framing in the category of risk of bankruptcy.

Based on Table X the values of the Z score-function can be considered as (Stratulat, 2009; Ţole, 2000):

Table 1. The Z-score Value in Altman Model case

lue of Z-score	The situation of the company	Risk of bankruptcy
Z = 3,0	Solvent	Low - none
1,8 < Z < 3,0	Weak	Indefinite
Z < 1,8	Insolvency / Bankruptcy	Imminent - maximum

Source authors based on (Ţole, 2000; Stratulat, 2009)

- A score greater than 3 will indicate lack of risks;
- A score lower than 1,8 will indicate insolvency;
- score between 1,8 and 3 will indicate the possibility of insolvency equal to 95% in one year and equal to 70% in years (Stratulat, 2009).

Concerns in order to identify the most relevant models for the analysis of the risk of insolvency and bankruptcy continued, and in literature are made numerous references to another model used as the one presented earlier, similar to the model Altman which was accomplished by J. Conan and M. Holder in 1979 and has the form as it is shown below (Ţole, 2000; Borlea & Achim, 2014; Mraihi, 2015; Khemakhem Boujelbènea, 2015; Spatacean, 2015):

$$CH = 0.24xr_1 + 0.22xr_2 + 0.16xr_3 - 0.87xr_4 - 0.1xr_5,$$

where,

$$r_1 = \frac{\text{Gross operating surplus}}{\text{Total debt}}.$$

$$r_2 = \frac{\text{Permanent Equity}}{\text{Total balance}}$$

$$r_3 = \frac{\text{Current assets} - \text{inventory}}{\text{Total balance}}.$$

$$r_4 = \frac{\text{Staff expenses}}{\text{Value added}}.$$

Table 2. Vulnerability to bankruptcy- Conan-Holder Model

Score Z value	Company status	Insolvency risks
CH>9	Solvent	Low – inexistent
4< Z <9	Weak	Indefinite
Z < 4	Insolvent	High – maxim

Source: authors based on (Ţole, 2000)

BACKGROUND

e Evolution of the Main Indicators on Economic Performance

The analysis of the company's performance is necessary in order to know the evolution of the financial indicators that are reflecting this process. In the following sectis based on the company's financial data during 2008-2014, it will be presented the calculation indicators and the analysis, tracking their evolution. There are evaluated six categories of indicators, liquidity indicators, and solvability indicators. In this context six categoriesf financial indicators are analyzed during the process, staring with liquidity indicators, solvability indicator and indebtedness and ending with rate of return.

Liquidity Indicators, Solvability Indicator and Indebtedness

The analysis of the liquidity indicators, solvability indicators and indebtedness is carried on using the methodology described in studies as (Avare et al., 2000; Georgescu & Robu, 2001; Vasilescu, 2002; Petcu, 2003; Iacovoiu et al., 2011).

The evolution of the liquidity indicators is presented in Figure 1, showing that the values of those three rates of liquidity is increasing in the analyzed period, as it is presented in the next graphic which shows the evolution in the years following

Figure 1. Evolution of main trends in rates of wound up of the analyzed company, 2008-2014
Source: authors own computations

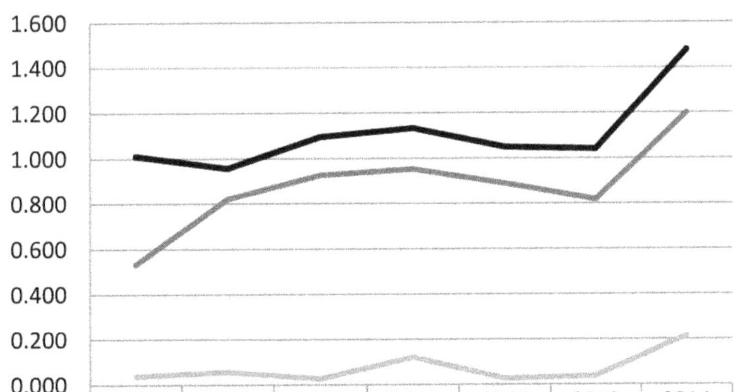

	2008	2009	2010	2011	2012	2013	2014
Current ratio	1.011	0.957	1.095	1.132	1.049	1.041	1.478
Immediate liquidity ratio	0.532	0.821	0.926	0.953	0.888	0.819	1.199
liquidity at hand	0.039	0.057	0.026	0.121	0.026	0.037	0.215

the economic crisis(2008). As it can be seen in the data below, in the following years of the economic crisis (2008) there was a slight decrease in liquidity, while both immediate liquidity and current liquidity showed a slight increase from 0.532 in 2008 to 0.821 in 2010 and from 0.039 to 0.057 for current liquidity.

As it can be noticed from the data presented below, in the immediate economic crisis (2008) is found a slight trend downward of current liquidity, while both immediate liquidity and liquidity of the current exhibit shows a slight upward trend from 0.532 in 2008 to 0.821 in 2010, respectively from 0.039 to 0.057 in case of current liquidity.

In 2011, there was a slight increase in all analyzed indicators, which does not keep on growing over the next two years (2012-2013), so the company suffers from a lack of liquidity during this period. However, in 2014, the analyzed company records an increase in all indicators of liquidity, the greatest belonging to the current period, 1.478, followed by the immediate liquidity, with 1.199.

The data presented in Figure 1, points out that in 2014 the value of immediate liquidity exceeds the values from the recommended range, i.e. 0.8 to 1, thus, the possibility of current assets materialized in receivables and treasury to finance current liabilities decreases. Regarding the analysis of visual liquidity, it appears that its values are within normal limits, between 0.2 - 0.3.

For the period under review, the liquidity at sight ratio suffers small fluctuations, but from 2008 to 2014 records an increase of 0.176, from 0.039 in 2008 to 0.215 in 2014. So, the company's capacity of paying its due to settlement debts increases, based on its available funds.

Regarding the solvency of the company, from the data presented in Figure 2, it is remarked a decrease of the overall solvency ratios and patrimonial solvency for

Figure 2. The solvency trend in case of the analyzed company, 2008-2014
Source: Authors own computations

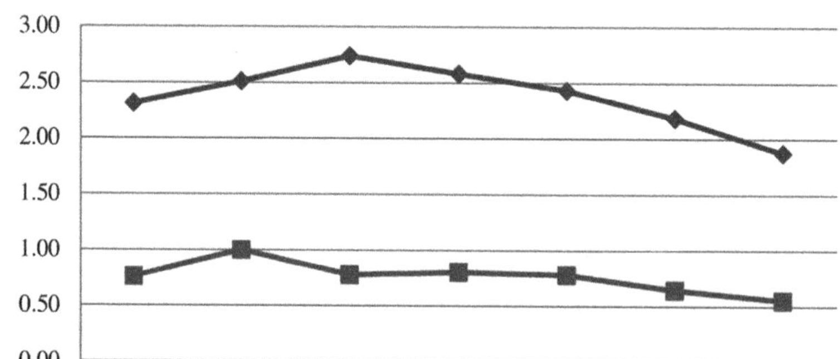

	2008	2009	2010	2011	2012	2013	2014
General solvency	2.31	2.51	2.74	2.58	2.43	2.18	1.87
Patrimonial solvency	0.76	1.00	0.78	0.80	0.78	0.65	0.55

2008-2014. Thus, the overall solvency records a slight increase during 2008-2010, the maximum value being 2.74, reached in 2010. During the period of 2010 to 2014, its value decreases from 2.74 to 1.87, with 2.19. This decrease does not influence in a crucial way the company's ability to cover the total debt of total assets, the solvency exceeding the minimum accepted value of 1.4. The matrimonial solvency underwent the same changes, recording a maximum value of 1.00 in 2009, followed by a decrease in growth with slight fluctuations in 2011, where it recorded an increase of 0.02, followed by a continuous decrease to the value of 0.55.

Indicators of Activity

In the analysis of company economic activity, it was taken into consideration the calculation of the rotational speeds for certain categories, such as: assets, stocks of goods, debts-clients or consumer's credits. In Figure 3 the evolution of these indicators is presented the analyzed company, from 2008 until 2014.

The evolution of rotational speeds in 2008-2014 fluctuate similar to the growth trend, recording maximum values in 2009 for the rotation speed of stocked goods (58.05 days), the rotation speed of debt-clients (117.94 days) and for the rotation speed of supplier's credits (221.92 days) and minimum values towards the end of the analyzed period, in 2013 – 2014.

Figure 3. Evolution of rotational-speed selector at the analyzed company, 2008-2014
Source: Authors own computations

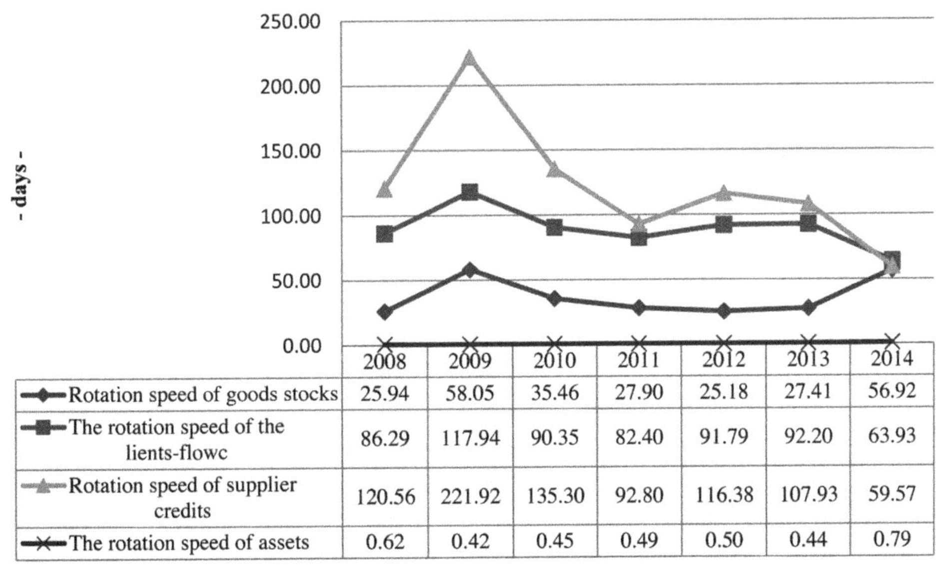

	2008	2009	2010	2011	2012	2013	2014
Rotation speed of goods stocks	25.94	58.05	35.46	27.90	25.18	27.41	56.92
The rotation speed of the lients-flowc	86.29	117.94	90.35	82.40	91.79	92.20	63.93
Rotation speed of supplier credits	120.56	221.92	135.30	92.80	116.38	107.93	59.57
The rotation speed of assets	0.62	0.42	0.45	0.49	0.50	0.44	0.79

According to Figure 3, concerning the stocks of goods, it is noted that in 2014 the number of days that the goods are stored in the company has increased. The calculation of the reverse ratio indicates that the stock has been rolled 6.41 times throughout the financial exercise of 2014.

Regarding the values of the rotation speed of assets, we can see that they remain relatively constant, fluctuating slightly, about -0.20 between 2008 and 2009. However, in 2014 the maximum value is recorded, namely 0.79 times, a difference of 0.17 times compared to 2008, observing that in 2014 the number of days that the goods remained stored in the unit has increased.

Profitability Indicators

The company profitability analysis took into account productivity developments work and earnings per share. In Figure 4 and Figure 5 these indices are presented. Through an analysis of labor productivity in the analyzed company (Figure 4) we can see a slight decrease of this indicator in 2008-2009 due to the economic crisis in 2008.

However, the company manages to increase productivity value by 2014 at the value of 348,595.56 lei/employer, registering a difference of approximately 50% compared to 2008, which highlights an increase in the company's profitability.

Figure 4. Developments of labor productivity at the analyzed company, 2008-2014
Source: Authors own computations

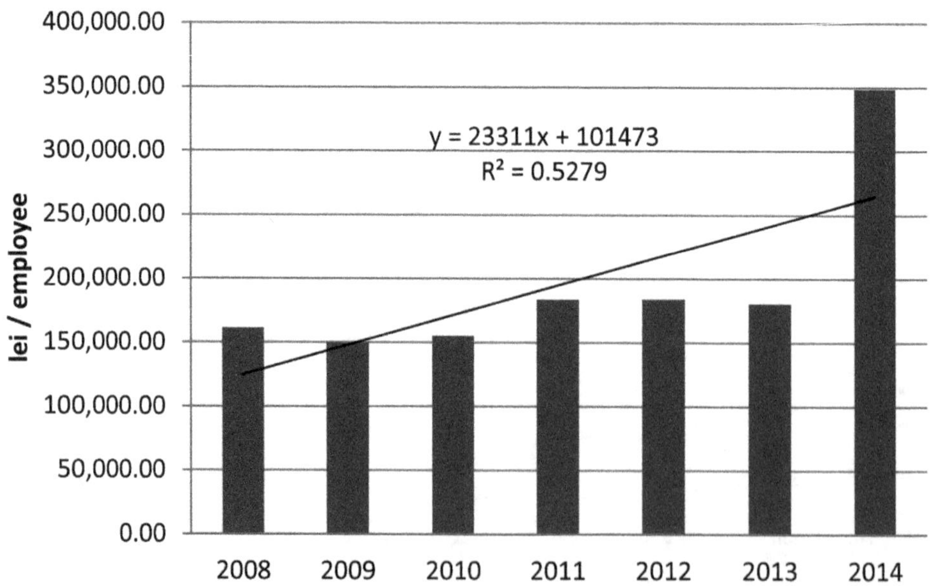

Figure 5. Evolution of the earnings per share at the analyzed company, 2008-2014
Source: Authors own computations

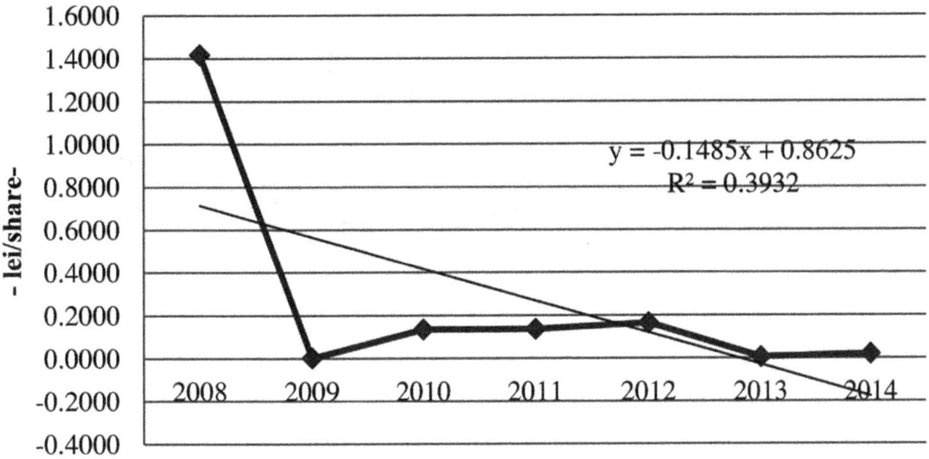

Regarding earnings per share, we can see in Figure 5 that its amount suffers a sharp drop in the period following the economic crisis, decreasing the value of 1.4181 lei/share in 2008, to 0.0014 lei/share in 2009. This sharp decrease is followed by a slight increase in earnings per share, rising until 2012 to the value of 0.1643 lei/share, but this growth is not maintained, reaching in 2014 0.0192 lei/share.

Indicators of Economic Resources Structure and Financial Sources

In Figure 6 to Figure 9 indicators are presented on the resource structure of economic developments and financial sources for the analyzed company for 2008-2014. Thus, Figure 6, financial stability presents the evolution rate for these companies.

Through an analysis of financial stability rate in the 2008-2014 period (Figure 6) it can be noticed an increase in financial stability by almost 50% from 130.91% in 2008 to 244.47% in 2014, reflecting the large share of funding sources that remain available to the company for more than a year in the total of sources covering economic means.

The analysis of global autonomy rate shown in Figure 8 highlights an irregular increase, of 18.53% for the value of the overall autonomy rate from 2008 until 2014, this growing from 129.99% to 148.52% in 2014. Thus, it is observed that the share of own resources in the total of resources used to finance an economic activity increased in the next 6 years after the economic crisis.

Figure 6. Evolution of financial stability rate at the analyzed company, 2008-2014
Source: Authors own computations

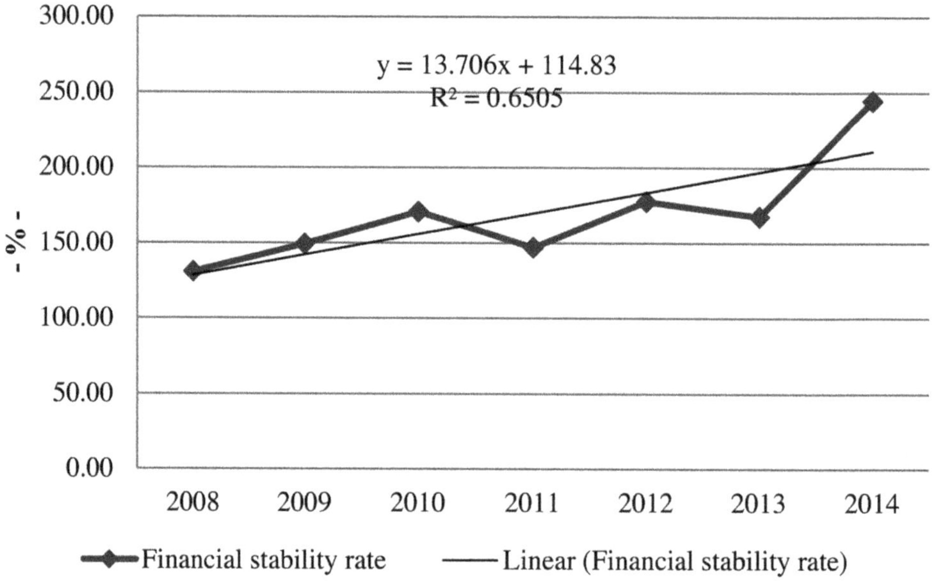

Figure 7. Evolution of the rate of global autonomy at the analyzed company, 2008-2014
Source: Authors own computations based on the company's financial documents

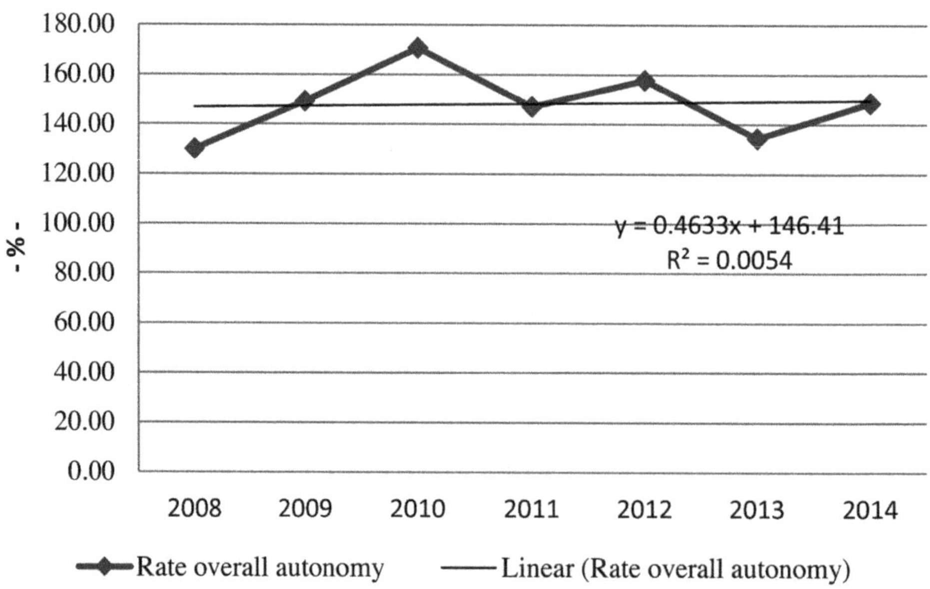

Figure 8. Evolution of assets at rates for the analyzed company, 2008-2014
Source: Authors own computations

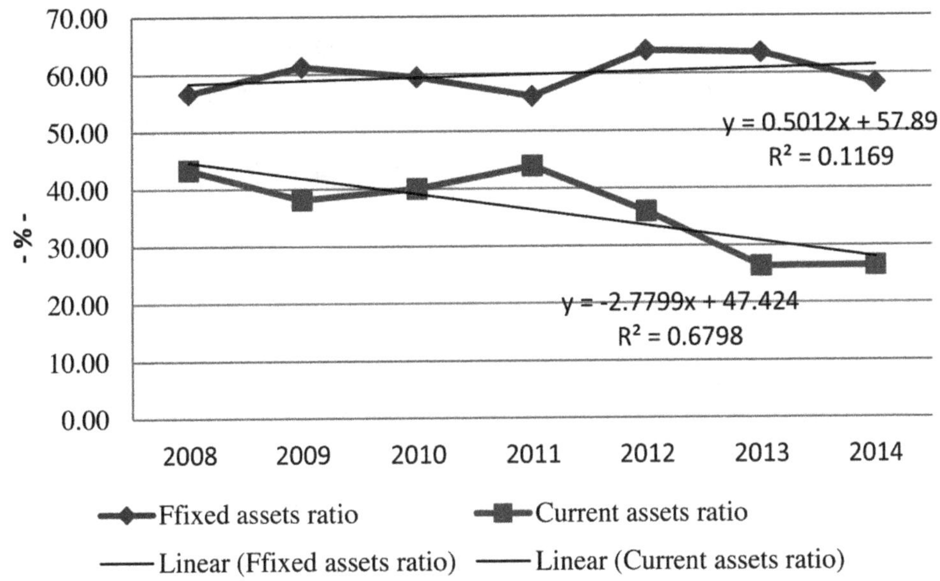

From the analysis of asset's rates at the analyzed company during 2008-2014 (Figure 9) it is found that the rate of fixed assets is inversely proportional to the rate of current assets. It is noted that the largest share of total assets is held by fixed assets, about 60%. This highlights the importance of long-term assets in total assets. Analyzing the rate of current assets, it is observed that the share of current assets to total assets, although about 40% in 2008-2011 is negatively disrupted, reaching a value of about 26% in 2014.

Analyzing the development of debt rates it is noted that the size ratio of total debt has great value, which must be commented always closely related to the business. If this high rate may be accepted by trade and service activities, in the case of manufacturing activities, the rate level may show a precarious financial position. Furthermore, although in 2008, short-term debt ratio coincides with the total debt rate, it is noted that since 2011 the rate of short-term debt decreased by approximately 10 percent, ranging from 38.78% to 27, 22%, and the total debt increases by approximately 15%, from 38.78% to 53.40%, also highlighting a precarious financial position.

Figure 9. Evolution of debt rates at the analyzed company, 2008-2014
Source: Authors own computations based on the company's financial documents

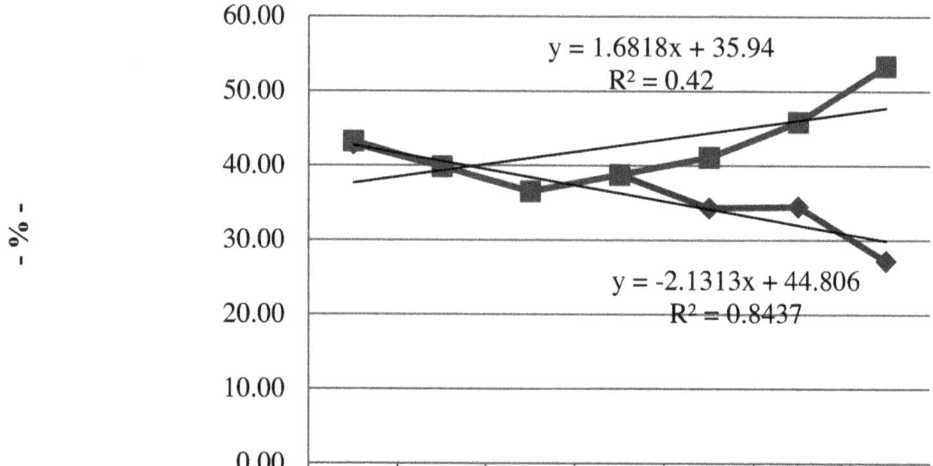

	2008	2009	2010	2011	2012	2013	2014
Short-term debt rate	42.83	39.81	36.52	38.78	34.32	34.48	27.22
Total debt ratio	43.21	39.83	36.52	38.78	41.12	45.80	53.40

Rate of Return

In analyzing the profitability indicators shown in Figure 10 is found that all analyzed rates of return follow the same process of yearly development. Since the economic crisis in 2008, return rates dropped considerably, reaching in 2009 values below 0.50%. At the end of 2009, the indicator of profitability begins to increase, indicating more efficient use of invested capital, of all the material and financial resources involved in the company's activity. The highest growth was recorded by the commercial rate, ranging from 0.02% in 2009 to 1.61% in 2012, showing the effectiveness of the company's commercial function and appreciating the company's return. In 2014, all three rates analyzed drop again at values lower than 0.50%, due to inefficiently use of the invested capital and the material and financial resources owned by the company.

The Evolution of the Cost-Productivity-Profits Trinom: A Case Study for the Period 2008-2013

The issue as evolution of the trinom cost-productivity-profits represents a milestone in literature as (Mărgulescu & Mărgulescu, 2011) staring from this study we have carried out an analysis regarding the current study case. The analysis and under-

Figure 10. Evolution of the rates of return at the analyzed company, 2008-2014
Source: Authors own computations

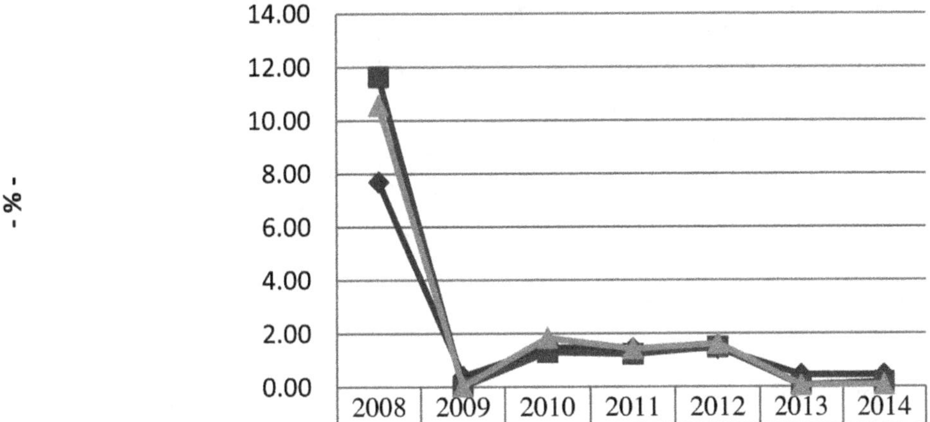

	2008	2009	2010	2011	2012	2013	2014
Economic rate of return	7.69	0.39	1.47	1.44	1.44	0.44	0.44
Financial rate of return	11.64	0.01	1.31	1.23	1.48	0.05	0.17
The commercial rate	10.56	0.02	1.83	1.42	1.61	0.06	0.09

standing of the development of the trinom cost-productivity-profit at the analyzed companies is an essential element for optimizing the production process, but also in raising the performance of the company.

Starting from earlier findings, taking into consideration the level indicators already compiled and analyzed, it is noted that the company's activity is one that recorded profits, even in a situation of crisis, which denotes the fact that it is a profitable activity and, at the same time effective, given that costs are kept at a lower level than the revenue.

The most important resource of a company is human resources, being the main factor necessary to achieve effective and successful activities. For a better example, in Table 3 is shown the evolution of the staff of the analyzed company, during the period 2008-2014.

From the data presented in Table 3, are found throughout the analysis period (2008-2014) the number of employees classified on their level of training within the enterprise has a tendency of reduction. Thus, this period stands out due to a reduction by approximately 13.12% of personnel, from 404 employees in 2008, to 351 employees in 2014. Although the total number of staff is reduced, the tendency of increasing the higher educated human resources is maintained, thereby the number of staff with specialized training being increased from 89 in 2008 to

Table 3. Number of employees by the level of preparedness during the period 2008-2014

Years	2008	2009	2010	2011	2012	2013	2014
Personnel with tertial education	89	67	61	71	75	88	103
Personnel with high school education, school for craftsmen	16	15	6	17	15	29	83
Skilled workers	292	209	180	209	200	211	164
Unskilled workers	7	5	3	3	4	8	1
Total employees	404	296	250	300	294	336	351

Source: Authors own computations

103 employees in 2014, as well as the number of personnel with higher education, from 16 employees in 2008 to 83 in 2014.

At the opposite pole lie qualified workers and the unskilled, of which numbers are lowering drastically in this period. The number of skilled workers decreases since 2008, until 2014 by almost 50%, from 292 employees to 164, and the number of unskilled workers decreases from 7 employees in 2008, to one employee in 2014. The primary method of raising labor productivity, efficiency of employees and maintaining the structure and level of training is represented by staff's salaries. Thus, Figure 11 presents an analysis of the evolution of expenditures and salaries recorded during the period 2010-2014.

Figure 11. Evolution of salaries at the analyzed company, 2010-2014
Source: Authors own computations

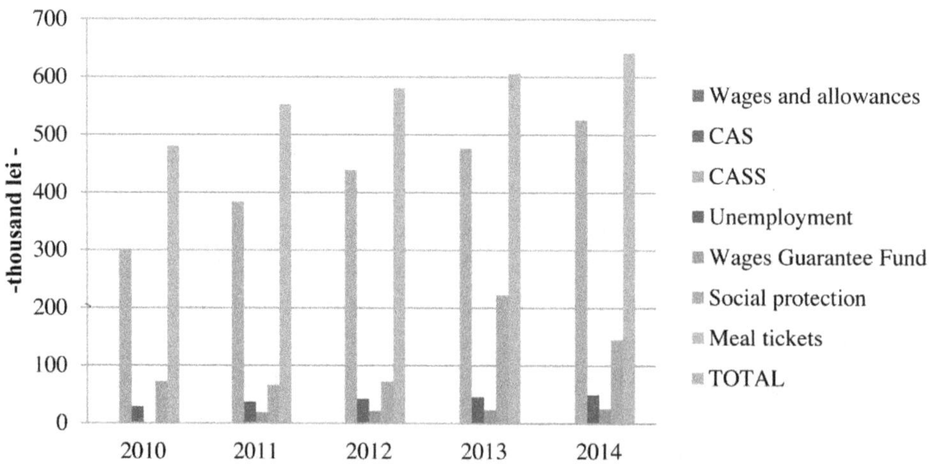

**For a more accurate representation of this figure, please see the electronic version.*

From the data presented in Figure 12 is discovered that, in the period under analysis, 2010-2014, the level of wages and allowances increase steadily, affecting the expenditures and salaries, which will automatically increase. Thus, the average annual gross income accomplished in 2011 is 26950 lei/employee, being greater with 33% of the average gross income in 2010. In 2012 the average annual gross income is $ 28917 employee, being greater with 7.30% of gross average income in 2011. In 2013, the average annual gross income level increases with 3.82% from the gross income achieved in the year 2012, reaching the amount of MDL 30023 employee.

By the end of 2014, it is found that the average annual gross income accomplished is 31226 lei per employee, being greater with 4.01% from the gross income achieved in 2013. The amount of the average annual gross income in 2014 is significantly higher than that in 2010. Thus, the average annual gross income achieved per employee in 2014 was 31226 lei, being greater with 4.01% than the gross income achieved in 2013 and with 4276 lei compared to the average gross achieved in 2010. The increase was mainly due to an increase in gross base wages by introducing the holiday bonus.

In Figure 12 it is shown the structure of the main categories of expenditure of the analyzed company, for the period 2008-2014, and it can be observed their share in total expenses of the company.

Figure 12. Structure of the main categories of expenditure at the analyzed company, 2008-2014
Source: Authors own computations

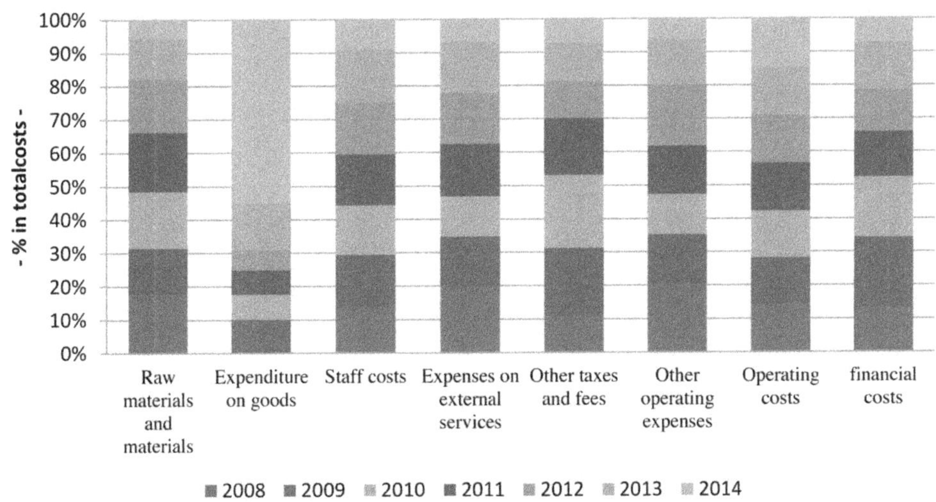

**For a more accurate representation of this figure, please see the electronic version.*

From the data presented in Figure 12 it can be noted that, in general, all categories of expenses are maintained at approximately equal odds along the analyzed period, other taxes and levies making an exception due to their higher values compared to other expense categories. Moreover, it is found that, in 2008, expenditure on goods had very low values of 207.071 lei. Since 2009, the level of spending on goods increases, its peak being in 2014 with the amount of 47,428,130 lei.

As regards the analysis of operating expenses, it is found between 2008 and 2014, a difference of 50,516,534 lei. Also it can be seen in 2014 and increase of 55,976,481 million for operating expenses in relation to the previous year, 2013, from 57,357,633 lei operating expenses to 113,334,114 lei in 2014, the difference being about 50%

It can be seen that the expense of the company grew significantly from year to year until 2014, compared with 2008. Steady growth is recorded at the expense of personnel, starting with 2011, with approximately 1,000,000 Euro/year, its peak being in 2014 with the amount of 13,407,007 lei.

In close connection with the expenditure incurred by the company in the course of a financial year is its revenue, income, financial income, operating income and revenue from sales of goods. Evolution of the total revenue achieved by the analyzed company largely reflects developments in the economic environment from Romania which is affected by a serious economic instability and high inflation rates. (Figure 13)

As can be inferred from the data shown in Figure 15, in 2009, one year after the onset of the financial crisis, the total revenues of the company were accounted for

Figure 13. Evolution of major categories of expenditure at the analyzed company, 2008-2014 (2008=100)
Source: Authors own computations

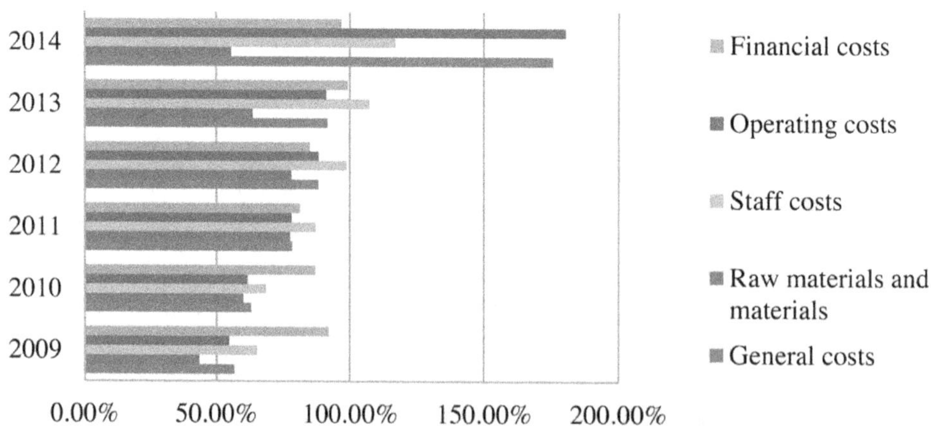

**For a more accurate representation of this figure, please see the electronic version.*

Figure 14. Evolution of the main categories of income, the analyzed company, 2008-2014
Source: Authors own computations

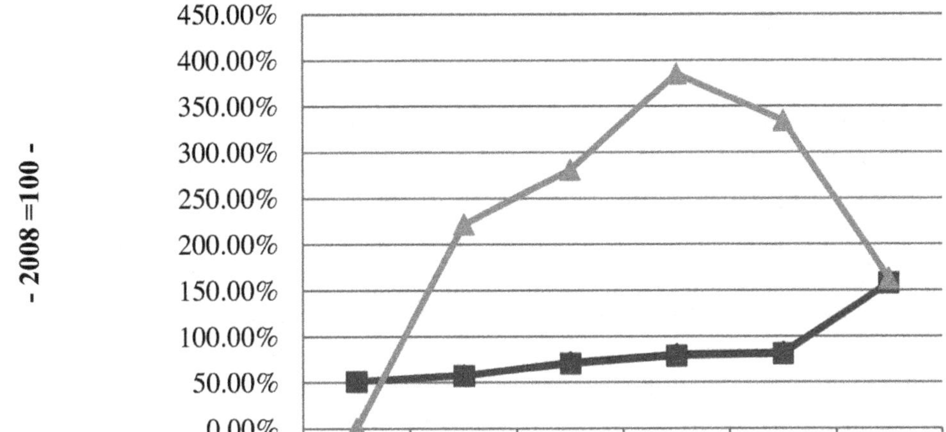

	2009	2010	2011	2012	2013	2014
Total income	51.28%	58.09%	71.84%	80.75%	82.55%	157.61%
Operating income	51.10%	57.06%	70.52%	78.83%	80.97%	157.58%
financial income	0.08%	221.77%	280.92%	385.23%	333.90%	162.51%

Figure 15. Structure of the main categories of income to the analyzed company
Source: Authors own computations

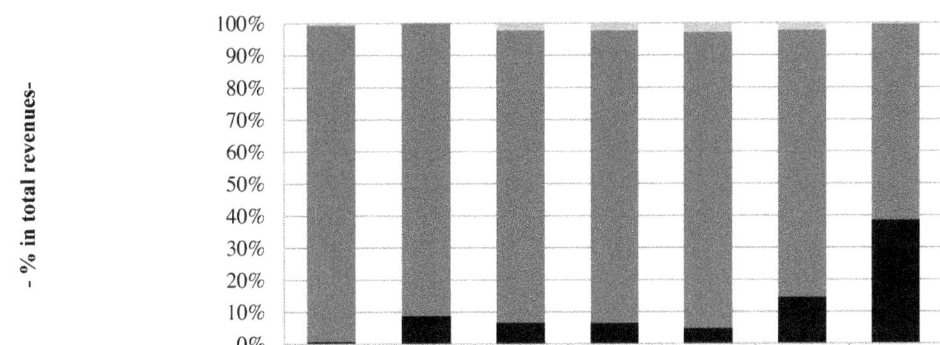

	2008	2009	2010	2011	2012	2013	2014
financial income	0.63%	0.00%	1.39%	1.76%	2.42%	2.10%	1.02%
Operating income	99.37%	50.78%	56.70%	70.08%	78.34%	80.46%	156.59%
Income from sale of goods	0.74%	4.84%	4.04%	4.90%	4.10%	13.97%	98.73%

only 51.28% compared to those recorded at the beginning of the analyzed period, respectively, compared with 2008. Overall, a slight increase in the level of total income in relation to 2008, from 51.28% in 2009 to 157.61% in 2014. Thus, it appears that the total revenue increased 57.51% from 2008 until 2014, from 74,565,452 lei in 2008 to 515 117,520 in 2014.

The incomes from the sale of goods are the main category of income that influences the total revenues increase of the analyzed company. Developments is diverse, with low rates, varying with growth, as for example happens in 2008 when it register its lowest level of revenue from the sale of goods, i.e. 0.74% in total, followed by an increase in years to come, until the level of around 4% in total revenue in the period 2009-2012.

Their evolution is varied, with low levels, varying with growth, as it happens, for example, in 2008 when it records its lowest level of revenue from the sale of goods, i.e. 0.74% in total, followed by an increase in years to come, until the level of around 4% in total revenue in the period 2009-2012.

Starting with 2013, the share of revenues from the sale of goods in total income begins to be considerably higher, reaching in 2014 the level of 98.73% revenue from selling goods in total, their level being strongly influenced by the evolution of the inflation rate and the leu/ dollar or leu/euro.

In the analysis of financial revenue, it is found from the data presented in Figure 16 that, during the period 2008-2014, it has a very small share in total income, starting from 0.63% in 2008, reaching a maximum in 2012 of 2.42% financial income in

Figure 16. Evolution of total expenditure, total income, and gross profit for the analyzed company, 2008-2014
Source: Authors own computations

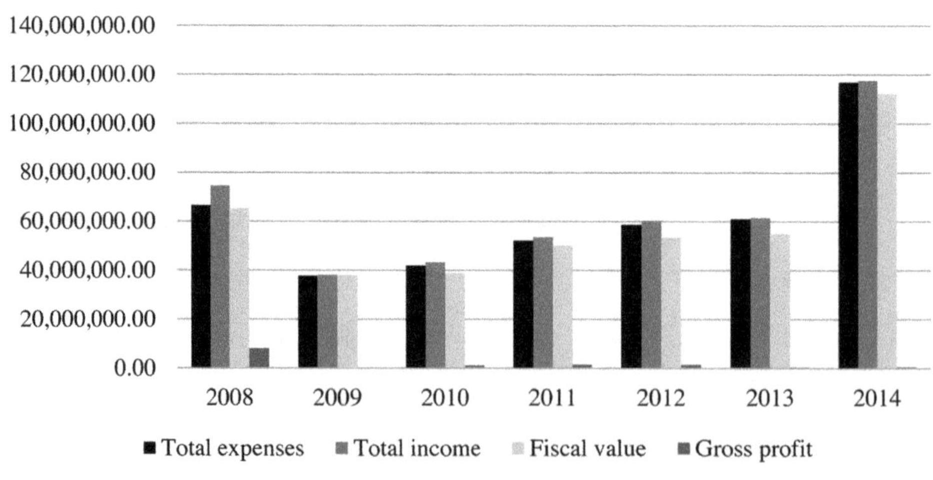

total income, and in 2014 diminishing until it reaches 1.02%. However, the largest share in the total revenue is the income from exploitation. In 2008 it represent 99.37% of total revenues, and in 2014 it reach at the level of 156.59% of the total revenue.

From the data presented in Figure 17 it can be found an increase in the fiscal value of the company the analyzed company throughout the period analyzed, hence being affected by the economic crisis in 2008, it records in 2009 a decrease of about 40% of the value of fiscal value, from 65,116,582 lei in 2008 to 38,021,811 lei in 2009. From 2010, the company recorded a turnover growth, its peak being in 2014 with the amount of 112,247,770 lei, with 47,131,188 lei higher than the one in 2008. In the period under review, 2008-2014, gross profit recorded declining values. The smallest value of gross profit is observed in 2009, 348,868 lei, although within 2010-2012, its value increases to 1,543,945 lei. In 2014 the gross profit declines again, reaching 631,972 lei, two times higher than that recorded in 2009.

According to the analysis of the data presented in Figure 17, it can be noticed an annual fluctuation in the levels of indicators envisaged. If in 2009 are recorded decreases of the 4 main indicators compared to 2008, starting with 2010 indicators begin to increase. The exception is the gross profit in 2009 which records a decrease with 95.68% from 2008, but in 2010 increases at a value with 268.13% higher than in 2009, and continues to increase slightly, until 2013 when it falls again, with a lower value than in 2012 with 64.37%.

Figure 17. Evolution of fiscal value, gross profit and total costs at the analyzed company, 2008-2014
Source: Authors own computations

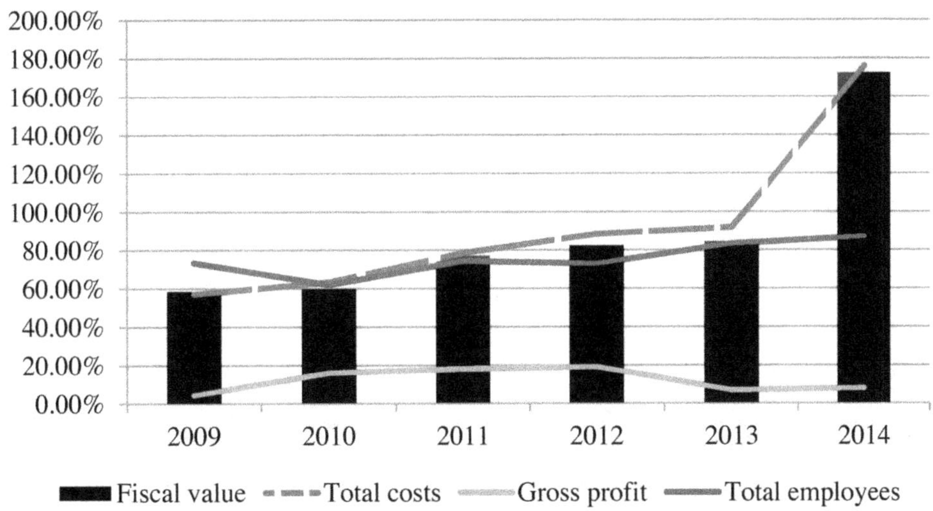

Risk Computation in Business

In the determination of the risk of business for the analyzed company it was used in the analysis Model Altman applied to private businesses, having the following form (Stratulat, 2009):

$$Z = 1.2xr_1 + 1.4xr_2 + 3.3xr_3 + 0.6xr_4 + 1.0xr_5,$$

According to the score obtained, a company can be allocated to one of the two categories-companies that are bankrupt or companies that are in solvency, estimating at the same time and the likelihood of bankruptcy of the company. Applying Altman Model for 2014 it has been obtained the following Z-score function:

$$Z = 1.2 \times 0.554 + 1.4 \times 0.006 + 3.3 \times 0.033 + 0.6 \times 0.172 + 1.0 \times 1.081 = 1.97 .$$

where,

$$r_2 = \frac{631.972}{103.841.198} = 0.006 .$$

$$r_3 = \frac{3.426.042}{103.841.198} = 0.033$$

$$r_4 = \frac{13.150.632,50}{76.332.123} = 0.172 .$$

In table 4 have been determined the Z-score values for the analyzed company, for the period 2008-2014.

From the calculations made it is noted that the value of the function Z-score is in a down trend, from 2.95 recorded in 2008 to 1.97 in 2014, respectively, from the area of the solvency to deficiency. In Figure 18 is presented the change in Z-score r the analyzed company, 2008-2014.

In Figure 18 is presented the variation of the Z-score of model Altman for the analyzed company, during 2008-2014. Thus, it can be noted that in 2008, the company is located in a solvent area, with almost non-existent risk of bankruptcy. Due to the economic crisis, the values of all the indicators that define the enterprise's profitability declined, and the Z-score value decreased, reaching a minimum value of 1.59, which indicates a risk of bankruptcy. Economic results of the analysis done

Table 4. Risk analysis in business - Altman Model applied to the analyzed company, 2008-2014

	2008	2009	2010	2011	2012	2013	2014
r_1	0.758	0.633	0.634	0.717	0.550	0.550	0.554
r_2	0.134	0.006	0.023	0.023	0.022	0.7	0.006
r_3	0.188	0.062	0.063	0.050	0.041	0.033	0.033
r_4	0.244	0.413	0.413	0.334	0.297	0.232	0.172
r_5	1.084	0.702	0.707	0.806	0.760	0.678	1.081
Z	2.95	1.92	1.96	2.07	1.76	1.59	1.97

Source: Authors own computations based on the company's financial documents

Figure 18. Variation of score Z, the analyzed company, 2008-2014
Source: Authors own computations

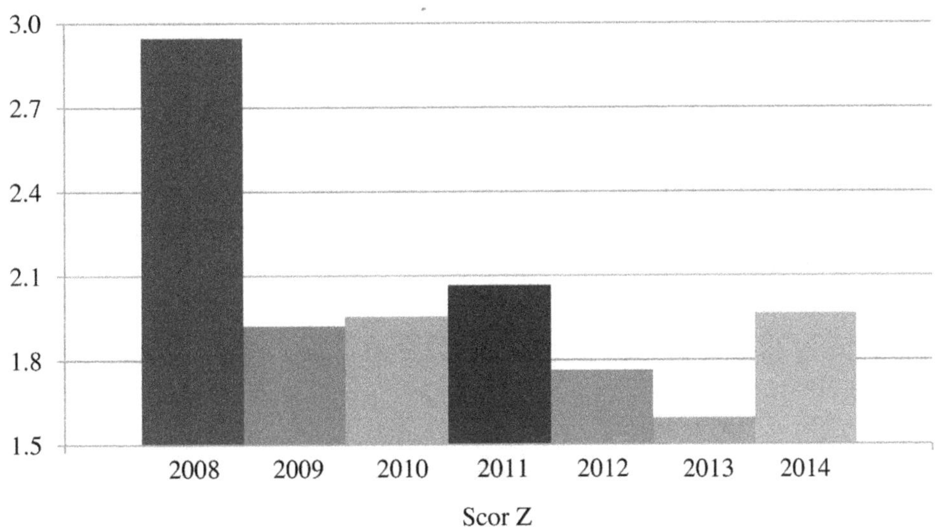

in 2014 at the analyzed company shows that the company falls in a poor area with a risk of bankruptcy indeterminate, Z-score value being of 1.97.

The adaptation of the company to the requirements imposed by the developments of the economic environment, internal or external, calls for an integrated approach in understanding the risks. From the analysis of the evolution of the financial level the analyzed company and from the perspective of cost-productivity-profit during the period 2008-2013, it can be remarked an increase in the value of the main indicators, turnover, total expenses and total revenue. This is more than an estimation of the required financial developments of the analyzed company in terms of cost-productivity-profit for 2015-2020. In fig.19 is shown the evolution of the main economic indicators.

From Figure 19, it can be noted that for the period 2015-2020, both total revenue and total expenditure recorded a continuous increase. However, the amount of expenses exceeds the income value recorded. Also, it can be recorded an increase in the value of the fiscal value for the said period, an increase direct proportion to the total income. In Figure 20 is presented the evolution of labor productivity for the period 2015-2020.

Starting from the analysis of labor productivity during the period 2008-2013, in which it could be noted a rise in the value of this indicator along the whole period, described in Figure 20 shows the estimation of the indicator in the perspective of 2015-2020. As it can be seen in Figure 20, labor productivity is growing during 2015-2020, which highlights a further increase in the profitability of the company.

CONCLUSION

As a result of the study of efficiency, profitability and the economic performance of the enterprise, but also indicators of achievement of economic activity obtained in the study, it was found a positive evolution of society in crisis due to the actions and measures taken by the management of the company, which led to an increase in turnover in 2008, until 2014, but which, however, it have not led to an increase

Figure 19. Evolution of total revenues, fiscal value and total expenditures, the analyzed company, 2015-2020
Source: Authors own computations

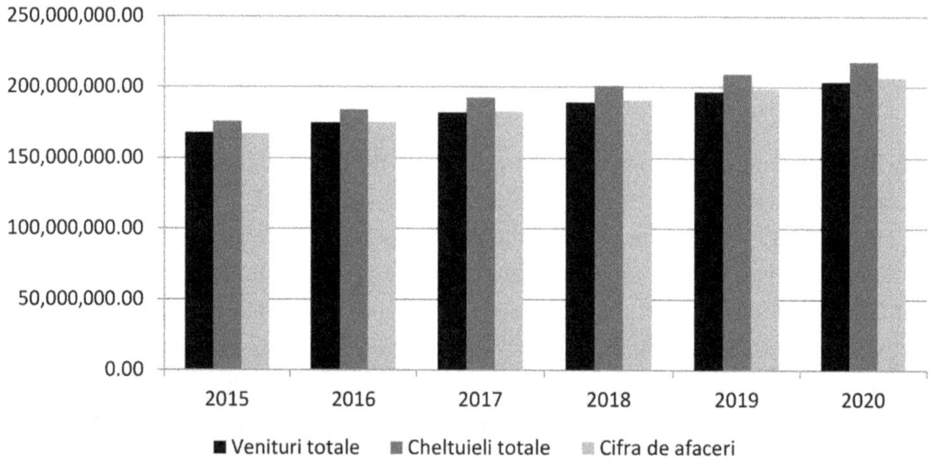

Figure 20. Evolution of labor productivity, the analyzed company, 2015-2020
Source: Authors own computations

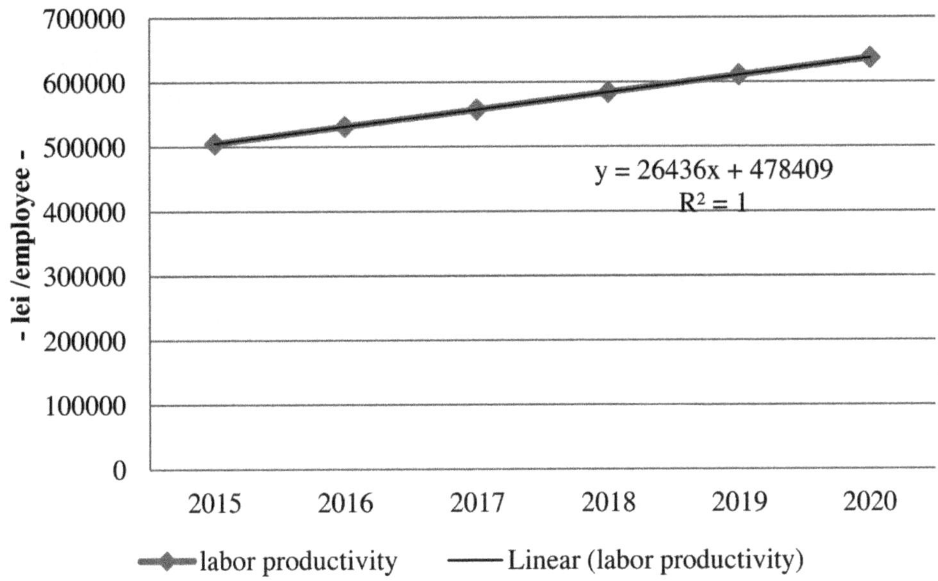

in gross profit level, but to a significant decline. From the analysis undertaken at the analyzed company it has been established the following:

The net turnover achieved in 2014 has registered a value of 112,247,770 lei, establishing an increase of 47,131,188 lei compared to 2008 and with 57,340,288 lei compared to 2013. The expense of the enterprise register also increased with 55,882,126 lei compared with the values in 2013, the related gross profit or turnover recording a slight increase of 81858 lei compared with that achieved in the financial year 2013.

During the period 2008-2014, the spending on goods increased by 47,221,059 lei and operating costs increased by 50,516,534 lei, while the category operating income registered an increase of 42,662,591 lei. In these circumstances the result from operations decreased with 7,853,943 lei compared with that achieved in the financial exercise from 2004. The result of the increase in exploitation, in terms of an increase in turnover with 104,43%, is due to the diversification of the business company unfolded in parallel with the reduction of manufacturing costs and general expenses by the administration.

It can be noted a significant reduction in the share of raw materials in total expenditures from 40.80 percent in 2008 to 12.93 percent in 2014, while expenditure on goods recorded an increase from 0.31% in 2008 to 40.58% in 2014. During the same period under review it is found a decrease in the share of expenditure on staff in total, even if there are small fluctuations, from 17.26% in 2008, to 11.47% in 2014 and spending with taxes ranging from 1.13% in 2008, to 0.77% in 2014.

In the current liquidity is found an increase in the value of these installments, from 1.011 in 2004, to 1.478 in 2014. The current liquidity increase reflects an improvement in the financial situation of the company and thus, improves the coverage of current debts generated by the activity of the company. In order to obtain an image as closely to the company is calculated the immediate liquidity rate which also records an increase from 0.532 in 2004, to 1.199 in 2014.

If in 2004 the exercise ended with a net profit of 6,875,933 lei, in 2014 the net profits are recorded to have decreased, reaching the amount of 100,819 lei.

In 2014 the company liquidity continued to be affected by the elements and factors specific to the market economy in the period of economic and financial crisis, of which the most important are:

- The instability of the agreements concluded -a significant reduction in their number -reducing quantities -waiving of contracts during the year;
- Supply fluctuations;
- Reducing the possibilities of suppliers.

With regard to solvency, it can be seen a decrease of the indicators of overall solvency and the solvency assets for the period 2008-2014. Thus, the overall solvency has a slight increase recorded in the interval 2008-2010, the maximum value attained being of 2.74 in 2010. In the intervening period 2010-2014, it decreases with 2.19, from 2.74 to 1.87. This drop does not affect in any significant way the company's ability to cover its total debts, total assets exceeding solvency by the minimum value accepted by 1.4.

As regards to the evolution of the company's total revenue, they accounted in 2009, a year after the onset of the financial crisis, 51.28 percent from those recorded in 2008. Overall it is found a slight increase in the level of total income from 2008; 51.28% in in 2009 to 157.61% in 2014. Thus, it appears that the total revenue increased by 57.51% from 2008 to 2014, from 74,565,452 lei in 2008 to 515 117,520 in 2014.

From the analysis of the development of labor productivity for the analyzed company, we can observe a slight decrease in this indicator for the period 2008-2009, due to the economic crisis of 2008. However, the company manages to grow the value of productivity by the year 2014 from the value of 348,595.56 lei/employee, with a difference of about 50% in comparison with 2008, which emphasizes an increase in the profitability of the company. Assessing the risk of bankruptcy of the analyzed company by applying Atman Model is found that the company's situation deteriorated in meantime. If in the year 2008, the company stood out in the area with a bankruptcy risk almost non-existent, six years later it is situated in an area of uncertainty. In 2008 the value of the function Z-score was 2.95, while in 2014 it has reached 1.97, placing the company in from the area of the solvency to the one of deficiency.

REFERENCES

Andronic, B. C. (2000). *Performanţa firmei. Abordare transdisciplinară în analiza microeconomică.* Iaşi: Ed. Polirom.

Artene, A.E., Sabău, C., & Domil, A. (2009). Analiza performanţelor companiilor şi standardizarea situaţiilor financiare, Analele Seria Ştiinţe Economice. *Timişoara,* (15), 715-719.

Avare, P., Ravary, L., Legros, G., & Lemonnier, P. (2000). Gestiune şi analiză financiară. Ed. Economică, Bucureşti.

Bamadio, B., & Lebedev, K. A. (2015). Development of Altman Five-Factor Model of Assessing the Creditworthiness of an Enterprise. *Modern Economy, 6*(07), 797–807. doi:10.4236/me.2015.67075

Bertoncelj, A., & Kovac, D. (2008). The influence of management capital on enterprise performance. *International Journal of Management and Enterprise Development, 5*(4), 444–461. doi:10.1504/IJMED.2008.018761

Borlea, S. N., & Achim, M. V. (2014). Assessing bankruptcy risk for Romanian metallurgical companies. *Metalurgija, 53*(2), 279–282.

Brunnert, A., & Krcmar, H. (2015). Continuous performance evaluation and capacity planning using resource profiles for enterprise applications. *Journal of Systems and Software.*

Burlton, R. T. (2015). Delivering business strategy through process management. In *Handbook on Business Process Management 2* (pp. 45–78). Springer Berlin Heidelberg.

Ciora, C. (2013). *Analiza performanţei prin creare de valoare.* Bucureşti: Ed. Economică.

Criste, A., Mosneanu, E. A., & Glod, A. G. (2008). O abordare a conceptului de competitivitate naţională[Financial Studies]. *Studii Financiare, 12*(4), 51–59.

Dinu, E. (2004). *Rentabilitatea firmei în practică* (C. H. Beck, Ed.). Bucureşti.

Estrin, S., & Bevan, A. (2003). Determinants of Russian enterprise performance: Conclusions from the symposium. *Comparative Economic Studies, 45*(2), 192–203. doi:10.1057/palgrave.ces.8100010

Folan, P., & Browne, J. (2005). A review of performance measurement: Towards performance management. *Computers in Industry, 56*(7), 663–680. doi:10.1016/j.compind.2005.03.001

Folan, P., Higgins, P., & Browne, J. (2006). A communications framework for extended enterprise performance measurement. *International Journal of Computer Integrated Manufacturing, 19*(4), 301–314. doi:10.1080/09511920500340858

George, J. A., & Rodger, J. A. (2010). *Smart data: enterprise performance optimization strategy* (Vol. 71). John Wiley & Sons. doi:10.1002/9780470583067

Georgescu, N., & Robu, V. (2001). *Analiza economico-financiară.* Bucuresti: Ed.ASE.

Gordon, L. A., Loeb, M. P., & Tseng, C. Y. (2009). Enterprise risk management and firm performance: A contingency perspective. *Journal of Accounting and Public Policy, 28*(4), 301–327. doi:10.1016/j.jaccpubpol.2009.06.006

Grace, M. F., Leverty, J. T., Phillips, R. D., & Shimpi, P. (2015). The Value of Investing in Enterprise Risk Management. *The Journal of Risk and Insurance, 82*(2), 289–316. doi:10.1111/jori.12022

Gunasekaran, A., Williams, H. J., & McGaughey, R. E. (2005). Performance measurement and costing system in new enterprise. *Technovation, 25*(5), 523–533. doi:10.1016/S0166-4972(03)00176-7

Haţegan, C. D., & Imbrescu, C. M. (2011). Contabilitatea şi performanţa economico-financiară. *Studia Universitatis Vasile Goldiş, Arad-Seria Ştiinţe Economice*, (1-2), 38-45.

Helfert, E. (2006). *Tehnici de analiză financiară. Ghid pentru crearea valorii.* B. M. T. Publishing.

Hu, Y., Song, F., & Zhang, J. (2004). *Competition, ownership, corporate governance and enterprise performance: Evidence from China.* Hong Kong Institute of Economics and Business Strategy Working paper, 1111.

Iacovoiu, V. B., Străoanu, B. M., & Teodorescu, C. D. (2011). Instrumente şi tehnici de analiză a stării economico-financiare a firmei. Ed. Karta Graphic, Ploieşti.

Imbrescu, I., Băbăiţă, I., Spiridon, C.A. (2010). Performanţa–o abordare macroeconomică, Studia Universitatis Vasile Goldiş. *Arad-Seria Ştiinţe Economice*, (1), 370-380.

Işfănescu, A., Hristea, A. M., & Vasilescu, C. (2003). *Analiză economico-financiară*. Bucuresti: Ed. ASE.

Isfanescu, A., Robu, V., Hristea, A. M., & Vasilescu, C. (2002). *Analiza economico-financiara*. Bucuresti: Ed. ASE.

Jan, A., & Marimuthu, M. (2015). Altman Model and Bankruptcy Profile of Islamic Banking Industry: A Comparative Analysis on Financial Performance. *International Journal of Business and Management*, *10*(7), 110. doi:10.5539/ijbm.v10n7p110

Kato, T., & Long, C. (2006). CEO turnover, firm performance, and enterprise reform in China: Evidence from micro data. *Journal of Comparative Economics*, *34*(4), 796–817. doi:10.1016/j.jce.2006.08.002

Khemakhem, S., & Boujelbènea, Y. (2015). Credit risk prediction: A comparative study between discriminant analysis and the neural network approach. *Journal of Accounting and Management Information Systems*, *14*(1), 60–78.

Mărgulescu, D., Mărgulescu, S. (2011). Cauzalitate şi determinism în trinomul: productivitate--cost--profit şi utilizare în analiza economico--financiară a firmei. *Internal Auditing & Risk Management*, *6*(1).

McAfee, A. (2002). The impact of enterprise information technology adoption on operational performance: An empirical investigation. *Production and Operations Management*, *11*(1), 33–53. doi:10.1111/j.1937-5956.2002.tb00183.x

Mraihi, F. (2015). Distressed Company Prediction using Logistic Regression: Tunisians Case. *Global Journal of Management and Business Research*, *15*(3).

Nicolaou, A. I. (2004). Firm performance effects in relation to the implementation and use of enterprise resource planning systems. *Journal of Information Systems*, *18*(2), 79-105.

Petcu, M. (2003). *Analiza economico-financiară a întreprinderii*. Bucureşti: Ed. Economică.

Režnáková, M., & Karas, M. (2015). The Prediction Capabilities of Bankruptcy Models in a Different Environment: An example of the Altman Model under the Conditions in the V4 Countries. *Ekonomicky Casopis*, (06): 617–633.

Robu, V., Sandu, R. (2006). Problematica analizei performanţelor–o abordare critică în contextul teoriilor informaţiei şi guvernanţei corporative. *Revista Economie Teoretică şi Aplicată*, (8), 15-28.

Schoar, A. (2002). Effects of corporate diversification on productivity. *The Journal of Finance*, *57*(6), 2379–2403. doi:10.1111/1540-6261.00500

Shannak, R. O. (2015). The Impact of Implementing an Enterprise Resource Planning System on Organizational Performance Using Balanced Scorecard. *Journal of Management Research*, *8*(1), 37–54. doi:10.5296/jmr.v8i1.8523

Spatacean, I. O. (2015). Ensuring Business Continuity Assumption for Romanian Investment Firms–An Expression of Good Governance in Financial Reporting. *Procedia Economics and Finance*, *26*, 967–974. doi:10.1016/S2212-5671(15)00917-X

Stănescu, C., Işfănescu, A., & Băicuşi, A. (1996). *Analiza economico-financiară*. Bucureşti: Ed. Economică.

Ştefănescu, A. (2005). *Performanţa financiară a întreprinderii între realitate şi creativitate*. Bucureşti: Ed. Economică.

Stratulat A.A.(2009). Simularea Riscului Financiar prin Metoda Altmanin, Buletinul Ştiinţific Al Universităţii Creştine "Dimitrie Cantemir". *Braşov, 10*(2), 244.

Tabara, N., & Dicu, R. M. (2011). Indicatori de performanţă în contextul reglementărilor contabile internaţionale. *EIRP Proceedings, 2*.

Teece, D. J. (2014). The foundations of enterprise performance: Dynamic and ordinary capabilities in an (economic) theory of firms. *The Academy of Management Perspectives*, *28*(4), 328–352. doi:10.5465/amp.2013.0116

Ţole, M. (2000). Analiza economico-financiară a firmelor. Ed. Fundaţiei "Romania de Mâine".

Troie, L., Zaharia, O., Roman, M., & Hurduzeu, M. (2003). *Analiza statistică a activităţii economice şi a gestiunii financiare a întreprinderii*. Bucureşti: Ed. Economică.

Turner, P., Kane, R., & Jackson, C. (2015). Implementing performance improvement through the enterprise culture. *British Journal of Healthcare Management*, *21*(11), 523–527. doi:10.12968/bjhc.2015.21.11.523

Vasilescu, G. (2002). Analiza statistică economică şi metode de evaluare a firmei. Ed.Didactică şi Pedagogică, Bucureşti.

Wijewardena, H., Nanayakkara, G., & De Zoysa, A. (2008). The owner/managers mentality and the financial performance of SMEs. *Journal of Small Business and Enterprise Development*, *15*(1), 150–161. doi:10.1108/14626000810850892

ADDITIONAL READING

Ailenei, D., Mosora, L. C.(2011). Economia dezvoltării sustenabile. Competitivitate şi creştere economică, Economie Teoretică şi aplicată, (2), 555.

Akimova, I., & Schwödiauer, G. (2004). Ownership structure, corporate governance, and enterprise performance: Empirical results for Ukraine. *International Advances in Economic Research*, *10*(1), 28–42. doi:10.1007/BF02295575

Auzina-Emsina, A. (2014). Labor Productivity, Economic Growth and Global Competitiveness in Post-crisis Period. *Procedia: Social and Behavioral Sciences*, *156*(256), 317–321. doi:10.1016/j.sbspro.2014.11.195

Bose, R. (2006). Understanding management data systems for enterprise performance management. *Industrial Management & Data Systems*, *106*(1), 43–59. doi:10.1108/02635570610640988

Botezatu, M., & Andrei, J. (2012). Implications of the environmental factors on the economic efficiency of capital investments. A Romanian perspective in terms of a sustainable economy. *Journal of Environmental Protection and Ecology*, *13*(1), 382–391.

Bouquet, C., Morrison, A., & Birkinshaw, J. (2009). International attention and multinational enterprise performance. *Journal of International Business Studies*, *40*(1), 108–131. doi:10.1057/jibs.2008.64

Burtică, M., Pop, V. (2008). Calitate-productivitate-competitivitate factori esentiali de crestere a performantei economice, Studia Universitatis Vasile Goldiş, Arad-Seria Ştiinţe Economice, (1-1), 486-492.

De Rosa, D., Gooroochurn, N., & Goerg, H. (2015). Corruption and Productivity: Firm-level Evidence.[Jahrbuecher fuer Nationaloekonomie und Statistik]. *Journal of Economics and Statistics*, *235*(2), 115–138.

Dethier, J. J., Hirn, M., & Straub, S. (2008). Explaining enterprise performance in developing countries with business climate survey data. World Bank Policy Research Working Paper Series, Vol.

Dethier, J. J., Hirn, M., & Straub, S. (2010). Explaining enterprise performance in developing countries with business climate survey data. *The World Bank Research Observer*.

Dumitru, C., Danciu, F. R. (2008). Rolul informaţiei contabile în evaluarea riscului la creditare prin analiza indicatorilor de performanţă, Studia Universitatis Vasile Goldiş, Arad-Seria Ştiinţe Economice, (1-1), 228-239.

Eniola, A. A., & Entebang, H. (2015). Government Policy and Performance of Small and Medium Business Management. *International Journal of Academic Research in Business and Social Sciences*, *5*(2), 237–248. doi:10.6007/IJARBSS/v5-i2/1481

Fakhfakh, F., & Perotin, V. (2000). The effects of profit-sharing schemes on enterprise performance in France. *Economic Analysis*, *3*(2), 93–111. doi:10.1080/713663558

Fan, C. S., & Hu, Y. (2008). Imports of capital goods and enterprise performance: A firm-level analysis in China. *Applied Economics Letters*, *15*(5), 391–394. doi:10.1080/13504850600690004

Gronum, S., Verreynne, M. L., & Kastelle, T. (2012). The Role of Networks in Small and Medium-Sized Enterprise Innovation and Firm Performance. *Journal of Small Business Management*, *50*(2), 257–282. doi:10.1111/j.1540-627X.2012.00353.x

Haralambie, G. A. (2008). *Planurile expermentale statistice în turism studiu de caz-Judeţul Prahova. Editura Universităţii Petrol-Gaze din Ploieşti, Romania.*

Hendricks, K. B., Singhal, V. R., & Stratman, J. K. (2007). The impact of enterprise systems on corporate performance: A study of ERP, SCM, and CRM system implementations. *Journal of Operations Management*, *25*(1), 65–82. doi:10.1016/j.jom.2006.02.002

Imbrescu, C. M., & Haţegan, C. D. (2011). Contabilitatea şi performanţa economico-financiară, Studia Universitatis "Vasile Goldiş" Arad, Seria Ştiinţe Economice 21:38-45. http://studiaeconomia.uvvg.ro/images/2001/v2/7.%20CONTABILITATEA%20SI%20PERFORMANTA%20ECONOMICO-%20FINANCIARA.pdf

Imbrescu, I., Spiridon, C. A. (2010). Performanţă şi competitivitate în economie. Studia Universitatis Vasile Goldiş, Arad-Seria Ştiinţe Economice, (1-3), 236-245.

Ionascu, I., Ionascu, M. (2007). Aspecte controversate privind raportarea si auditarea informatiilor referitoare la performanta companiilor, Audit financiar, 5(12), 18-26.

Ionaşcu, M. (2013). Raportarea financiară şi previziunile analiştilor financiari în contextul crizei economice: consideraţii privind mediul românesc, Audit Financiar, 11(97).

Ionita, I., Popescu, F. A., Andrei, J. V., & Voicu, A. (2011). Redesigning the A B. com 1 test suite through value engineering: A new approach for using economic efficiency methods. *African Journal of Business Management*, *5*(10), 3942.

Kallunki, J. P., Laitinen, E. K., & Silvola, H. (2011). Impact of enterprise resource planning systems on management control systems and firm performance. *International Journal of Accounting Information Systems*, *12*(1), 20–39. doi:10.1016/j.accinf.2010.02.001

Kiselakova, D., Horvathova, J., Sofrankova, B., Soltes, M. (2015). Analysis of risks and their impact on enterprise performance by creating Enterprise Risk Model. Polish Journal of Management Studies, 11.

Kotey, B., & Meredith, G. G. (1997). Relationships among owner/manager personal values, business strategies, and enterprise performance. *Journal of Small Business Management*, *35*(2), 37.

Liu, G., Eng, T. Y., & Takeda, S. (2013). *An investigation of marketing capabilities and social enterprise performance in the UK and Japan*. Entrepreneurship Theory and Practice.

Lizal, L., Singer, M., & Svejnar, J. (2001). Enterprise breakups and performance during the transition from plan to market. *The Review of Economics and Statistics*, *83*(1), 92–99. doi:10.1162/003465301750160063

Masakure, O., Henson, S., & Cranfield, J. (2009). Performance of microenterprises in Ghana: A resource-based view. *Journal of Small Business and Enterprise Development*, *16*(3), 466–484. doi:10.1108/14626000910977170

Matei, M., & Voica, M. C. (2013). Social Responsibility in the Financial and Banking Sector. *Economic Insights-Trends & Challenges*, *65*(1), 115–123.

Neamtu, M. (2007). Preocupari si Tendinte Actuale in Procesul de Evaluare a Performantelor Profesionale, Rev. Stiinte Juridice, 169.

Ng, Y. C., & Siu, N. Y. (2004). Training and enterprise performance in transition: Evidence from China. *International Journal of Human Resource Management*, *15*(4-5), 878–894. doi:10.1080/0958519042000192997

Otto, N. (2008). Producţia şi costul. Studia Universitatis Vasile Goldiş, Arad-Seria Ştiinţe Economice, (1-3), 432-441.

Payne, A., Holt, S., & Frow, P. (2003). Equal opportunities practices and enterprise performance: A comparative investigation on Australian and British data. *International Labour Review*, *142*(4), 471–505. doi:10.1111/j.1564-913X.2003.tb00541.x

Pribadi, H., & Kanai, K. (2011). Examining and exploring Indonesia small and medium enterprise performance: An empirical study. *Asian Journal of Business Management, 3*(2), 98–107.

Rolstadås, A. (1998). Enterprise performance measurement. *International Journal of Operations & Production Management, 18*(9/10), 989–999. doi:10.1108/01443579810225577

Shaik, M., & Abdul-Kader, W. (2012). Performance measurement of reverse logistics enterprise: A comprehensive and integrated approach. *Measuring Business Excellence, 16*(2), 23–34. doi:10.1108/13683041211230294

Subic, J., Vasiljevic, Z., & Andrei, J. (2010, June). The impact of FDI on the European economic development in the context of diversification of capital flows. In *The 14th IBIMA Conference on Global Business Transformation through Innovation and Knowledge Management, Istanbul, Turkey* (pp. 23-24).

Tan, W., Shen, W., Xu, L., Zhou, B., & Li, L. (2008). A business process intelligence system for enterprise process performance management.Systems, Man, and Cybernetics, Part C: Applications and Reviews. *IEEE Transactions on, 38*(6), 745–756.

Tan, W., Shen, W., & Zhao, J. (2007). A methodology for dynamic enterprise process performance evaluation. *Computers in Industry, 58*(5), 474–485. doi:10.1016/j.compind.2006.10.001

Teece, D. J. (2007). Explicating dynamic capabilities: The nature and microfoundations of (sustainable) enterprise performance. *Strategic Management Journal, 28*(13), 1319–1350. doi:10.1002/smj.640

Teece, D. J. (2007). The role of managers, entrepreneurs and the literati in enterprise performance and economic growth. International Journal of Technological Learning. *Innovation and Development, 1*(1), 43–64.

Valerdi, R., & Blackburn, C. (2010). Leveraging measurement systems to drive enterprise transformation: Two case studies from the US aerospace industry. *Information, Knowledge, Systems Management, 9*(2), 77–97.

Van Aken, E. M., Letens, G., Coleman, G. D., Farris, J., & Van Goubergen, D. (2005). Assessing maturity and effectiveness of enterprise performance measurement systems. *International Journal of Productivity and Performance Management, 54*(5/6), 400–418. doi:10.1108/17410400510604557

Vatankhah Barenji, R., Hashemipour, M., & Guerra-Zubiaga, D. A. (2015). A framework for modelling enterprise competencies: From theory to practice in enterprise architecture. *International Journal of Computer Integrated Manufacturing*, *28*(8), 791–810. doi:10.1080/0951192X.2014.901563

Verdecho, M. J., Alfaro-Saiz, J. J., & Rodriguez-Rodriguez, R. (2012). Prioritization and management of inter-enterprise collaborative performance. *Decision Support Systems*, *53*(1), 142–153. doi:10.1016/j.dss.2011.12.011

Yu, Y. C., & Hung, T. Y. (2012). The Application of Rolling Examine to Improve Enterprise Performance. *Journal of Convergence Information Technology*, *7*(14).

KEY TERMS AND DEFINITIONS

Economic Profitability Rate: Reflects the link between economic results and economic means necessary (capital), for its effectiveness, with invested capital of all financial and material resources involved in the business.

Enterprise Sustainability: Designs a concept which implies a high rate of company survival from the performance concept point of view.

Immediate Liquidity Rate: Reflects current assets resulting in debts and Treasury to cover its debts; the stocks decrease because they have the least liquidity character of current assets (the assets most likely occurring in the event of loss). The value of this pointer must be between 0.8 and 1.

Labor Productivity: A qualitative index which measures the quantity of product obtained in a unit of time or through the labor expense which returns on the unit produced and it is determined by the reporting of the quantity of products obtained in the time it takes to obtain them.

Overall Borrowing Rate (Lever Rate): Reflects the degree to which the company ensures the financing of the enterprise, but also the extent to which long-term commitments is guaranteed by the company.

The Rate of Global Autonomy: Presents the share of the total sources of funds used to finance the activity of an operator. In practical work, the share of own financing sources is at least 33% of the total funding sources used by the enterprise.

The Rate of Circulating Assets: Represents a measure of the company's financial flexibility, insofar as it highlights the relative importance of the assets easily converted to cash. The size of this indicator reflects the share's current assets in total assets.

ENDNOTES

1 Z score function is a function proposed by Altman, a function based on Fisher, shape like (Stratulat, 2009):

$Z(r_1,r_2,\ldots,r_n)=\alpha_0+\alpha_1\times r_1+\alpha_2\times r_2+\ldots+\alpha_n\times r_n$,

where:

$r_1,r_2,\ldots,r_n$ = rates considered to develop model classification;

$\alpha_1, \alpha_2,\ldots,\alpha_n$ = financial rates coefficients considered;

α_0 = free term classification tool.

Chapter 3
Integrated Sustainability Reports:
Historical Survey, Theoretical Proposals and Best Practices

Massimo Costa
University of Palermo, Italy

Giuseppe Valenza
University Mediterranea of Reggio Calabria

ABSTRACT

Disclosure of corporate social and environmental sustainability, resumed in 'sustainability reports', have occupied most of the attention of accounting thought and practice over the last few decades. Evaluation of ecological footprint and social sensitiveness is becoming relevant also for the investors. The chapter presents institutional disclosure concerning social, environmental, and integrated (financial, social and environmental) issues in a threefold perspective. The first is a historical one: after some definitions the birth and development of sustainability reports are presented to the reader. The second is a theoretical one: a paradigm or framework is developed for including what various experiences and literature have supplied until nowadays. The third is an empirical one presenting the main sustainability scoring criteria mostly used today, and an empirical survey on the car industry. Some concluding notes follow from the comparison of the aforementioned perspectives.

DOI: 10.4018/978-1-5225-2075-7.ch003

INTRODUCTION[1]

For many decades the accounting has expanded its content, focusing beyond the narrow field of financial information and considering the social and environmental information. The increased focus on non-financial information is paradoxically started by big company, typically focused on creating shareholder value (Tinker, 1984).

The need for information required by stakeholders (not only shareholders and equity investors) concerned the issue of sustainable development in the second half of the twentieth century. Initially, corporate sustainability has been interpreted as social sustainability against the unacceptable exploitation of workers and social disintegration. Then, corporate sustainability has also been considered as environmental sustainability, so as ecological sustainability for the production of goods and services, to preserve the rapid consumption of non-renewable resources and to reduce the impact of pollution caused by production processes (Mintz, 2014).

The reasons for this need for information are multiple and often conflicting, but they all stem from the opportunity to involve stakeholders in their business to converge corporate goals with stakeholder objectives. Therefore, the first academic studies on this subject were included in the field concerning the stakeholder theory (Freeman, 1984; Freeman & Evan, 1988). Specifically, the need to provide information to the stakeholders is derived from a new social sensitivity towards the issue of sustainability, which is interpreted as: strategy for creating sustainable value added (Figge & Hahn, 2004); social commitment of the company to safeguard the rights of the community (Vallance et al., 2011); request of ethics by the community (van Marrewijk, 2003; Di Giandomenico, 2008); a result of an expansion of the stakeholders (Dawkins, 2003); possibility to ensure human development (Anand & Sen, 2000). Today the communication of information reaches social and environmental objectives that coincide with the goals of investors and management, at least in the most advanced companies and in the advanced countries.

The social and environmental disclosure is traditionally divided into two parts. This distinction is derived from a difference between the two 'new' areas of reporting. Social accounting concerns the reporting of the impact of business on human and social aspects, which can be both economic and non-economic (e.g. value added distribution, employment, social well-being created), instead environmental accounting concerns the reporting of the consequences and any benefits of the business on the ecological environment (e.g. protection of environmental balance, environmental sustainability, use of energy resources) (Gray et al., 1996; Unerman, 2000; Adams, 2004). According to the most recent literature and best practices, the chapter also argue the issue of integrated reporting, which considers financial, social and environmental information, focusing corporate communication towards value creation over time (Busco et al., 2013). Recent literature (Guthrie & Yongvanich,

2006) also highlighted the need to coordinate the Balanced Scorecard, Intellectual Capital and social and environmental reporting to provide more complete account of the management and performance of a corporation.

The expansion of the disclosure from a traditional conception (financial accounting) to a social concept (social accounting) is not simply a generalization of the focus of reporting to other variables. This perspective considers only the formal aspects of the phenomenon. Material aspects depend instead by political and philosophical changes that have encouraged the diffusion of Corporate Social Responsibility (CSR). The principles and structure of CSR have been defined in previous decades, but the latest developments of the debate concerned the implementation of the CSR on corporate performance (Carroll, 1991, 1998, 2000). The empirical literature on CSR has studied many aspects of this issue: e.g. the market reaction to social responsibility disclosures (Patten, 1990) or correlations between CSR and financial performance (McWilliams & Siegel, 2000). Other contributions (Margolis & Walsh, 2001), criticizing the previous studies based on correlations between CSR and financial performance, supported redirecting the empirical analysis of the most useful aspects to guide corporate social initiatives.

CSR begins when the classical economic paradigm (liberalism) is abandoned. According to the liberal paradigm, social welfare is maximized when the selfishness of individuals and competition of businesses are greatest. This paradigm has greatly influenced the development of economics and accounting, thus summarize in a few elements that process of evolution is impossible. However, the most important elements are certainly the neoclassical economic assumptions about profit maximization and competitive markets for the best allocation of economic resources.

Scholars, governments and analysts did not consider the inconsistencies of the classical economic paradigm as abnormal. The assumptions remained valid, therefore the contradictions were considered 'corrections' of a model that was never disputed. Market failures were treated with empirical solutions, often conceived as ethical necessity for the benefit of the community. Alternatives to the individualist paradigm were proposed, some of them disputing any economic organization based on selfishness and market exchanges, such as the Marxist paradigm (the only real alternative to the predominant system).

Accounting followed the economic interests of the companies, thus maximizing the net worth or profit, considering only the perspective of the owners or the companies (conceived as institutions). In the debate of the nineteenth and twentieth centuries the economic postulate was never really criticized.

The egoistic postulate became the *only* economic postulate, designed as a certain and indisputable 'law'. The egoistic limits were seen only as 'constraints' to egoistic actions, established by an external body to protect public interests. The maximization of the utility function was the main objective of economic agents, companies and individuals. Opposite behaviours were considered 'subversive' (Friedman, 1962).

The assumption of this postulate is an economic growth without limits and contradictions of the capitalist system of production, but this assumption is inevitably falsified by logic, and then from history. Economic growth does not seem compatible with the unlimited exploitation of the economic, energy and human resources, because it will inevitably fail. Therefore, the attention of public interest to the community and the environment arose from the observation of the contradictions and inconsistencies of the capitalist system.

The social and environmental reporting stems from the opening of the company aims to altruism and solidarity (collective interests), not denying the egoistical characteristics of the companies related to the achievement of profits. This process is not linear because the 'social welfare' outside the exchange market and financial perspective loses the monetary assessment, which is the unit of measure and the conventional sign for comparing economic resources.

The social and environmental accounting concerns measurement problems of physical, quantitative and qualitative values, which cannot be expressed in a single unit of measurement. The 'quality' is certainly a subjective concept: assessing or measuring quality performance is a process of interpretation, certainly not objective. Therefore, the main problem of social and environmental reporting is not to define principles of objective and universal evaluation (Nicolò, 1997), but to explain and clarify the qualitative assumptions.

Corporate reporting is divided into two sections: (a) accounting and financial statements, which have systematic features; (b) non-accounting reporting (also called statistical reporting), which has fragmented characteristics. Non-accounting reporting is more flexible than financial reporting, therefore it handles better the complexity of qualitative and subjective assessments. It promotes processes of cooperation and expectations between the company and stakeholders, who are promoters of concrete projects for sustainable and socially responsible corporate policies.

Non-financial reporting has serious limitations: different methods, notions, classifications and units of measurement. Financial accounting may instead provide for the systematic integration of data and concepts. It shall be therefore regulated (ex ante) and revised (ex post) to ensure reliability and neutrality of accounting systems, although it is possible that companies intend the financial accounting as a fulfilment. For this reason, the chapter will discuss the social and environmental accounting following a systematic view.

The aim of this chapter is not to deal with the social and environmental aspects included in corporate purposes but to focus on reporting, also analysing the best practices of the companies. A brief diachronic synthesis will follow, also considering literature, historical development, laws, empirical observations, but without providing a comprehensive review.

The chapter aims to explain the historical origin of the social, environmental and integrated reporting, considering successively two points of view: the first one is an integrated reporting based on a systemic approach, while the second one is based on a non-systemic approach. Then, an empirical study will analyse the evaluation of sustainability performance of the companies based on integrated assessment of economic, social and environmental dimensions, according to the criteria of RobecoSAM and Dow Jones Sustainability Indices (DJSI). This study will also show the best practices of companies in the automobile industry. Finally, conclusions will compare theoretical deductions with empirical evidences.

The chapter does not explore some issues because there are space limitations, in particular: (a) a list of legal requirements for social and environmental reporting in the advanced countries, despite its importance; (b) national social and environmental accounting; (c) internal accounting (e.g. cost accounting and management accounting).

For this reason, after this Introduction and before Conclusions, the chapter is articulated into the following sections. Sections 1 and 2 are devoted, respectively, to the birth and diffusion of social reporting and to the following emerging of environmental reporting. They are mainly of historical nature. Sections 3 and 4 concern, respectively, the presentation of social/environmental reporting in corporations, and its strategic role. Section 5 concern the integration between financial, social and environmental reporting. They are mainly of descriptive and theoretical nature. Sections 6 and 7, finally, deal with the best practices, and, respectively, with the international practice of sustainability evaluation in general and with the automobile industry in particular. They are mainly of empirical nature.

1. HISTORICAL SURVEY OF SOCIAL REPORTING

The history of social reports is relatively recent: fifty years ago the first studies on this topic spread. The classical accounting developed its scientific theories when the first big companies were born during the second industrial revolution, while the big state administrations were spreading (Lipari & Costa, 2005).

At that time only the financial accounting was predominant. It considered two opposite points of view: the first one was the 'assets and liabilities view' (also called 'balance sheet view'), whose main contributions were proposed by Anthony, Moonitz, Kester, Solomons and Sprouse, instead the second one was the 'revenues and expenses view' (also called 'income statement view'), based on the theories of Brade, Dixon and Paton (Lionzo, 2012). This duality also existed in national variants:

'Statik Bilanz' vs. 'Dinamische Bilanz', in Germany, and 'Sistema del Patrimonio' vs. 'Sistema del Reddito', in Italy.

The social reports, and consequently the social accounting, is explicitly an extension of the traditional field of financial accounting. The spread of Corporate Social Responsibility has been the cause of this extension, therefore there is a strong connection between them. CSR has different definitions and notions, therefore it is impossible to summarize all the literature on this topic. Green Paper (2002) defined CSR as "a concept whereby companies integrate social and environmental concerns in their business operations and in their interaction with their stakeholders on a voluntary basis".

However, this notion seems restrictive and narrow. Therefore, a wider notion could be the following: "a concept whereby companies integrate, among its institutional purposes, social and environmental goals, also considering financial and economic aspects, expanding its range of stakeholders, and adapting their strategies and actions, as well as its corporate communications towards these stakeholders".

In the light of this perspective, social reports express a wide corporate communication, including social information (communication in the strict sense) or social and environmental information (communication in the broad sense), which is a part of the larger CSR. Therefore, business communication and CSR are not the same thing, despite the solid connections between them.

Focusing the discussion on the history, an Italian record is recognized in the field of social reports when other countries did not feel sensitivity to social issues. The generalist approach of the Italian accounting shifted the attention of scholars to the third sector enterprises in the early years of the twentieth century. In those years, the only non-profit organizations were called 'Opere Pie', ie religious institutions of charity, in relation to which it was proposed a report that summarized the results of their mission and purpose. The 'mission report' had very limited impact in other areas different from the non-profit sector. There were no similar experiences outside of Italy, because until the end of World War II there were no conditions for the development of a social sensitiveness in the reporting field.

The Germany showed signs of sensibility on social issues like Italy, where AEG Company published the first Social Report in 1938. At that time there was a culture of corporatism in Italy and Germany, thus the first studies of social economy began to spread, where scholars theorized a 'third way' between socialism and capitalism and the active intervention of States over national economies. It is no coincidence that the first 'business administrations' were born in Germany and Italy, as evolution of the corporate administration and accounting. Both Italian 'Economia aziendale' and German 'Betriebswirtschaftslehre' proposed studies about intermediate economic systems, and their contribution to domestic production (GDP), seen as the predominant purpose with respect to the distribution of profit for shareholders. In this cultural climate the income theories of Gino Zappa (1937) spread, where income was seen as the result of a durable combination of factors of economic production, considering a social and holistic view of the company. As well as the 'Dinamische Bilanz' of Eugen Schmalenbach (1919), which proposed the income statement configured in value and cost of production obtained, indicating the company's social contribution to domestic production. But it would be wrong to attribute this sensibility only to the authoritarian regimes of the past, since similar theoretical and practical experiences are found in socialist countries of Northern Europe, like Sweden, or in countries with a long liberal tradition, like the Netherlands. This sensitivity - as mentioned - does not invest the entire theme of the social report but caused the first phase of the 'socialization' of the traditional report, incorporating indexes and values in it out of the traditional reporting aimed at investors. After World War II the first social democratic governments were born in Europe, therefore the studies about socialized reports continued to major developments (on the concept of 'socialized reports' and 'social reports', see Gabrovec Mei, 1990). The more invasive role in the economy by the states, the growing social sensitivity and trade unionists, strengthen the focus on social reports.

In this light, dirigiste orientations of France and Spain can be interpreted, where the government, through a mandatory accounting plan, proposed to guide the industrial policy of private companies and direct them to national and social purposes.

However, the issue of sustainability has appeared everywhere with social, political and economic movement of the sixties. 1968 is the year in which the cultural process achieved full maturity, it is the moment when the literature and practice on the social statement really began to develop. The Anglo-Saxon countries were a little back, only in the following decade they remained fully involved in the new cultural scene. The seventies are certainly those in which both the literature and the practice on the social report finally implement their scientific contents. In the United States, following the model of the traditional disclosure, the Survey on Social Responsibility Disclosure is published. Similarly, a White Paper is published in the UK. In Germany, the practice of publishing social reports spreads more, becoming widespread among big companies. In Italy there is a discussion of doctrine, but also the first publication of a social report, by Merloni in 1978. In France, a country of traditional legal regulation, a law on the social report is published.

In summary, the most advanced countries were opened to social reports, each one according to their cultural, economic and legal traditions. The theoretical models are, however, fragmented and undeveloped at that time. The most consistent theoretical model was proposed by Solomons (1974), but it was difficult its practical applicability. This model in fact adopted only the monetary unit of measurement, limiting the field to only those elements capable of economic assessment. In summary, the model can be summarized in the following formal expression:

Overall Value generated by the production process (*Added Value*)
+ External Benefits (for external subjects or for the community)
– External Costs (as before)
= 'Social' Profit/Loss

In the following decade, the scientific debate on the social budget is consolidated. It is important to remember IX International Congress of Strasbourg in 1983, when the first structure of the social report was proposed, based on the German experience. In contrast, there was a reaction of the scholars of the traditional report against all forms of socialization of the financial statements.

This reaction was in accordance with neoliberal environment in those years was consolidated, especially in Anglo-Saxon countries, but it was an opportunity for a complete emancipation of the debate on the social report against the themes of traditional accounting.

The debate on the environmental report was born in the nineties, reducing attention to the social report, which has become mature. The gradual broadening of the range of stakeholders also determined the consideration of 'future citizens', therefore sustainability became an intertemporal concept impacting on the reproduction ability of resources consumed in production processes. In this context, the social report had two meanings: as a broad meaning, the social report considered both social and environmental information; according to a narrow sense, it considered only the social dimension reporting, leaving further information to the environmental report. In the same years the researchers attempted to assess the 'quality' of corporate performance, using non-financial approaches. In this direction, a significant contribution is certainly the balanced scorecard (Kaplan and Norton, 1996). Literature and practice in the last fifteen years are not easily summarized, since the contributions and proposals are very numerous, but here highlighting at least a process of standardization of rules for the preparation of the social report (such as the EU Green Book, 2002).

European Union, which summarizes literatures and practice of European countries, is perhaps the most advanced in the world for attention to social issues. Directive 2003/51/EC regarding the 'Modernization' establishes the need to include financial and economic indicators for better understanding of the development or performance of the company, considering also non-financial indicators (employees and environment) when appropriate. However, all proposals for standardization and promotion of social disclosures have never been legislatively mandatory. The information society is now therefore purely voluntary. The international network of scholars of CSR has been consolidated in recent years. Among these it is important to remember the Encyclopedia of CSR (edited by S. Idowu, 2012) and other publishing initiatives in the same field, as well as the First World Congress on CSR (London, 2014), followed by other world conferences (Nanjing, 2015; Cologne, planned for 2016).

2. THE SPRING OF ENVIRONMENTAL REPORTING FROM SOCIAL REPORTING

Environmental Reporting is much shorter and more recent. As it was said before the environmental sensitivity found its way just in the '90s (Amendola, 2006). Scientific studies had already showed that a continuous development would imply a more and more intensive deployment of not renewable resources and a so deep consumption of renewable ones to make them will be not recovered in the future. According to authoritative studies already in 1985 global consumption of renewable resources exceeds the ability to reconstitute them, and since then such a ratio worsened rapidly year by year. Since '90s, then, the public opinion acknowledges the fact an unlimited growth is not sustainable. The same concept of 'sustainable development' was formulated in 1987 'Brundtland Report' (WCED, 1987) by the World Commission on Environment and Development. After some years one arrives to the signature of a joint document among various countries (the so called 'Agenda 21'), in the Rio de Janeiro Conference of 1992: for the first time principles, objectives and actions for a more equilibrated development are determined under an economic, social and environmental perspective. Rio de Janeiro 'Agenda 21' was still a transition document: the unlimited development was not still denied, but it is theorized a possibility for it is sustainable. The same environmental sensitivity is finally outlined, but beside to the more traditional social one, and then it was not still an autonomous field at all.

Anyway, since then a new literature is to be recorded, this time specific to environmental reporting (Harte & Owen, 1991; Roberts, 1991; Lehman, 1995; Gamble et al., 1996; Krut & Moretz, 2000; Wilmshurst & Frost, 2000) and parallel to the 'social' one. It enjoyed a relevant fortune and more rapid growth in attention. The first efforts, however, were driven toward 'environmental accounts' conceived as parallel to the traditional economic ones of the 'national accounting'. 'Environmental accounting' remains along as a branch of statistics, while corporate environmental accounting finds it hard to take on its own identity. Notwithstanding this, after two decades, a literature and a practice is spread so much to allow some comparative valuations respect to the wider literature on 'social accounting'.

A very relevant document, which resumes the actual sensitivity toward sustainability themes, even for its possible reference to every kind of organization is that one issued in 2011 by the FEE (Fédération des Expert Comptable Européens), which gives an introductive framework on integrated disclosure, by means of 'key indicators' on social and environmental issues, as well as on governance, meant as the qualitative side of information on management. In this document is very relevant the distinction between separated sustainability reporting and integrated sustainability reporting, where 'integration' is meant with reference to traditional financial reporting. The document does not want to choose between them, but indicates both as directed to different stakeholders, then indicating both as opportune in different contexts of reporting. One observes an apparent paradox in the not symmetric relationship between the two kinds of sustainability reporting, namely social and environmental, at least in literature. Literature on social reporting tends, in fact, to include environmental one, as one relevant chapter of the former, and, then, it loses its self-sufficiency in a strict 'social' discourse. Of course there are important exceptions in some national traditions, as in the Italian case, where there is a self-sufficient and robust stream of studies on social reports (Vermiglio, 2000). On the contrary literature on environmental accounting indicates a stronger autonomy, tending to reject specifically social issues, even if it was born just from this previous literature. At a simple glance on scientific contributions on main international reviews it is evident a disproportion between the many articles on environmental accounting and the few on social accounting, these last ones often including the previous ones.

Another difference in comparison is the difference on the point of view. Social accounting and reporting is nearly always from a 'corporate' point of view, starting from firms and progressively expanding toward other kinds of organizations. Environmental one, on the contrary, finds hard to distinguish itself from 'national accounting'. The latter shows official documents (even at a UN level) that are absent in the former, but the 'corporate' dimension remains quite atrophic. What both share, anyway, is the inspiration for a systematic language, then by means of true accounts and not by means of statistic tables or rhetoric clauses. The same term 'reports' for both sustainability fields, reveals, more than a full balancing of stocks and flows as in financial reports, a theoretical trend toward integrated or systematic statements.

Inside specific contents of environmental reports (INTOSAI, 2010), willing to give a sort of systematic view, we find some general premises, largely common to social disclosure, but more agreed information, concerning mainly the following 4 fields of disclosure: (1) Flows of resources, energy and similar issues, external to the reporting entity, or between entity and its environment, expressed in non-monetary terms; (2) Distinction of the specific 'environmental' inside financial accounting (e.g. the costs for environmental recovery); (3) Measurement of stocks, or positions, of environmental resources, and of flows, or variations, in parallel physical and monetary terms; (4) Financial measurement for environmental outcome of economic activity, and in terms of not renewable resource consumption, and in terms of production/consumption residuals (solid, liquid, aeriform), and – more rarely – in terms of positive effects of environmental recovery (e.g. a reforestation action).

3. SUSTAINABILITY REPORTING IN CORPORATION: GENERAL ASPECTS

Sustainability reporting in practice has followed three different ways in correspondence with the three main groups of organizations: enterprises, public bodies, no profit organizations (Hinna, 2005). In enterprises, and particularly in the big corporations, sustainability disclosure belongs mainly to what is called as Corporate Social Responsibility (about reviews on CSR definition, see: Moir, 2001; Dahlsrud, 2008). It is, then, a tool integrating the more traditional financial disclosure to actual and potential investors, which keeps its core business and role. In a nutshell, sustainability disclosure is, for corporation, a projection of traditional disclosure on a broader scenario (Werther and Chandler, 2011). In our opinion, the full understanding of it need a recall of basic features of its historical precedent.

Classical financial disclosure is 'relevant for economic decisions' (*decision useful approach*), and, secondarily, for the 'discharge of manager responsibility' (*stewardship approach*). These two objectives are reached by a comprehensive disclosure on performance, both in terms of controlled financial stocks (resources, when positive, and claims, when negative), and in terms of cash and economic flows, where 'economic' means 'adjusted for competence' cash flows (income and owners contributions, when positive, and expenses and owners distributions, when negative).

Starting from this resumed framework, CSR imagines a sort of 'social contract' (Gray et al., 1988; Sacconi, 2004), similar but wider than corporation contracts, between corporation and a broad set of 'investors' and 'stakeholders'. This time 'investment' is no longer only a capital investment, but also an investment in terms of 'job', 'consumption', and, generally speaking, an 'entrustment' respect to wider social ends. Now stakeholders are not only single persons or categories, but also the society as a whole, and even future generations, as when we account for the consumption of not renewable resources. Thus, accountability reporting, in order to address decisions, interests this set of actual and potential users, and who represents institutionally their interests (e.g. 'state' in the name also of future generations, as abstract titular of the 'common wealth'). Which kinds of decisions to address? Of course not only economic decisions, but the basic decision to renew the 'trust' toward the corporation, so allowing its life and development or not. And, furthermore, there is also an appraisal on management performance in sustainability issues, perhaps with rewards and punishments, even of virtual character, like social consensus or blame.

In the specific contents, respectively, of social and environmental statements, it is impossible – at the state of art – to present a generally agreed framework. Moreover, doctrine is not uniform in deciding if it is opportune to set a rigid and homogeneous structure, or, at the contrary, a flexible and heterogeneous one. We can just observe first recurring nuclei of contents among the various theoretical proposals and practical experiences. There is always a 'descriptive' part, where social and/or environmental phenomena are presented qualitatively, on its turn shared into two parts: one concerning what is 'inside' the corporation, the other what concerns 'outside', that is relationships with not directed involved in production stakeholders. There is, more, a quantitative part, on its turn shared according different criteria. A distinction is between the part of reports that is derived form or linked to financial reports, and the part where social/environmental variables and relations are autonomously disclosed. Another distinction, partially similar to the previous one, is the distinction between the monetary and non-monetary part. The former shows issues like the formation and distribution of the added value, the reclassification of expenses according social or environmental criteria, the monetary translation of positive and negative externalities. The latter affects not monetary variables, expressed in physical quantitative terms (like, e.g., in environmental statements, acquisition and consumption of energy) or in qualitative ones. Another distinction, this time inside the only quantitative part of the reports, is between the strict social/environmental statements and the various information, by means of ratios or other not systematic tools, which accounts for social/environmental performance. The lack of a unit of measurement that makes homogeneous and comparable the different variables seems, till now, to represent an obstacle for the affirmation of a systematic tool, which expresses in a 'bottom line' the environmental/social available value created or destroyed in an administrative period.

To give some examples, issues dealt by social reporting concern, typically: ethical codes, employment, distribution of added value by means of wages or other income, work conditions, life conditions inducted by the corporate, professional training activities, industrial relations, and generally speaking external relations, definitions of stakeholders and of specific activity directed to or for involving them, social investments, quality of good/service and related trade initiatives, contributions to consumers' health, and more.

To give other examples, issues dealt by environmental reporting concern, typically: even here themes related to health and security, environmental sustainability for what concerns consumption renewable and not renewable resources, quantification of pollution, environmental expenses or investments, environmental ratios for positions and variations of environmental variables, stocks and flows of employed resources, both in physical quantitative terms and in monetary terms, environmental impact of life cycle of products, and more. Environmental reporting, for its nature, shows a greater degree of structured information and quantitative languages than the social one, and, more, a more incisive intervention by the law, even if still relatively fragmented. When 'environmental costs' are presented, of course in monetary terms, they are classified into the following categories: costs of prevention and environmental protection, costs of environmental management, costs of recovery and reparation, depreciation of environmental assets.

4. SUSTAINABILITY REPORTING IN CORPORATION: THE ROLE OF STRATEGY

In recent years the international financial crisis is hampering the development of the real economy. Selfish behaviours of companies and financial organizations have guided their decision to short-term choices aimed at maximizing profits. These choices were guided by a partial view in decision-making, which were based exclusively on economic and financial considerations.

In light of the economic disasters caused by the crisis, companies today are changing their paradigm and points of view. Companies are realizing that the maximization of economic and financial objectives in a short-term perspective is counterproductive for themselves, but also for the ecological and socio-cultural environment. The behaviour of firms oriented only to the achievement of profits could compromise the survival of companies, while also reducing the quality of the ecological environment and the quality of life of the communities. The investment decisions of investors consider not only the economic and financial aspects, but also social and environmental ones. This happens not only for ethical reasons, but mainly because it guarantees more security in the investment risk, closely linked with the long-term durability of the company identified for investment (Krosinsky & Robins 2008; Fulton et al., 2012).

Therefore, the predominant concept of current times is 'sustainable development' (Gladwin et al. 1995; Bansal, 2005; Hopwood et al., 2005; Robert et al., 2005; Steurer et al., 2005; Crowther and Aras, 2009) which implies that in the future investors and shareholders will consider investment decision processes more oriented to a long-term and multidimensional perspective. The sensitivity towards sustainability seems to move with the need for a reporting that considers financial, social and economic parameters.

In addition to problems linked to the economic crisis, companies are competing in increasingly large and globalized markets and competitive sectors, where it is much more difficult to defend their competitive advantages and strengths. According to some authors (Nicolò, 2015), the survival of companies depends mainly on their reputation. Consequently, although economic and financial performance is important for the survival of companies, the importance of social and environmental issues is growing. Current and potential customers are increasingly sensitive to sustainability issues when implementing their purchasing processes: quality and safety of goods and services, conditions of workers and environmental protection are variables that customers consider to orient their purchasing decisions. The workers with excellent skills decide to work in companies that have a high reputation, because they are more reliable in meeting the needs expected from employees. Raw material suppliers, service providers and lenders may decide to lower their contractual claims if the corporate reputation is good and shared between stakeholders (e.g. companies can obtain lower costs or more time to fulfil their obligations). Finally, shareholders may choose to invest in companies with high reputation for two reasons: (a) investors want to reward companies that implement social and environmental objectives within their business strategy; (b) investors see safer companies that follow sustainable development strategies, because shareholder value is better guaranteed by financial risks, business failure risks or environmental and ethical scandals.

Companies must define corporate strategy by incorporating in it financial, social and environmental factors. In this way, the strategy of companies can enhance corporate reputation, creating long-term competitive advantages fully compatible with sustainable development. Therefore, companies have to increase corporate reputation, communicating it adequately to stakeholders.

To achieve these objectives, companies can use sustainability reports used not only to account for and report on financial, social and environmental data, but also as a strategic tool to support corporate communication to achieve an increase in reputation.

Managers should follow the steps below to use sustainability reports for effective corporate communication in support of the reputation of the company:

- Clearly define issues, aspects and objectives of corporate sustainable development;
- Involve internal and external stakeholders in defining the issues above (not only shareholders and investors);
- Explain how the strategy of sustainable development (social and environmental objectives) has a positive impact on financial and economic results;
- Communicate sustainability information to stakeholders;
- Make, year by year, the gap analysis between planned objectives of sustainability and actual results.

In the first step, managers identify the relevant issues regarding their sustainability strategy. Second, companies involve stakeholders in order to understand whether the issues identified are really important and shared by them. In the third step, companies intend to convey to stakeholders, especially investors, the link between sustainability objectives and financial aspects of corporate businesses. Then companies show the information on financial, social and environmental objectives to stakeholders, summarized in the corporate sustainability strategy. Finally, through gap analysis, managers give high credibility to the sustainability report, avoiding the risk of using it as a tool to disseminate news on the corporate objectives not actually pursued.

5. TOWARD AN INTEGRATED DISCLOSURE: A PROPOSED MODEL OF SYNTHESIS

All the aforesaid doctrine and practice, as for social accounting and reporting as for environmental accounting and reporting, shares an easily recognizable common denominator.

It is the belonging to all relations, be they internal or external to the entity, of 'not financial' character. In words we are speaking about 'non-financial' accounting. The other main feature is the widening of potential stakeholders, far beyond the classic providers of capital.

The same investors are not only passive subjects respect to sustainability reporting as an external bond, but they are really involved and interested in it, because this is perceived like a tool for evaluating the overall risk of business. Anyway, it is not deniable an evident progressive trend to the integration of various kind of disclosure, between social and environmental reporting for a unique sustainability reporting, and between this last one and traditional financial accounting.

Such an integration has not still got a recognized path. In this section, then, we will try a model of synthesis as a contribution toward a rational and compact synthesis of the three main fields of accountability.

Of course the aim of this proposal is not the pretension to be the 'best way' to consolidation of reports along different sets of variables, but it is assumed as an eventual starting point, among other possible ones, to be criticized and overcome by other more mature approaches. In other words, it is time – in authors' opinion – to go beyond the recurrent vague claims for integration and to experiment concrete operational solutions, even though they could be risky under some methodological points of view.

The first choice we do is toward the privileged single corporate reference. Social reports and, more, environmental reports are to consider distinct from disclosure on a 'national' or 'regional' basis, in order it can be considered to have reached an adequate level of maturity. This means that we neglect flows that are totally external to the organization, because they do not belong to the entity. Flows can concern only either inside the entity or relations between inside and outside, not exclusively outside the entity. These last ones will be able to be considered by a parallel 'national' sustainability accounting, which can share methods and system with corporate accounting (as it happens between classic national accounting and corporate financial accounting). Only by this sharp distinction the corporate dimension could get an adequate methodological development for the required disclosure to stakeholders.

The second choice is the fact that social/environmental disclosure is founded upon some general principles: sustainability, accountability, transparency (Crowther & Aras, 2008). These principles define CSR before the same disclosure on it, and the same business ethics, meant as the discussion on the final ends of corporate. From those ends and from those principles the features of sustainability reporting derive for the benefice of stakeholders.

Every statement of this kind, whichever is its name, looks to have always the following two parts: (1) descriptive part; (2) systematic part.

The former, like in traditional financial statements includes generalities on reporting entity, an introductive part, a definition of entity's social identity, a definition of areas of disclosure and of subjects to whom the information is directed. A broad part of this will be devoted to the tools of implementation for social/environmental policies, to their coordination and finally to their representation and auditing. In it there will be a methodological section that will be the greater the more social and environmental variables communication will not have a generally agreed corpus of representation and communication methodologies.

The latter is made of input/output tables for defined classes of values in their relations between inside the entity and outside it. It is, then, a flow statement, whereas rarer will be the stock accounts, i.e. the accounts representing, in physical unit or in monetary terms, availability of social/environmental value in defined instants of time. This part represents the 'strict' financial statements; it can derive its values from financial accounting by means of satellites accounts, but also charging autonomously other classes of values. The reclassification of accounts from financial accounts is simply the same traditional method adopted by management accounting, on the UN Model of 2003, named IEEA (Integrated Economic and Environmental Accounting).

Social and environmental variables are, and are expressed, both in physical quantities and in monetary terms. The great challenge of the last years is to found a measure, which is both monetary, and then useful for comparisons, and conventional, for including every kind of complexity that is not possible to express in exchange values. Conventions might be the most various, let one thinks at least to the environmental recovery cost, and it is not possible to recall them here. Just for giving a very recognized example of translation of qualitative outcomes to economic proxies we can mention the birth and diffusion of SROI analysis (Social Return on Investments) in the last years.

There are not so many attempts to summarize the three traditional domains, economic, social, and environmental, into a unique account or statement, notwithstanding the wide literature on integrated reporting. Until now, unfortunately, integration seems to be only the putting 'side-by-side' the three dimension, even without a common unit for the only social and environmental variables.

An innovative idea might be the one of pursuing a real systemic approach that combines the three dimension each other. Thus, corporate integrated statements should be ideally shared into three parts, each for a class of values. However, all variables, by means of an opportune convention, would be translated in monetary terms.

Let us look, then, at the following proposal:

Financial Section

Income

- Expenses

= Net Profit or Loss

+ Other Income from Primary Factors of Productions (Earnings not included in Net Profit, Interests, Wages, Rents, Taxes)

= Added Value (AV)

Social-Ethical Section

AV

+ Social Benefits in Money Terms

– Social Costs in Money Terms

= Social-economic Added Value (SEAV)

Environmental-Energetic Section

SEAV

+ Environmental Recovery Actions in Money Terms

– Net Consumption of Natural Resources in Money Terms

= Integrated Environmental-Social-Economic Added Value (ISEAV).

The above model deserves some explicative notes.

First of all, this is 'monetary' disclosure, where 'money' is the unit of size selected for measuring well-being. Thus, it has two explicit boundaries. The former is that it does not take into account what does not belong to the domain of 'translatable' to money. The descriptive part of integrated reports serves for such duties. The systematic part, instead, could only concern what is liable to be systemized. The latter is that 'money' is here only a proxy for measuring net benefits; while it measures 'economic dimensions', it does not represent an 'exchange value' as it does in the traditional domain of financial accounting. Its weakness could be the need for a generally agreed convention in defining criteria of translation to monetary proxies; its strength the power allowed by monetary comparisons in space and time.

Secondly, the label adopted try to cover the most general field liable to disclosure. Out of the financial section, one can give information about a potentially unlimited set of variables and indicators. The model tries to gather them into two main classes. The *former* concerns whatever is linked to manhood and society as a whole. It has been named 'social/ethical' because part of literature assesses social variables for what they simply are or seem to be, without no reference to peculiar ideological or cultural points of view, while others assume a defined set of 'value judgments' and evaluates ethically what is being disclosed. The *latter* concerns whatever is linked to physical and natural contexts. It has been named 'environmental/energetic' to stress, in the second term, the recurrent 'input/output' reporting in terms of energy consumed and produced, while in the first term, position and variations in environmental 'net assets' is underlined.

Third, and finally, some criticism about the sum is possible, considered the heterogeneous spring of the different sources. But the comparability of 'money value' deriving from different sources is necessarily to be entrusted to further research, considered that neither financial accounting, nor non-financial one could ever only deal with strictly homogeneous values. In the same traditional financial accounting, in fact, doctrine and practitioners sum each other cash values, exchange values, historical costs and conventional amounts. A strict choice for homogeneous accounting could make accounting regress toward an archaic cash accounting. There is no reason, then, for not undertaking new roads including new fields of disclosure.

It is possible to affirm that today research has not still invested along this direction. We have no available data, but it would be possible that an implementation of the proposed model could lead to unpleasant results, like that ISEAV could be always, in a societal aggregation, negative and then this model gives the analytical proof that unlimited capitalistic development does not belong to the realm of possible and then that it is condemned to a historical failure. Sustainability accounting could give times and costs of this historical failure.

An alternative model of integrated reporting could be a 'non-systemic' one. In this approach the economic domain, even inserted in a broad social reporting, keeps its own autonomy.

The 'not economic', in this model, results shared into the social and environmental fields of reporting.

The 'social' one should concern the following areas of disclosure: distribution of income, acquisition and/or variations in availability for corporation of 'not financial' resources, like, e.g. organization culture or know-how, creation or destruction of job opportunities and professional growth in the social context of relation, creation or destruction of social security, spreading of the corporation culture outside the boundaries of the organization, civic sense or legality promotion, fight against social exclusion, discrimination, marginalization, and similar things. A focus on basic research funding or culture funding or other similar activities of social impact, could be opened; or, otherwise on infrastructure investments, tangible or intangible be they, which are permanent and of social fruition, then distinguished from contingent entity's investments; or, finally, on 'societal influences', that is social and cultural resources absorbed by the organization from its social context.

The 'environmental' one should concern, more, the following areas of disclosure: physical flows of materials, services and energy, inside the corporation and between inside and outside it, reclassification of financial flows (economic or cash) under an environmental point of view, economic measurement of resources withdrawals from environment, renewable or not be they, economic measurement of solid, liquid and gas waste, economic measurement of environmental recovery.

6. INTEGRATED ASSESSMENT OF CORPORATE SUSTAINABILITY PERFORMANCE: BEST PRACTICES USED BY INTERNATIONAL RATING AGENCIES AND PERFORMANCE ANALYSIS COMPANIES

The previous sections have shown the historical development of sustainability reports. At first, the accounting considered only financial information, because the reporting was exclusively addressed to the owners of the company (shareholders and investors). Then, social information began to be important, therefore reporting was also addressed to a wider group of stakeholders through social reports (community, employees, trade unions, customers, public bodies, etc.). Finally, environmental information assumed great importance with business increasingly impacts on the ecological environment, therefore reporting was addressed to a group of stakeholders interested in the conditions of the environment (employees, customers, environmental groups, animal rights organizations, non-profit organization, public bodies, etc.). Now, as mentioned, companies are focused on integrated reporting, which jointly considers economic, social and environmental information under the concept of 'sustainability' or 'sustainable development'.

In this section, an empirical study is proposed to analyse approaches and techniques used by international rating agencies and performance analysis companies about the assessment of corporate sustainability. This empirical study allows to identify the best practices used in integrated assessment of sustainability, in order to understand whether the techniques followed are aligned with the theoretical approach proposed in paragraphs (see section 5).

Standard & Poor's prepares the listing of sustainable enterprises by the Dow Jones Sustainability Index (DJSI). Literature has focused on the framework used by the Dow Jones Sustainability Group Index (DJSGI) for identifying and ranking companies according to their corporate sustainability performance (Knoepfel, 2001), while other scholars have proposed different empirical studies on the DJSI (Cerin & Dobers, 2001; López et al., 2007; Robinson et al., 2011). Therefore, one of the best known and highly regarded Socially Responsible Investing (SRI) indexes is the Dow Jones Sustainability World Index (Sariannidis et al., 1999).

The quotations of the sustainability performance consider both global indices (World Index World Enlarged Index, World Developed Index) and area indices (Australia Index, Chile Index, Emerging Markets Index, Europe Index, Eurozone Index, Korea Index, Nordic Index, North America Index, United States Index). In this way, S & P highlights the corporate sustainability performance of sustainable enterprises, including both global perspective and limited geographical areas.

The oscillations of DJS indices measure the performance of sustainability based on an integrated evaluation approach, which considers jointly: (a) economic and financial results; (b) social results; (c) environmental results. Consequently, positive oscillations of DJS indices show an increase of the sustainability performance of listed companies in terms of economic, social and environmental results. Conversely, negative oscillations represent lower integrated sustainability performance.

The listing of the companies and their sustainability performance within 'integrated markets' enables investors, and stakeholders in general, to guide their decision-making process more consciously, giving the company the ability to create reputation and enhance its corporate image.

The 'integrated rating' provides reliable information for the choices of the stakeholders, as the sustainability of companies listed on the DJSI market is subjected to an external evaluation by RobecoSAM. In fact, S&P cooperates with RobecoSAM, company that has the task of developing the criteria for integrated assessment of the sustainability of companies ('Corporate Sustainability Assessment' – CSA).

The techniques used by S & P and RobecoSAM represent international best practices for performance evaluation of corporate sustainability, because the evaluation of sustainability performance is based on the criteria proposed by GRI (Global Reporting Initiative[2]), the international leader in the preparation of the sustainability reporting standards. For this reason, they are generally accepted as international best practices. The literature has highlighted the importance of best practices promoted by the GRI, considering both theoretical and empirical contributions (Hussey et al., 2001; Hedberg & von Malmborg, 2003; Willis, 2003; Brown et al., 2009; Levy et al., 2010; Skouloudis, 2010; Brown, 2011; Marimon et al., 2012; Milne & Gray, 2013). In addition, all the biggest and best-known multinational companies adopt these criteria for the preparation of their sustainability reporting (e.g. 3M Co, Adidas AG, AXA SA, Bayer AG, Bombardier Inc, Bridgestone Corp, Cisco System Inc, Danone, Electrolux AB, Eni SpA, Finmeccanica SpA, Henkel AG & Co KGaA, Hewlett-Packard Co, Intel Corp, Johnson & Johnson, LG Electronics Inc, Panasonic Corp, Pirelli & C. SpA, Samsung Electronics Co Ltd, Sony Corp, Unilever NV).

According to the principles adopted by RobecoSAM in official documents (Measuring Intangibles 2015), sustainability performance of companies are assessed using a 'comprehensive approach' (or 'integrated approach') that considers the overall results that affect corporate sustainable development. In particular, valuation practices adopted are based on:

- Economic, social and environmental results;
- Long-term perspective.

Techniques used by S & P and RobecoSAM are based on an integrated assessment approach that is not restricted only to economic and financial factors, but also extends to social and environmental aspects. In addition to this, performance evaluation involves not only shareholders and investors, but certainly a wider audience of stakeholders, such as customers, employees, communities, institutions and associations that are related to the companies evaluated.

The importance of three different evaluative dimensions (economic, social and environmental) is needed because the only financial factors are not useful in evaluating corporate performance excluding non-financial factors. Only if companies define their competitive strategy according to an integrated vision of sustainability can improve their ability to create shareholder value in the long term (Greenwald, 2015).

Companies subject to integrated assessment of sustainability are those that can identify and exploit business opportunities related to the field of sustainability, taking advantage of the emerging chances within the dynamic of industries and markets in which they operate. Rating is based on 'a truly integrated approach to analysing sustainability performance', since specific scores obtained from the assessment in relation to economic, social and environmental dimensions are summarized in an overall score, called 'Total Sustainability Score'. Companies are classified in a ranking; this allows identification of the the leading companies of sustainability in the international context. Through this assessment, companies can highlight and focus on the sustainability factors associated with their business success and value creation. Companies with a higher Total Sustainability Score have a greater chance of high performance resulting from the adoption of best practices of integrated sustainability.

RobecoSAM identifies 59 economic sectors ('industries'), in which companies listed on S&P's DJSI are classified. Economic, social and environmental aspects of businesses are measured using specific parameters. These parameters are 'general', then valid for all the industries, or 'specific', then only valid for a particular industry (to reflect specific sector characteristics). The parameters are weighted with a specific 'weight' based on the parameter importance within the industry.

Assessment methodology is based on questionnaires in relation to which companies respond to questions. Each answer has to be accompanied by a specific documentation to show proof that supports the veracity of the answers. If the issues are relevant or critical, RobecoSAM also requires that such documents are public, then spread among stakeholders.

Parameters for integrated assessment of sustainability are identified with reference to the G4 Sustainability Reporting Guidelines (2015) issued by GRI. A list given by the GRI organization includes parameters that measure dimensions of the Corporate Sustainability Assessment for all industries. The following list does not include all the parameters, but it is useful to provide an overview of the economic, environmental and social measurements of corporate sustainable development:

- **Economic Dimension:** Antitrust policy; brand management; codes of conduct/compliance/corruption & bribery; corporate governance; customer relationship management; financial stability & systemic risk; health & nutrition; independence of content; IT security & system availability; payment transparency; principles of sustainable insurance; privacy protection; product quality and recall management; risk & crisis management; supply chain management; tax strategy.
- **Environmental Dimension:** Biodiversity; climate strategy; environmental policy/management system; environmental reporting; genetically modified organisms; low carbon strategy; operational eco-efficiency; product stewardship; releases to the environment; resource conservation and resource efficiency; water related risks.
- **Social Dimension:** Bioethics; controversial issues, dilemmas in lending/financing; corporate citizenship and philanthropy; human capital development; Labor Practice Indicators and Human Rights; Local Impact of Business Operations; Occupational Health and Safety; Promoting Responsible

Gaming; Responsibility for Alcoholic Products; Responsibility of Content; Responsible Marketing Policies; Social Impacts on Communities; Social Reporting; Stakeholder Engagement; Talent Attraction & Retention.

As mentioned above, some parameters are only used for specific industries. For example, the following fundamental parameters ('highlighted criteria') are considered in relation to the automobile sector (see RobecoSAM Sustainability Yearbook 2015):

- **Economic Dimension:** Health & Nutrition; Innovation Management; Strategy for Emerging Markets.
- **Environmental Dimension:** Climate Strategy; Operational Eco-Efficiency; Water Related Risks.
- **Social Dimension:** Human Capital Development; Labor Practice Indicators and Human Rights; Talent Attraction & Retention.

7. PERFORMANCE ASSESSMENT OF INTEGRATED CORPORATE SUSTAINABILITY: INTERNATIONAL REPORTING PRACTICES FROM AUTOMOBILE COMPANIES

This section shows the results from an analysis of the sustainability reports of automobile companies that have achieved the best sustainable development goals. The decision to study automobile industry is justified by the importance of this economic sector for international economies and for the social and environmental impacts on society and territories. Specifically:

- Automobile companies are faced with many challenges, including the need to define and implement a clear strategy of market positioning in a competitive environment with over-capacity, intense competition and the need for large investments in research and development (R & D). These aspects are certainly critical to economic and financial dimensions of corporate sustainable development.
- Increasingly strict regulations on greenhouse gases emissions and air pollutants, as well as dependence on oil, cause management problems for automobile company, which need to improve energy efficiency and reduce the intensity of carbon emissions (the recent scandal involving Volkswagen group is particularly representative). These aspects are important for environmental dimension of corporate sustainability.
- The impact on society of automobile companies activities is remarkable, considering the number of workers, institutions, trade unions, government agen-

cies and associations involved. These factors are relevant for social dimension of sustainable businesses.

Therefore, accounting practices adopted by carmakers are a particularly representative field of investigation to identify international best practices for the preparation of integrated sustainability reports. In this way, the most recent sustainability reports published by companies that have obtained the best results in RobecoSAM evaluations were analysed in their statements, values and parameters. The sustainability reports analyzed are:

- BMW – Bayerische Motoren Werke AG (Germany) – Gold Class [Sustainable Value Report 2014];
- FCA – Fiat Chrysler Automobile NV (United Kingdom) – Silver Class [Sustainability Report 2014];
- Nissan Motor Co Ltd (Japan) – Silver Class [Sustainability Report 2015];
- Peugeot SA (France) – Bronze Class [CSR Report 2014];
- Renault SA (France) – Bronze Class [Registration Document 2014; CSR Report 2013].

All sustainability reports adopt a comprehensive/integrated approach to reporting. The tables below list the economic, environmental and social parameters used in all integrated reports. In this way, best practices of integrated reporting were identified. The terminology used for the parameters were taken from the 'G4 Sustainability Reporting Guidelines'.

Besides the parameters shown in the table, some sustainability reports consider additional aspects and parameters. Referring to the economic dimension, some companies also consider the following aspects: market presence (e.g. Proportion of

Table 1. Economic aspects and parameters of integrated reporting (best practices)

CATEGORY: ECONOMIC
Aspect: Economic Performance
Direct economic value generated and distributed
Financial implications and other risks and opportunities for the organization's activities due to climate change
Coverage of the organization's defined benefit plan obligations
Aspect: Indirect Economic Impacts
Development and impact of infrastructure investments and services supported
Significant indirect economic impacts, including the extent of impacts

Table 2. Environmental aspects and parameters of integrated reporting (best practices)

CATEGORY: ENVIRONMENTAL
Aspect: Materials
Materials used by weight or volume
Percentage of materials used that are recycled input materials
Aspect: Energy
Energy consumption within the organization
Energy consumption outside of the organization
Energy intensity
Reduction of energy consumption
Reductions in energy requirements of products and services
Aspect: Water
Total water withdrawal by source
Aspect: Biodiversity
Operational sites owned, leased, managed in, or adjacent to, protected areas and areas of high biodiversity value outside protected areas
Aspect: Emissions
Direct greenhouse gas (GHG) emissions (Scope 1)
Energy indirect greenhouse gas (GHG) emissions (Scope 2)
Other indirect greenhouse gas (GHG) emissions (Scope 3)
Greenhouse gas (GHG) emissions intensity
Reduction of greenhouse gas (GHG) emissions
NOX, SOX, and other significant air emissions
Aspect: Effluents and Waste
Total water discharge by quality and destination
Total weight of waste by type and disposal method
Total number and volume of significant spills
Aspect: Products and Services
Extent of impact mitigation of environmental impacts of products and services
Aspect: Compliance
Monetary value of significant fines and total number of non-monetary sanctions for non-compliance with environmental laws and regulations
Aspect: Transport
Significant environmental impacts of transporting products and other goods and materials for the organization's operations, and transporting members of the workforce

Table 3. Social aspects and parameters of integrated reporting (best practices)

CATEGORY: SOCIAL
SUB-CATEGORY: LABOR PRACTICES AND DECENT WORK
Aspect: Employment
Total number and rates of new employee hires and employee turnover by age group, gender, and region
Benefits provided to full-time employees that are not provided to temporary or part-time employees, by significant locations of operation
Aspect: Occupational Health and Safety
Percentage of total workforce represented in formal joint management–worker health and safety committees that help monitor and advise on occupational health and safety programs
Type of injury and rates of injury, occupational diseases, lost days, and absenteeism, and total number of workrelated fatalities, by region and by gender
Health and safety topics covered in formal agreements with trade unions
Aspect: Training and Education
Average hours of training per year per employee by gender, and by employee category
Programs for skills management and lifelong learning that support the continued employability of employees and assist them in managing career endings
Aspect: Diversity and Equal Opportunity
Composition of governance bodies and breakdown of employees per employee category according to gender, age group, minority group membership, and other indicators of diversity
SUB-CATEGORY: HUMAN RIGHTS
Aspect: Investment
Total hours of employee training on human rights policies or procedures concerning aspects of human rights that are relevant to operations, including the percentage of employees trained
SUB-CATEGORY: SOCIETY
Aspect: Anti-corruption
Communication and training on anti-corruption policies and procedures
Aspect: Supplier Assessment for Impacts on Society
Significant actual and potential negative impacts on society in the supply chain and actions taken
SUB-CATEGORY: PRODUCT RESPONSIBILITY
Aspect: Customer Health and Safety
Percentage of significant product and service categories for which health and safety impacts are assessed for improvement
Aspect: Product and Service Labeling
Results of surveys measuring customer satisfaction

senior management hired from the local community at significant locations of operation); procurement practices (e.g. Proportion of spending on local suppliers at significant locations of operation). Referring to the environmental dimension, additional aspects are considered: overall (e.g. Total environmental protection expenditures and investments by type); Supplier Environmental Assessment (e.g. Percentage of new suppliers that were screened using environmental criteria; Environmental Grievance Mechanisms (e.g. Number of grievances about environmental impacts filed, addressed, and resolved through formal grievance mechanisms). With reference to the social dimension, additional aspects are: Equal Remuneration for Women and Men (e.g. Ratio of basic salary and remuneration of women to men by employee category, by significant locations of operation); Supplier Assessment for Labor Practices (e.g. Percentage of new suppliers that were screened using labor practices criteria); Non-discrimination (e.g. Total number of incidents of discrimination and corrective actions taken); Child Labor (e.g. Operations and suppliers identified as having significant risk for incidents of child labor, and measures taken to contribute to the effective abolition of child labor); Forced or Compulsory Labor (e.g. Operations and suppliers identified as having significant risk for incidents of forced or compulsory labor, and measures to contribute to the elimination of all forms of forced or compulsory labor); Indigenous Rights (e.g. Total number of incidents of violations involving rights of indigenous peoples and actions taken); Local Communities (e.g. Percentage of operations with implemented local community engagement, impact assessments, and development programs); Anti-competitive Behaviour (e.g. Total number of legal actions for anti-competitive behaviour, anti-trust, and monopoly practices and their outcomes); Customer Privacy (e.g. Total number of substantiated complaints regarding breaches of customer privacy and losses of customer data).

Empirical analysis highlights the best international practices, which consider the sustainability performance reporting in accordance with a global vision, measured through multi-dimensional parameters. The *common* aspects and parameters of the five companies observed belonging to automobile industry have identified integrated reporting best practices in this specific industrial sector. Additional parameters identified in some sustainability reports indicate that the integrated reporting practices are still developing, which tend toward expansion of the range of aspects and parameters for measuring corporate sustainability results.

The results of the empirical analysis of sustainability reports are summarized in the following key points:

- The sustainability reports adopt a holistic approach, according to which sustainability performance is measured by analysing the economic, social and environmental results jointly achieved.
- The sustainability reports analysed contain various types of information: qualitative information (e.g. Descriptions of management approaches and future lines of action); quantitative-monetary information (e.g. investment to

ensure safety at workplaces and environmental security); quantitative-technical information (e.g. consumption of energy and natural resources).

- The sustainability reports have two different perspectives: the first one is an 'ex-post reporting' (closing perspective), used by companies to highlight corporate sustainability results achieved; the second one is an 'ex-ante reporting' (preventive perspective), used to program the future goals of corporate sustainable development.
- The sustainability reports are aimed at a wide range of stakeholders: not only shareholders, but also employees, customers, suppliers, communities, territories, associations, non-profit organizations, trade unions, non-governmental organizations, public bodies, states and governments.
- The sustainability reports adopt information representation criteria that are also designed for non-expert users, therefore 'user-friendly' information to facilitate their understanding of the content (e.g. digital interaction on the reports contents, summary tables with the most important data, photos, images, graphics, summary and interpretation schemes, description of approaches used to simplify the learning data, interviews, appendices with more detailed information).
- The sustainability reports have characteristics that enable them to support the communication strategy of companies to spread, increase and maintain their corporate reputation.
- The sustainability reports analysed adopt an integrated, but not systemic, approach because there is no single measure that summarizes and expresses economic, social and environmental results achieved.

CONCLUSION

In this chapter we presented the theme of sustainability reports for as concerns the social dimension, the environmental one, the integrated one (financial-social-environmental). The chapter, then, deals with the corporate institutional communication in a broader sense than the traditional financial disclosure.

The chapter, after having presented and defined its object, shows the historical progress toward the sustainability reports in its different dimensions in the last decades, proposes a theoretical basis for the integrated reports, verifies a correspondence of this last one with general agreed criteria for evaluating the sustainability performance, and, particularly, endeavors an empirical survey on the car production sector, considered one of the most environment sensitive industry of the world.

It is time, now, for some conclusive clauses about the main results of this reconstruction.

Management and accounting literature, in these last years, gave a pressure for broadening disclosure on the social impact of corporate activity.

This broadening, before limited to strict social issues, after to environmental ones, is now generally conceived in a more integrated shape. But the attitude of disclosure is not so different from the traditional one, at least in a logical sense. We observe information useful for decisions (not only and no longer only economic decisions) and we observe information useful for a discharge of responsibility (not only and no longer only toward ownership of corporate). As well as investors entrust their capital to management, so society, in a wider sense, entrusts a role to single corporate.

The set of stakeholders is now greater than in the past, and includes also generic 'subjects' like 'public opinion' or the 'future generations', but social issues matter also for traditional stakeholders, even the same investors who could be very interested on the sustainability of their investment.

Sustainability reports as the main tangible outcome of CSR on one hand discovers a new field for corporate ends, i.e. the business ethics, giving substance and verifiability to it, and, on the other hand, strengthens the traditional ends of value creation, with a long-sighted vision.

Corporations realize, just in the years of the great crisis (after 2007) that a short-sighted perspective can endanger the same long-time survival of themselves. In a more and more integrated and globalized arena, environmental and social reputation becomes a core strategic issue, to which customers (and not only them) are more and more sensitive. The same value of shares looks influenced by the risk of environmental scandals and investing on a social-environmental sustainable corporation is not only a fact of ethics but simply a rational attitude.

Of course sustainability reports may not be kept separated from financial ones. Integration looks the natural outcome for a clear disclosure toward stakeholders.

Focus of disclosure, then, is on the risk it can become a propaganda exercise, not verifiable by an independent auditing.

This risk could be avoided, exactly as happened since '30 years in U.S.A. after the Great Depression in traditional accounting, by a regulation; regulation that now is moving just its first steps.

In any case, regulation needs a doctrinal effort for designing a framework, an ideal model for this integrated reports. Our contribution could be read in this perspective. In this paper we propose two models of integration. A first one – non-systemic – gives a regulation on single items of disclosure but does not integrate the three dimensions into a unique value. A second one – systemic – tries to integrate the three dimensions, expressing in money terms externalities, i.e. benefits and costs for society in the widest sense, financial, social or environmental could they be.

The two theoretical solutions show vantages and disadvantages because the strength of one single bottom line (in the second approach) could face the risk of over-simplification for externalities that, by their nature, cannot be translated in money terms, even by the help of proxies.

Analysis of praxis seems to corroborate our general suggestions. Integration of disclosure is now real, and all three are resumed in a general discourse on sustainability. Scoring of Dow Jones and RobecoSAM seem to enforce the idea that success in competition is due to a harmonic and systematic combination of financial success inside corporation and financial-social-environmental success outside it.

Comparison between theory and law, by one side, and empirical analysis, by the other side, looks a progressive reduction of the gap between what corporations do and what they should. What it is still weak, perhaps, seems the relationship between a defined and clear ex ante perspective (programming, forecasting about social-environmental impact of business activity) and the ex post one (the sustainability reports, in words).

Empirical observation confirms theoretical intuition of the need for a really integrated reporting. Financial, Social and Environmental Reports are generally now parts of integrated 'sustainability' reports. What it is not confirmed, however, is the trend toward what we called the 'systemic approach'. Translation of social and environmental benefits and costs in terms of money or economic proxies is moving just its first steps, being generally preferred what we called the 'non systemic approach'.

Another feature emerging from the survey is the great variance in structure, recognition, evaluation, presentation, disclosure from one corporation to another.

These two main results may suggest two practical indications for research and regulation in this field.

First one is the theoretical investment on the 'systemic approach'. Lack of a unique unit of measurement, in fact, is a weakness for sustainability reporting.

Second one is the need for a compulsory regulation on sustainability reporting, not necessarily only on a global basis, because of the importance of 'national' or 'sector' classes of stakeholders (but here regulation could intervene by means of G.A.A.P.).

The challenge of the next years seems to be the enhancement along these two dimension, in order disclosure in environment and social issues can establish really a link between corporation and stakeholders and not only is an unreliable rhetoric mean of corporation propaganda.

REFERENCES

Adams, C. A. (2004). The ethical, social and environmental reporting-performance portrayal gap. *Accounting, Auditing & Accountability Journal*, *17*(5), 731–757. doi:10.1108/09513570410567791

Amendola, C. (2006). *La gestione ambientale e i suoi strumenti – Il bilancio ambientale per la rilevazione dei costi*. Roma: Aracne.

Anand, S., & Sen, A. (2000). Human Development and Economic Sustainability. *World Development*, *28*(12), 2029–2049. doi:10.1016/S0305-750X(00)00071-1

Bansal, P. (2005). Evolving sustainably: A longitudinal study of corporate sustainable development. *Strategic Management Journal*, *26*(3), 197–218. doi:10.1002/smj.441

Brown, H. S. (2011). Global Reporting Initiative. In Handbook of Transnational Governance. Cambridge, UK: Polity Press.

Brown, H. S., de Jong, M., & Lessidrenska, T. (2009). The rise of the Global Reporting Initiative: A case of institutional entrepreneurship. *Environmental Politics*, *18*(2), 182–200. doi:10.1080/09644010802682551

Busco, C., Frigo, M. L., Riccaboni, A., & Quattrone, P. (Eds.). (2003). Integrated Reporting Concepts and Cases that Redefine Corporate Accountability. Springer.

Carroll, A. B. (1991). The Pyramid of Corporate Social Responsibility: Toward the Moral Management of Organizational Stakeholders. *Business Horizons*, *34*(July-August), 39–48. doi:10.1016/0007-6813(91)90005-G

Carroll, A. B. (1998). The Four Faces of Corporate Citizenship. *Business and Society Review*, *100/101*(1), 1–7. doi:10.1111/0045-3609.00008

Carroll, A. B. (2000). Ethical Challenges for Business in the New Millennium: Corporate Social Responsibility and Models of Management Morality. *Business Ethics Quarterly*, *10*(1), 33–42. doi:10.2307/3857692

Cerin, P., & Dobers, P. (2001). What does the performance of the Dow Jones Sustainability Group Index tell us? *Eco-Management and Auditing*, *8*(3), 123–133. doi:10.1002/ema.159

Commission of the European Communities. (2001). Green Paper: Promoting a European framework for Corporate Social Responsibility. Brussels: Author.

Crowther, D., & Aras, G. (2008). *Corporate Social Responsibility*. BookBoon.

Crowther, D., & Aras, G. (2009). *The Durable Corporation: Strategies for Sustainable Development*. Gower.

Dahlsrud, A. (2008). How corporate social responsibility is defined: An analysis of 37 definitions. *Corporate Social Responsibility and Environmental Management*, *15*(1), 1–13. doi:10.1002/csr.132

Dawkins, J., & Lewis, S. (2003). CSR in Stakeholder Expectations: And Their Implication for Company Strategy. *Journal of Business Ethics*, *44*(2), 185–193. doi:10.1023/A:1023399732720

Di Giandomenico, M. E. (2008). *Il bilancio sociale e il modulo aziendale etico*. Milano: Giuffrè.

European Parliament and Council. (2003). *DIRECTIVE 2003/51/EC amending Directives 78/660/EEC, 83/349/EEC, 86/635/EEC and 91/674/EEC on the annual and consolidated accounts of certain types of companies, banks and other financial institutions and insurance undertakings*. Author.

Fédération des Experts-comptables Européens. (2011). *Integrated Reporting. Debates and developments around the concept of integrated reporting are growing in importance*. Author.

Figge, F., & Hahn, T. (2004). Sustainable Value Added – measuring corporate contributions to sustainability beyond eco-efficiency. *Ecological Economics*, *48*(2), 173–187. doi:10.1016/j.ecolecon.2003.08.005

Freeman, R. E. (1984). *Strategic management: A stakeholder approach*. London: Pitman.

Freeman, R. E., & Evan, W. (1988). A stakeholder theory of the modern corporation: Kantian capitalism. In T. L. Beauchamp & N. E. Bowie (Eds.), *Ethical theory and business*. Englewood Cliffs, NJ: Prentice Hall.

Friedman, M. (1962). *Capitalism and Freedom*. Chicago: University of Chicago Press.

Fulton, M., Kahn, B. M., & Sharples, C. (2012). *Sustainable Investing: Establishing Long-Term Value and Performance. In Climate Change Investment Research*. Deutsche Bank Group.

Gabrovec Mei, O. (1990). *Il linguaggio contabile – Itinerario storico e metodologico*. Torino: Giappichelli.

Gamble, G. O., Hsu, K., Jackson, C., & Tollerson, C. D. (1996). Environmental disclosures in annual reports: An international perspective. *The International Journal of Accounting*, *31*(3), 293–331. doi:10.1016/S0020-7063(96)90022-9

Gladwin, T. N., Kennelly, J. J., & Krause, T. S. (1995). Shifting Paradigms for Sustainable Development: Implications for Management Theory and Research. *Academy of Management Review*, *20*(4), 874–907.

Global Reporting Initiative. (2015). *G4 Sustainability Reporting Guidelines. Reporting Principles and Standard Disclosure*. Amsterdam: GRI.

Gray, R., Owen, D., & Adams, C. (1996). *Accounting & accountability: Changes and challenges in corporate social and environmental reporting*. London: Prentice Hall.

Gray, R., Owen, D., & Maunders, K. (1988). Corporate Social Reporting: Emerging Trends in Accountability and the Social Contract. *Accounting, Auditing & Accountability Journal*, *1*(1), 6–20. doi:10.1108/EUM0000000004617

Greenwald, C. (2015). *Focus on Financial Materiality. Measuring Intangibles. In ROBECOSAM's Corporate Sustainability Assessment Methodology*. Zurich: RobecoSAM AG.

Group, B. M. W. (2014). *Sustainable Value Report 2014*. Bayerische Motoren Werke AG.

Group, F. C. A. (2014). Sustainability Report 2014. Fiat Chrysler Automobile NV.

Guthrie, J., & Yongvanich, K. (2006). An extended performance reporting framework for social and environmental accounting. *Business Strategy and the Environment*, *15*(5), 309–321.

Harte, G., & Owen, D. (1991). Environmental Disclosure in the Annual Reports of British Companies: A Research Note. *Accounting, Auditing & Accountability Journal*, *4*(3), 09513579110144442. doi:10.1108/09513579110144442

Hedberg, C. J., & von Malmborg, F. (2003). The Global Reporting Initiative and corporate sustainability reporting in Swedish companies. *Corporate Social Responsibility and Environmental Management*, *10*(3), 153–164. doi:10.1002/csr.38

Hinna, L. (2005). *Come gestire la responsabilità sociale dell'impresa. Processi, strumenti e modelli*. Milano: Il Sole 24 Ore.

Hopwood, B., Mellor, M., & OBrien, G. (2005). Sustainable development: Mapping different approaches. *Sustainable Development*, *13*(1), 38–52. doi:10.1002/sd.244

Hussey, D. M., Kirsop, P. L., & Meissen, R. E. (2001). Global Reporting Initiative Guidelines: An Evaluation of Sustainable Development Metrics for Industry. *Environmental Quality Management*, *11*(1), 1–20. doi:10.1002/tqem.1200

Idowu, S. (Ed.). (2012). Encyclopedia of CSR. Springer.

Kaplan, R. S., & Norton, D. P. (1996). *The Balanced Scorecard - translating strategy into action*. Boston: Harvard Business School Press.

Knoepfel, I. (2001). Dow Jones Sustainability Group Index: A Global Benchmark for Corporate Sustainability. *Corporate Environmental Strategy*, *8*(1), 6–15. doi:10.1016/S1066-7938(00)00089-0

Krosinsky, C., & Robins, N. (2008). *Sustainable Investing: The Art of Long-Term Performance*. London: Heartscan.

Krut, R., & Moretz, A. (2000). The state of global environmental reporting: Lessons from the global 100. *Corporate Environmental Strategy*, *7*(1), 85–91. doi:10.1016/S1066-7938(00)80117-7

Lehman, G. (1995). A Legitimate Concern for Environmental Accounting. *Critical Perspectives on Accounting*, *6*(5), 393–412. doi:10.1006/cpac.1995.1037

Levy, D. L., Brown, H. S., & de Jong, M. (2010). The Contested Politics of Corporate Governance The Case of the Global Reporting Initiative. *Business & Society*, *49*(1), 88–115. doi:10.1177/0007650309345420

Lionzo, A. (2012). *Gli studi di financial accounting di matrice nordamericana. Fondamenti epistemologici e percorsi scientifici*. Milano: Franco Angeli.

Lipari, C., & Costa, M. (2005). Istituzionalismi di imprese e di bilancio tra passato, presente e futuro. Atti dell'VIII Convegno Nazionale della Società Italiana di Storia della Ragioneria. Teramo.

López, M. V., Garcia, A., & Rodriguez, L. (2007). Sustainable Development and Corporate Performance: A Study Based on the Dow Jones Sustainability Index. *Journal of Business Ethics*, *75*(3), 285–300. doi:10.1007/s10551-006-9253-8

Margolis, J. D., & Walsh, J. P. (2003). Misery Loves Companies: Whither Social Initiatives by Business. *Administrative Science Quarterly*, *48*(2), 268–305. doi:10.2307/3556659

Marimon, F., del Mar Alonso-Almeida, M., del Pilar Rodríguez, M., & Alejandro, K. A. C. (2012). The worldwide diffusion of the global reporting initiative: What is the point? *Journal of Cleaner Production*, *33*, 132–144. doi:10.1016/j.jclepro.2012.04.017

McWilliams, A., & Siegel, D. (2000). Corporate social responsibility and financial performance: Correlation or misspecification? *Strategic Management Journal*, *21*(5), 603–609. doi:10.1002/(SICI)1097-0266(200005)21:5<603::AID-SMJ101>3.0.CO;2-3

Milne, M. J., & Gray, R. (2013). W(h)ither Ecology? The Triple Bottom Line, the Global Reporting Initiative, and Corporate Sustainability Reporting. *Journal of Business Ethics*, *118*(1), 13–29. doi:10.1007/s10551-012-1543-8

Mintz, S. (Ed.). (2014). Accounting for the Public Interest – Perspectives on Accountability, Professionalism and Role in Society. Springer.

Moir, L. (2001). What do we mean by corporate social responsibility?. *Corporate Governance: The International Journal of Business in Society*, *1*(2), 16 – 22.

Nicolò, D. (2000). Il bilancio sociale come strumento di governo delle relazioni con gli stakeholder. In F. Vermiglio (Ed.), *Nuovi strumenti di comunicazione aziendale. Confronto di esperienze in tema di bilancio sociale*. Torino: Giappichelli.

Nicolò, D. (2015). Towards a theory on corporate reputation and survival of young firms. *Procedia Economics and Finance*, *22*, 296–303. doi:10.1016/S2212-5671(15)00289-0

Nissan Motor Corporation. (2015). *Sustainability Report 2015*. Nissan Motor Co Ltd.

Patten, D. N. (1990). The market reaction to social responsibility disclosures: The case of the Sullivan principles signings. *Accounting, Organizations and Society*, *15*(6), 575–587. doi:10.1016/0361-3682(90)90035-S

Peugeot, S. A.Group. (2014). *CSR Report 2014*. PSA Peugeot Citroën.

Renault, S. A.Group. (2013). *CSR Report 2013*. Groupe Renault.

Renault, S. A.Group. (2014). *Registration Document 2014*. Groupe Renault.

Robeco, S. A. M. (2015). *Measuring Intangibles. ROBECOSAM's Corporate Sustainability Assessment Methodology*. Zurich: RobecoSAM AG.

Robeco, S. A. M. (2015). *The Sustainability Yearbook 2015*. Zurich: RobecoSAM AG.

Robert, K. W., Parris, T. M., & Leiserowitz, A. A. (2005). What is Sustainable Development? Goals, Indicators, Values, and Practice. *Environment: Science and Policy for Sustainable Development*, *47*(3), 8–21. doi:10.1080/00139157.2005.10524444

Roberts, C. B. (1991). Environmental Disclosures: A Note on Reporting Practices in Mainland Europe. *Accounting, Auditing & Accountability Journal*, *4*(3), 09513579110005536. doi:10.1108/09513579110005536

Robinson, M., Kleffner, A., & Bertels, S. (2011). Signaling Sustainability Leadership: Empirical Evidence of the Value of DJSI Membership. *Journal of Business Ethics*, *101*(3), 493–505. doi:10.1007/s10551-011-0735-y

Sacconi, L. (2004). Corporate Social Responsibility (CSR) as a Model of 'Extended' Corporate Governance: An Explanation Based on the Economic Theories of Social Contract, Reputation and Reciprocal Conformism. *LIUC, Ethics, Law and Economics*, Paper No. 142.

Sariannidis, N., Koskosas, I., Kartalis, N., & Konteos, G. (2009). Macroeconomic Effects on D.J.S.I. - World Returns. *International Journal of Economic Sciences and Applied Research*, *2*(2), 95–110.

Schmalenbach, E. (1919). Grundlagen dynamischer Bilanzlehre. Zeitschrift für handelswissenschaftliche Forschung, 13.

Skouloudis, A., Evangelinos, K., & Kourmousis, F. (2010). Assessing non-financial reports according to the Global Reporting Initiative guidelines: Evidence from Greece. *Journal of Cleaner Production*, *18*(5), 426–438. doi:10.1016/j.jclepro.2009.11.015

Solomons, D. (1974). Corporate social performance: a new dimension in accounting reports? In H. Edey & B.S. Yamey (Eds.), Debits, Credits, Finance and Profits. London: Sweet & Maxwell.

Steurer, R., Langer, M. E., Konrad, A., & Martinuzzi, A. (2005). Corporations, Stakeholders and Sustainable Development I: A Theoretical Exploration of Business–Society Relations. *Journal of Business Ethics*, *61*(3), 263–281. doi:10.1007/s10551-005-7054-0

Tinker, T. (Ed.). (1984). Social Accounting for Corporations. Private Enterprises versus Public Interest. Manchester, UK: Manchester University Press.

Unerman, J. (2000). Methodological issues: Reflections on quantification in corporate social reporting content analysis. *Accounting, Auditing & Accountability Journal*, *13*(5), 667–680. doi:10.1108/09513570010353756

United Nations. (1992). *Agenda 21.United Nations Conference on Environment & Development, Rio de Janerio*, Brazil.

United Nations, European Commission, International Monetary Fund, Organization for Economic Cooperation and Development, & World Bank (2003). The Handbook of National Integrated Environmental and Economic Accounting. New York: ONU.

Vallance, S., Perkins, H. C., & Dixon, J. E. (2011). What is social sustainability? A clarification of concepts. *Geoforum*, *42*(3), 342–348. doi:10.1016/j.geoforum.2011.01.002

Van Marrewijk, M. (2003). Concept and definitions of CSR and corporate sustainability: Between agency and communion. *Journal of Business Ethics*, *44*(2), 95–105. doi:10.1023/A:1023331212247

Vermiglio, F. (Ed.). (2000). Nuovi strumenti di comunicazione aziendale. Confronto di esperienze in tema di bilancio sociale. Torino. Giappichelli.

WCED. (1987). *Our Common Future. World Commission on Environment and Development*. Oxford University Press.

Werther, W. B., & Chandler, D. (2011). Strategic Corporate Social Responsibility: Stakeholders in a Global Environment. *Sage (Atlanta, Ga.)*.

Willis, A. (2003). The Role of the Global Reporting Initiatives Sustainability Reporting Guidelines in the Social Screening of Investments. *Journal of Business Ethics*, *43*(3), 233–237. doi:10.1023/A:1022958618391

Wilmshurst, T. D., & Frost, G. R. (2000). Corporate environmental reporting: A test of legitimacy theory. *Accounting, Auditing & Accountability Journal*, *13*(1), 10–26. doi:10.1108/09513570010316126

Working Group on Environmental Auditing. (2010). *Environmental Accounting: Current Status and Options for SAIs*. INTOSAI.

Zappa, G. (1937). *Il reddito d'impresa: Scritture doppie, conti e bilanci di aziende commerciali*. Milano: Giuffrè.

ENDNOTES

1 Massimo Costa is the author of the Introduction, section 1, 2, 3, 5, and the Conclusion. Giuseppe Valenza is the author of sections 4, 6, 7.

2 As reported in the official website, 'GRI is an international independent organization that helps businesses, governments and other organizations understand and communicate the impact of business on critical sustainability issues such as climate change, human rights, corruption and many others'. See: https://www.globalreporting.org.

Chapter 4
A Game Theory Coopetitive Perspective for Sustainability of Global Feeding:
Agreements Among Vegan and Non-Vegan Food Firms

David Carfì
University of California – Riverside, USA

Alessia Donato
University of Messina, Italy

Dania Panuccio
University of Messina, Italy

ABSTRACT

Throughout this study, the authors propose possible agreements among different food producers, in order to develop a new better conceived diet for the future generations, by using a coopetitive approach and game theory. Specifically, the authors shall consider food producers and sellers of vegan (respectively, vegetarian) and non-vegan (or non-vegetarian) food. The coopetitive approach used by the authors provides a mathematical game theory model, which could help producers of vegan food a simpler entry in the market and free significant publicity. Meanwhile, the

DOI: 10.4018/978-1-5225-2075-7.ch004

model could allow producers of non-vegetarian food a smooth transaction to vegetarian and vegan production. In particular, authors propose an agreement setting among McDonald's and Muscle of Wheat, because they think that Muscle of Wheat cannot enter a global market without the help of a large food producer already in the market. The game theory model represents an asymmetric R&D alliance between McDonald's and Muscle of Wheat.

INTRODUCTION

General Perspective and Objectives

In this chapter, the authors study a game theory model for the sustainability of food production. Specifically, we construct a coopetitive model suggesting general possible alliances among vegan and non-vegan food producers. It is now well known that the meat production has begun non-sustainable, from several points of view. Moreover, the meat consumption reveals linked with heart strokes, cancers, diabetes and several other diseases. Indeed, affluent citizens in middle-income and low-income countries are adopting similar high-meat diets and experiencing increased rates of those chronic diseases. The industrial agricultural system (nowadays, the predominant form of agriculture in the USA and increasingly world-wide) - required for the meat and dairy production - determines consequences for public health, owing to:

- Its extensive use of fertilizers and pesticides;
- Strongly unsustainable use of resources (such as water and fertile soil);
- High environmental pollution.

Moreover, in industrial animal production, we emphasize the strong public health concerns for feed formulations, including animal tissues, arsenic and antibiotics. We underline also the strong concerns for the induced laborer health risks - coming from such unsustainable work - and also for the consequent related health hazards regarding the communities living close to the meat production factories.

A Game Theory Approach

We shall consider possible agreements among different food producers, in order to develop a new better conceived diet for the future generations, by using a coopetitive approach and game theory. Our coopetitive approach provides a mathematical game theory model, which could help producers of vegan food a simpler entry in the market and free significant publicity. Meanwhile, our model could allow producers of non-vegetarian food a smooth transaction to vegetarian and vegan production.

Economic Perspective

Everywhere, during the last years, the industry is taking increasingly more note of the evident circumstance that vegetarians and vegans worlds represent a very attractive economic target. Nowadays, indeed, the major brands of the food industry are trying to create more space for themselves in a food market increasingly less niche and continuously widening.

Vegan Consumption in Europe

In Europe, the "average" consumer shows an increasing interest for alternative foods with respect to meat and dairy products: it is evident the gradual growth in sales of products based on soy, almonds, coconuts, legumes, seeds, beans and other noble vegetables - coming from, also, a thorough marketing campaign which in recent years has extolled the virtues of the legumes health benefits (see Seclì, 2007).

BACKGROUND

Literature Reviews on Food Production

In this section we present, by citing some relevant sentences, some of the literature we used for the construction of our ideas about the sustainability of food production.

Problems with Meat Production

In an article of 2005 written by Walker, Rhubart-Berg, McKenzie, Kelling, and Lawrence, we read: "We live in a world of contradictions, where one billion people are overweight or obese and another one billion lack adequate food resources, despite the fact that current world food production could feed the 6.3 billion people on Earth (now 7.5 billion people), if distributed equitably and based on a diet with only moderate amounts of animal products Animal products, however, are the primary source of saturated fat responsible for higher risk of cardiovascular disease, diabetes mellitus and some cancers. Meat itself is also associated with increased risk of some cancers. An important public health challenge is to provide adequate amounts of protein and essential nutrients without also causing over-consumption of saturated fat" (see Walker et al., 2005).

Costs of Non-Vegan Food Production

Consider the following data about the costs of meat production as reported by Fiala (2008): "Current production processes for meat products have been shown to have a significant impact on the environment, accounting for between 15% and 24% of current greenhouse gas emissions. Meat consumption has been increasing at a fantastic rate and is likely to continue to do so into the future" (see Fiala, 2008).

Moreover, in Nguyen, Hermansen, and Mogensen (n.d.), we read: "The environmental costs of meat are displayed as characterized results at different midpoint categories e.g. global warming, nature occupation, acidification, eutrophication, ecotoxicity, etc.

In decreasing order of importance, nature occupation has been found to be the main contributor to the costs (55%), followed by global warming (21%) and respiratory inorganics (18%).

A breakdown of the external costs into three damage categories shows that impacts on ecosystems obtain high importance with 80% contribution to the costs whereas impacts on human well-being and impacts on resource productivity carry relatively low importance with 15% and 5% contribution, respectively.

Approximately 75.4% of the environmental costs of pig meat production is related to feed production and the remaining is distributed among the other sub processes, "emissions from housing and manure storage", "manure utilization for crop fertilization", "feed transport and direct energy use" by 16.3%, 3.2%, 3.7% and 1.2% respectively.

As for the detailed information about on which part (or component) of the pig meat life cycle, the highest load of different environmental impacts occurs or the largest potential for improvements lies, Figure 1 summarizes the results of such analysis".

For a deeper study you can read Nguyen et al. (n.d.).

Meat and Sustainability: Data of the Consumption of Meat in the World

Recent data, however, show that in the US, with a population of 316 million in habitants, but also in other European countries, the consumption of animal products is decreasing: 6% between 2006 and 2010. Aided by the economic downturn, but even healthier lifestyles, responsible and sustainable - for example, is increasing in the number of vegetarians or vegans. Western countries are slightly changing their

Figure 1. Breakdown of contributing sub-processes and contributing impact categories
Source: Nguyen et al., n.d.

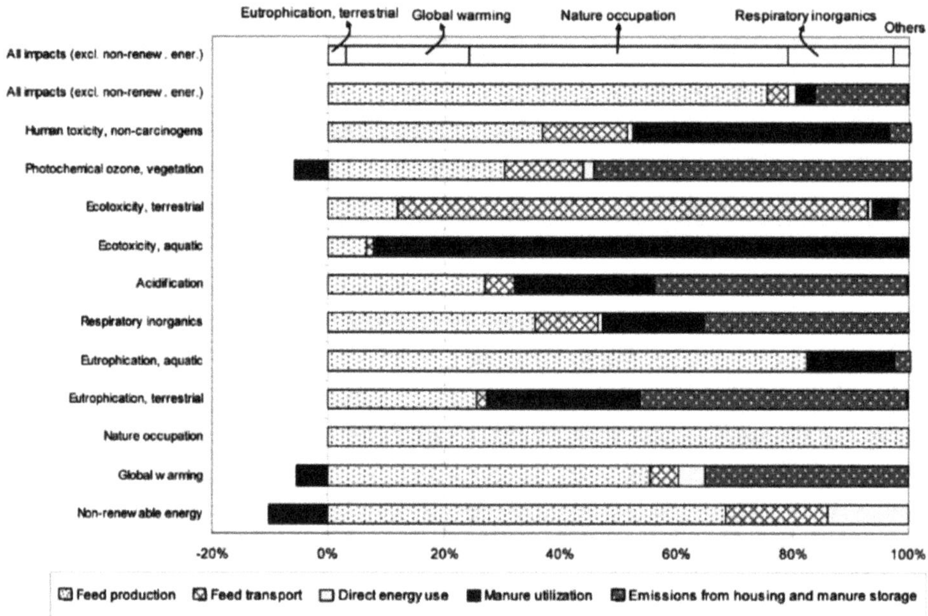

eating habits or keeping them less stable. Other countries see their meat consumption increase, i.e., very large and densely populated countries experiencing a period of strong economic growth. They are the BRICS countries (Brazil, Russia, India, China, South Africa) (see Figure 2).

What the W.H.O. Said on Meat

Epidemiological studies suggest that increases in the risk of several cancers are associated with high consumption of red meat or processed meat. These risks are very important for public health because many people worldwide eat meat and meat consumption is increasing in low- and middle - income countries (See Figure 3).

A group of 22 international experts, from 10 countries, examined more than 800 different studies on cancer in humans, and summarized the data in a document of IARC, the International Agency for Research on Cancer. Red meat was classified as "Group 2A - probably carcinogenic to humans", and processed meat was classified as "Group 1 - carcinogenic to humans". Processed meat has been classified in the same category as causes of cancer such as tobacco smoking and asbestos (IARC Group 1, carcinogenic to humans i.e. there is sufficient evidence of carcinogenicity in humans from epidemiological studies). The IARC classifications describe the

Figure 2. Estimated consumption of meat for person in kilograms in 2010-12, and forecast in 2022
Source: Böll-Stiftung (2014, pp. 49)

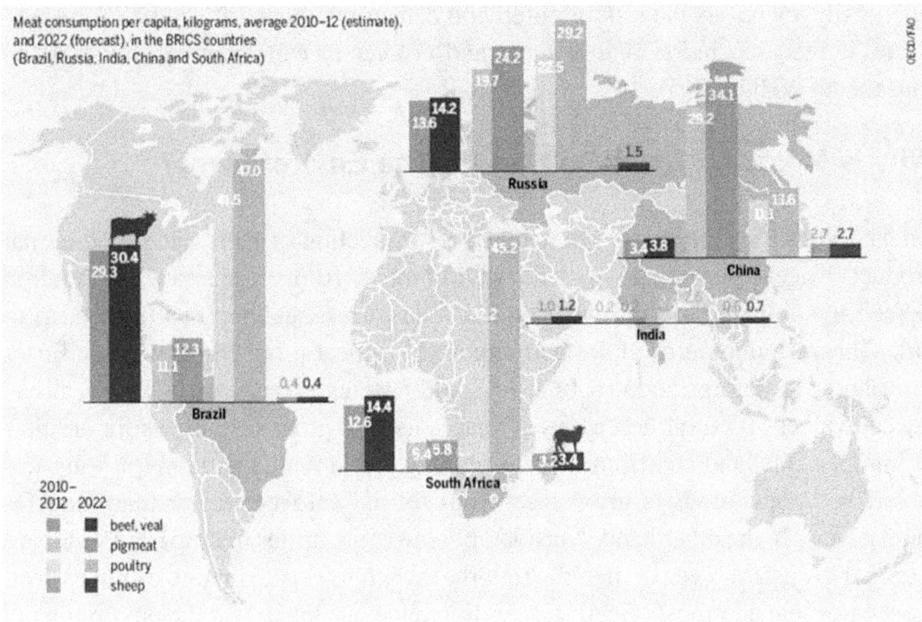

Figure 3. Worldwide Annual Meat Consumption per capita - Source: ChartsBin (2009)

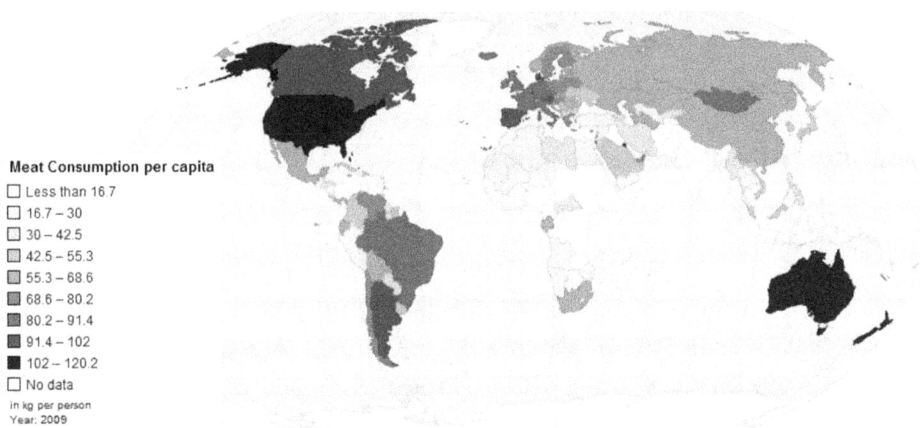

strength of the scientific evidence about an agent being a cause of cancer, rather than assessing the level of risk. An analysis of data from 10 studies estimated that every 50 gram portion of processed meat and every 100 gram portion of red meat, eaten daily, increases the risk of colorectal cancer by about 18% and 17% respectively, if the association of red meat and colorectal cancer were proven to be causal (see WHO, 2015).

Why is Meat and Dairy So Bad for The Environment?

On The Vegan Society (n.d.) we read: "The production of meat and other animal products places a heavy burden on the environment - from crops and water required to feed the animals, to the transport and other processes involved from farm to fork. The vast amount of grain feed required for meat production is a significant contributor to deforestation, habitat loss and species extinction. In Brazil alone, the equivalent of 5.6 million acres of land is used to grow soya beans for animals in Europe. This land contributes to developing world malnutrition by driving impoverished populations to grow cash crops for animal feed, rather than food for themselves. On the other hand, considerably lower quantities of crops and water are required to sustain a vegan diet, making the switch to veganism one of the easiest, most enjoyable and most effective ways to reduce our impact on the environment" (see The Vegan Society, n.d.).

Leitzmann (2014) writes: "The future of vegetarian nutrition is promising because sustainable nutrition is crucial for the well-being of humankind. An increasing number of people do not want animals to suffer nor do they want climate change; they want to avoid preventable diseases and to secure a livable future for generations to come" (see Leitzmann, 2014).

Readings About Sustainability

In this chapter we used several additional by bibliography and sitography about sustainable food succeed: Gourmandelle (2015), Vegan Outreach (2014), MacMillan (n.d.), Universo Vegano (n.d.), Turnbull (2015), One Green Planet (n.d.), Knutson (n.d.), Gavin (2014), Vegan Starter Kit (n.d.), Messina (2010), Vegans of Color (2009), Staying Vegan (2010), Pimentel, D. and Pimentel, M. (2003), Wheeler (2015), Boston University (n.d.), Thomas (n.d.), Wick (2011), National Sustainable Sales (n.d.), AMP (n.d), Albanesi (2013), Lugano (2012), AdnKronos (2015), Oscar Green (2015), Veganblog (2015), Dutto (2015), Sclaunich (2015), Sacchi Hunter (n.d.), Etica Vegana (2016), Zanni (2013), Animalvibe (2015), Fiala (2008), Four Seasons Natura e Cultura (n.d.), Worldwatch Institute (2004), Whole Foods market (n.d.), Petroff (2015), Giambarrresi (2013), Leitzmann (2003), The

Vegetarian Resource Group (n.d.), Shanker (2015), Mingolia (2015), Lusk and Bailey Norwood (2007), Mission 2015 (n.d.), Four Seasons Natura e Cultura (n.d.), Saint Louis (2015), Kjaernes, 2010.

Food Sustainability

Food sustainability implies several aspects, already considered widely in literature, for example (see Figure 4):

- Impact of production and distribution on the environment in terms of the use of land and resources, pollution and emissions, genetic diversity.
- Consequences on the external environment in health hazards and in the satisfaction of basic needs.

Why Go Vegan?

In this section we shall consider some common motivations to go vegan.

- **For Your Health**: Increased energy, younger looking skin due to diets rich in protein, iron, calcium and other essential vitamins and minerals, high in fiber and packed with antioxidants, helping mitigate some of the modern world's biggest health issues like obesity, heart disease, diabetes and cancer.

Figure 4. Sustainable development - Source: Drolc (2013)

- **For the Animals**: Because no animal is killed, abused and exploited for the preparation of a vegan meal (it does not include any animal products, even eggs, dairy products, milk, cheese, honey).
- **For the Environment**: Because eating vegan means less impact on the resources of our planet, less energy consumption, less water consumption, less pesticides adoption, less pollutants dispersion, less need for land and therefore less deforestation. Moreover a plant-based diet requires only one third of the land needed to support a meat and dairy diet.
- **For Those Who Are Dying of Hunger**: Because if we ate vegan food there would be more than enough for everyone (the land used to feed one person who eats meat would be enough to feed well 20 vegans)

(see The Vegan Society, n.d.).

Vegan Diet and Impact on the Territory

The vegan diet is clearly different than in vegetarian and omnivorous because it does not provide any form of intensive animal husbandry, truly responsible for the large consumption of resources caused by the major diets common in the West. Those practicing vegan chooses to minimize the burden on the company due to the chain of transformation of raw materials into food on our tables.

The calculation of the natural resource consumption for meat production is expressed taking into account the energy required for the collection of raw materials, the environmental costs of transportation of animals, the washing of animals, the animal feed and environmental costs also due to distribution. In assessing the impact of different diets on the environment, it does not come into play only quantitative assessments:

- Opting for vegan will also limit the impact in terms of greenhouse food production;
- It is in fact demonstrated how animal breeding on a large scale, especially if aimed at the production of beef, dries up the soil and promotes the destruction of wetlands as forests to pasture land;
- Feeding vegan, on the contrary, easier uses raw materials at 0 km;
- Vegan recipes use organic ingredients, which do not require for their production the adoption of chemicals or genetically modified organisms;
- Even vegetarian feeding, contemplates egg consumption, which poses sustainability problems in establishments where poultry is exploited industrially.

(see Non solo Vegan, 2014).

Case Study: The "Muscle of Wheat"

We will analyze the case of the "Muscle of wheat", a food created by the Italian-Calabrese Enzo Marascio, from high quality agricultural product of his land.

It is a real evolution in the food industry, because it shows a nutrient value similar to that of meat, while it results totally vegetable. Wheat and pulses reveal the basic ingredients and make the muscle of wheat more complete than seitan, soy and tofu. It represents a good substitute for those who decide to limit or abolish the own consumption of meat and fish, by following a diet free of dangerous animal fat and cholesterol.

Thanks to a special processing and fermentation, a mixture of wheat flour and pulses it assumes a consistency surprisingly similar to that of meat. Marascio is able to reproduce, with this new raw material - from himself named "Muscle of wheat", given his impressive consistency - many traditional plates of meat, such as dried beef, some salami, roast beef, etc (see Figure 5, Figure 6, Figure 7).

Figure 5. Image of Muscle of Wheat dish: "arrosto con verdure"
Source: Muscolo di Grano (n.d.)

Figure 6. Image of Muscle of Wheat dish: "Muscolo di Grano alla Pizzaiola"
Source: Muscolo di Grano (n.d.)

Figure 7. Image of Muscle of Wheat dish: roast beef
Source: Muscolo di Grano (n.d.)

There seems to exist a big difference between the invention of Marascio and substitutes meat more known and consumed by vegans, like seitan, tempeh, soy steaks. While the latter are derived from a de-structuring of the raw material used, Muscle of wheat develops exclusively on the basis of a dough, without the intervention of artificial modifications of the basic molecules. Moreover, this new product gains a specificity from legumes and cereals put together, not from a major modification of a single raw material: for this reason, the nutrient profile of the muscle of wheat is better.

Muscle wheat has undergone numerous surveys: in particular, in 1992 was analyzed by Prof. Fernando Tateo of the University of Milan and, surprisingly, turned out to be a food very particular: it contains, in fact, 20 amino acids, including the essential 7 amino-acids from 8, is composed of a type of protein which is not found either in the derivative of soy or in food of animal origins. It contains no fat, nor cholesterol - if we except the good cholesterol of extra virgin olive oil - or carbohydrates, resulting therefore be an ideal food for diabetic and celiac people, despite coming from grain.

According to many tasters, the taste of Muscle of Wheat is strikingly similar to that of meat.

Marascio found, proportionally, a greater interest from people out of the universe of vegetarians and vegans, because very often these individuals react with surprise, admitting the goodness of food consisting exclusively on vegetable.

The invention of Marascio is truly innovative, the traditional dishes may be reformulated without significant changes, as it is not the case with traditional seitan, tempeh, soy nuggets, tofu, that frequently require an additional food that gives them flavor. In addition, this food is not derived from soy beans, whose massive use, especially by some vegans, is currently the subject of frequent discussions, but from veggie products traditionally adopted in Italy - in particular, the grain used to produce "Muscle of Wheat" belongs to the "cultivar Senatore Cappelli", renowned for its nutritional qualities (see Seclì, 2007).

Muscle of Wheat Wins the Oscar Green Prize at Expo Milan 2015

Muscle of Wheat wins the first prize in the category WeGreen in the occasion of the national competition *Oscar Green* at Expo Milan, in Italy, as the best and original truly innovative food (see Figure 8, Figure 9). The victory of Muscle of Wheat represents an historical steps towards the production of eco-sustainable food, because it stimulates world's attention upon a product that will solve many problems, both ethical and healthy, for generations to come. The population is increasing exponen-

Figure 8. Muscle of Wheat wins Oscar Green 2015
Source: Oscar Green (2015)

tially and consequently, to meet the protein need, we see an unsustainable adoption of intensive farming, at the expense, of course, of the quality and ethical issues. Intensive farming goes against nature, by modifying the natural cycles of growth of animals, all with the addition of hormones that, as a result, we assimilate by feeding. Muscle of wheat, contains all the necessary proteins, right calories, zero carbohydrates and zero saturated fat, does not intend to eliminate meat, but stands as an alternative food, at least in the days that you want to save a bit your body, and especially our liver (see Napolitano, 2015).

MAIN FOCUS OF THE CHAPTER

In this chapter the authors propose the possible agreement among a large globalized food producer and Muscle of Wheat. We think that Muscle of Wheat cannot enter a global market without the help of a large food producer already in the market, for example like McDonald's or other globalized food chains. At this aim, we propose a game theory model based on a coopetitive reasoning, representing a possible asymmetric R&D alliance between two subjects: McDonald's and Muscle of Wheat. This asymmetric alliance will benefit different players in the game, Muscle of Wheat

Figure 9. Muscle of Wheat wins Oscar Green 2015
Source: Napolitano, U. (2015)

will enter a globalized market and export its production worldwide, McDonald's will gain another part of the global food market and society will gain from health improvement.

The Economic Model

Assumption 1: The authors assume that, to achieve its goals, McDonald's, our 1st player, is forming horizontal alliances (that is food-food alliances), instead of producing new innovative food, with the small (but research-oriented and highly efficient) Muscle of wheat firm, our 2nd player.

Assumption 2: The Muscle of wheat firm (2nd player) is engaged in the discovery eco-sustainable development, creation of new food produced entirely from eco-sustainable sources.

Assumption 3: To cope with global competitive pressures, McDonald's is allying in triad with another mid-size or small-size food firm (our Muscle of wheat) and with a venture capitalist (let us call VC or Cap), our 4th player (which we won't consider one of our principal players, because of its elementary actions and simple payoffs) in order to spin out a new food development program into a new renewable joint venture firm (the authors call RJV, research joint venture), our 3rdplayer.

Semi-Quantitative Description of the Payoffs

At the end of this R&D alliance, the benefits for the three partners can be summarized as follows:

- McDonald's buys a certain amount x of food from RJV and gains from the selling of the product x on the Market;
- Muscle of wheat firm produces a bi-quantity $z = (z_1, z_2)$ of a new 100% safe and eco-sustainable food; MW gains by selling a quantity z_1 to RJV and a quantity z_2 on the Market;
- RJV gains by selling x of the *Muscle of wheat* production to McDonald's and $z_1 - x$ of the food on the Market;
- Cap receives from McDonald's (at time 2) the capitalization k' of its initial investment k (money given to McDonald's at time 1);
- Market/Italy gains from the sunk costs k of RJV, from the research-costs y of *Muscle of wheat* and it gains a value $b(z_1+z_2)$ by improving food production and health.

The Formal Construction of the Game Model

Axiom 0: We consider a five-player game.

The players are:

1. McDonald's (or LF, large firm);
2. Muscle of Wheat (or SF, small firm);
3. the 3rd player is the RJV (Research Joint Venture) constituted by McDonald's and MW;
4. VC (venture capitalist);
5. Market.

The authors distinguish between principal players and side players: principal players are **LF** and **SF**, side players are **RJV**, **VC** and the **Market** (civil society).

Strategies

Axiom 1 (strategies of the 1st player): Any real number x represents the production that **McDonald's** decides to buy (x in **E**, compact interval of the positive real semi-line) from the **Research Joint Venture** founded by **McDonald's** and **MW.**

Axiom 2 (strategies of the 2nd player): Any real number y represents investments for research and food production (y in **F**, compact interval of the real line, with first end-point greater or equal to 1) employed by **MW**, we assume that an investment in research of at least 1 is needed for creating the 100% eco-sustainable food.

Axiom 3 (strategies of the 3rd player - coopetitive strategies of the first two players): Any vector $z = (z_1, z_2)$, with z in $\mathbf{C} = C_1 \times C_2$, where C_1 and C_2 are compact intervals of the real line, such that the first end-point of C_1 results greater or equal to the maximum of **E,** represents the bi-production of MW.

We assume that:

- The vector z is decided together by McDonald's and MW;
- The RJV buys only the z_1 component of z;
- By convention, the strategy of the third player;
- The vector z represents, equivalently, the coopetitive strategy of the first two players.

In other terms, we shall use the strategy *z* of the 3rd player as a cooperative strategy of the couple (LF, SF) in a coopetitive game.

Axiom 4 (strategies of the 4th player): *The number k represents the loan that VC decides to offer to the McDonald's (the strategy set of VC is reduced to the singleton {k}).*

Axiom 5 (strategies of the 5th player): *Any couple z represents the coopetitive production branded by RJV that the Market decides to buy: we assume, by classic microeconomic assumption, that this z coincides with the bi-production branded by RJV, decided together by McDonald's and* MW.

Payoffs

Axiom 6: *The payoff function of McDonald's is defined by*

$f_1(x, y, z) = (p - p')x - k' - ay,$

where:

1. px is the profit from selling x at price p in the Market;
2. *p'x is the cost to buy x from RJV at price p';*
3. *k' are the sunk costs faced by McDonald's itself;*
4. ay is the extra-payment to MW for research and development y (a > 1).

Axiom 7: *The payoff function of MW is defined by*

$f_2(x,y,z) = p''z_1 + ay - y - F + p''' z_2,$

where:

1. *$p''z_1$ is the payment received from RJV selling the product z_1;*
2. ay is extra-payment for research y, (with a >1), received from McDonald's; y is the investment in research;
3. F is the fixed cost to produce energy, this cost is not afforded by RJV, which pay only the variable cost;
4. $p'''z_2$ is the revenue obtained by selling z_2 in the Market of price p''', with $p''<p'''<p$.

Axiom 8: *The payoff function of the RJV is defined by*

$f_3(x,y,z) = p'x + p(z_1 - x) - cz_1 - p''z_1 - cz_2;$

where:

1. *p'x is the profit from selling x at price p' to McDonald's;*
2. *$p(z_1 - x)$ is the profit from selling $z_1 - x$ at price p > p' on the Market;*
3. (z_1+z_2) is the variable cost for the production of (z_1+z_2), faced by MW and paid by RJV;
4. *$p''z_1$ is the payment paid to MW to buy the product z_1, with $p > c + p''$.*

Axiom 9: *The payoff function of VC is defined by*

$f_4(x,y,z) = k' - k$

where:

1. k’ represents the money which **1st** player has to give back to VC;
2. k is the number that represents the loan that VC decides to offer to the McDonald’s.

Axiom 10: The payoff function of the Market is defined by

$$f_5(x,y,z) = - p(z_1 - x) + cz_1 + k - px + y + bz_1 + cz_2 - p'''z_2 + bz_2$$

where:

1. px is the cost from buying x at price p from LF;
2. $p(z_1 - x)$ is the cost from buying $(z_1 - x)$ at price p from RJV;
3. $c(z_1+z_2)$ is the indirect gain from the production of z, faced by MW and paid by RJV;
4. y is the indirect gain coming from the research activity of MW;
5. k is the indirect gain coming from the foundation of RJV;
6. $b(z_1 + z_2)$ is the social indirect gain (beneficial effects) coming from the use of the quantity $z_1 + z_2$ of the new sustainable food.

The following Figure 10 shows the formal situation.

Figure 10. Formal representation of the game

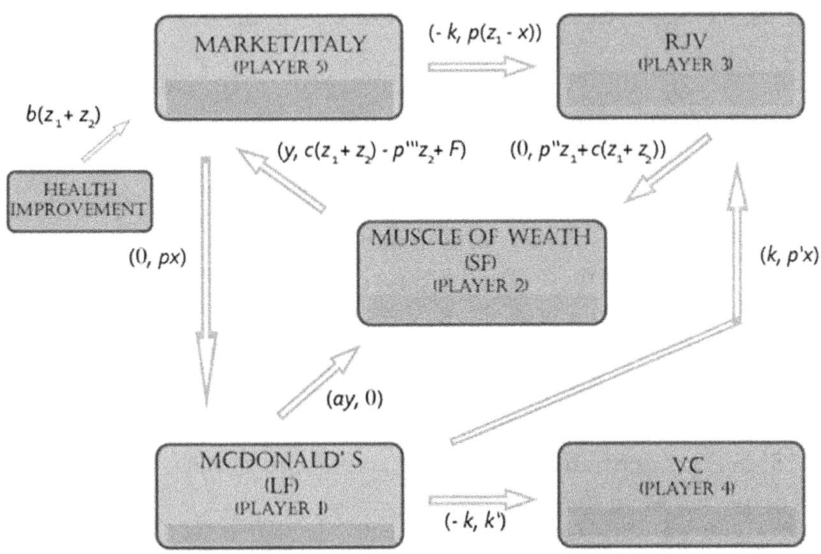

Economic Interpretation

Axiom 11: In this model we have three formal players interacting together and one player, the venture capitalist **VC**, acting only at the beginning of the interaction (time 1) and at its end (time 2).

Axiom 12: We assume that:

- Our 1st player is a Large Firm (LF) (in our study case, it is the McDonald's) that, in order to develop new totally eco-sustainable, decides to form an horizontal alliance with a Small Firm (SF) (in our case, it is the MW), our 2nd player, operating in the same sector (food production).
- 1st and 2nd player, in order to cooperate, constitute a Research Joint Venture (RJV), our 3rd player. The RJV is financially supported by the VC, our 4th player, at the level of initial costs, and it supports SF, at the level of variable costs.

Axiom 13: The 2nd player produces a quantity z (decided together by 1st and 2nd player) of new vegan food and sells a quantity z_1 to the RJV, at price p'' (fixed by contract).

When the research of the RJV of the good (in our case the food) has already begun, then the production of sustainable food is conducted by 2nd player and the Large Firm decides the amount x of production to buy from the RJV.

Axiom 14: The revenue of LF is given by the difference between the sale price p'x and the purchase price px, of the quantity x of production bought by the RJV at price p'.

To begin the RJV research, the VC offers a financial support k to RJV, to cover the initial sunk costs.

After the cooperative production of 2nd player is started, the 1st player pays the capitalized sunk costs k'>k to the RJV, in order to compensate the VC and to conclude the participation of the VC in the game.

Moreover, at the beginning of the RJV, 1st player funds directly the researches of the small firm SF, by a sum ay, for any investment y in research of the 2nd player, with $a > 1$.

Axiom 15: When, cooperatively, 1st player and 2nd has decided the pair z that the 2nd player has to produce and sell.

Revenues for the 2nd player are equal to

$p''z_1 + p'''z_2$,

where:

1. p'' is the unit price at which 2nd player sells to RJV;
2. z_1 is the quantity of production sold to RJV;
3. p''' is the unit price at which 2nd player sells to Market;
4. z_2 is the quantity of production sold to the Market.

The cost is represented by the investment for research and is equal to y.

Axiom 16: For the Research Joint Venture revenues are calculated as

$p'x + p(z_1 - x) + k$

where:

1. p'x is the profit from selling x at price p' to LF;
2. $p(z_1 - x)$ represents the profit from selling $(z_1 - x)$ at price $p > p'$ on the Market;
3. k is a positive constant for the RJV because the sunk costs are paid by the 1st player.

Axiom 17: Lastly, the authors assume that the cost cz for the production of z (by the second player) is paid by the RJV and so the costs for the RJV are equal to:

$cz_1 + cz_2 + p''z_1 + k$,

where:

1. $c(z_1 + z_2)$ is the cost of $z_1 + z_2$ (paid by RJV to 2nd player);
2. $p''z_1$ is the payment given to the small firm for the product z_1;
3. k is a sunk cost payed by RJV to the Market.

SOLUTIONS AND RECOMMENDATIONS

Once defined numerically the Payoff functions and strategies of the players, we can develop and analyze completely the numerical game and find classic and less classic solutions of the game: from a competitive, cooperative and coopetitive perspectives. As usual, such solutions show specific economic meanings.

Specifically, we suggest to analyze the game following the general lines proposed by David Carfì in his complete analysis of a differentiable game.

Complete analysis of differentiable game consists in the following points of exam:

0a: Classify the game (linear, semi-linear, symmetric, invertible, symmetric in the strategies, ...);
0b: Find the critical zone of the game and its image by f;
0c: Determine the bi-gain space im(f) (image of the function f);
0d: Determine inf and sup of the game and see if they are shadow optima;
0e: Determine the Pareto boundaries of the bi-strategy space and their images by f;
1a: Specify the control of each player upon the boundaries;
1b: Specify the non-cooperative reachability and controllability of the Pareto boundaries;
1c: Find the possible Pareto solutions and crosses;
1d: Find devotion correspondences and devotion equilibria;
1e: Specify the efficiency and non-cooperative reachability of devotion equilibria;
2a: Find best reply correspondences and Nash equilibria;
2b: Study the existence of Nash equilibria (Brouwer and Kakutany);
2c: Evaluate Nash equilibria: non-cooperative reachability, position with respect to and, efficiency, devotion;
2d: Find, if there are, dominant strategies;
2e: Find strict and dominant equilibria, reduce the game by elimination of dominated strategies;
3a: Find conservative values and worst gain functions of the players;
3b: Find conservative strategies and crosses;
3c: Find all the conservative parts of the game (in the bi-strategy and bi-gain spaces);
3d: Find core of the game and conservative knots;
3e: Evaluate Nash equilibria by the core and the conservative bi-value;
4a: Find the worst offensive correspondences and the offensive equilibria;
4b: Specify non-cooperative reachability of the offensive equilibria and their efficiency;
4c: Find the worst offensive strategies of each player and the corresponding gain of the other;
4d: Find the possible dominant offensive strategies;
4e: Confront the possible non-cooperative solutions;
5a: Find the elementary best compromises (Kalai-Smorodinsky solutions) and corresponding bi-gain;
5b: Find the elementary core best compromise and its corresponding bi-gain;
5c: Find the Nash bargaining solutions and corresponding bi-gains;
5d: Find the solutions with closest bi-gains to the shadow minimum;

5e: Find the maximum collective utility solutions;
5f: Confront the possible cooperative solutions;
6a: Study the transferable utility case.

In the present work, we do not analyze completely the game but we propose a complete, general and detailed economic model. For some examples, of similar economic models, completely studied by using the technic of a differentiable game completely analysis, you can find in Baglieri, Carfì and Dagnino (2016a, 2016b, 2012), Carfì and Donato (in press), Carfì and Lanzafame (2013), Carfì and Musolino (2015a, 2015b, 2014a, 2014b, 2013a, 2013b, 2013c, 2012a, 2012b, 2012c, 2012d, 2012e, 2011a, 2011b), Carfì and Romeo (2015), and Carfì and Schilirò (2014a, 2014b, 2013, 2012a, 2012b, 2012c, 2012d, 2012e, 2011a, 2011b, 2011c, 2011d).

In particular, we want to emphasize the following solution points:

1. Nash equilibria, those representing the (static non-coopetitive) competitive solution.
2. The purely coopetitive solution: representing the best Nash equilibrium (payoff) of the coopetitive game, or, more correctly, a compromise solution on the Pareto boundary of the coopetitive Nash zone, that is the dynamic trajectory determined by the Nash equilibria during the coopetitive evolution of the game.
3. Super-cooperative solution without the 3rd player: representing a possible compromise solution determining the maximum collective gain of the first two players without taking into account of the gains of the third player, which (in this case) remain outside the sharing a solution maximizing the collective profit for both players.
4. Super-cooperative solutions with the 3rd player: representing a possible compromise solution determining the maximum collective gain of the first three players, taking into account of the gains of third player, which (in this case) remain inside the sharing.

Remark

Maximum-collective solutions consists in finding a compromise maximum collective gain solution (if any) and in sharing fairly the corresponding total profit.

The share of collective gains among players can respect the Kalai-Smorodinsky method.

Sharing the maximum collective profit by using a Kalai-Smorodinsky method allows to obtain a win-win solution, in the sense that, our solution will be better than the initial Nash payoff for both players.

FUTURE RESEARCH DIRECTIONS

Future and Emerging Trend

It appears now clear, without any possible doubt, that the world future of feeding goes towards non-meat and non-seafood consumption, essentially because of global environmental issues, linked with a severe climate change and an exponential growing of the current mass extinction. The food production and veggie-products, feasible for that new future feeding scenarios, reveals perfectly matching the Marascio's production of the Muscle of Wheat. Our research and solutions proposal appears perfectly fitting the future scenarios and obliged emerging trends. This consideration provides an insight about the future of the book's theme from the perspective of the chapter focus.

From an economic point of view, the viability of the proposed paradigm and model is shown by the already employed successful similar R&D alliances in bio-pharmaceutical industry. The implementation issues of the proposed program might be devised in the difficulties of proposing new feeding habits to an entire society. But, as we explained before, the right way - from an economical, political, health, environmental, ethical and social points of view - appears the road which we traced.

Future Research Opportunities within the Domain of the Topic

Our economic model allows to find easily the optimal transferable utility solutions for the two main participants, when the real data come into the arena. In the future we shall consider numerical models and computer simulations for realistic case, considering also probabilistic scenarios.

As we said above, knowing the data relative to the economic problem, that is:

- Selling prices in the Market,
- Market interest rates,
- Maximum possible quantities of product, which the players can produce and sell,
- The research costs,
- The precise agreements between the two main participants of the game

it becomes possible to analyze and solve the game by calculating all the Carfì's solutions and - among all - those solutions of cooperative nature that give to the main players the optimal solution on a rich Pareto boundary.

We recall two fundamental aspects of our approach:

- First of all, the optimization problem we face is not mono-variate but multivariate, so, in general it does not exist a maximum of the problem but we construct various optimal boundaries, on which we shall find and select special solutions;
- The most convenient of those optimal boundaries could be obtained by a multiple stage cooperation among the main economic players involved in order to adopt a transferable utility approach (examples of such analytical approach could be found in Baglieri, Carfì and Dagnino (2016a, 2016b, 2012), Carfì and Donato (in press), Carfì and Lanzafame (2013), Carfì and Musolino (2015a, 2015b, 2014a, 2014b, 2013a, 2013b, 2013c, 2012a, 2012b, 2012c, 2012d, 2012e, 2011a, 2011b), Carfì and Romeo (2015), and Carfì and Schilirò (2014a, 2014b, 2013, 2012a, 2012b, 2012c, 2012d, 2012e, 2011a, 2011b, 2011c, 2011d).

Another possible future research consists in the observation that our model allows us to forecast, at the beginning of the game, the future gains in the case of uncertain selling scenarios, that is, we can consider scenarios in which we don't know how much product will be bought by the Market and only a part of the total production is actually sold. We shall introduce parameters indicating what percentages of production is actually sold. Such complete approach could be found in Carfì and Donato (in press).

More, assuming the existence of probability distributions on the space of possible sold production we can calculate the aleatoric variable representing the uncertain gains in function of the selling parameters.

CONCLUSION

In this chapter, we propose a possible coopetitive agreement among a large globalized food producer/seller and Muscle of Wheat, a small, local but strongly innovative healthy food producer of southern Italy.

We think that the small enterprise Muscle of Wheat cannot enter significantly a global market, without the help of a large and famous food producer, already in the global market: for example, McDonald's or other globalized food chains.

On the other hand, we strongly believe that Muscle of Wheat should enter the globalized market because of the quality of its food innovation, which is capable to address global issues such as climate change and even the current mass extinction, human-determined and linked with the extreme soil exploitation, due to all the necessities induced by the meat industry, for the feeding of animals.

Muscle of wheat represents an extremely good alternative to meat and seafood, with optimal healthy features and a minimal environmental impact.

Moreover, McDonald's might see great motivations to change towards the vegan and vegetarian productions, because the world food politics are changing in those directions.

At this aim, we propose a game theory model based on a coopetitive reasoning, representing a possible asymmetric R&D alliance between two subjects: McDonald's and Muscle of Wheat.

This asymmetric alliance will benefit different players in the game:

- Muscle of Wheat will enter a globalized market and export its production worldwide,
- McDonald's will conquer another part of the global food market,
- Society will gain from health (and ethical) improvement.

In this chapter, specifically, we use D. Carfì's new coopetitive game definition, which considers both collaboration and competition together and simultaneously. Coopetition may advance the understanding and control of asymmetric R&D alliances, those between small (and/or young) firms and large (e.g. Multinational Enterprises).

The results of the mathematical study has proved that we can find more solutions advantageous both for the firms involved for the

- World environment,
- Human healthy,
- Human population sustainability,
- Climate change.

The mathematical solution we propose are:

- Purely coopetitive solutions;
- Super-cooperative solutions without the 3rd player;
- Super-cooperative solutions with the 3rd player;
- Maximum-collective solutions.

Our contribution is twofold:

- Firstly, we have explained the advantages of a vegan diet for the human health, environmental issues, food sustainability, population sustainability and how global food producers could improve environmental, social and health conditions of world population;

- Secondly, we have shown how game theory normal-form and extensive-form games can be used in coopetition studies
  - To increase health conditions of people,
  - To address climate change,
  - To address hunger in the world,
  - To improve welfare in a particular market.

So, we encourage McDonald's and other large food companies to look more closely at the model to understand that compete with biological and vegan small producers and innovators is not always the right way to "get rich" and to create wealth.

From an Economic point of view, we are sure that the competition is not the right way to have success.

Food enterprises should decide not to "fight" with other small food companies to grab a good share of the market, but they have to cooperate to reach the maximum collective gain, for them and for the social communities. Indeed, it's important, for a world looking to the future, to study what is the best combination of richness for enterprises and welfare for the community and for our planet.

Our study, as it is presented, is fully applicable. It can be surely implemented by other scholars and entrepreneurs interested in the food area, and/or in living conditions of all humans and/or in sustainable food production.

Surely, the model can be improved by widening the points of view, for example by studying not only a particular global food producer and only one innovators, but taking into account entire firm-clusters, by using other innovative vegan food resources, that - during time - could be discovered.

If we want to live all in good conditions, we'll have to be more smart and more "green" to save our life and our future and so we hope that enterprises should think the same to increase world health conditions and welfare.

Nowadays, we also need that McDonald's and other food companies should use more sustainable vegan food product, in order to use less primary resources; so we're looking to stimulate more interest on these global issues.

ACKNOWLEDGMENT

The authors wish to thank two anonymous referees for their precious and stimulating remarks about the work, which help to improve significantly the subject matter and the form of the present chapter.

REFERENCES

AdnKronos. (2015). Ecco il 'muscolo di grano', la carne vegetale nata per amore. *Focus*. Retrieved April 9, 2015, from http://www.focus.it/ambiente/ecologia/ecco-il-muscolo-di-grano-la-carne-vegetale-nata-per-amore

Agreste, S., Carfì, D., & Ricciardello, A. (2012). An algorithm for payoff space in C^1 parametric games. *Applied Sciences, 14*, 1-14. Retrieved from http://www.mathem.pub.ro/apps/v14/A14-ag.pdf

Albanesi, R. (2013). *Muscolo di grano*. Retrieved from http://www.albanesi.it/alimentazione/cibi/muscolo.htm

Albert, S. (1999). E-commerce Revitalizes Co-opetition. *Computerworld, 33*(15), 36.

Alvarez, S. A., & Barney, J. B. (2001). How Entrepreneurial Firms Can Benefit from Alliances with Large Partners. *The Academy of Management Executive, 15*(1), 139–148. doi:10.5465/AME.2001.4251563

AMP. (n.d.). *Veganism*. Retrieved from http://www.abbotsmillproject.co.uk/what-we-do/veganism/

Animalvibe. (2015). *Muscolo di grano*. Retrieved September 23, 2015, from http://animalvibe.org/2015/09/muscolo-di-grano/

Arthanari, T., Carfì, D., & Musolino, F. (2015). Game Theoretic Modeling of Horizontal Supply Chain Coopetition among Growers. *International Game Theory Review, 17*(2). doi:.10.1142/S0219198915400137

Asch, S. E. (1952). *Social Psycology*. Englewood Cliffs, NJ: Prentice Hall. doi:10.1037/10025-000

Aubin, J. P. (1997). *Mathematical Methods of Game and Economic Theory* (Revised Edition). North-Holland.

Aubin, J. P. (1998). Optima and Equilibria. Springer Verlag. doi:10.1007/978-3-662-03539-9

Baglieri, D., Carfì, D., & Dagnino, G. (2010). Profiting from Asymmetric R&D Alliances: Coopetitive Games and Firms' Strategies. In *Proceedings of 4th Workshop on Coopetition Strategy "Coopetition and Innovation"*. doi:10.13140/RG.2.1.2072.9043

Baglieri, D., Carfì, D., & Dagnino, G. (2016a). *A Coopetitive Game Model for Asymmetric R&D Alliances within a generalized "Reverse Deal"*. Aracne editrice.

Baglieri, D., Carfì, D., & Dagnino, G. (2016b). Asymmetric R&D Alliances in the Biopharmaceutical Industry. *International Studies of Management & Organization, 46*(2(3)), 179–201. doi:10.1080/00208825.2016.1112154

Baglieri, D., Carfì, D., & Dagnino, G. B. (2012a). Asymmetric R&D Alliances and Coopetitive Games. In *Advances in Computational Intelligence: 14th International Conference on Information Processing and Management of Uncertainty in Knowledge-Based Systems, IPMU 2012,Proceedings, Part IV*. Springer-Verlag. doi:10.1007/978-3-642-31724-8_64

Baglieri, D., Carfì, D., & Dagnino, G. B. (2012b). Asymmetric R&D Alliances and Coopetitive Games. Cornell University Library. Retrieved from http://arxiv.org/abs/1205.2878 doi:10.1007/978-3-642-31724-8_64

Baum, J. A. C., Calabrese, T., & Silverman, B. S. (2000). Dont Go It Alone: Alliance Network Composition and Startups Performance in Canadian Biotechnology. *Strategic Management Journal, 21*(3), 267–294. doi:10.1002/(SICI)1097-0266(200003)21:3<267::AID-SMJ89>3.0.CO;2-8

Bengtsson, M., & Kock, S. (2014). Coopetition-Quo Vadis? Past Accomplishments and Future Challenges. *Industrial Marketing Management, 43*(2), 180–188. doi:10.1016/j.indmarman.2014.02.015

Biondi, Y., & Giannoccolo, P. (2012). Complementarities and Coopetition in Presence of Intangible Resources: Industrial Economic and Regulatory Implications. *Journal of Strategy and Management, 5*(4), 437–449. doi:10.1108/17554251211276399

Böll-Stiftung, H. (2014). Meat Atlas. Fact and figures about the animals we eat. *Friends of the Earth Europe*. Retrieved January 9, 2014, from https://www.foeeurope.org/sites/default/files/publications/foee_hbf_meatatlas_jan2014.pdf

Boston University. (n.d.). *Vegetarian Society*. Retrieved from http://www.bu.edu/sustainability/what-you-can-do/join-a-club/vegetarian-society/

Brandenburger, A., & Stuart, H. (2007). Biform Games. *Management Science, 53*(4), 537–549. doi:10.1287/mnsc.1060.0591

Brandenburger, A. M., & Nalebuff, B. J. (1995). The Right Game: Use Game Theory to Shape Strategy. *Harvard Business Review, 64*, 57–71.

Branderburger, A. M., & Nalebuff, B. J. (1996). *Coopetition*. New York: Currency Doubleday.

Campbell, M., & Carfì, D. (2015). Bounded Rational Speculative and Hedging Interaction Model in Oil and U.S. Dollar Markets. *Journal of Mathematical Economics and Finance*, *1*(1), 4–28. Retrieved from http://asers.eu/journals/jmef.html

Carayannis, E. G., & Alexander, J. (1999). Winning by Co-opeting in Strategic Government University-industry R&D Partnerships: The Power of Complex, Dynamic Knowledge Networks. *The Journal of Technology Transfer*, *24*(2-3), 197–210. doi:10.1023/A:1007855422405

Carfì, D. (2004a). Geometric aspects of a financial evolution. *Atti della Reale Accademia della Scienze di Torino*, *138*, 143–151.

Carfì, D. (2004b). S-bases and applications to Physics and Economics. Annals of Economic Faculty, University of Messina, 165-190.

Carfì, D. (2004c). S-linear operators in quantum Mechanics and in Economics. *Applied Sciences*, *6*(1), 7-20. Retrieved from http://www.mathem.pub.ro/apps/v06/A06.htm

Carfì, D. (2004d). The family of operators associated with a capitalization law. *Physical, Mathematical, and Natural Sciences*, *81-82*, 1–10. doi:10.1478/C1A0401002

Carfì, D. (2006a). An S-Linear State Preference Model. *Communications to SIMAI*, *1*, 1–4. doi:10.1685/CSC06037

Carfì, D. (2006b). S-convexity in the space of Schwartz distributions and applications. *Rendiconti del Circolo Matematico di Palermo, 77.*

Carfì, D. (2007a). Dyson formulas for Financial and Physical evolutions in S'n. *Communications to SIMAI Congress, 2*, 1-10. doi:10.1685/CSC06156

Carfì, D. (2007b). S-Linear Algebra in Economics and Physics. *Applied Sciences, 9*, 48-66. Retrieved from http://www.mathem.pub.ro/apps/v09/A09-CA.pdf

Carfì, D. (2008a). Optimal Boundaries for Decisions. *Physical, Mathematical, and Natural Sciences*, *86*(1), 1–11. doi:10.1478/C1A0801002

Carfì, D. (2008b). Superpositions in Prigogine's approach to irreversibility for Physical and Financial applications. *Physical, Mathematical, and Natural Sciences, 86*(S1), 1-13. doi:10.1478/C1S0801005

Carfì, D. (2008c). Structures on the space of financial events. *AAPP | Physical. Mathematical, and Natural Sciences*, *86*(2), 1–13. doi:10.1478/C1A0802007

Carfì, D. (2009a). Decision-Form Games. In *Communications to SIMAI Congress - Proceedings of the 9th Congress of SIMAI, the Italian Society of Industrial and Applied Mathematics*. doi:10.1685/CSC09307

Carfì, D. (2009b). Differentiable Game Complete Analysis for Tourism Firm Decisions. *Proceedings of the 2009 International Conference on Tourism and Workshop on Sustainable Tourism within High Risk Areas of Environmental Crisis*. Retrieved from http://mpra.ub.uni-muenchen.de/29193/

Carfì, D. (2009c). Fibrations of financial events. *Proceedings of the International Geometry Center - Prooceding of the International Conference "Geometry in Odessa 2009*. Retrieved as MPRA Paper 31307 from http://mpra.ub.uni-muenchen.de/31307/

Carfì, D. (2009d). Payoff space in C^1-games. *Applied Sciences, 11*, 35-47. Retrieved from http://www.mathem.pub.ro/apps/v11/A11-ca.pdf

Carfì, D. (2009e). Globalization and Differentiable General Sum Games. *Proceedings of the 3rd International Symposium "Globalization and convergence in economic thought"*. Bucaresti: Editura ASE. doi:10.13140/RG.2.1.2215.8801

Carfì, D. (2010a). *A model for Coopetitive Games*. MPRA Paper 59633. Retrieved from http://mpra.ub.uni-muenchen.de/59633/Carf

Carfì, D. (2010b). *Topics in Game Theory*. Il Gabbiano; doi:10.13140/RG.2.1.4203.9766

Carfì, D. (2010c). *Decision-Form Games*. Il Gabbiano. doi:10.13140/RG.2.1.1320.3927

Carfì, D. (2011a). Financial Lie groups. *Proceedings of the International Conference RIGA 2011*. Bucharest University. Retrieved as MPRA Paper 31303 from http://mpra.ub.uni-muenchen.de/31303/

Carfì, D. (2011b). Financial Lie groups. Cornell University Library. Retrieved from http://arxiv.org/abs/1106.0562

Carfì, D. (2011c). Fibrations of financial events. Cornell University Library. Retrieved from http://arxiv.org/abs/1106.1774

Carfì, D. (2011d). Reactivity in Decision-form Games. Cornell University Library. Retrieved from http://arxiv.org/abs/1103.0841

Carfì, D. (2012). Coopetitive Games and Applications. In Advances and Applications in Game Theory. doi:10.13140/RG.2.1.3526.6005

Carfì, D. (2015). A model for coopetitive games. *Journal of Mathematical Economics and Finance, 1*(1), 46–75. Retrieved from http://asers.eu/journals/jmef.html

Carfì, D., & Caristi, G. (2008). Financial dynamical systems. *Differential Geometry - Dynamical Systems, 10*, 71–85. Retrieved from http://www.mathem.pub.ro/dgds/v10/D10-CA.pdf

Carfì, D., Caterino, A., & Ceppitelli, R. (2015). *State preference models and jointly continuous utilities*. doi:10.13140/RG.2.1.3689.0966

Carfì, D., & Cvetko Vah, K. (2011). Skew lattice structures on the financial events plane. *Applied Sciences, 13*, 9-20. Retrieved from http://www.mathem.pub.ro/apps/v13/A13-ca.pdf

Carfì, D., & Donato, A. (in press). A critical analytic survey of an Asymmetric R&D Alliance in Pharmaceutical industry: Bi-parametric study case. *Journal of Mathematical Economics and Finance*.

Carfì, D., & Fici, C. (2012). The government-taxpayer game. *Theoretical and Practical Research in Economic Fields, 3*(1), 13-26. Retrieved from http://www.asers.eu/journals/tpref/tpref-past-issues.html

Carfì, D., & Gambarelli, G. (2015). Balancing Bilinearly Interfering Elements. *Decision Making in Manufacturing and Services, 9*(1), 27-49. Retrieved from https://journals.agh.edu.pl/dmms/article/view/1676/1410

Carfì, D., Gambarelli, G., & Uristani, A. (2013). Balancing pairs of interfering elements. *Zeszyty Naukowe Uniwersytetu Szczecińskiego 760*, 435-442.

Carfì, D., & Lanzafame, F. (2013). A Quantitative Model of Speculative Attack: Game Complete Analysis and Possible Normative Defenses. In M. Bahmani-Oskooee & S. Bahmani (Eds.), Financial Markets: Recent Developments, Emerging Practices and Future Prospects. Nova Science. Retrieved from https://www.novapublishers.com/catalog/product_info.php?products_id=46483

Carfì, D., & Magaudda, M. (2009). Complete study of linear infinite games. *Proceedings of the International Geometry Center - Prooceding of the International Conference "Geometry in Odessa 2009"*. Retrieved from http://d-omega.org/category/books-and- papers/

Carfì, D., Magaudda, M., & Schilirò, D. (2010). Coopetitive Game Solutions for the eurozone economy. Retrieved as MPRA Paper from http://mpra.ub.uni-muenchen.de/26541/1/MPRA_paper_26541.pdf

Carfì, D., & Musolino, F. (2011a). Fair Redistribution in Financial Markets: A Game Theory Complete Analysis. *Journal of Advanced Studies in Finance*, *2*(2(4)), 74–100.

Carfì, D., & Musolino, F. (2011b). Game Complete Analysis for Financial Markets Stabilization. In Proceedings of the 1st International On-line Conference on Global Trends in Finance (pp. 14–42). ASERS. Retrieved from http://www.asers.eu/asers_files/conferences/GTF/GTF_eProceedings_last.pdf

Carfì, D., & Musolino, F. (2012a). A coopetitive approach to financial markets stabilization and risk management. In *Advances in Computational Intelligence, Part IV. 14th International Conference on Information Processing and Management of Uncertainty in Knowledge-Based Systems, IPMU 2012*. doi:10.1007/978-3-642-31724-8_62

Carfì, D., & Musolino, F. (2012b). Game Theory and Speculation on Government Bonds. *Economic Modelling*, *29*(6), 2417-2426. doi:10.1016/j.econmod.2012.06.037

Carfì, D., & Musolino, F. (2012c). *Game Theory Models for Derivative Contracts: Financial Markets Stabilization and Credit Crunch, Complete Analysis and Coopetitive Solution*. Lambert Academic Publishing. Retrieved from https://www.lap-publishing.com/catalog/details//store/gb/book/978-3-659-13050-2/game-theory-models-for-derivative-contracts

Carfì, D., & Musolino, F. (2012d). A game theory model for currency markets stabilization. University Library of Munich. Retrieved from https://mpra.ub.uni-muenchen.de/39240/

Carfì, D., & Musolino, F. (2012e). Game theory model for European government bonds market stabilization: a saving-State proposal. University Library of Munich. Retrieved from https://mpra.ub.uni-muenchen.de/39742/

Carfì, D., & Musolino, F. (2013a). Credit Crunch in the Euro Area: A Coopetitive Multi-agent Solution. In Multicriteria and Multiagent Decision Making with Applications to Economic and Social Sciences: Studies in Fuzziness and Soft Computing, 305, 27-48. doi:10.1007/978-3-642-35635-3_3

Carfì, D., & Musolino, F. (2013b). Game Theory Appication of Monti's Proposal for European Government Bonds Stabilization. *Applied Sciences*, *15*, 43-70. Retrieved from http://www.mathem.pub.ro/apps/v15/A15-ca.pdf

Carfì, D., & Musolino, F. (2013c). Model of Possible Cooperation in Financial Markets in Presence of Tax on Speculative Transactions. *Physical, Mathematical, and Natural Sciences*, *91*(1), 1–26. doi:10.1478/AAPP.911A3

Carfì, D., & Musolino, F. (2014a). Dynamical Stabilization of Currency Market with Fractal-like Trajectories. *Scientific Bulletin of the Politehnica University of Bucharest, Series A-Applied Mathematics and Physics, 76*(4), 115-126. Retrieved from http://www.scientificbulletin.upb.ro/rev_docs_arhiva/rezc3a_239636.pdf

Carfì, D., & Musolino, F. (2014b). Speculative and Hedging Interaction Model in Oil and U.S. Dollar Markets with Financial Transaction Taxes. *Economic Modelling*, *37*, 306–319. doi:10.1016/j.econmod.2013.11.003

Carfì, D., & Musolino, F. (2015a). A Coopetitive-Dynamical Game Model for Currency Markets Stabilization. *Physical, Mathematical, and Natural Sciences*, *93*(1), 1–29. doi:10.1478/AAPP.931C1

Carfì, D., & Musolino, F. (2015b). Tax Evasion: A Game Countermeasure. *AAPP | Physical. Mathematical, and Natural Sciences*, *93*(1), 1–17. doi:10.1478/AAPP.931C2

Carfì, D., Musolino, F., Ricciardello, A., & Schilirò, D. (2012). Preface: Introducing PISRS. *AAPP | Physical, Mathematical, and Natural Sciences, 90*. doi:10.1478/AAPP.90S1E1

Carfì, D., Musolino, F., Schilirò, D., & Strati, F. (2013). Preface: Introducing PISRS (Part II). *AAPP | Physical, Mathematical, and Natural Sciences, 91*. doi:.91S2E1 doi:10.1478/AAPP

Carfì, D., & Okura, M. (2014). Coopetition and Game Theory. *Journal of Applied Economic Sciences, 9*, 457-468. Retrieved from http://cesmaa.eu/journals/jaes/files/JAES_2014_Fall.pdf#page=123

Carfì, D., Patanè, G., & Pellegrino, S. (2011). Coopetitive Games and Sustainability in Project Financing. In *Moving from the Crisis to Sustainability: Emerging Issues in the International Context*, (pp. 175-182). Franco Angeli. Retrieved from http://www.francoangeli.it/Ricerca/Scheda_libro.aspx?CodiceLibro=365.906

Carfì, D., & Perrone, E. (2011a). Asymmetric Bertrand Duopoly: Game Complete Analysis by Algebra System Maxima. In *Mathematical Models in Economics*, (pp. 44-66). ASERS Publishing House. Retrieved from http://mpra.ub.uni-muenchen.de/35417/

Carfì, D., & Perrone, E. (2011b). Game Complete Analysis of Bertrand Duopoly. *Theoretical and Practical Research in Economic Fields, 2*. Retrieved from http://mpra.ub.uni-muenchen.de/31302/

Carfì, D., & Perrone, E. (2011c). Game Complete Analysis of Bertrand Duopoly. In *Mathematical Models in Economics*, (pp. 22-43). ASERS Publishing House. Retrieved from http://mpra.ub.uni-muenchen.de/31302/

Carfì, D., & Perrone, E. (2012a). Game complete analysis of symmetric Cournout duopoly. University Library of Munich. Retrieved from http://mpra.ub.uni-muenchen.de/ 35930/

Carfì, D., & Perrone, E. (2012b). *Game Complete Analysis of Classic Economic Duopolies*. Lambert Academic Publishing. Retrieved from https://www.lap-publishing.com/catalog/details//store/ru/book/978-3-8484-2099-5/game-complete-analysis-of-classic-economic-duopolies

Carfì, D., & Perrone, E. (2013). Asymmetric Cournot Duopoly: A Game Complete Analysis. *Journal of Reviews on Global Economics*, *2*, 194–202. doi:10.6000/1929-7092.2013.02.16

Carfì, D., & Pintaudi, A. (2012). Optimal Participation in Illegitimate Market Activities: Complete Analysis of 2 Dimimensional Cases. *Journal of Advanced Research in Law and Economics, 3*, 10-25. Retrieved as MPRA Paper from at https://mpra.ub.uni-muenchen.de/37822/

Carfì, D., & Ricciardello, A. (2009). Non-reactive strategies in decision-form games. *Physical, Mathematical, and Natural Sciences*, *87*(2), 1–12. doi:10.1478/C1A0902002

Carfì, D., & Ricciardello, A. (2010). An algorithm for payoff space in C^1 Games. *Physical, Mathematical, and Natural Sciences*, *88*(1), 1–19. doi:10.1478/C1A1001003

Carfì, D., & Ricciardello, A. (2011a). *Topics in Game Theory*. Il Gabbiano. doi:10.13140/RG.2.1.2368.9685

Carfì, D., & Ricciardello, A. (2011b). Mixed extensions of decision-form games. Cornell University Library. Retrieved from http://arxiv.org/abs/1103.0568

Carfì, D., & Ricciardello, A. (2012a). Algorithms for Payoff Trajectories in C1 Parametric Games. In *Advances in Computational Intelligence: 14th International Conference on Information Processing and Management of Uncertainty in Knowledge-Based Systems*. Springer-Verlag. doi:10.1007/978-3-642-31724-8_67

Carfì, D., & Ricciardello, A. (2012b). *Topics in Game Theory*. Balkan Society of Geometers. Retrieved from http://www.mathem.pub.ro/apps/mono/A-09-Car.pdf

Carfì, D., & Ricciardello, A. (2013a). An Algorithm for Dynamical Games with Fractal-Like Trajectories. In *Fractal Geometry and Dynamical Systems in Pure and Applied Mathematics II: Fractals in Applied Mathematics. PISRS 2011 International Conference on Analysis, Fractal Geometry, Dynamical Systems and Economics*. doi:10.1090/conm/601/11961

Carfì, D., & Ricciardello, A. (2013b). Computational representation of payoff scenarios in C[1] families of normal-form games. *Uzbek Mathematical Journal, 1*, 38-52. Retrieved from https://www.researchgate.net/publication/259105575_Computational_representation_of_payoff_scenarios_in_C1-families_of_normal-form_games

Carfì, D., & Romeo, A. (2015). Improving Welfare in Congo: Italian National Hydrocarbons Authority Strategies and its Possible Coopetitive Alliances with Green Energy Producers. *Journal of Applied Economic Sciences, 10*(4), 571–592. Retrieved from http://cesmaa.eu/journals/jaes/files/JAES_summer%204(34)_online.pdf

Carfì, D., & Schilirò, D. (2011a). Coopetitive Games and Global Green Economy. In *Moving from the Crisis to Sustainability: Emerging Issues in the International Context*. Retrieved as MPRA Paper from http://mpra.ub.uni-muenchen.de/32035/

Carfì, D., & Schilirò, D. (2011b). Crisis in the Euro Area: Coopetitive Game Solutions as New Policy Tools. *Theoretical and Practical Research in Economic Fields, 2*(1), 23-36. Retrieved as MPRA Paper from http://mpra.ub.uni-muenchen.de/27138/

Carfì, D., & Schilirò, D. (2011c). Crisis in the Euro Area: Co-opetitive Game Solutions as New Policy Tools. In *Mathematical Models in Economics*, (pp. 67-86). ASERS. Retrieved from http://www.asers.eu/asers-publishing/collections.html

Carfì, D., & Schilirò, D. (2011d). A model of coopetitive games and the Greek crisis. Cornell University Library. Retrieved from http://arxiv.org/abs/1106.3543

Carfì, D., & Schilirò, D. (2012a). A coopetitive Model for the Green Economy. *Economic Modelling, 29*(4), 1215-1219. doi:10.1016/j.econmod.2012.04.005

Carfì, D., & Schilirò, D. (2012b). A Framework of coopetitive games: Applications to the Greek crisis. *Physical, Mathematical, and Natural Sciences, 90*(1), 1–32. doi:10.1478/AAPP.901A1

Carfì, D., & Schilirò, D. (2012c). A Model of Coopetitive Game for the Environmental Sustainability of a Global Green Economy. *Journal of Environmental Management and Tourism, 3*(1), 5-17. Retrieved as MPRA Paper from https://mpra.ub.uni-muenchen.de/38508/

Carfì, D., & Schilirò, D. (2012d). Global Green Economy and Environmental Sustainability: A Coopetitive Model. In *Advances in Computational Intelligence,14th International Conference on Information Processing and Management of Uncertainty in Knowledge-Based Systems, IPMU 2012*. Springer Berlin Heidelberg. doi:10.1007/978-3-642-31724-8_63

Carfì, D., & Schilirò, D. (2012e). Global Green Economy and Environmental Sustainability: A Coopetitive Model. Cornell University Library. Retrieved from http://arxiv.org/abs/1205.2872

Carfì, D., & Schilirò, D. (2013). A Model of Coopetitive Games and the Greek Crisis. In *Contributions to Game Theory and Management*. Saint Petersburg State University. Retrieved from http://www.gsom.spbu.ru/files/upload/gtm/sbornik2012_27_05_2013.pdf

Carfì, D., & Schilirò, D. (2014a). Coopetitive Game Solutions for the Greek Crisis. In *Design a Pattern of Sustainable Growth, Innovation, Education, Energy and Environment*. Retrieved from http://mpra.ub.uni-muenchen.de/54765/Carfì

Carfi, D., & Schilirò, D. (2014b). Improving Competitiveness and Trade Balance of Greek Economy: A Coopetitive Strategy Model. *Journal of Applied Economic Sciences*, *9*(2), 211–220. Retrieved from http://www.ceeol.com/aspx/issuedetails.aspx?issueid=583d6083-2bbf-4d8c-af1f-3b5786c6e087&articleId=8c9be4cb-86d9-43f1-b555-58b8cb28bbeb

Carfì, D., & Trunfio, A. (2011). A Non-linear Coopetitive Game for Global Green Economy. In *Moving from the Crisis to Sustainability: Emerging Issues in the International Context*, (pp. 421-428). Franco Angeli. Retrieved as MPRA Paper from http://mpra.ub.uni-muenchen.de/32036/

ChartsBin. (2009). *Current Worldwide Annual Meat Consumption per capita*. Retrieved from http://chartsbin.com/view/12730

Chen, M., & Hambrick, D. C. (1995). Speed, Stealth, and Selective Attack: How Small Firms Differ from Large Firms in Competitive Behavior. *Academy of Management Journal*, *38*(2), 453–482. doi:10.2307/256688

Clarke-Hill, C., Li, H., & Davies, B. (2003). The Paradox of Co-operation and Competition in Strategic Alliances: Towards a Multi-Paradigm Approach. *Management Research News*, *26*(1), 1–20. doi:10.1108/01409170310783376

Craig, W. G. (2009). Health effects of vegan diets. *The American Journal of Clinical Nutrition*, *89*(5), 1627S–1633S. doi:10.3945/ajcn.2009.26736N PMID:19279075

Drolc, T. (2013). Education for sustainable development. *EFnews*. Retrieved January 10, 2013, from http://efnet.si/en/2013/01/10/education-for-sustainable-development/

Dutto, A. (2015). Muscolo di grano: la "carne" vegan inventata in Calabria sta conquistando l'Italia. *La cucina italiana*. Retrieved October 28, 2015, from http://www.lacucinaitaliana.it/news/trend/muscolo-di-grano-carne-vegetale/

Etica Vegana. (2016). *Muscolo di grano*. Retrieved from http://eticavegana.it/index.php?route=product/category&path=59

FAO - Food and Agriculture Organization of the United Nations. (n.d.). *Sustainable food consumption and production*. Retrieved from http://www.fao.org/ag/ags/sustainable-food-consumption-and-production/en/

Fiala, N. (2008). Meeting the demand: An estimation of potential future greenhouse gas emissions from meat production. *Ecological Economics*, *67*(3), 412–419. doi:10.1016/j.ecolecon.2007.12.021

FSNC - Four Seasons Natura e Cultura. (n.d.). Retrieved from http://www.viagginaturaecultura.it

Gavin, M. L. (2014). Vegan Food Guide. *TeensHealth*. Retrieved March 2014, from http://kidshealth.org/teen/food_fitness/nutrition/vegan.html

Ghobadi, S., & D'Ambra, J. (2011). Coopetitive Knowledge Sharing: An Analytical Review of Literature. *Electronic Journal of Knowledge Management*, *9*(4), 307–317.

Giambarrresi, F. (2013). *La dieta vegana è per tutti? Pro e contro*. Retrieved from http://www.greenstyle.it/la-dieta-vegana-e-per-tutti-pro-e-contro-50271.html

Gnyawali, D. R., & Park, B. J. R. (2009). *C*o-opetition and Technological Innovation in Small and Medium-Sized Enterprises: A Multilevel Conceptual Model. *Journal of Small Business Management*, *47*(3), 308–330. doi:10.1111/j.1540-627X.2009.00273.x

Gomes-Cassares, B. (1997). Alliance Strategies of Small Firms. *Small Business Economics*, *9*(1), 33–44. doi:10.1023/A:1007947629435

Gourmandelle. (2015). *Vegetarian on a Budget | How Much Does a Vegetarian Diet Really Cost?* Retrieved September 19, 2015, from http://gourmandelle.com/vegetarian-on-a-budget-cost-diet/

Gulati, R., & Higgins, M. C. (2003). Which Ties Matter When? The Contingent Effects of Interorganizational Partnerships on IPO Success. *Strategic Management Journal*, *24*(2), 127–144. doi:10.1002/smj.287

Hagedoorn, J., Carayannis, E., & Alexander, J. (2001). Strange Bedfellows in the Personal Computer Industry: Technology Alliances between IBM and Apple. *Research Policy*, *30*(5), 837–849. doi:10.1016/S0048-7333(00)00125-6

Hagel, J. III, & Brown, J. S. (2005). Productive Friction: How Difficult Business Partnership Can Accelerate Innovation. *Harvard Business Review*, *83*(2), 82–91. PMID:15724576

iVegan. (n.d.). Retrieved from http://shop.ivegan.it/28-muscolo-grano

Jorde, T. M., & Teece, D. J. (1990). Innovation and Cooperation: Implications for Competition and Antitrust. *The Journal of Economic Perspectives*, *4*(3), 75–96. doi:10.1257/jep.4.3.75

Key, T. J., Appleby, P. N., & Rosell, M. S. (2008). Health effects of vegetarian and vegan diets. *The Proceedings of the Nutrition Society*, *65*(1), 35–41. doi:10.1079/PNS2005481 PMID:16441942

Kjaernes, U. (2010). Sustainable Food Consumption. Some contemporary European issues. *Sustainable Consumption Research Exchange*. Retrieved from http://www.sifo.no/files/file76709_prosjektnotat_nr.1-2010-web.pdf

Knutson, P. (n.d.). Let's Uncover the Truth Behind The Vegan Food Pyramid. *Vegan Coach*. Retrieved from http://www.vegancoach.com/vegan-food-pyramid.html

Lado, A. A., Boyd, N. G., & Hanlon, S. C. (1997). Competition, Cooperation, and the Search from Economic Rents: A Syncretic Model. *Academy of Management Review*, *22*(1), 110–141.

Laine, A. (2002). *Hand in Hand with the Enemy: Defining a Competitor from a New Perspective*. Paper Presented at the EURAM Conference: Innovative Research in Management, Stockholm, Sweden.

Leitzmann, C. (2003). Nutrition ecology: the contribution of vegetarian diets. *The American Journal of Clinical Nutrition*. Retrieved from http://ajcn.nutrition.org/content/78/3/657S.long

Leitzmann, C. (2014). Vegetarian nutrition: past, present, future. *The American Journal of Clinical Nutrition*. Retrieved from http://ajcn.nutrition.org/content/early/2014/06/04/ajcn.113.071365

Lugano, M. (2012). Gli ingredienti della cucina naturale: muscolo di grano. *TuttoGreen*. Retrieved July 12, 2012, from http://www.tuttogreen.it/gli-ingredienti-della-cucina-naturale-muscolo-di-grano/

Lusk, J. L., & Bailey Norwood, F. (2007). *Some Economic Benefits and Costs of Vegetarianism*. Retrieved October 16, 2007, from http://citeseerx.ist.psu.edu/viewdoc/download?doi=10.1.1.549.1689&rep=rep1&type=pdf

MacMillan, A. (n.d.). 14 Best Vegan and Vegetarian Protein Sources. *Health Magazine*. Retrieved from http://www.health.com/health/gallery/0,20718479,00.html

McKinsey & Company. (2011). *The moment Is Now. Successful Pharmaceutical Alliances in Japan*. Retrieved from http://www.mckinsey.com/global_locations/asia/japan/en/latest_thinking

Messina, G. (2010). The high cost of ethical eating. *The Vegan RD*. Retrieved January, 20, 2010, from http://www.theveganrd.com/2010/01/the-high-cost-of-ethical-eating.html

Mingolia, S. (2015). *A Expo 2015, il "muscolo vegetale" made in Italy*. Retrieved from http://www.econewsweb.it/it/2015/05/05/muscolo-di-grano/#.VpqaLFKR4dU

Mission 2015. (n.d.). *Problems With Current Meat Production*. Retrieved from http://web.mit.edu/12.000/www/m2015/2015/meat_production.html

Muscle of Wheat. (n.d.). Retrieved from http://www.muscolodigrano.com/#!page3/cee5

Muscolo di Grano. (n.d.). Retrieved from https://www.facebook.com/muscolo.digrano/photos_stream

Musolino, F. (2012). Game theory for speculative derivatives: a possible stabilizing regulatory model. *Physical, Mathematical, and Natural Sciences, 90*(S1), 1-19. doi:10.1478/AAPP.90S1C1

Napolitano, U. (2015). Muscolo di Grano, la carne vegetale del futuro, trionfa a Expo Milano quale unico prodotto alimentare veramente innovativo. *Famiglie d'Italia*. Retrieved September 27, 2015, from https://famiglieditalia.wordpress.com/2015/10/04/muscolo-di-grano-la-carne-vegetale-del-futuro-trionfa-a-expo-milano-quale-unico-prodotto-alimentare-veramente-innovativo/

National Sustainable Sales. (n.d.). *What is Vegan/Vegetarian?* Retrieved from http://www.nationalsustainablesales.com/vegan-vegetarian

Ngo, D. D., & Okura, M. (2008). Coopetition in a Mixed Duopoly Market. *Economic Bulletin, 12*(20), 1–9.

Nguyen, T. L. T., Hermansen, J. E., & Mogensen, L. (n.d.). *Environmental costs of meat production: The case of typical EU pork production*. Retrieved from http://www.researchgate.net/publication/251624206

Non solo Vegan. (2014). *Alimentazione vegana e sostenibilità ambientale*. Retrieved November 30, 2014, from http://www.nonsolovegan.it/alimentazione-vegana-e-sostenibilita-ambientale/

Ohkita, K., & Okura, M. (2014). Coopetition and Coordinated Investment: Protecting Japanese Video Games Intellectual Property Rights. *International Journal of Business Environment, 6*(1), 92–105. doi:10.1504/IJBE.2014.058025

Okura, M. (2007). Coopetitive Strategies of Japanese Insurance Firms: A Game-Theory Approach. *International Studies of Management & Organization, 37*(2), 53–69. doi:10.2753/IMO0020-8825370203

Okura, M. (2008). Why Isnt the Accident Information Shared? A Coopetition Perspective. *Management Research, 6*(3), 219–225. doi:10.2753/JMR1536-5433060305

Okura, M. (2009). Coopetitive Strategies to Limit the Insurance Fraud Problem in Japan. In Coopetition Strategy: Theory, Experiments and Cases (pp. 240-257). Routledge.

Okura, M. (2012). An Economic Analysis of Coopetitive Training Investments for Insurance Agents. In *Advances in Computational Intelligence: 14th International Conference on Information Processing and Management of Uncertainty in Knowledge-Based Systems, IPMU 2012*. Springer-Verlag. doi:10.1007/978-3-642-31724-8_61

One Green Planet. (n.d.). Retrieved from http://www.onegreenplanet.org/channel/vegan-food/

Oscar Green. (2015). *Oscar Green 2015 WeGreen a Muscolo di Grano*. Retrieved October 2, 2015, from http://www.oscargreen.it/notizie/oscar-green-2015-a-muscolo-di-grano-per-wegreen/

Padula, G., & Dagnino, G. B. (2007). Untangling the Rise of Coopetition: The Intrusion of Competition in a Cooperative Game Structure. *International Studies of Management & Organization, 37*(2), 32–53. doi:10.2753/IMO0020-8825370202

Pesamaa, O., & Eriksson, P. E. (2010). Coopetition among Nature-based Tourism Firms: Competition at Local Level and Cooperation at Destination Level. In *Coopetition: Winning Strategies for the 21st Century*. Edward Elgar Publishing.

Petroff, A. (2015). Processed meat causes cancer, says WHO. *CNNMoney (London)*. Retrieved October 26, 2015, from http://money.cnn.com/2015/10/26/news/red-meat-processed-cancer-world-health-organization/

Pimentel, D., & Pimentel, M. (2003). Sustainability of meat-based and plant-based diets and the environment. *The American Journal of Clinical Nutrition*, *78*, 660S–663S. Retrieved from http://ajcn.nutrition.org/content/78/3/660S.full PMID:12936963

Porter, M. (1985). *Competitive Advantage. Creating and Sustaining Superior Performance*. New York: Free Press.

Quintana-Garcia, C., & Benavides-Velasco, C. A. (2004). Cooperation, Competition, and Innovative Capability: A Panel Data of European Dedicated Biotechnology Firms. *Technovation*, *24*(12), 927–938. doi:10.1016/S0166-4972(03)00060-9

Rodrigues, F., Souza, V., & Leitao, J. (2011). Strategic Coopetition of Global Brands: A Game Theory Approach to Nike + iPod Sport Kit Co-branding. *International Journal of Entrepreneurial Venturing*, *3*(4), 435–455. doi:10.1504/IJEV.2011.043387

Sacchi Hunter, E. (n.d.). Muscolo di grano. *Cure Naturali*. Retrieved from http://www.cure-naturali.it/muscolo-di-grano/4188

Saint Louis, C. (2015). Meat and Cancer: The W.H.O. Report and What You Need to Know. *The New York Times*. Retrieved October 26, 2015, from http://www.nytimes.com/interactive/2015/10/26/health/meat-cancer-who-report.html?_r=2

Sakakibara, K. (1993). R&D Cooperation among Competitors: A Case Study of the VLSI Semiconductor Research Project in Japan. *Journal of Engineering and Technology Management*, *10*(4), 393–407. doi:10.1016/0923-4748(93)90030-M

Sakakibara, M. (1997). Heterogeneity of firm capabilities and cooperative research and development: An empirical examination of motives. *Strategic Management Journal*, *18*(S1), 143–164. doi:10.1002/(SICI)1097-0266(199707)18:1+<143::AID-SMJ927>3.3.CO;2-P

Sclaunich, G. (2015). La Regione Calabria punta sul muscolo di grano per Expo. *Veggo anch'io*. Retrieved April 10, 2015, from http://veggoanchio.corriere.it/2015/04/10/expo-muscolo-di-grano-regione-calabria/

Seclì, R. (2007). *VEG-ECONOMY. Fondamenti, realtà e prospettive dell'impresa "senza crudeltà"*. Retrieved from http://www.societavegetariana.org/site/uploads/570e7bd1-6289-f2b9.pdf

Shanker, D. (2015). *The US meat industry's wildly successful, 40-year crusade to keep its hold on the American diet*. Retrieved October 22, 2015 from http://qz.com/523255/the-us-meat-industrys-wildly-successful-40-year-crusade-to-keep-its-hold-on-the-american-diet/

Shy, O. (1995). *Industrial Organization: Theory and Applications*. Cambridge, MA: The MIT Press.

Società Scientifica di Nutrizione Vegetariana. (n.d.). Retrieved from http://www.scienzavegetariana.it/

Staying Vegan. (2010). *Is eating vegan more expensive than a "normal" diet?* Retrieved April 26, 2010, from http://stayingvegan.com/2010/04/is-eating-vegan-more-expensive-than-a-normal-diet/

Stein, H. D. (2010). Literature Overview on the Field of Co-opetition. *Verslas: Teorija ir Praktika, 11*(3), 256-265.

Stiles, J. (2001). Strategic Alliances, in Rethinking Strategy. Sage Publications.

Stuart, T. E. (2000). Interorganizational Alliances and the Performance of Firms: A Study of Growth and Innovation Rates in High-technology Industry. *Strategic Management Journal, 21*(8), 791–811. doi:10.1002/1097-0266(200008)21:8<791::AID-SMJ121>3.0.CO;2-K

Sun, S., Zhang, J., & Lin, H. (2008). Evolutionary Game Analysis on the Effective Co-opetition Mechanism of Partners within High Quality Pork Supply Chain. *Service Operations and Logistics, and Informatics, 2008, IEEE/SOLI 2008. IEEE International Conference on*, (pp. 2066-2071). IEEE.

The Vegan Society. (n.d.). *Why go vegan?* Retrieved from https://www.vegansociety.com/try-vegan/why-go-vegan

The Vegetarian Resource Group. (n.d.). Retrieved from https://www.vrg.org/nutshell/market.htm

Thomas, K. (n.d.). *Dairy sustainability made me rethink being vegan*. Dairy Council of Utah & Nevada. Retrieved from http://thecowlocale.com/2014/04/22/dairy-sustainability-made-me-rethink-being-vegan/

Turnbull, S. (2015). *How to eat vegan at any restaurant (and not order salad)*. Retrieved June 22, 2015, from http://itdoesnttastelikechicken.com/2015/06/22/eat-vegan-restaurant-order-salad/

Universo Vegano. (n.d.). Retrieved from http://www.universovegano.it/

Vegan Outreach. (2014). *What Do Vegans Eat?* Retrieved from http://veganoutreach.org/what-to-eat/

Vegan Starter Kit. (n.d.). *Eating*. Retrieved from http://vegankit.com/eat/

Veganblog. (2015). Muscolo di grano sbriciolato. *Ricette di Terra*. Retrieved December 22, 2015, from http://www.veganblog.it/2015/12/22/muscolo-di-grano-sbriciolato/

Vegans of Color. (2009). *Does being vegan cost more money?* Retrieved February, 20, 2009, from https://vegansofcolor.wordpress.com/2009/02/20/does-being-vegan-cost-more-money/

von Hippel, E. (1987). Cooperation between Rivals: Informal Know-how Trading. *Research Policy*, *16*(6), 291–302. doi:10.1016/0048-7333(87)90015-1

Walker, P., Rhubart-Berg, P., Mckenzie, S., Kelling, K., & Lawrencw, R. S. (2005). Public health implications of meat production and consumption. *Public Health Nutrition*, *8*(4), 348–356. doi:10.1079/PHN2005727 PMID:15975179

Walley, K. (2007). Coopetition: An Introduction to the Subject and an Agenda for Research. *International Studies of Management & Organization*, *37*(2), 11–31. doi:10.2753/IMO0020-8825370201

Wheeler, L. (2015). Vegan diet best for planet. *The Hill*. Retrieved May 4, 2015, from http://thehill.com/regulation/237767-vegan-diet-best-for-planet-federal-report-says

WHO. (2015). *Q&A on the carcinogenicity of the consumption of red meat and processed meat*. Retrieved October, 2015, from http://www.who.int/features/qa/cancer-red-meat/en/

Whole Foods Market. (n.d.). Retrieved from http://www.wholefoodsmarket.com/healthy-eating/special-diets/vegan

Wick, A. (2011). The Conscious Case Against Veganism. *Ecosalon*. Retrieved March 17, 2011, from http://ecosalon.com/reasons-not-to-be-vegan/

Wilkinson, I., & Young, L. (2002). On Cooperating: Firms, Relations and Networks. *Journal of Business Research*, *55*(2), 123–132. doi:10.1016/S0148-2963(00)00147-8

Worldwatch Institute. (2004). Is Meat Sustainable? *World Watch Magazine, 17*(4). Retrieved from http://www.worldwatch.org/node/549

Zanni, M. (2013). Il Muscolo di grano: una valida e gustosa alternativa alla carne. *Saggi e Assaggi*. Retrieved January 30, 2013, from http://www.saggieassaggi.it/il-muscolo-di-grano-una-valida-e-gustosa-alternativa-alla-carne/

Chapter 5
Green Information System for a Sustainable Enterprise

Laura-Diana Radu
Alexandru Ioan Cuza University of Iasi, Romania

ABSTRACT

The changes made in the environment as a consequence of massive industrialization led to a change in the vision of mankind on how organizations should interact with the ecosystem. In the same time information system has a key role in their activity. The increasing their use is accompanied by positive effects. This chapter presents the changes necessary for transformation traditional information systems in green information system. The organization's motivations to develop and implement strategies and regulations for environmental protection are varied. They can be the organization's internal drivers, such as reducing delivery costs, increasing efficiency, improving market reputation, and external, such as government legislation or policies, regulations, competition. Changes necessary to implement green information system are presented based on agile model life cycle and in accord with organizations objectives.

INTRODUCTION

The field of environmental sustainability has been studied by marketing researchers, management researchers, operation researchers or business economists (Walker et al., 1998; Bazerman & Hoffman, 1999; Corbett & Kirsch, 2001; King & Lenox, 2001; Midgley & Reynolds, 2004; Collins et al., 2007; Lyon & Maxwell, 2007; White &

DOI: 10.4018/978-1-5225-2075-7.ch005

Lee, 2009). Its benefits have been put to profit from various perspectives, but they have also been criticized mainly due to the way in which they are perceived and implemented. Until 2010, there had been made quite a few studies which presented the way in which environmental sustainability could be engulfed by the information systems (IS) (Melville, 2010). After this year some organizations adopted certain strategies of ecological sustainable development, some important changes came up, in the technical or non-technical fields and currently it is seen as a necessity. In our days *a business that fails to have sustainable development as a top priorities could receive considerable public criticism and subsequently lose market legitimacy* (Du et al., 2013).

For an organization, "going green" means going through an analysis of the current situation as regards the influence on the environment, identifying the drawbacks on organizational level, then developing models to describe the state which the company aims to reach and turn them into business projects in order to improve the equilibrium between the organizational inputs and outputs and the environment (Beal, 2011).

During the last decades, in some countries, by regulation, education and life conditions there have been made attempts to turn sustainable consumption into a lifestyle. The reduction in the electric energy consumption or the use of alternative sources, less non-renewable resources, diminishing waste and encouraging selective waste collection have been assimilated into the natural behavior of some community members.

The studies have shown that technology, including IT, can help with increasing eco-efficiency, which is the ratio between environmental and economic performance, or, more concretely, between (product or service) value added and environmental impact added by that activity (Hack & Berg, 2014).

In these circumstances an important role is held by the IS of the organization which should be green in its turn in order to meet the demands of the international organizations interested in the field of environment protection, but also of a wide range of consumers. This is how the concept of *green IS* appeared and it expands the meaning of phrases such as green IT, ecoinformatics, green computing etc. and it analyses in real terms how the IS within the organization can contribute to the environment protection and how its negative effects can be diminished.

BACKGROUND

Considering the degree of involvement of organizations in promoting sustainable ecological development, Hart (1997) identifies three objectives: (1) preventing pollution by minimizing the waste and CO_2 emissions, (2) manage the product characteristics after consideration the partners/clients' opinions and optimize the whole life-cycle, (3) sustainable ecological development accomplished by diminishing the influence of the organization on the environment and assuming a vision on long-term ecological research. IT and IS can contribute to the accomplishment of these objectives as object and subject of the ecological sustainable development by reducing their influence on the environment, as well as by improving the influence of products and services on the accomplishment they participate in.

The literature in the field identifies six key points which might lay the basis for the ecological sustainability: (1) prevent pollution; (2) more production with less resources; (3) reduce impact on the environment; (4) clean production; (5) environmental performance; (6) output equals input (Tu and Huang, 2015). These key points apply in the IT as well to prove that green design increase efficiency, produce benefits in companies and reduce environmental pollution. The concept of green IS has appeared as a normal extension of green IT. It was introduced in research and practice in 2008 as a consequence of wider ICT use and becoming aware of their impact on the environment, in the production process and later also during the use and after use.

The aim of replacing IS and IT with those considered green is to intensify the way in which these technologies support sustainable development by and in different organizations. The literature in the field as well the practice present different opinions and these, together with the growing interest for this topic make it quite a challenge to clearly define and delineate this concept. For this reason, at the beginning, there will be clarified the notions of green IT and green IS, as well as the differences and resemblances, based on literature. The following table presents a few definitions, considered relevant by the author for the two concepts (Table 1).

The opinions regarding the resemblances and differences between the two concepts are not unitary. Some authors consider that green IT refers exclusively to the technical part of the field, while others include the economic side as well. At the same time, some authors, such as Dedrick, 2010; Molla, 2013; Sarkis et al., 2013; Esfahani et al., 2015 highlight the close relationship between green IS and green IT, but they do not consider that they have different interests and goals. In their opinion, green IT aims to bring the negative effects of IT on the environment to a minimum by producing, using and discharging the equipment and applications only in ecological terms (Murugesan, 2008; Molla et al., 2011; Molla, 2013). On the other side, green IS refers to the use of IS in organizations in order to support the sustainable ecological development by automatisation and changing the products, processes as well as business relationships and practices (Chen et al., 2008; Melville, 2010; Molla, 2013).

In the opinion of other authors as Watson et al. (2010), green IT is a component of green IS, since the first concept's approach focuses on technology, thus its meaning is limited. They consider green IS the design and implementation of IS that contrib-

Table 1. ICT and environment: different approaches

Author	Green ICT (Green computing) is...
Murugesan (2008)	... the designing, manufacturing, using and disposing all ICT equipment with minimal impact on the environment or with no negative impact. These equipment include monitors, printers, storage devices, networking and communication devices.
Molla (2009)	... the interest of the company to apply environmental sustainability criteria (pollution, clean technologies and production, e-waste management etc.) in the processes of product design, production, use and disposal of the IT infrastructure (including equipment, human resources and managerial components).
Andreopoulou et al. (2013)	... the design, construction and information diffusion in order to achieve ecologically sustainable development and to improve the company's operational process by adopting and applying technological innovations from ICT industry.
Author	**Green IS refers to...**
Esty and Winston (2006)	... information system modified and used to monitor environmental practices and outcomes.
Jenkin et al. (2011)	... design, development and use of information system in order to support environmental sustainability initiatives and that has direct or indirect favorable impact on the environment.
Löser et al. (2012)	... all information system components (products, service and business operations) in order to minimize the negative impact on the environment manifested by managerial perspective on the investments in information system, his design, his development and use.

ute to sustainable business process. The table below shows the differences between green IS and green IT in the opinion of the above-mentioned authors (Table 2).

Brooks et al. (2012) offers a complete and correct definition of the concept of green IS considering its technical side, as well as the non-technical side. In these authors opinion, they represent the improving of the energy efficiency and the introducing of more environmentally friendly products and services to decrease negative influences on the environment through initiatives concerning the use of IT infrastructures to change organizational practices and processes. Green IS addresses a wider issue and consequently, it is expected to offer more complex solutions. Their impact on the environment is more favorable than green IT. Green IS make entire activity of the organization more sustainable and this includes the use of IS to increase sustainability across the global economy (Watson et al., 2008) and improving, in this way, efficiency in industries that are major sources of GHG emissions, such as the transportation, manufacturing, and energy sectors (Dedrick, 2010). In another definition, given by Watson et al. (2010) green IS is the investments in design, development, management and use of IS in order to decrease or even to eliminate the negative impact of IS, business operations and its specific products and services on the environment. As it can be seen, in this approach, the authors do not mention IT explicitly, as they are considered an implicit component of IS, thus

Table 2. Green IS vs. Green IT

Green IS	Green IT
• Using a fleet management system and dynamic routing of vehicle to reduce transportation costs through less energy consumption and the avoidance of the traffic congestion; • Collecting and using information on the environmental impact in the production and in the supply of service; • More effective management of operational emission and waste product; • A better information of the consumers about the influence of the products and the services on the environment. They can make green choices more conveniently and effectively; • Using online communication for teamwork and meeting in the case of companies with offices distributed to the world.	• Designing and using green hardware; • Using thin clients instead of personal computers; • Using cloud computing to run applications and operating systems; • Replacing brown sources of energy with green sources in data centers; • Minimizing energy consumption in data centers; • Minimizing e-waste from computing equipment; • Reduce transportation through online communication and remote computer administration.

(Watson el al., 2008)

promoting the more complex and wider role of the latter. However, regardless of the adopted approach, it is clear that the aim remains unchanged, namely: introduce and potentiate some advanced methods and techniques to protect the environment, in agreement with the extended use of ICT.

GREEN IS ADOPTION: MOTIVATIONS FOR ENTERPRISES AND FOR SOCIETY

In order to understand how green IS can be introduced in organizations aiming to support a sustainable ecological development, some authors consider that the starting point could be the concept of environmental technologies. It is defined as product design, acquisition and use of production equipment, methods and procedures, delivery and after-sale service through methods and mechanisms that ensure energy conservation and minimize negative influences on the natural balance and protect the environment (Shrivastava, 1995). Without explicitly mentioning green IS, this definition highlights the way in which they can contribute to the protection of the environment by increasing the efficiency in using the resources associated to procedures, equipment and products destined to the end user. A significant role is played by the management team who should propose strategies to encourage the protection of the environment, if they are interested in this aspect.

Based on this interpretation, the researchers identified three stages in the green IT and IS evolution up to the present day (Löser, 2015). The first stage refers to *reducing the negative impact of IT on the environment, mainly that of CO_2 emissions,* *by promoting green IT*. In the second stage, green IS takes shape in the *innovation of process* which points to the way in which IS contributes to the reducing of the negative effects caused by other fields of activity, such as transport, production or energy. In the end, there was identified a third stage which considers *the innovation of product* and this is accomplished by developing and putting on the market certain products with smaller negative effect on the environment, in the form of diminishing the consumption of resources, the CO_2 emissions and the e-waste and also by creating a smart or intelligent infrastructure. A previous analysis on the green IT and green IS stage underlined the fact that different organizations are going through different stages since the adoption of these concepts (Radu, 2014, 2015a, 2015b). Also, a significant part does not arouse any interest for the purchase, development and use of ICT in agreement with the protection of the ecosystem.

Fighting the negative impact on the environment by adopting green IS requires a series of actions and decisions among which we consider these are significant: choose the hardware and software suppliers considering their environmental policies, as regards the presence and compliance to the standard (as ISO 14000 series or EMAS), as well as the offer actually present on the market, a rational replacement of the equipment, limited use of IT depending on the organizational needs, policies of eliminating e-waste favorable to the environment and so on. This last aspect is very controversial. The growing countries prove to be the deposit of a great volume of e-waste, even under the conditions of laws in force which actually forbid such practices. The motivations are the following: little awareness on the issue, lack of resources in the hands of the authorities or the presence of corruption. For instance, in China there is exported a great volume of e-waste, although it is legally forbidden since 2000 and 2002 (Li et al., 2006). Approximately 80% of the totals of 40 million tons of e-waste generated yearly is exported to the developing countries (UNEP, 2010). The main importers are China, Pakistan, India, Vietnam, Philippines, Malaysia, Nigeria, Ghana and Peru according to a report of Basel Action Network (Puckett et al., 2005). The presence of contaminants as beryllium or brominated flame retardants as well as dangerous metals such as mercury, arsenic, chromium, cadmium which can be found in e-waste and can affect the population's state of health. Also, an interesting analysis shows that a modern microprocessor requires around 60 elements (more than a half of all existing elements on earth) while in the 1980s, it was produces with 12 chemical elements (Löser, 2015). The responsibility assumed for such practices cannot be found on both parties, whereas finding a solution remains a problem of social consciousness.

Another controversial aspect of this topic is the moment when a piece of equipment is considered e-waste, since sometimes; they are hidden under the form of transactions of functional equipment. In this case, when liability no longer functions as a determining factor in applying the specific green IT practices, the developers end up with the task of finding less invasive solutions for the environment. The positive effects should be spread from the developed countries, which have the proper legal frame and can limit the production of polluting equipment and applications, consuming energy as well, towards the less developed countries which assume mainly the position of consumers, but this status is not given as a rule (China and India for example have important positions on both sides of the market). Another critical aspect is given by the growing purchase of IT equipment in the developing countries which, in a rather short period of time, considering the evolution in the field, will also turn into e-waste and the lack of laws and education in the field of recycling will lead to their improper discharge. According to the estimations, by 2018 the number of computers used in the developing countries will have been greater than in the developed countries (Yu et al., 2010).

Another controversial aspect, specific to IT, is the storage capacity. The increase in the information volume requires more or more efficient storage devices, an increase in the transfer speed, enlarging the access time, hence, more efficient equipment. According to some studies made by IBM, a quantity 2.5 quintillion bytes of data is created daily – this is so huge that 90% of the current volume of data has been created in the last two years (Zikopoulos et al., 2014).

From an organizational perspective, the effects related to the use of IT on the environment suggest the necessity of a holistic approach along the whole life-cycle which actually corresponds to the concept of green IS. The measures currently applied by the organizations interested in the protection of the environment refer to the consolidation and virtualization, intelligent power management functions, dynamically adjustable cooling, separation of hot and cold air flows, and optimized uninterruptable power supplies (USPs), thin clients, mobile instead of desktop computers, power management software, LED displays and multifunction printers, refurbishing, reusing and recycling outdated hardware at the end of life.

The role played by the IS is obvious when it comes to implementing the measures mentioned above. They are able to render the information as well as the necessary instruments so as to engulf the characteristics of the sustainable ecological development within the operations and the decision-making process in the organizations. On the other hand, adopting green IS brings significant economic benefits to the organizations due to the following: *increase competition* (Dao et al., 2011; Chou, 2013), *increase efficiency and effectiveness* (Chen et al., 2009; Molla & Abareshi, 2011) and *reduce costs* (Vykoukal et al., 2009; Way, 2009; Mithas et al., 2010; Marett et al., 2013; Talebi & Chou, 2013; Loock, 2013). They are the result of the important role IS play within the organizations. They are considered the core of the business processes and due to this, they might become the main trigger of organizational changes (Ramirez et al., 2010; Popescul & Georgescu, 2015; Löser, 2015).

As it can be seen, the adoption of green IS brings numerous benefits to the companies as well as to the society. There are also many motivations to take measures in this field, reflected mainly by the environment conditions. Even under the current circumstances of technological progress, there are not enough technologies, methods and initiatives to neutralize the negative effects of ICT on the environment. The influences on the environment appear during all cycles of life and take the shape of using non-renewable resources in the production process, consumption of energy, e-waste, and CO_2 emissions. These are the most important and visible. For this reason, the major investments focus in this direction. Nowadays, there would be needed 1.5 planets to meet the demands of all the people and unless essential changes appear, it is estimated that by the middle of the century, 2 planets will be needed (Maclean et al., 2010). Innovation in green IS is essential in order to restore the natural balance.

From the ethical point of view, the motivations which encourage the companies to get involved in the development and innovation in green IS are the problems of our planet reflected in *global warming, scarce non-renewable resources and pollution.* Nevertheless, in reality, in most situations, they are constrained by *legal regulations*. According to Porter's conclusion, *the regulations which aim getting results and not processes will force the companies to redesign their technology, so that they could increase the efficiency of their activity by cutting costs and increasing the product quality and produce less polluting goods* (Porter, 1991 in Ashford, Hall, 2011). Being open to the legal changes regarding the environment protection as well as anticipating them might offer an advantage of the *temporary monopolies* to the companies and this is similar to any technological innovation, in the ICT field even more, being considered extremely dynamic.

THE CHANGES REQUESTED BY GREEN IS

The motivations which determine the companies to adopt changes in IS are varied. They can be internal as well as external and they are closely related to the objectives and priorities of the organization. Complying IS with the organizational objectives and strategies have been an important concern of the management teams during the last decades, once the important role they play has been identified. On the other hand, any possible failure in this process might lead to the loss of certain opportunities, wasting resources and not meeting the proposed goals (Bush et al., 2009).

In case of most organizations the objectives are of a financial side or are related to the finances. Green IS often requires partial or total replacement of the infrastructure, which means making a significant investment while the profit will be obtained on the long term: green practices can affect system requirements related to hardware, software, and business processes (Beal, 2010). The characteristics which should be included in IS in order to become green can be identified starting from the IS components mentioned by Löser (2015): IT (physical servers, personal and office computers and network devices), shared services (database or storage), business applications (ERP systems), IT human resources (skill and knowledge) and managerial capabilities for organizational process and business transformation related to IS. The first component involves mainly the technical part and it actually represents green IT (Figure 1).

In what follows, starting from the agile life-cycle model, considered the most efficient nowadays, we present the way in which the green concept might be integrated in all stages of the life-cycle of the IS. The model we mention has four main stages (Figure 2)

The interest in green IS might appear from the *project selection and approval stage*. In this stage, a *team of managers, developers and clients agree on the goals,*

Figure 1. Green IS components

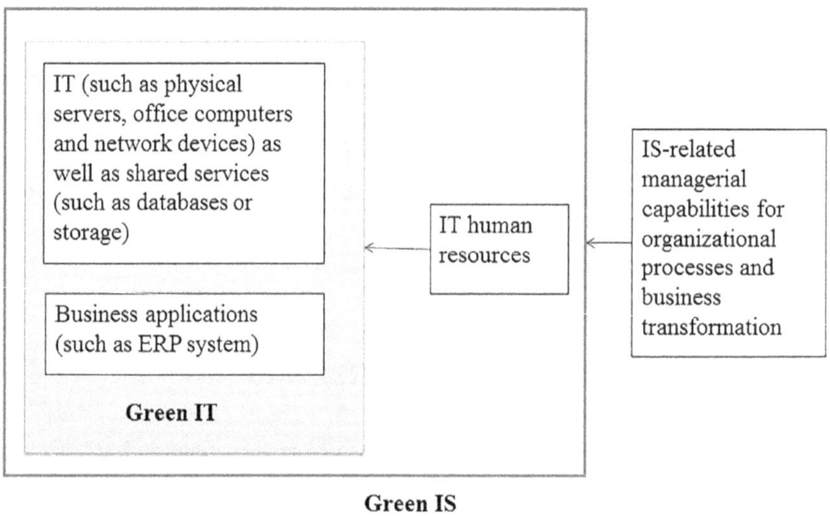

Figure 2. Agile development life-cycle
Source: adapted from Isaias and Issa, 2015

objectives and requirements of the product, they evaluate the alternatives and estimate the risks. Introducing a new IS, replacing the current one or updating it can have the issue of the influence on the environment as the starting point. Such a decision can be made either by introducing some new regulations or by adopting a protection strategy for the environment or even both. The most visible influences on the environment, from the point of view of the end user, are CO_2 emissions, in direct proportion to the consumption of energy and also the waste generated at the end of the product life. The negative influences are not always visible. For example, a significant quantity from the resources used in the production process (energy, material and chemical substances) will not appear in the final product. Sarkis et al. (2013) considers that an average desktop computer and monitor requires ten times its weight in fossil fuels, water and chemicals as material and resources inputs. In case the environment considerations are different than the approach, the protection principles could be integrated into the requirements of the new system. In this stage there is established the purpose of the new system, there are estimated the necessary resources, there are made feasibility studies and there are described the expected benefits. Regardless of the vastness of the system which will be implemented and of the changes it might bring, the objectives of the new system should be in agreement with the organizational goals. The concern for the environment during the selection and approval stage can be clearly seen in the following:

- Analysis of the opinions and directions adopted by partners and the business environment generally speaking, as regards the world trends on ecology but also the trends specific to the field in which the organization operates.
- Clear definition of the organizational goals considering the environment and the strategies that should be adopted in order to accomplish them.
- Formulation of a set of environmental requirements to be included in the non-functional requirements of the new system.
- Analysis of the regulations on the environment in force in the country in which the company activates or, if it is the case, international regulations for the multinational companies. It would also prove useful to make an analysis of the trends on the long run in this field considering there are a larger and larger number of constraints regarding the use of natural resources, pollution and waste.
- Elaborate a viable proposal for green IS which could highlight the financial benefits as well, not only those specific to the environment protection. The analysis of the cost-benefit proportion should be based on detailed measurements regarding the influence on the environment. From the financial point of view, the main advantage is currently given by saving energy.

During this stage there are also made the feasibility studies. There are analyzed the following types of feasibility: economic, operational, technical, schedule and legal. There is made a list of potential criteria and risks which should be considered when making a decision regarding the continuity of the project depending on the obtained results expressed in key milestones. In the context of an increased importance awarded to the environment, there could be introduced a new analysis of *environmental feasibility* as a distinct component. It will undertake components from other types of studies in order to develop them, for example, the influence of technologies used nowadays or those which are necessary to implement a new system on the environment, identify the most environmental-friendly equipment, the volume of waste as a consequence of replacing the current equipment with a new one required by the functioning of the new system, organize the network so as to generate minimum negative effects, reducing the costs by less energy consumption.

The feasibility study on the environment will bring new elements, such as the analysis of a potential development of *green and sustainable software*. This concept was defined by Naumann et al. (2011) as *software with minimum negative on the environment and on the society effects in all stages of cycle-life (design, development and usage) or software with positive effects on sustainable development.* The above-mentioned authors consider that the direct impact refers to the consumption of resources and energy during the design and production and then use of the software. The indirect impact refers to the effects from the use of the applications in order to accomplish the processes within the organizations and to the systematic effects on the environment on the long run.

In case the protection of the environment plays a leading role in the development of the new system, the *environmental feasibility* should clearly show the consequences on the environment as well as the benefits the project implementation might bring. This analysis will be continued during the design and development of the system in order to estimate the consumption of non-renewable resources and the level of pollution entailed by the new system. Environmental feasibility has to answer to the following questions (Lopez-Lopez, 2011):

- **Carbon Footprint:** How much CO_2 a software development, management or maintenance phase will emit?
- **Energy:** How much energy is consumed in the development phase?
- **Travel:** How much traveling time is required in the development phase?
- **Waste:** How much resources are consumed in activities that create no visible value to software end users?

Similar to the other types of feasibility, the one specific to the environment will bring the following benefits to the project: it strengthens the general frame as well as the motivation behind accomplishing the proposed system, it contributes to the increase of the success chances due to the detailed analysis of the elements which influence the success of each project, it allows the identification of the business alternatives, it helps in making a decision when choosing one particular project out of several proposals, it offers a detailed documentation on the situation of the company, according to each feasibility category. It will also allow the identification of the internal and external restrictions in the accomplishment of the project, as well as an objective estimation of the success chances.

During the second stage of *project initiation,* there is established the team which will take part in it and contribute to its accomplishment, there are identified the available funds and financial sources, there is designed the initial architecture of the system, there is configured the environment in which the project will be developed, there are purchased the necessary tools and there is estimated a life span of the project based on the abilities displayed by the team, the demands and the initial architecture. The issue of the environment protection could be introduced in this stage, as part of the activity of purchase of the necessary equipment and establish the initial architecture of the system. It can shape in the following:

- Correct evaluation of the equipment and applications used in the company as regards the effects on the environment, estimate the need to replace them or a re-design of the current processes would be enough, hence energy could be saved, CO_2 emissions reduced without increasing the volume of waste. Another important aspect, in this case, is the evaluation of the consequences of the changes required by green IS and to what extent they comply with the organizational goals and could be included in the adopted strategies regarding the environment.
- Identify the changes imposed by the purchase, use and discharge of the current IT resources, including establishing the criteria which should be met by the equipment which is planned to be bought and also be eco-friendly. Very useful in this situation is the eco-labeling of the IT products introduced by the International Organization for Standardization in 1992, at the United Nations Conference on Environment and Development, at Rio de Janeiro, shaped in the standards from the ISO 14000 family.

The third stage, *construction iterations*, actually designates the accomplishment of the project in successive stages. Each of them includes the planning, construction as well as adaptation to the changes required by the interested parties. The efficient communication is essential in the agile model since the final success of the project depends on it. At each iteration the users can formulate requirements on the influence they expect the future system to have on the environment and the developers should consider and include in the project. They can also demand an estimation of the impact on the environment made by specialized companies or require that the created system should comply with the regulations on the environment adopted by the organization.

During this stage, the green and sustainable software concept that was presented earlier can be applied. The problems referring to the environment, presented by Naumann et al. (2011) are specific to fixing errors (bugs) and, in the Greensoft Model, are referring to electrical energy and other resources used by: employees' workstation, IT infrastructure (as networking devices, servers and storages), heating and air conditioning, office lighting, transportation in case of business trip for meetings with customers and even the employees' daily way to work. Also, they propose three categories of sustainability criteria and metrics for software products: *Common Quality Criteria and Metrics, Directly Related Criteria and Metrics, and Indirectly Criteria and Metric* (Naumann et al., 2011) each of them referring to first, second and third-order impacts identified by Berkhout and Hertin. The latter refer to: indirect effects of ICT production and usage over the environment (first order impacts), indirect effects that result from economy structural changes, production processes, the products themselves and the distribution (second order impact) and the indirect effects resulted from stimulating consumption, economic growth as a result of ICT usage („rebound effect") and the impact on the way of life and the value systems (third level impact). According to the mentioned model, each iteration is followed by a review of the impact over the environment. After each application component is created, it becomes quite easy to measure and monitor the energy consumption. The results obtained can then be used to optimize the energy consumption in the next iterations. But the Greensoft Model is not the only software development model that takes into consideration the impact upon the existing environment. Shenoy and Earatta (2011) have proposed another model in which they suggest measures that can be adopted in order to reduce carbon emissions during the software lifetime circles.

Mahmoud and Ahmad (2013) are proposing a green model for sustainable software engineering that offer a full picture over the way software affects the environment, in two stages: how the life-cycle of a software product effects the environment through ICT and how software itself can aid in keeping the environment green or not by monitoring and utilizing resources efficiently, thus contributing to creating a green ICT. They mention the following set of general operational or low-level software goals for satisfying environmental sustainability: use of environmentally approved products for development, reduce transportation means and instead use the Internet for communication, use of cloud computing in terms of IaaS (Infrastructure as a Service), use of service oriented software, sacrificing performance above a limit for energy efficiency, running the system on computers with power profiles, reduce the number unnecessary activities in the system and use of a reusable system (Mahmoud and Ahmad, 2013). As can be observed the essential element in all approaches is to improve energy efficiency. It can be estimated as the ratio of useful work done and used energy (Johann, 2012):

$$Energy\,Efficience = \frac{Useful\,Work\,Done}{Used\,Energy}$$

Other important aspects that need to be considered during this stage refer to reducing the volume of data to a reasonable and relevant level for the organization, as well as developing and implementing some techniques of organizing the data in a manner that favors the diminishing of negative influence over the environment. Another aspect that can be considered is the possibility of migrating towards cloud computing. The benefits brought by this process are: less energy consumption and CO_2 emission, less equipment needed to run the IS and less e-waste (Kumar & Buyya, 2012; Beloglazov el al., 2012; Elgelany & Nada, 2013).

Finally, the last stage of the agile life-cycle is the *product release*. This stage encompasses two components: final testing of the entire system, as well as any necessary final reworks and documentations and the product is provided to the users in order to maximize operational integration (Isaias & Issa, 2015). During this stage, users can verify if the final product is in agreement with the chosen environmental standards. They can ask for a final report regarding the IS influence over the environment and can request changes. The direct effects of this stage over the ecosystem are similar to those during the iteration construction phase.

INTEGRATING GREEN IS WITH THE ORGANIZATION'S OBJECTIVES

To have a favorable impact over the organization's activity, IS must be designed to answer the five dimensions proposed through Delone and McLean IS success model (2004), analyzed and developed by Gable et al. (2008) and furthermore by Isaia and Issa (2015). Including environment protection as a priority of IS involves adding it to the mentioned model (Figure 3).

Even the "green IS" name itself makes it impossible to exclude this component from the requirements that the IS, if it is to be successfully implemented and used by organizations. Beyond the particular company traits, it must answer specific general requirements regarding the environment, previously presented in both the agile life-cycle model analysis, and it must also be integrated in the organization's financial and strategic objectives.

Figure 3. The conceptual basis for the IS-impact measurement model
Source: adapted from Gable et al., 2008; Isaia and Issa, 2015

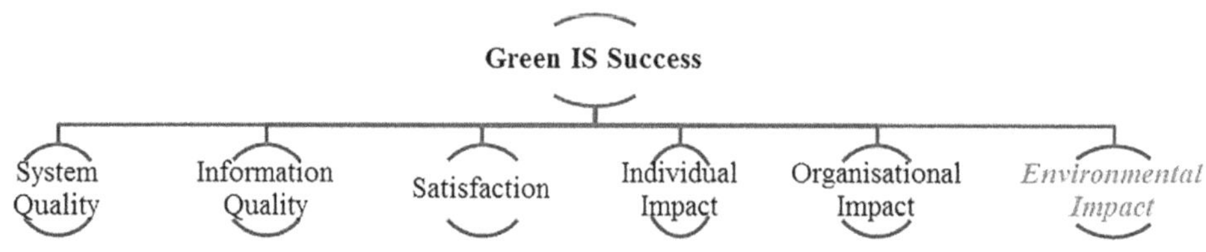

Green IS has a key role in both the tactical short-term and in transforming businesses in the longer-term (Sherringham and Unhelkar, 2010). As a result, adopting a green IS must be designed in agreement to the organization's objectives in order for it to be successful. References can be made to both financial objectives (turnover, profit, dividends, stock exchange listing, and cash flow) and to strategic ones (market share, product quality, position at the top, reputation, consumer satisfaction, extending the product diversity).

Financially, a green IS can contribute to accomplishing the company objectives by reducing cost through energy economy, recycling equipment, reducing or eliminating environmental taxation by implementing appropriate regulations, resource economy. From a strategic point of view, green IS contribution to accomplishing the company objectives is noted by attracting new customers, increased competitiveness, diversifying the portfolio of products that take the environment into account and increasing the overall company image.

Another essential element is maintaining the company's ability to face technology changes. Due to keeping ICT as an essential element, full or partial IS changes will trigger technology changes. From an environmental perspective, these changes are bi-directional. It was proven that changing hardware generations to newer ones will trigger an increased beneficial environmental relationship, but the same changes trigger an increase in the amount of waste. Another important characteristic is that management-level employees should sustain environmental protection. By their attributions, they can help or hinder the adoption of a green IS.

SOLUTIONS AND RECOMMENDATIONS

Starting from the organization's objectives, the potential of shifting from an IS to a green IS can be appreciated by evaluating the activity and company features on three lanes: the speed of adopting new green IS findings; the interest for direct and indirect effects of these findings to environmental changes and the financial implications. The next table presents the way in which enterprise sustainability can be appreciated in the context of green IS adoption (Table 3).

Evaluating the organization's activity and features on these three lanes can be a trigger of IS change. The result of this evaluation can offer an estimation of the organization's ability to assimilate a new system and to capitalize its benefits over the environment. It must secure a growth of efficiency, calculated as the ratio between effort and effect, but the expected value of this indicator remains an option of the management of each organization.

Table 3. The enterprise sustainability in the context of green IS adoption

Indicators	The speed in adopting new green IS findings	The interest for direct and indirect effects of green IS findings	Financial implications of green IS findings
Application of environmental standards within the organization	-	Promoting environmental protection and reducing the negative effects on the environment.	The costs of the application of standards and certification.
Participation in trainings regarding the environment and IS potential in this area, organized inside the company	Increased training of employees on green IS; Stimulate involvement in activities with creative potential.	Environmental awareness; Framing environmental protection as a priority in ICT product characteristics	Reducing the time to create own products; Labor productivity growth; Staff training expenses (if committed outside the firm).
Participation in trainings regarding the environment and IS potential in this area, organized by other organizations			Costs of the courses; Growth in labor productivity.
Organization's participation in pro-environmental actions.	Identifying creative ideas for new products development.	Dissemination of environmental values of the company employees; Improving the company's image.	Costs of time allocation; Expenditure on the financing of such actions; Income from improved company image.
Individual participation of employees in pro-environmental actions		Dissemination of environmental values of employees at the firm; Reducing environmental impacts through access to information on measures to protect it.	Expenses related to the financing of participation (if applicable).
The existence and use of a system for monitoring energy consumption	-	Minimize negative effect of energy consumption on the environment; Reducing emissions of greenhouse gasses.	Savings from reduced energy consumption.
The diversity of areas of activity of the organization	Increases the innovative potential; Reduce the risks of failure innovations.	Balancing environmental impact through various activities.	Diversified allocation of costs; Balancing profitability between activities.

continued on following page

Table 3. Continued

<table>
<tr><th colspan="3">Indicators</th><th>The speed in adopting new green IS findings</th><th>The interest for direct and indirect effects of green IS findings</th><th>Financial implications of green IS findings</th></tr>
<tr><td colspan="3">The novelty of ICT use in firm (generation of hardware / software)</td><td>Familiarity with the latest generation of equipment and applications that support innovation and the emergence of new ideas;
Better information on the ICT area.</td><td>New equipment are less polluting and consume less energy;
New applications demand more resources.</td><td>Increased acquisition costs;
Updating applications trigger, in many cases, the replacement of equipment;
Increase work efficiency.</td></tr>
<tr><td colspan="3">The volume of investments in equipment and applications</td><td>-</td><td>-</td><td>Expenses generated through investment in infrastructure.
Additional investments for introducing environmental features of products.</td></tr>
<tr><td colspan="3">Dissemination of information on green benefits of IS in the company (innovation / adoption)</td><td>Familiarity with features that allow employment in green ICT and knowledge of their potential;
Expansion of product characteristics by incorporating environmentally friendly characteristics.</td><td>Reducing emissions of greenhouse gasses;
Lower power consumption;
Lower volume due to the trend of waste minimization;
Reducing the amount of toxic substances on board.</td><td>-</td></tr>
<tr><td rowspan="4">Characteristics of human resources</td><td colspan="2">Employee diversity training areas</td><td>-</td><td>Increase / decrease of environmental concerns relative to employee culture.</td><td>-</td></tr>
<tr><td rowspan="2">Affiliation</td><td>Foreign</td><td>Collection of products for which the company acquires ownership.</td><td>Increase / decrease of environmental concerns relative to the culture of the employees in other countries.</td><td>Differences in relation to local salaries</td></tr>
<tr><td>Native</td><td>Degree of readiness influences the quality of products made;
Collection of products for which the company acquires ownership.</td><td>-</td><td>Bonuses allocated to reward creative ideas</td></tr>
<tr><td colspan="2">The degree of training and experience</td><td>It positively influences the creative potential in innovation and value realization chances for a higher level of training and / or experience in the field.</td><td>Usually supports favorable environmental concerns through a level of culture and civilization in proportion to preparation;
Favorably / Unfavorably influences according to the rules of the organizations where they were formed.</td><td>Employment costs, usually proportionate to the level of training and experience</td></tr>
<tr><td colspan="3">The number of abandoned projects in the Green IS on the first failure</td><td>Lack of stimulating creativity; Reduces the chances of potential innovative ideas materializing.</td><td>Limiting the negative effects in the use of traditional ICT.</td><td>Financial security by not assuming additional risks.</td></tr>
<tr><td colspan="3">The number of green projects in the area continued despite more one or more failures</td><td>It stimulates creativity.</td><td>Increased negative effects of using traditional IS.</td><td>The increase in expenditures for each assumed failure / product.</td></tr>
</table>

FUTURE DIRECTIONS AND CONCLUSION

This chapter explored the necessity and applicability of green IS. Organizations are interested in adopting green technologies regardless if they refer to production processes, parts design or other activities that just secure the proper organization's functioning, as it results from recent studies. Considering these results, it is demanded that the green concept is assimilated in both the development and usage phase. Literature has made it clear that this leads to environmental benefits, but it cannot guarantee that these initiatives will also benefit the organizations that implement green concepts. A long-term return of investment can only be estimated. Even so, green IS should be a social priority.

The criteria proposed for early evaluation of the conditions needed to for green IS implementation can be used in the selection and approval phase of the agile life-cycle project model, in order to identify the organization's ability to adapt to these changes. It would be essential to create a model that allows evaluation of green IS implementation consequences and the way in which it can be aligned to long-term organization strategy.

Green enterprise is a necessity, not a choice, and changing IS in order to comply with environmental protection requests must be a priority due to their important role. They hold a huge potential due to their ability to contribute to entire industry changes (transportation, energy, production). To ensure the environment is protected, green IS must adhere to this tendency in the development phase and also in the lifetime and until its end.

REFERENCES

Andreopoulou, Z., Stiakakis, E., & Vlachopoulou, M. (2013). *E-Innovation for Sustainable Development of Rural Resources During Global Economic Crisis (Practice, Progress, and Proficiency in Sustainability)*. New York: IGI Global.

Ashford, N. A., & Hall, P. R. (2011). The Importance of Regulation-Induced Innovation for Sustainable Development. *Sustainability*, *3*(1), 270–292. doi:10.3390/su3010270

Bazerman, M., & Hoffman, A. (1999). Sources of Environmentally Destructive Behavior: Individual, Organizational, and Institutional Perspectives. *Research in Organizational Behavior*, *21*, 39–79.

Beal, A. (2010). The Role of the Business Analyst in Green ICT. In B. Unhelkar (Ed.), *Handbook of Research on Green ICT: Technology, Business and Social Perspectives* (pp. 42–50). New York: IGI Global.

Beloglazov, A., Abawajy, J., & Buyya, R. (2012). Energy-aware resource allocation heuristics for efficient management of data centers for Cloud computing. *Future Generation Computer Systems*, *28*(5), 755–768. doi:10.1016/j.future.2011.04.017

Boudreau, M. C., Chen, A. J., & Huber, M. (2007). Green IS: Building Sustainable Business Practices. In R. T. Watson (Ed.), *Information Systems*. Athens, GA: Global Text Project.

Brooks, S., Wang, X., & Sarker, S. (2012), Unpacking Green IS: A Review of the Existing Literature and Directions for the Future. In Green Business Process Management. Springer Berlin Heidelberg.

Bush, M., Lederer, L. A., Li, X., Palmisano, J., & Rao, S. (2009). The alignment of information systems with organizational objectives and strategies in health care. *International Journal of Medical Informatics*, *78*(7), 446–456. doi:10.1016/j.ijmedinf.2009.02.004 PMID:19307148

Calero, C., & Piattini, M. (Eds.). (2015). *Green in Software Engineering*. Springer International Publishing Switzerland. doi:10.1007/978-3-319-08581-4

Chen, A. J., Watson, R. T., Boudreau, M. C., & Karahanna, E. (2009). Organizational Adoption of Green Is & It: An Institutional Perspective. In ICIS 2009 Proceedings.

Chen, A. J. W., Boudreau, M. C., & Watson, R. T. (2008). Information systems and ecological sustainability. *Journal of Systems and Information Technology*, *10*(3), 186–201. doi:10.1108/13287260810916907

Chou, C. D. (2013). „Risk identification in Green IT practice. *Computer Standards & Interfaces*, *35*(2), 231–237. doi:10.1016/j.csi.2012.10.001

Collins, C., Steg, L., & Koning, M. (2007). Customers Values, Beliefs on Sustainable Corporate Performance, and Buying Behavior. *Psychology and Marketing*, *24*(6), 555–577. doi:10.1002/mar.20173

Corbett, C. J., & Kirsch, D. A. (2001). International Diffusion of ISO 14000 Certification. *Production and Operations Management*, *10*(3), 327–342. doi:10.1111/j.1937-5956.2001.tb00378.x

Dao, V., Langella, I., & Carbo, J. (2011). From green to sustainability: Information Technology and an integrated sustainability framework. *The Journal of Strategic Information Systems*, *20*(1), 63–79. doi:10.1016/j.jsis.2011.01.002

Dedrick, J. (2010). Green IS: Concepts and Issues for Information Systems Research. *Communications of the Association for Information Systems*, *27*(11), 174–184.

Du, W., Pan, S. L., & Zuo, M. (2013). How to balance sustainability and profitability in technology organizations: an ambidextrous perspective. In *Proceedings of IEEE Trans Eng Manag* (vol. 60, pp. 366–385). doi:10.1109/TEM.2012.2206113

Elgelany, A., & Nada, N. (2013). Energy Efficiency for Data Center and Cloud Computing: A Literature Review. *International Journal of Engineering and Innovative Technology*, *3*(4).

Esfahani, M. D., Rahman, A. A., & Zakaria, N. H. (2015). Green IT/IS Adoption as Corporate Ecological Responsiveness: An Academic Literature Review. *Journal of Software Computing and Decision Support Systems*, *2*(1), 35–43.

Esty, D. C., & Winston, A. S. (2006). *Green to Gold: How Smart Companies use Environmental Strategy to Innovate, Create Value, and Build Competitive Advantage*. John Wiley & Sons Publishers.

Hack, S., & Berg, C. (2014). The Potential of IT for Corporate Sustainability. *Sustainability*, *7*(6), 4163–4180. doi:10.3390/su6074163

Hart, L. S. (1997). Beyond Greening: Strategies for a Sustainable World. *Harvard Business Review*, (January-February), 67–79.

Isaias, P., & Issa, T. (2015). *High Level Models and Methodologies for Information Systems*. Springer Science+Business Media New York.

Jenkin, A. T., Webster, J., & McShane, L. (2011). An agenda for Green information technology and systems research. *Information and Organization*, *21*(1), 17–40. doi:10.1016/j.infoandorg.2010.09.003

Johann, T., Dick, M., Naumann, S., & Kern, E. (2012). How to Measure Energy-Efficiency of Software: Metrics and Measurement Results. In *Proceedings of the First International Workshop on Green and Sustainable Software (GREENS)*. doi:10.1109/GREENS.2012.6224256

King, A. A., & Lenox, M. J. (2001). Lean and Green? An Empirical Examination of the Relationship between Lean Production and Environmental Performance. *Production and Operations Management*, *10*(3), 244–256. doi:10.1111/j.1937-5956.2001.tb00373.x

Kumar Garg, S., & Buyya, R. (2012). Green Cloud Computing and Environmental Sustainability. In S. Murugesan & G. R. Gangadharan (Eds.), *Harnessing Green IT: Principles and Practices* (pp. 76–87). Wiley-IEEE Press. doi:10.1002/9781118305393.ch16

Li, J. H., Tian, B. G., Liu, T. Z., Liu, H., Wen, X., & Honda, S. (2006). Status quo of e-waste management in mainland China. *J. Mater. Cycles Waste Manag*, *8*(1), 13–20. doi:10.1007/s10163-005-0144-3

Loeser, F., Erek, K., & Zarnekow, R. (2012). Towards a Typology of Green IS Strategies: Insights from Case Study Research.*Proceedings Thirty Third International Conference on Information Systems.*

Loock, C. M., Staake, T., & Thiesse, F. (2013). Motivating Energy Efficient Behavior with Green IS: An Investigation of Goal Setting and the Role of Defaults. *Management Information Systems Quarterly*, *37*, 4.

Loos, P., Nebel, W., Gómez, J. M., Hasan, H., Watson, R. T., vom Brocke, J., & Recker, J. et al. (2011). Green IT: A Matter of Business and Information Systems Engineering? *Business & Information Systems Engineering*, *3*(4), 245–252. doi:10.1007/s12599-011-0165-5

Lopez-Lopez, J. C., Sissa, G., & Natvig, L. (2011). Green ICT: The Information Society's Commitment for Environmental Sustainability. *The European Journal for the Informatics Professional*, *12*(4).

Löser, F. (2015). *Strategic Information Systems Management for Environmental Sustainability. Enhancing Firm Competitiveness with Green IS.* Universitätsverlag der TU Berlin.

Lyon, T., & Maxwell, J. (2007). Environmental Public Voluntary Programs Reconsidered. *Policy Studies Journal: the Journal of the Policy Studies Organization*, *35*(4), 723–750. doi:10.1111/j.1541-0072.2007.00245.x

Maclean, D., Akoh, B., & Egede-Nissen, B. (2010). ICTs, sustainability and the green economy. *Reconect Review*, *2*(3), 161–165.

Mahmoud, S. S., & Ahmad, I. A. (2013). Green Model for Sustainable Software Engineering. *International Journal of Software Engineering and Its Applications*, *7*(4).

Marett, K., Otondo, R. F., & Taylor, G. S. (2013). Assessing the Effects of Benefits and Institutional Influences on the Continued Use of Environmentally Munificent Bypass System in Long-Haul Trucking. *Management Information Systems Quarterly*, *37*(4).

Melville, P. N. (2010). Information Systems Innovation for Environmental Sustainability. *Management Information Systems Quarterly*, *34*(1), 1–21.

Midgley, G., & Reynolds, M. (2004). Systems/operational research and sustainable development: Towards a new agenda. *Sustainable Development*, *12*(1), 56–64. doi:10.1002/sd.218

Mithas, S., Khuntia, J., & Roy, P. K. (2010). Green information technology, energy efficiency, and profits: Evidence from an emerging economy. In ICIS 2010 Proceedings.

Molla, A. (2009). Organizational Motivations for Green IT: Exploring Green IT Matrix and Motivation Models. *PACIS 2009 Proceedings*.

Molla, A. (2013). Identifying IT sustainability performance drivers: Instrument development and validation. *Information Systems Frontiers*, *15*(5), 705–723. doi:10.1007/s10796-013-9415-z

Molla, A., & Abareshi, A. (2011). Green IT Adoption: A Motivational Perspective. *Proceedings of the 15th Pacific Asia Conference on Information Systems* (PACIS), (pp. 1-14).

Molla, A., Cooper, V., & Pittayachawan, S. (2011). The Green IT Readiness (G-Readiness) of Organizations: An Exploratory Analysis of a Construct and Instrument. *Communications of the Association for Information Systems*, *29*(1), 4.

Murugesan, S. (2008). *Harnessing Green IT: Principles and Practices*. IEEE IT Professional.

Naumann, S., Dick, M., Kern, E., & Johann, T. (2011). The GREENSOFT model: A reference model for green and sustainable software and its engineering. *Sustain Comput Informat Syst*, *1*(4), 294–304. doi:10.1016/j.suscom.2011.06.004

Popescul, D., & Georgescu, M. (2015). Social Networks Security in Universities: Challenges and Solutions. *Scientific Annals of the "Alexandru Ioan Cuza" University of Iaşi Economic Sciences*, *62*(SI), 53-63.

Puckett, J., Westerwelt, S., Gutierrez, R., & Takamiya, Y. (2005). *The Digital Dump: Exporting Re-use and Abuse to Africa*. Seattle: Basel Action Network.

Radu, L. D. (2014). The Ecological Behaviour Related to Green Information and Communication Technology in Romanian Organizations. *The Romanian Statistical Review*, *4*, 73–88.

Radu, L.D. (2015a, February). Investments in Technological Innovations: A Literature Review of Organization Determinants. *European Scientific Journal*.

Radu, L.D. (2015b). Green Information Systems: New Trend of Information Systems Development from the Perspective of Sustainability Improvement. *Proceedings of Globalization and Higher Education in Economics and Business Administration*.

Ramirez, R., Melville, N., & Lawler, E. (2010). Information Technology Infrastructure, Organizational Process Redesign, and Business Value: An Empirical Ansalysis. *Decision Support Systems*, *49*(4), 417–429. doi:10.1016/j.dss.2010.05.003

Sarkis, J., Koo, C., & Watson, R. (2013). Green information systems & technologies – this generation and beyond: Introduction to the special issue. *Information Systems Frontiers*, 1–10.

Shenoy, S., & Earatta, R. (2011). Green Software Development Model: An Approach towards Sustainable Software Development. *Proceedings of IEEE Annual India Conference (INDICON)*. doi:10.1109/INDCON.2011.6139638

Sherringham, K., & Unhelkar, B. (2011). Strategic Business Trends in the Context of Green ICT. In B. Unhelkar (Ed.), *Handbook of research on green ICT: technology, business, and social perspectives* (pp. 66–83). New York: IGI Global. doi:10.4018/978-1-61692-834-6.ch005

Shrivastava, P. (1995). Environmental Technologies and Competitive Advantage. *Strategic Management Journal*, *16*(S1), 183–200. doi:10.1002/smj.4250160923

Taleby, M., & Way, T. (2009). Methods, Metrics and Motivation for a Green Computer Science Program.*Proceedings of the 40th ACM technical symposium on Computer science education*, (pp. 362-366). doi:10.1145/1508865.1508995

Tu, J. C., & Huang, D. S. (2015). Analysis on the Relationship between Green Accounting and Green Design for Enterprises. *Sustainability*, *7*(5), 6264–6277. doi:10.3390/su7056264

UNEP. (2010). *Recycling – from E-waste to Resources*. Berlin, Germany: Oktoberdruck AG.

Vykoukal, J., Wolf, M., & Beck, R. (2009). Does Green It Matter? Analysis of the Relationship between Green It and Grid Technology from a Resource-Based View Perspective.*Proceedings of the Pacific Asia Conference on Information Systems.*

Walker, R. H., & Hanson, D. J. (1998). Green marketing and green places: A taxonomy for the destination marketer. *Journal of Marketing Management, 14*(6), 623–639. doi:10.1362/026725798784867671

Watson, R. T., Boudreau, M. C., Chen, A., & Huber, M. H. (2008). Green IS: Building Sustainable Business Practices. In R. T. Watson (Ed.), *Information Systems*. Athens, GA: Global Text Project.

White, L., & Lee, J. G. (2009). Operational research and sustainable development: Tackling the social dimension. *European Journal of Operational Research, 193*(3), 683–692. doi:10.1016/j.ejor.2007.06.057

Yu, J., Williams, E., Ju, M., & Yang, Y. (2010). Forecasting Global Generation of Obsolete Personal Computers. *Environmental Science & Technology, 44*(9), 3232–3237. doi:10.1021/es903350q PMID:20302363

Zikopoulos, P., deRoos, D., Bienko, C., Andrews, M., & Buglio, R. (2014). *Big Data Beyond the Hype: A Guide to Conversations for Today's Data Center*. McGraw-Hill Professional.

KEY TERMS AND DEFINITIONS

Agile Development Life Cycle: It is a set of principles that promotes adaptive planning, evolutionary development, early delivery, and continuous improvement for software development.

Energy Efficiency: Is the goal to reduce the energy consumption of products, services and processes related to ICT field. It has favorable effects on the environment mainly by reducing carbon footprint.

Environment Protection: All actions, regulations and policies that aim the conservation of the natural environment, preserving his current state or, if it is possible, reversing its degradation.

Green Technology: A green technology does not negatively affect the environment (through pollution, energy consumption, increasing the volume of e-waste, etc.) or diminish the negative effects of the similar technologies.

Green: A green company tries to minimize the negative influences of its products, services and business processes on the environment by implementing strict rules and regulations at all levels and across its entire value chain.

Rebound Effect: It is the reduction of the estimated effects of the green ICT or green IS because of consumer behavior or other systemic reactions.

Sustainable: It is a company's ability to remain in business a long time. This concept has three dimensions in present: economic viability, environmental responsibility and social equitability.

Chapter 6
The Role of Waste Management in the Green Economy:
An Empirical Analysis of Economic Data of the Business

Massimo Saita
University of Milano Bicocca, Italy

Maria Vittoria Franceschelli
University of Milano Bicocca, Italy

ABSTRACT

Green economy has become highly relevant over the last years. We are currently experiencing pollution issue and environmental decay that had its origin, however, in the previous centuries. The development of industrial economy inevitably entails the production of waste, in such a quantity that the environment is incapable of assimilating and transforming it naturally. Therefore, it is believed that one of the main green economy sectors is the waste retrieval and recycling, that means waste management. In the existing literature, this sector has not been deeply analyzed from a viewpoint of performance business analysis. Although a European legislation exists, every country manages this business by itself. After a historical introduction, this study, using the regression model, analyses the variables that influence the Italian business of waste retrieval and recycling, in the process establishing which of them has a deeper impact on performance.

DOI: 10.4018/978-1-5225-2075-7.ch006

INTRODUCTION

Environment and Human Beings: A Historical Background

Animal and vegetable organisms carry out their lives in the biosphere, i.e. in the environment surrounding them. Such physical and biological components have neither been designed not built by man.

No doubt, the environment undergoes an ongoing evolution, and accordingly changes as years elapse by virtue of nature itself. Not only that. The activities engaged in by man have altered the terrestrial biosphere; thereby have occasioned changes in soil, air and water. Such transformations may result in environmental decay.

The natural environment changes by the action of endogenous or exogenous agents. These agents modify the earth demolishing a part and constituting another, to thereby maintain a balance.

Classical literature describes Germany as entirely covered by forests (Tacitus in *Germania)* and Egypt and Mauritania as the granaries of the Empire. In the first case, human settlements of Germanic tribes expanded the vital space by creating glades to locate the settlements and develop agriculture. In the second one natural events transform it in desert.

Human activity has often transformed the landscape through destructive actions, which have irreversibly compromised the environmental balance. At the beginning of agricultural activity that the human species started causing deep changes to the territory. Man has exploited the environment for the sake of his personal sustentation. Over time, this exploitation increased ever more, because it was related to the country development. The trend began to abuse the available resources, as if they were at no cost (which was, after all, the case from the perspective of sheer economic cost). The Earth was offering resources to man, and men were using them.

Through the cultural development, spread awareness that such resources were not "free of charge". One of the first environmental protection laws dated back to 1769, when it was decreed that forests on the island of Mauritius should be safeguarded. As Grove (1996) stated, the most important and innovative aspect of French's environmental protection in Mauritius, was the acknowledgment of a link between deforestation and local climatic changes. Deforestation, after all, is the work of man, implemented in order to set aside the soil for a different use than the preservation of forests, generally by using the soil first for agricultural purposes and then for industrial ones. Consciousness was thus undergoing a change. The development of industrial economy was deemed by many scientists to represent "a threat to mankind's survival". Well-known, among others, is Wilson's (1858) study on the drying up of the earth and the atmosphere, in which his concern surfaced: changes in the atmosphere are slowly drawing close to the state in which it will be impossible for man to live on the Earth. *This paper can be said to mark the onset of a truly international environmental debate in which processes operating at a global scale were being considered* (Grove, 1995, p. 159).

This realization burst forth in the 70s of the XX century. So a new branch of economic discipline, viz. "environmental economy", was born for the sake of picking up the interactions between environment and development, by setting a limit on the constant growth of production and on the use of resources, and by implementing the environment's ability, to receive the only product unable to transform itself, save across millennia: waste.

Environmental economy may be defined as the study of the regulation of polluting activities and the assessment of environmental beauties. Famous is the exemplification of the economy-environment relationship by the economist Kenneth Boulding (1966). He used the "metaphor of the space shuttle": the economy experienced up to this moment was compared to a cowboy who saw the far west as a «frontier» capable of being continuously shifted by acquiring new lands, and thus new resources to exploit. The economy, instead, should be considered as an astronaut aboard a space shuttle, who can solely enjoy a limited kit of resources, which he must try to save and recycle as much as possible.

In this period, there was no way of severing the link between environment and economy. Politics began to adapt to these new ideas and realizations. Companies began to adapt to the policies and the new legislative provisions, until they arrived at a system where health and environmental integrity acquired an ever-increasing relevance.

Pollution

The term "environmental pollution" means the change in the biosphere composition caused by pollutants and emitted from many human activities. This change has a negative connotation; in fact, it interferes with the growth rate of the species and causes damage both to human health and territory.

The effect of the different agents depend on their own characteristics and on the quantity released.

There are different types of pollution categorized according to the polluted site. For each site the causes, sources and the effects are different. They are: air pollution that changes the composition of air; water pollution that changes the composition of the water; soil pollution that changes the composition of the territory; noise pollution that changes the sound in a given environment; electromagnetic pollution that alters the natural values of the electromagnetic field.

Pollution is a direct result of industrial development. Human activities, which are promoted for the economic development, produce most of the contaminants.

The economic processes (mining, processing or manufacturing and consumption), generate necessarily waste that will inevitably come back to nature. This involves a biological change, damaging animals, plants, and then the ecosystem, i.e. a contamination that is defined pollution (Turner et al., 1993, p. 16). It has a direct effect on the economy. One of the first researcher in this field was Pigou (1920), who introduced the concept of "externalities": pollution causes external costs that result in a gap between private costs and social costs.

Sustainable Development and Waste

In order to fulfil human's needs, it is necessary to obtain goods and services. Their fulfilment is strictly linked to economic development, and in order to obtain goods and services, the use of energy is required. Yet its use inevitably entails repercussions on the environmental balance, such as "negative externalities".

Already Malthus (1798) had concerned himself with the limits, which he had termed absolute that existed in the relationship between population and economic resources.

The fact that the availability of resources was limited, gave rise the problem of a sustainable development; in other words, the tendency is to promote social-economic growth that might be sustained over time both by the natural environment and by society.

The best-known definition is the one given in the *Brundtland Report* 1987 (WECD): *the "Green Development"* (Adams, 2001) is *development that meets the needs of the present without compromising the ability of future generations to meet their own needs (Brundtland, 1987)*[1]. Companies simultaneously consider their financial, social, and environmental performance (Marshall & Brown, 2003, p.101), keeping services and quality of natural resources.

Inevitably, economy is linked also to natural resources: renewable and nonrenewable. Gray and Hotelling were the firsts who studied the relationship between economy and non-renewable resources.

By resorting to the manufacturing industry as a case study, they identify an optimal rate of exploitation of resources, so that the current extracting activity does not affect the future extraction quantity. In order to achieve that, they identify a value, and thus a cost of utilizing the non-renewable resource, which includes extraction and user cost (Gray, 1914). Nevertheless, user cost should increase over time based on the discount (Hotelling, 1931).

Two types of approach to sustainable development have been classified in accordance with the hypothetical replaceability scenario between natural capital and artificial (man-made) capital (Pippo, 2011): can be achieved the same level of well-being by replacing the natural capital with the artificial (man-made) one?

The "Strong substitutability current", believes that the artificial capital is not able to produce the same well-being given by natural capital, i.e. there is a very weak and limited compensation level. You need to preserve the natural capital because is irreplaceable by human activities. The risk of damaging environmental resources irreversibly must be minimized. According to this approach the economic growth should be slowed down or even stop in order to preserve the environmental capital integrity.

Instead, according to the "weak sustainability current", there is an almost perfect substitution between the two types of capital (environmental and human), since the satisfaction derived from human can easily equal or exceed that received by the natural capital. This approach believes in the possibility of decoupling between environmental growth and degradation. Technological progress allows more efficient use of resources and the reduction of human activities.

The objective of sustainable development is therefore to achieve simultaneously both socio economic growth and environmental care. Emerge the three pillars of the concept sustainability: economy, environment, society (Williamson, Lynch-Wood, & Ramsay, 2006). The link among these tree aspect is deeply developed in literature. Lounsbury et al. (2003) have found that industries are shaped by social structures of meanings and resources. Lounsbury et al., have explained that the waste management is strongly interconnected with the political, social, and cultural situation. The both social movement and political practices transform the extant socio-economic practices. Given this background the authors believe that a complete analysis of the Green Economy should include both environmental aspects (in this case the waste management), and economic aspects (in this case an analysis of a green business) through the study of economic performance using indicators such as EBITDA.

WASTE

Maybe one of the most relevant issue is to identify waste. The problem may seem trivial, but it is not. Economic operations such as produce, research and develop, create inevitably the existence of products or waste products. While there have always been, during the last two decades of the 1900s waste has started to be a great issue for States and policy. As a consequence of that, it was formed ad hoc legislation on waste management.

To define uniquely waste, here is used the legislative definition that is found in the Basel Convention: *Waste are substances or objects which are disposed of or are intended to be disposed of or are required to be disposed of by the provisions of national law*[2].

At European level, the previously mentioned legislation is possibly the first and most exhaustive legislation in the waste field. The Basel Convention was signed in 1989 and came into force on 5 May 1992. It was born out of the need to contain the production of a wide range of waste categories and the possibility of handling and disposing of it as close to the place of production as possible, with a view to reducing the environmental risk associated with handling activities and combating transport towards developing Countries, a then frequent phenomenon (Marzetti, 2001).

The Basel Convention made a change in the environmental situation, now unsustainable, that many developing countries or "economies of the transaction" were living. In fact, many large industries were using these countries for disposal of waste, as easy way, less "controlled" and certainly cheaper. In doing so, however, it is threatened not only the environment but also human health. Therefore, with the Convention of 1989 it was decided to establish a genuine system of checks in respect of both imports and exports, both disposal of hazardous and non-hazardous.

The Italian legislation, in article 184 of Legislative Decree No. 205/2010, regulates the classification of waste categories, which are differentiated according to their origin into urban and special waste, and according to their dangerous characteristics into dangerous and non-dangerous waste.

The function of waste classification is the prerogative of the producer (or holder), who bears the obligation and thus the responsibility to assess it carefully for purposes of allocating the CER code.

Such classification is important because indicates the type of waste involved and distinguishes between "waste" and "non-waste" (i.e. "end of waste"). **R**etrieval activity, as regulated by Legislative Decree 152/2006 in article 181, is the reuse, recycling and the other forms of recovery. The result is a departure[3] from the regulations in the field of waste of substances or objects in question.

Directive 2008/98/CE: Waste Management

Article 4 has a great relevance. It establishes a waste hierarchy as a priority order in waste prevention and management legislation and policy[4].

The hierarchical order, as established by the Directive is:

1. Prevention;
2. Preparing for re-use;
3. Recycling;
4. Other recovery, e.g. energy recovery;
5. Disposal.

Member States shall take measures to encourage the options that deliver the best overall environmental outcome. However, they must ensure that waste management does not jeopardize human health and does not affect the environment. When they are subjected to a salvage operation, they stop to be regarded as waste and therefore they are no longer subject to this law.

The Directive lays down measures to protect the environment and human health by preventing or reducing the adverse impacts of the generation and management of waste and by reducing overall impacts of resource use and improving the efficiency of such use[5]

The said hierarchy sums up whatever has been asserted so far, namely, that all the activities pertaining to waste management are of equal environmental impact. Nay, the legislator, in his intent to promote an ecologically rational management of those substances or objects which must be necessarily disposed of, wanted to specify the fact that certain activities have a lesser impact on environment and health, and that they should be favoured over the others.

The legislation does not promote "the removal of existing waste", but first the prevention, and only subordinately, the waste management through the reuse or processing of waste, to cause the least possible. When it is not possible, it will be necessary to dispose waste in precisely demarcated places, equipped in conformity to the law. In this work, it is studied the economic performance of a green business: the waste business. Particularly retrieval and recycling business.

RECYCLING AND WASTE MANAGEMENT

The recycling process could be implemented in a very broad range of sectors and fields, through infinite methodologies and motivations. Accordingly, it becomes hard to find in the literature, a unique definition of waste recycling, without focusing on any specific sector or any specific type of recycling.

It is believed that, even in this instance, the broadest definition of recycling may be drawn from the legislation in force, Directive 2008/98/CE of the European Parliament and of the Council:

'Recycling' means any recovery operation by which waste materials are reprocessed into products, materials or substances whether for the original or other purposes. It includes the reprocessing of organic material but does not include energy recovery and the reprocessing into materials that are to be used as fuels or for backfilling operations[6].

Therefore, the very same European directive identifies the recycling activity as one of the main paths for a sustainable waste management.

As the authors were pointing out, the said specific activity is strictly interconnected with many sectors and thus with several subjects, such as health care, public administration, local legislation, education etc. Suffice it to think of the repercussions which inappropriately managed waste causes to the health of living beings and to the proper functioning of civilization.

An efficient waste retrieval system, in fact, must involve both the citizens and the companies. In other words, is necessary to pay heed both to the phase "at source", i.e. where the waste is produced, and the "end-of-pipe" phase, i.e. where the waste is managed. In such a system, efficiency is accordingly determined both by producers and by consumers. As regards the former, they may contribute from different viewpoints: by devising a "sustainable product", they may facilitate both a lesser waste of resources at the time of transforming the input into finished product and an easier retrieval of the utilized products. The consumers may instead contribute by efficiently managing the products capable of being retrieved (for instance through waste separation). Uncertainty concerning the quality of recycled materials and the incapacity of laying down a «common language» of dialogue between buyers and sellers may not only engender problems caused by asymmetrical information but also, more generally, give rise to significant transaction costs (D'Amato, 2008, p. 436).

Other research studied the "organizational citizenship behaviour", defined by Organ as *individual behavior that is discretionary, not directly or explicitly recognized by the formal reward system, and that in the aggregate promotes the effective functioning of the organization*'' (1988, p. 4). These researches suggest that such ''organizational citizenship behaviors for the environment'' are a distinct and important aspect of organizational behavior and there is a strong relation between citizenship behaviors and environmental performance (Organ, 1988; Boiral 2009; LePine and Erez 2002; Podsakoff et al. 2000; Boiral and Paille 2012; Daily et al. 2009).

For example, in this field it has been carried out a research that presented a *case study of recycling at a large University, that does not have a formal organizational structure to address sustainability concerns*, and they *found that recycling behavior was influenced in important ways by the university context and by processes designed to promote recycling* (Weaver et al., 2015, p.427).

Companies have used recycling as a sustainable strategy. Many studies analyze the effects and reasons for the implementation of environmental strategies. It has been shown that more and more companies implement environmental strategies as a key success factors (Maas et al., 2014; Siegel, 2009; Aragon-Correa & Sharma, 2003; Sharma & Vredenburg, 1998; Gouldson, 2004; Ambec & Lanoie, 2008; Anderson & Anderson, 2009; Al-Najjar & Anfimiadou, 2012).

To the best of our knowledge, little attention has been devoted on recycling retrieval as core business and not only as an environmental strategy implemented to gain competitive advantage.

Having the aim to study the performance of the waste business, it seems that this study is not broadly connected to the research on environmental performance. It is significant, however, that some studies using environmental performance as variable, the percentage of total waste that is treated, recycled or recovered as a percentage of total waste generated (Dobler et al., 2014, p. 8)

The Italian Context

Already in the past years, studies on environmental issues have been conducted in our jurisprudential doctrine (A.A. V.V., 1998; Catturi, 1990; Ferrara, 1998; Matacena, 1984; Miolo Vitali, 1978).

Within the Italian background, researches have been carried out in the green economy field. More specifically, studies have been undertaken on social reporting (Campedelli, 2005; Secchi, 2006) as well as on the more specific environmental report (Noci, 2000), on Corporate Social Responsibility (Masini, 1970; Fiori et al., 2007), and on voluntary environmental disclosure (Quagli & Teodori, 2005; Andrei & Pesci 2009; Garzella et al., 2011).

To the best of our knowledge, neither at an Italian level nor at the level of other nations, have specific studies been conducted on the retrieval/recycling business.

This research has deliberately focused on a single country, given that business is undoubtedly influenced by national politics and culture. It is moreover undoubted, based on the different current episodes that a link exists between the said sector and mafia, at the Italian level as well as at the level of other countries.

Prior to developing the linear regression model, we deem it useful to provide some information of a general character about the Italian recycling business.

The Foundation for sustainable development (2014) has elaborated, based on the CONAI[7] data, a table setting out the amount of recycling of packages. As evinced by the following table, results have improved. This is no doubt due both to a higher "environmental consciousness" and to a better waste management.

REGRESSION ANALYSIS ON WASTE BUSINESS

Development of Hypotheses

Given the scant literature in the field of business analysis of retrieval and recycling companies, are used some variables utilized in the analyses of other businesses. The

Table 1. Recycling of packages, data in kt and %. Years 2011-2013

	2011		2012		2013		Variazione % delle quantità 2013/2012	Variazione % delle percentuali 2013/2012
	kt[8]	%	kt	%	kt	%	kt	%
Steel	353	73	332	76	320	74	-4	-2
Aluminum	41	59	41	61	44	65	8	4
Paper	3.526	80	3.594	84	3.531	86	-2	2
Wood	1.272	55	1.257	54	1.353	55	8	1
Plastic	749	36	770	38	789	39	2	1
Glass	1.570	69	1.568	71	1.596	73	2	2
Total	**7.511**	**65**	**7.562**	**67**	**7.633**	**68**	**1**	**1**

Source: Elaboration by the Foundation for Sustainable development upon CONAI data.

independent variables analyzed are deemed to be of a strategic nature. Regard was paid to two macro-categories: "where" and "what" determinants.

"Where" Determinants:

Localization

Waste is a European and world problem.

The Italian situation presents some peculiarities. In Italy, waste is mostly managed at regional level. For the purposes of this research, it is believed that the two macro areas distinction is sufficiently significant: the northern area and the central-southern area. This distinction is made because frequently, in the current news, come across several instances of mafia-like waste management and the legal or illegal trade in the same, mainly in the Centre-South area. Moreover, some reports by Italian companies (Amsa and Gruppo A2A, for instance) set out extremely positive data relate to northern Italy. As a consequence, the authors consider the retrieval and recycling companies performing in a different way, depending on their area: better in the north of Italy than the Centre-South, where companies have to manage higher waste levels and are obliged to interface with illegal organizations.

This work studies, first and foremost, the distribution of these companies in the North and Centre-South areas, in order to examine their performance level, in accordance with the following distribution:

- What is meant by north are the companies situated in the following regions: Emilia Romagna; Friuli Venezia Giulia; Liguria; Lombardia, Piemonte; trentino alto Adige, Valle d'Aosta e Veneto.
- What is meant by center are the companies situated in the following regions: Lazio; Marche; Toscana e Umbria.
- What is meant by south (and islands) are the companies situated in the following regions: Abruzzo; Basilicata; Calabria; Campania; Molise; Puglia; Sardegna e Sicilia.

The authors want to study, therefore, the relationship between the localization of retrieval and recycling companies and performance.

H1: There is a positive relation between localization in the North area and the performance level of Italian retrieval and recycling companies.

"What" Determinants

Company Size

Another relationship that is studied in literature is the relationship between company size and performance. The number of employees is a variable frequently used to indicate company size. European Union considers this parameter, together with the total balance sheet, liabilities and the net turnover, in order to assess the company size. Even recently, Directive 2013/34/UE of the European Parliament and Council, dated 26 June 2013, has stipulated that, in order to fall within one of the three defined categories, the company must have *exceed the limits of at least two of the three following criteria (article 3):*

Table 2. Directive 2013/34/UE

	Micro Undertakings	Small Undertakings	Medium Undertakings	Large Undertakings
Balance sheet total (euro)	≤ 350.000	4.000.000 ≤	≤ 20.000.000	> 20.000.000
Net turnover (euro)	≤ 700.000	≤ 8.000.000	≤ 40.000.000	> 40.000.000
Average number of employees	≤ 10	≤ 50	≤ 250	> 250

Based on previous literature, there is a positive relationship between profitability and company size. Many authors (Alexander 1949; Stekler, 1964; Hall and Weiss, 1967; Scherer, 1973; Ravenscraft & Scherer, 1987; Fiegenbaum & Karnani, 1991; Helfat et al., 2007; Jonsson, 2007Bayyurt, 2007; Dogan, 2013) theoretically supported this link. Prior research confirms the existence of a positive relation.

H2: There is a positive relationship between the size of a retrieval and recycling company and performance.

Shareholders

A peculiarity of the recycling business, which is deemed as a "sustainable business", is that it is thoroughly interconnected with many different sectors. In fact, the environment care is interconnected with many different fields, healthcare, politics and business.

Regarding human health, the number of people who need medical attention and therapeutic treatment because of pollution is increasing, and it is going to continue to grow. This of course strains the whole system and increases the financial burden of health care providers, the state, and ultimately the individual. An "environmental culture" has been growing in many ways: by educating children at school, originating new university classes, new jobs specialized on environmental care, pollution prevention, green economy etc...

There is a patent link with the "public sector" and the extent to which it might be interested in a waste management system. Consequently, in order to conduct a deep analysis of this business, it indispensable to study the equity participation by public Authorities, State and Government and if exist a relationship between this type of participation and the performance by retrieval/recycling companies. It is believed that, given the strong link between this business and various public sectors, the State is interested in intervening in the recycling business with a view to rendering it more efficient.

H3: There is a positive relation between participation by a public company in retrieval/recycling companies and performance.

Ageing

Undoubtedly, the recycling sector has been lively for a while. However, a substantial growth is being experienced by all the green economy sectors. No doubt, an increasingly greater number of companies have emerged in the recycling sector, by virtue also of the new legislative enactments, which enjoin a retrieval of waste. For this research the authors have considered only the companies which have drawn up the 2014 financial statement. Among the sample, the oldest company dates back to 1932, and it is a family business. From the 50s to the end of the 80s, have been founded 79 companies that are still active. 111 companies have been established in the 90s and the remaining 234 companies have come into being during the last 15 years.

These statistics evince that the business is certainly growing and that it is gaining considerable importance. Moreover, the specific legislation in the field of managing the retrieval and recycling of waste has become ever stricter, while technologies are more state-of-the-art.

Given that it is a very modern sector, the authors believe that, the most recent companies may attain a higher level of efficiency. In fact, they possess state-of-the-art equipment and technologies and, having been born in an age where the problem of the environment and in particular that of waste management, they are more capable of confronting the current situation.

H4: There is a positive relation between the age of retrieval/recycling companies and performance.

Presentation of the Sample

Using Aida database, 811 Italian companies have been identified (the main economic activity of which consists in the retrieval and preparation for recycling of solid urban, industrial and biomass waste). More specifically, this activity comprises the following:

- Crushing, cleaning and sorting of glass;
- Crushing, cleaning and sorting of other kinds of waste, such as demolition waste (rubble), in order to obtain secondary raw materials;
- Transformation of cooking oils and fats into secondary raw materials;
- Transformation of other types of waste relating to food, drinks, tobacco and residual substances in secondary raw materials.

Aida is a database produced by Bureau Van Dijk Electronic Publishing, which groups together financial, personal data and commercial information on Italian joint-stock companies.

In order to contextualize the selected sample, it is necessary to set out some general characteristics.

The total number of employees amounts to 8.263 units that means an average of ten employees per company.

Out of n.811, n.425 companies, i.e. 52.4%, have lodged their financial statements in 2014.

In this sector, only three companies out of 811 are registered under the Company Registry's special section as innovative Start-ups. They draw up financial statements in abbreviated form. In 2014, one of these start-ups has not lodged its financial statement. The other two, instead, have recorded negative results at EBITDA level. This obviously entails a negative net income, a loss for the financial year, and negative profitability ratios (ROE and ROI). These data indicate that the analysed sector has no special interest in developing along this new company characteristic.

As for the economic performance of the sector, we may observe that 124 companies record a negative ROE (i.e. 29.18%), with a ROE in excess of 3% (that is, a level indicating a par condition) as regards 235 companies, i.e. 55.29%. These initial remarks point to a rather positive business result, especially if we contextualize it within the current period of crisis.

Among the 811 companies, it was our intention to focus the research on those companies that had lodged their financial statements in 2014, in order to make them comparable in accordance with the latest available data. We excluded, instead, those companies that did not record the other variables analysed by us, such as the region of the registered office or the year of foundation.

Our sample, therefore, analyses 386 companies, i.e. 48% of total companies in the business, a sample felt to be undoubtedly representative.

Variables and the Model

Dependent Variable

Because the aim of this empirical analysis is to study the economic performance of a "green business", we have used **EBITDA** as performance indicator. It is believed that this data might highlight income based on the characteristic management (Saita, 2015), thereby excluding interest, taxes, depreciation and amortization.

No account was taken of sales, inasmuch as these companies may deal with extremely different types of waste. The company dealing with food waste, of course, will have a lower turnover than another company managing the same amount in ferrous waste or companies from which, for instance, one might extract substances with a high monetary value (such as copper, zinc, etc.).

Likewise, no regard was paid, as a business performance indicator, to the Net Income. As we deem it better not to consider some components, such as taxes and amortizations, that might impact differently depending on the type of company involved (possibly one with public shareholding) or on the localization of the same in a region, possibly one governed by a Special Act.

EBITDA it is a good variable for cash earnings. Depreciation and amortization are non-cash expenses. So, EBITDA is a good way to know how much cash a company is generating – cash that can be used to pay dividends or reinvest in the company EBITDA is the preferred metric. Furthermore, EBITDA mitigates the distortions to operating income caused by arbitrary asset depreciation schedules (Becker-Blease, et al., 2010).

Independent Variables

Localization

As previously explained, Italy is divided into 20 regions. Account has been taken of the region where the registered office is situated rather than the operational headquarters, given that this data was not always available. Having classified every region based on the area, the companies analysed in this database are equally apportioned between the two areas, as set out in the following table.

The area variable has been turned into a dummy variable, by assigning a value of 1 to companies in the northern area, and a value of 0 to those having their registered offices in the central-southern area.

The central-southern region with the largest number of retrieval and recycling companies is Campania (54); the northern region is instead Lombardy with 89 companies.

Company Size

The company size has been studied by paying regard to the number of employees. This choice has been made for two main reasons: the existing literature and the characteristics of the recycling business.

Table 3. Localization variable

	Independent Variable	**No. of Companies**	**% Companies Across Whole of Italy**
Where - localization	**Area**		
	North	192	49,74%
	Centre - South	194	50,26%
	Total for Italy	386	100%

The number of employees is a parameter widely used as a size indicator in the literature as well (Cavusgil & Nevin, 1981; Bilkey & Tesar, 1997; Burton & Schlegelmilch, 1987; Kaynak & Kothari 1984; Mugler & Miesenbock, 1986; Bonaccorsi, 1992; Cavusgil & Naor, 1987; Holzmuller & Kasper, 1991). The existence of a relationship between size and profitability has been proven in multiple sectors, such as the hotel one (Israeli 2002; Pine & Phillips 2005; Claver-Cortés et al. 2006; Ruggero & d'Angella 2011; Santoro, 2015).

The retrieval and recycling companies are considered as a service companies. In this kind of companies, the number of employees is seen as the most significant size parameter (Saita, 2012, p. 23)

Moreover, the analysed companies deal with different kinds of waste. It is thus inevitable that those which handle urban waste, for instance, will boast a mostly lower turnover or profit, and not just negligibly so, than other companies that deal with other types of waste, such as industrial waste. The number of employees is accordingly deemed to be a fair index of company size in this sector.

In the analysed sample, most are micro-companies, which thing is absolutely in line with the Italian structure (Saita, 2015, p. 21).

Shareholding

In the sample, the shareholders of more than half of the companies consist in physical persons or families. This data, too, is in line with the Italian business structure. Other reference shareholders are represented by "industrial companies", which hold shares in more than 34% of the sample businesses. Relatively few, instead, are the companies in which holdings are in the hands of "public authorities, the State or Government" (Public shareholding), nearly 2%. In order to study the relationship between public shareholding and performance level, the variable has been turned into a Dummy, by assigning a value of 1 to all the companies in which sharehold-

Table 4. Company size variable

	Independent Variable		**N. Companies**	**% Companies in Italy**
where	**Company Size**			
	Micro	x<10	257	66.67%
	Small	10<x<50	114	29,45%
	Medium	50<x<250	13	3,36%
	Large	x>250	2	0,52%
	Total Italy		386	100%

ing is in the hands of a public authority (including as a minority shareholder), and and a value of 0 to companies where shares are not held by pubic bodies, the State or Government.

Ageing

For the sake of a comprehensive business analysis, it is important to study the seniorities operating there.

As indicated by the previously mentioned data, the business of retrieval and recycling companies mostly consist in companies born in the 2000s. No doubt, the know how acquired over time is an important element, but in this specific business it is believed that to be in the forefront when it comes to systems and structure is a highly relevant factor.

In the literature, the age variable has often been paid heed to when assessing a business (Campa and Kedia, 2002; Villalonga, 2004; Radipere and Dhliwayo, 2014).

Other Controls

Other variables have been taken into account:

1. Total asset
2. Equity
3. Current asset
4. Sales
5. ROE (Return on equity)
6. Net income

These variables are deemed to be of great significance when conducting a business analysis. Just to give an example, among the selected control variables, total assets and sales are (besides the number of employees) the other two standards adopted by the European Union to measure company size. By contrast, is sufficiently independent from performance and is an index of stability. Current assets is an index of solvency, and points therefore to the capacity of duly meeting one's obligations. In order to avoid problems of multi-collinearity, the current asset, total asset, equity and sales variables have been clustered together in the Stability variable, as we are going to specify hereunder. In other words, a variable called "Stability", which groups together total asset, current asset, equity and sales variables, has been created.

As we may discern in the under-mentioned table, among the variables there are no problems of correlation, save to a slight degree between size and the variable by us established, i.e. stability. This correlation, however, is not particularly high, and the variables forming part of the Stability variable prove essential to the effectiveness of the model, indicated by the Rsquare.

As proven by the earlier literature, multi-collinearity has been studied through two tests: the Variance Inflation Factor (VIF) and the Condition Index. It should be noted that, apart from the "stability" variable, the maximum value of the VIF is less than 3, i.e. the threshold suggested by Hair et al. (2005). The variable reaches a value of 3, and is thus deemed thoroughly acceptable by the literature (Myers, 1990).

Model and Results

The gathered data relate to the year 2014.

The independent variables refer to the previously described what and where sizes.

The model utilized for the analysis of these variables is a model of multiple linear regression:

Table 5. Pearson correlation table

		Company size	Area	shareholding	Aiging	Stability	ROE %	Net income €
Company size	Pearson Correlation	1	-,043	,441**	-,048	,615**	,011	-,320**
	Sign.		,400	,000	,351	,000	,826	,000
Area	Pearson Correlation	-,043	1	,040	-,185**	-,016	-,002	,064
	Sign.	,400		,432	,000	,747	,974	,210
Shareholding	Pearson Correlation	,441**	,040	1	,038	,232**	,026	,016
	Sign.	,000	,432		,453	,000	,614	,750
Aging	Pearson Correlation	-,048	-,185**	,038	1	-,093	,001	-,072
	Sign.	,351	,000	,453		,069	,990	,155
Stability	Pearson Correlation	,615**	-,016	,232**	-,093	1	-,035	-,716**
	Sign.	,000	,747	,000	,069		,489	,000
ROE %	Pearson Correlation	,011	-,002	,026	,001	-,035	1	,125*
	Sign.	,826	,974	,614	,990	,489		,014
Net income €	Pearson Correlation	-,320**	,064	,016	-,072	-,716**	,125*	1
	Sign.	,000	,210	,750	,155	,000	,014	
**p < 0,01; * p < 0,05. (2-tailed).								

Table 6. Descriptive statistics

	Mean	SD	N
Company size	12,79	37,522	386
Area	,49	,500	386
Shareholding	,02	,143	386
Aging	36533,51	4159,287	386
Stability	3184649,2923	9039109,39601	386
ROE %	2,2318	35,42813	386
Net income €	12513,42	987663,072	386

$$yi = \beta 0 + \beta 1X1i + \beta 2X2i + \cdots \beta nXni + \varepsilon i$$

Where

- *Yi* = Dependent variable, i.e. the performance of Italian retrieval and recycling companies;
- *X1...Xn* = Independent variables;
- *β1... βn* = Regression coefficients;
- *Ɛ* = Stochastic error.

Empirical Results

For purposes of this research, after having studied the correlation between independent and control variables of the model, and after having detected some rather high correlations between total assets, current assets, equity and sales, the "Stability" variable was created through the "mean" operation in order to avoid problems of multi-collinearity. In conclusion, therefore, the model takes into account the relationship between the dependent performance variable, by resorting to EBITDA (Earnings Before Interest, Taxes, Depreciation and Amortization) as performance indicator, and the independent variables:

- *Company size,* by utilizing as indicator the number of employees;
- *Area,* by utilizing as indicator the region of the registered office;
- *Shareholding,* by distinguishing whether or not, among shareholders, there are public Authorities, the State or Government;
- *Ageing* of companies, by paying regard to the year of their foundation;
- *Stability,* which takes into account the total asset, current asset, equity and sales;

- *Net income,* i.e. the result for the 2014 financial year;
- *ROE,* i.e. the return on equity.

If we analyse the correlations more specifically, the Beta columns indicate the sign of the relationship between the dependent variable and the independent variables. We may observe how size and seniority are negatively linked to performance. This entails that the more recent the company, the worse is the performance result, and also that the bigger the company, the worse is its performance. Conversely, the higher the total assets, current assets, equity, sales, net income and return on equity (ROE), the better will be the company performance.

It is nevertheless important to observe that not all the variables have significant causal relationships with performance, in particular those variables that show p-value > 0.05. The variables indicating the type of shareholder, the age and the percentage ROE do not explain the performance variation. Despite that, the model is altogether thoroughly valid, as will be elucidated by the Table hereunder.

Among the other variables, instead, size, stability and net income have a higher impact on the level of company performance, given that they show a value of Sign. < 0,000. The where variable, too, proves to have an impact on performance.

By virtue of what has been asserted, the H3 and H4 hypotheses are refuted, in that the type of shareholder found in the companies and the age thereof do not impact at all on performance. The H1 hypothesis is accepted, whereas hypothesis H2 evinces the fact that size negatively impacts on the company performance.

Table 7. Coefficients

Coefficients(a)								
Model		Unstandardized Coefficients		Standardized Coefficients	t	Sign.	Collinearity Statistics	
		T	Std. Error	Beta			Tolerance	VIF
1	(Constant)	14125,765	151904,106		,093	,926		
	Company size	-3761,501	585,103	-,188	-6,429	,000	,516	1,939
	Area	71597,051	32219,715	,048	2,222	,027	,956	1,046
	Shareholding	148935,902	127077,466	,028	1,172	,242	,756	1,322
	Ageing	-,945	3,982	-,005	-,237	,813	,906	1,104
	Stability	,110	,003	1,320	34,581	,000	,302	3,314
	Net income €	,932	,025	1,225	37,531	,000	,413	2,422
	ROE %	462,122	450,130	,022	1,027	,305	,977	1,023
a. Dependent Variable: EBITDA €								

In order to assess the effectiveness of the model, we should bear in mind the value of the RSquare. In the model implemented by us, the RSquare equals .831, which represents a pretty satisfactory value, hence the model of the aforesaid seven variables proves to be significant and accordingly capable of explaining the 83% performance variance in the waste sector.

Analysis of Results

As shown by the model summary, the totality of utilized variables proves to be especially significant when trying to explain the performance trend of companies active in this waste business. That is further confirmed by the value 2 of the Durbin-Watson statistic indicating the absence of self-correlation in regression.

Relationships Between the Independent Variables

If we embark on an in-depth analysis of the relationships between control variables and independent ones (by breaking up the stability variable into the four variables it consists of), we will note that *current asset* is the item with a stronger correlation with control variables: net income, sales, total asset, equity and company size variable as well. This data is quite easy to deduce, in that current assets is an index of solvency, and thus of stability as well. As confirmed by the Pearson Correlation, as current asset increase the total activities, sales, equity and number of employees all increase. These data may be explained on the basis that companies with available liquidity generally have a wide turnover (hence large Sales), but at the same time need also to provide guarantees to their own customers and creditors (equity).

More singular is instead the significant and negative relationship (-0.66) with the fiscal year result. This may be explained if one pays regard to the items making up current assets in the Italian budget. Current assets consists of inventories, receivables, and financial assets other than fixed assets and cash. If, accordingly, some of these items, such as receivables and inventories, increase, there will be a simultaneous

Table 8. Model summary

Model Summary[b]					
Model	R	R square	Adjusted R Square	Std. Error of the Estimate	Durbin-Watson
1	,913[a]	,834	,831	309325,475	2,005
a. Predictors (constant), ROE %, Ageing, Shareholding, Net income€, Area, Company size, Stability					
b. Dependent variable: EBITDA €					

increase in financial need. Since, in fact, companies are small in size and with scant capital, they have to resort to market financing (we should not forget, moreover, that these companies have a limited self-financing capacity), save in the case of exceptions arising from the leverage (where investments are obviously made only until profitability exceeds the investment cost). The same explanation holds true for the negative relationship between the net profit and the stability variables. After all, if we analyse the correlation between net income and four variables grouped together under Stability, we may discern a negative link with each one of them.

The age of the companies, by contrast, is not specifically linked to any variable (the Pearson Correlation always shows values not exceeding 0.185). This indicates the fact that the year of foundation of the company does not impact on such fundamental budgetary variables as equity and net income or even on the company size.

The number of employees, hence the company **size** as well, besides showing a positive link with current assets and turnover, discloses a positive link (weak and yet existing) with the type of shareholder. We may infer from it that public shareholding in recycling/retrieval companies mostly occurs in medium- to large-size companies. That fact is confirmed by the data retrieved by the database, which indicate that 50% of companies with shares held by public authorities, State and Government, fall under the "medium- to large-size" category, which in turn represents only 3.63% of the total companies of the sample. This means that public bodies, State and Government hold shares especially in medium- to large-size companies.

Relationships between the Dependent Variable and the Independent Ones

Once the significant relationships have been clarified, we will now proceed to analyse the hypotheses that have not been accepted by virtue of the statistical results, given the lack of any correlation. The performance proves to be correlated neither with the company's seniority nor with the presence of public shareholders.

As far as the first relationship is concerned, different explanations might be put forward. Despite being a new sector, it does not means that companies established on a more recent date should record a higher level of performance. The new companies, in fact, must locate themselves in the most favourable areas, acquire sufficient know how to offer a good service, invest in state-of-the-art structures and in marketing operations, and thus establish a new customer base. Less recent companies must instead face problems of modernization and implementation of new structures and operations. On the other hand, however, they already boast good market shares and experience in the sector. Accordingly, a relationship between the company's seniority and its performance cannot be established, since the factors impact on the two variables in a radically different manner. Earlier, we had also discussed the presence of innovative start-ups in the Italian retrieval and recycling sector. Given the very negligible presence (3 companies out of 811) and the invariably negative result, account being taken of both EBITDA and the net income, we might assert that these innovative companies do not find in the Italian recycling and retrieval business a good sector wherein to operate and make profits.

The second unconfirmed hypothesis concerns the positive relationship between performance and the presence of public authorities, State and Government in the shareholding structures of Italian retrieval and recycling companies. The subject has been actually studied to an ample extent in other works as well as in various disciplines. In this sector, too, it is not possible to assert a better performance level in either public or private companies. This study indicates that performance is independent of the type of shareholding. This is an extremely significant element. It has in fact been explained that this business, and thus a sustainable waste management, is strictly linked to a Country's level of civilization and health care. The authors hold the view that a public presence in most of the sector companies might serve as an incentive to improve the performance level and standardize the sectorial management towards a more efficient and sustainable economy. Studies tackling economics often contend that, in Italy, public intervention, understood as public authorities, State and Government, most of the times does not entail efficient results. In the retrieval and recycling sector, however, it is believed, due to the abovementioned reasons, that the State has a specific interest in intervening in an efficient and constant fashion.

CONCLUSION

An analysis was conducted on a representative sample of the Italian retrieval and recycling sector, a sector of undoubtedly high relevance and importance within the green economy context. The analysed companies' record positive results altogether.

The companies are equally distributed between the Centre-South and Northern areas; the size thereof is in line with the Italian structure, and most of them have been set up during the last 15 years. We may notice that the most significant variables to explain the company performance are obviously represented by net profit and stability. Among the initially postulated hypotheses, the existence of a link between performance and size has been confirmed. The zero level of significance indicates in fact that the company size impacts on performance. The Beta value, however, indicates that this link is negative, hence as company size increases the performance level decreases. This data may be explained by the fact that the difficulty in organizing large-size companies and the inability to exploit economies of scale created thanks to the company's size expansion do not only entail the fact that an improvement in the performance level cannot be attained, but also an actual worsening thereof.

The authors may accept the second hypothesis, and thus the fact that performance is better in companies having their registered offices in Northern Italy. The economic growth gaps between the two areas are well known (Daniele and Malanina, 2007). This data, too, is in line with the Italian situation, which generally records better performances in the northernmost Italian region.

Limitation

The study suffers from a few limitations: 1) the analysis has been conducted by analysing solely the Italian retrieval and recycling companies which have lodged their financial statements in the last year; 2) reliance was placed exclusively on results from one year, the 2014 financial year; 3) The current market crisis, which has been already going on for several years, has undoubtedly impacted on company performances in general, hence those of the analysed companies as well; 4) exclusive reliance was placed on the data available from the Aida database; 5) since any reference to other studies in the recycling sector was lacking, studies from different sectors were taken into account.

REFERENCES

A.A. V.V. (1998). *Atti del Convegno Nazionale AIDEA - Lecce 1997*. Bologna: Clueb.

Adams, W. M. (2001). *Green Development: environment and sustainability in the third world*. London: Routledge.

Al-Najjar, B., & Anfimiadou, A. (2012). Environmental policies and firm value. *Business Strategy and the Environment*, *21*(1), 49–59. doi:10.1002/bse.713

Alexander, S. S. (1949). The effects of size of Manufacturing Corporation on the Distribution of Rate of Return. *The Review of Economics and Statistics*, *31*(3), 229–235. doi:10.2307/1927749

Ambec, S., & Lanoie, P. (2008). Does it pay to be green? A systematic overview. *The Academy of Management Perspectives*, *22*(4), 45–62. doi:10.5465/AMP.2008.35590353

Anderson, D. R., & Anderson, K. E. (2009). Sustainability risk management. *Risk Management & Insurance Review*, *12*(1), 25–38. doi:10.1111/j.1540-6296.2009.01152.x

Andrei, P., & Pesci, C. (2009). L'area di riferimento del bilancio socio-ambientale nei gruppi aziendali: spunti critici di riflessione emergenti da un'indagine empirica. *Financial Reporting*, (2), 45-70.

Aragon-Correa, J. A., & Sharma, S. (2003). A contingent resource based view of proactive corporate environmental strategy. *Academy of Management Review, 28*(1), 71–88.

Bayyurt, N. (2007). İşletmelerde Performans Değerlendirmenin Önemi ve Performans Göstergeleri Arasındaki İlişkiler. *Sosyal Siyaset Konferansları Dergisi, 53*, 577–592.

Becker-Blease, J. R., Kaen, F. R., Etebari, A., & Baumann, H. (2010). Employees, firm size and profitability in U.S. manufacturing industries. *Investment Management and Financial Innovations, 7*(2), 7–23.

Bilkey, W. J., & Tesar, G. (1977). Export behavior of smaller-sized Wisconsin manufacturing firms. *Journal of International Business Studies, 8*(1), 93–98. doi:10.1057/palgrave.jibs.8490783

Boiral, O. (2009). Greening the corporation through organizational citizenship behaviors. *Journal of Business Ethics, 87*(2), 221–236. doi:10.1007/s10551-008-9881-2

Boiral, O., & Paille, P. (2012). Organizational citizenship behavior for the environment: Measurement and validation. *Journal of Business Ethics, 109*(4), 431–445. doi:10.1007/s10551-011-1138-9

Bonaccorsi, A. (1992, December). (199). On the relationship between firm size and export intensity. *Journal of International Business Studies, 23*(4), 605–636. doi:10.1057/palgrave.jibs.8490280

Boulding, K. (1996). The economics of the coming Spaceship Earth. In H. Jarrett (Ed.), *Environmental quality in a growing economy* (pp. 3–14). Baltimore, MD: Johns Hopkins University Press.

Brundtland, G. H. (1987). *Our Common Future*. Report of the World Commission on Environment and Development. Retrieved from: http://www.un-documents.net/our-common-future.pdf

Burton, F. N., & Schlegelmilch. (1987). Profile analyses of non-exporters versus exporters grouped by export involvement. *Management International Review, 27*, 38–49.

Catturi, G. (1990). *Produrre e consumare, ma come? Verso l'ecologia aziendale*. Padova: Cedam.

Cavusgil, S., & Naor, J. (1987). Finn and management characteristics as discriminators for export behavior. *Journal of Business Research, 15*(3), 221–235. doi:10.1016/0148-2963(87)90025-7

Cavusgil, S. T., & John, R. N. (1981). Internal determinants of export marketing behavior: An empirical investigation. *JMR, Journal of Marketing Research, 23*(February), 114–119. doi:10.2307/3151322

Claver-Cortés, E., Molina-Azorín, J. F., & Pereira-Moliner, J. (2006). Strategic groups in the hospitality industry: Intergroup and intragroup performance differences in Alicante, Spain. *Tourism Management, 27*(6), 1101–1116. doi:10.1016/j.tourman.2005.11.006

D'Amato, A. (2008). Rifiuti, mercati del riciclo ed efficienza economica. *Economia dei Servizi, 3*(3), 423–440.

Daily, B. F., Bishop, J. W., & Govindarajulu, N. (2009). A conceptual model for organizational citizenship behavior directed toward the environment. *Business & Society, 48*(2), 243–256. doi:10.1177/0007650308315439

Daniele, V., & Malanina, P. (2007). Il prodotto delle regioni e il divario Nord-Sud in Italia (1861-2004). *Rivista di Politica Economica*, 1–49.

Dobler, M., Lajili, K., & Zèghal, D. (2014). Environmental performance, environmental risk and risk management. *Business Strategy and the Environment, 23*(1), 1–17. doi:10.1002/bse.1754

Dogan, M. (2013). Does Firm Size Affect the Firm Profitability? Evidence from Turkey. *Research Journal of Finance and Accounting, 4*(4), 53–59.

Ferrara, G. (1998). L'etica ambientale nella economia delle imprese tra conflitti e condivisioni. *Rivista italiana di ragioneria e economia aziendale*, 7-8.

Fiegenbaum, A., & Karnani, A. (1991). Output Flexibility–A Competitive Advantage for Small Firms. *Strategic Management Journal, 12*(2), 101–114. doi:10.1002/smj.4250120203

Fiori, G., Di Donato, F., & Izzo, M. F. (2007). *Corporate Social Responsibility and Firms Performance. An Analysis on Italian Listed Companies*. Retrieved from http://ssrn.com/abstract=1032851

Fondazione sviluppo sostenibile. (2014). *L'Italia del riciclo 2014*. Retrieved from http://www.fondazionesviluppososteniblie.org/f/Documenti/2014/Italia+Riciclo/04_parte_uno-italia_del_riciclo_2014.pdf

Franceschelli, V. (2010). *Diritto Privato*. Milano: Giuffrè.

Garzella, S., Fiorentino, R., & D'Antonio, C. (2011). Le strategie ambientali ed il green management nel sistema della comunicazione ambientale.*Financial Reporting Workshop*.

Gouldson, A. (2004). Risk, regulation and the right to know: Exploring the impacts of access to information on the governance of environmental risk. *Sustainable Development*, *12*(3), 136–149. doi:10.1002/sd.237

Gray, L. (1914). Rent under the Assumption of Exhaustibility. *The Quarterly Journal of Economics*, *22*, 432–440.

Grove, R. H. (1995). *A Historical review of institutional and conservationist responses to fears of artificially induced global climate change: The Deforestation-Desiccation Discourse in Europe and the Clonial Context 1500-1940. In Le sciences hors d'occident au XX siècle, Orstom èditions* (Vol. 3, pp. 155–174). Nature et Environment.

Grove, R. H. (1996). Green Imperialism: Colonial Expansion, Tropical Island Edens, and the Origins of Environmentalism 1600-1860. Cambridge University Press.

Hair, J. F. Jr, Black, W. C., Babin, B., Anderson, R., & Tatham, R. (2005). *Multivariate Data Analysis* (5th ed.). Upper Saddle River, NJ: Prentice-Hall.

Hall, M., & Weiss, L. (1967). Firms Size and Profitability. *The Review of Economics and Statistics*, *49*(3), 319–331. doi:10.2307/1926642

Helfat, C., Finkelstein, S., Mitchell, W., Peteraf, M. A., Singh, H., Teece, D. J., & Winter, S. G. (2007). *Dynamic Capabilities: Understanding Strategic Change in Organizations*. Oxford, UK: Blackwell.

Holzmuller, H. H., & Kasper, H. (1991). On a theory of export performance. *Management International Review*, *31*, 45–70.

Hotelling, H. (1931). The Economics of Exhaustible Resources. *Journal of Political Economy*, *39*(2), 137–175. doi:10.1086/254195

Israeli, A. A. (2002). Star rating and corporate affiliation: Their influence on room price and performance of hotels in Israel. *International Journal of Hospitality Management*, *21*(4), 405–424. doi:10.1016/S0278-4319(02)00037-3

Jónsson, B. (2007). Does the Size Matter? The Relationship between Size and Profitability of Icelandic Firms. Bifröst. *Journal of Social Sciences*, *1*, 43–55.

Kaynak, E., & Kothari, V. (1984). Export behavior of small and medium sized manufacturers. *Management International Review*, *24*, 61–69.

LePine, J. A., Erez, A., & Johnson, D. E. (2002). The nature and dimensionality of organizational citizenship behavior: A critical review and metaanalysis. *The Journal of Applied Psychology*, *87*(1), 52–65. doi:10.1037/0021-9010.87.1.52 PMID:11916216

Lounsbury, M., Ventresca, M., & Hirsch, P. M. (2003). Social movements, field frames and industry emergence: A cultural-political perspective on US recycling. *Socio-economic Review*, *1*(1), 71–104. doi:10.1093/soceco/1.1.71

Malthus, T. (1798). *An Essay on the Principle of Population*. London: Macmillan.

Marshal, R. S., & Brown, D. (2003). The strategy of sustainability: A Systems perspective on environmental initiatives. *California Management Review*, *46*(1), 101–126. doi:10.2307/41166234

Marzetti, L. (2001). *Manuale di diritto ambientale*. Padova: CEDAM.

Masini, C. (1970). *Lavoro e risparmio*. Torino: Utet.

Mass, S., Schuster, T., & Hartmann, E. (2014). Pollution prevention and service Stewardship strategies in the Third-part logistics industry: Effects on firm differentiation and moderating role of environmental communication. *Business Strategy and the Environment*, *23*(1), 38–55. doi:10.1002/bse.1759

Matacena, A. (1984). *Impresa e ambiente. Il bilancio sociale*. Bologna: Clueb.

Miolo Vitali, P. (1978). *Problemi ecologici nella gestione delle aziende*. Milano: Giuffrè.

Mugler, J., & Miesenbock, J. (1986). Determinants of increasing export involvement of small firms. *Proceedings, International Council of Small Business, World Conference*, (pp. 189-205).

Myers, R. (1990). *Classical and modern regression with applications* (2nd ed.). Boston, MA: Duxbury.

Noci, G. (2000). Environmental reporting in Italy: Current practice and future developments. *Business Strategy and the Environment*, *9*(4), 211–223. doi:10.1002/1099-0836(200007/08)9:4<211::AID-BSE248>3.0.CO;2-9

Organ, D. W. (1988). *Organizational citizenship behavior: The good soldier syndrome*. Lexington, MA: Lexington Books.

Pigou, A. C. (1920). *The economics of Welfare*. London: Macmillan.

Pine, R., & Phillips, P. A. (2005). Performance comparisons of hotels in China. *International Journal of Hospitality Management, 24*(1), 57–73. doi:10.1016/j.ijhm.2004.04.004

Pippo, R. (2011). *Economia dell'energia.* Bologna: Il Mulino.

Podsakoff, P. M., MacKenzie, S. B., Paine, J. B., & Bachrach, D. G. (2000). Organizational citizenship behaviors: A critical review of the theoretical and empirical literature and suggestions for future research. *Journal of Management, 26*(3), 513–563. doi:10.1177/014920630002600307

Quagli, A., & Teodori, C. (2005). *L'informativa volontaria per settori di attività.* Milano: Franco Angeli.

Radipere, S., & Dhliwayo, S. (2014). The role of age and business size on small business performance in the South African small enterprise sector. *Problems and Perspectives in Management, 12*(4), 7–12.

Ravenscraft, D. J., & Scherer, F. M. (1987). Life after Takeover. *The Journal of Industrial Economics, 36*(2), 147–156. doi:10.2307/2098409

Ruggero, S., & D'Angella, F. (2011). Strategie e performance delle imprese alberghiere di Milano. *Economia aziendale online, 2*(2), 209-221.

Saita, M. (2012). *Economia aziendale.* Milano: Giuffrè Editore.

Saita, M. (2015). *Economia d'azienda.* Milano: Giuffrè Editore.

Santoro, G. (2015). Evaluating Performance in the Hotel Industry: An Empirical Analysis of Piedmont. *Journal of Investment and Management. Special Issue: Attractiveness and Governance of Tourist Destinations, 4*, 17–22.

Scherer, F. M. (1973). The Determinants of Plant Sizes in Six Nations. *The Review of Economics and Statistics, 55*(2), 135–145. doi:10.2307/1926988

Secchi, D. (2006). The Italian experience in social reporting: An empirical analysis. *Corporate Social Responsibility and Environmental Management, 13*(3), 135–149. doi:10.1002/csr.96

Sharma, S., & Vredenburg, H. (1998). Proactive corporate environmental strategy and the development of competitively valuable organizational capabilities. *Strategic Management Journal, 19*(8), 729–753. doi:10.1002/(SICI)1097-0266(199808)19:8<729::AID-SMJ967>3.0.CO;2-4

Siegel, D. S. (2009). Green management matters only if it yields more green: An economic/strategic perspective. *The Academy of Management Perspectives*, *23*(3), 5–16. doi:10.5465/AMP.2009.43479260

Stekler, H. O. (1964). The Variability of Profitability with Size of Firm. *Journal of the American Statistical Association*, *59*, 1183–1193.

Tacito, P. C. (98). *De origine et situ Germanorum*. Mondadori.

The World Commission on Environment and Development. (1987). *Our Common Future, New York*. Oxford University Press.

Turner, R. K., Pearce, D. W., & Bateman, I. (1993). *Environmental Economics. An elementary introduction*. Baltimore, MD: Johns Hopkins University Press.

Villalonga, B. (2004). Diversification discount or premium? New evidence from the business information tracking series. *The Journal of Finance*, *59*(2), 475–502. doi:10.1111/j.1540-6261.2004.00640.x

Weaver, S., Ellen, P., & Mathiassen, L. (2015). Contextualist Inquiry into Organizational Citizenship: Promoting Recycling Across Heterogeneous Organizational Actors. *Journal of Business Ethics*, *129*(2), 413–428. doi:10.1007/s10551-014-2165-0

Williamson, D., Lynch-Wood, G., & Ramsay, J. (2006). Drivers of Environmental Behaviour in Manufacturing SMEs and the Implications for CSR. *Journal of Business Ethics*, *67*(3), 317–330. doi:10.1007/s10551-006-9187-1

Wilson, J. S. (1858). On the general and gradual desiccation of the earth and atmosphere. *Proceedings of the British Association for the Advancement of Science*.

ENDNOTES

1. Released in 1987 by the World Commission on Environment and Development (WCED). It introduces the concept of sustainable development.
2. Basel Convention, Article 2.
3. Directive 2008/98/CE of the European Parliament and of the Council of 19 November 2008, on waste and repealing certain Directives, art.6, "End-of-waste status": the substance or object is commonly used for specific purposes; a market or demand exists for such a substance or object; the substance or object fulfils the technical requirements for the specific purposes and meets the existing legislation and standards applicable to products; and the use of the

substance or object will not lead to overall adverse environmental or human health impacts.

4 Directive 2008/98/CE of the European Parliament and of the Council of 19 November 2008, on waste and repealing certain Directives, art.4, "Waste hierarchy".

5 Directive 2008/98/CE of the European Parliament and of the Council of 19 November 2008, on waste and repealing certain Directives, Art 1, "Subject matter and scope".

6 Directive 2008/98/CE of the European Parliament and of the Council of 19 November 2008, on waste and repealing certain Directives, Art 3.17, "Definitions".

7 CONAI, National Packageing Consortium, is a private non-profit Consortium and is a system which represents the answer to private companies and to a problem of collective interest, such as the environmental one, in due compliance with the guidelines and objectives laid down by the political system . More than 1.000.000 of companies producing and utilizing packages affiliate to the Consortium System. http://www.conai.org

8 Kiloton.

Chapter 7
Green Marketing:
A New Prospect in the Cosmetics Industry

Nur Suhaili Ramli
University of York, UK

ABSTRACT

This chapter proposes an important study of the cosmetics industry in relation to green marketing and sustainability concerns from the historical context and its evolution to the present day. The aim of this chapter is to explain the significant impact of green marketing on the cosmetics industry as a new future prospect that benefits all parties and what can be learned from history. This chapter intends to address the existence of sustainability concepts through history, which have become an interesting phenomenon in the present day. The aspects to be discussed include (1) new prospects and opportunities from green marketing for the cosmetics industry; (2) the evolution of the cosmetics industry; and (3) green marketing and green concepts in the cosmetics industry.

INTRODUCTION

Currently, concern for the environment is a global issue. This has been observed in various platforms, including consumer demand, lifestyle polls, political and activist campaigns, the media, and through marketing strategies and product offers. However, the academic literature does not reflect this popular movement in terms of its historical context and evolution. Previously, sustainability or green concepts

DOI: 10.4018/978-1-5225-2075-7.ch007

were not popular, with the exception of certain circumstances—for example, during the Second World War when some raw materials were rationed. However, industry, resources, and awareness are different in the present day. Currently, green marketing or sustainability is a new business direction that offers new prospects in the cosmetics industry. This is not limited solely to global brands such as L'Oreal, P&G, and Avon, but also attracts premium brands like Estee Lauder, Shiseido, and Clinique and encourages the success of new cosmetics brands like Lush, The Body Shop, Aveeno, Natura, and others. In relation to the past, the extent to which mainstream brands such as Avon, Estee Lauder, Maybelline, L'Oreal, and others have learned from history is a topic of debate, influencing their sustainable decisions in the present day.

Further, many cosmetics companies must react to changing customer needs, new regulations, and a new social preference, which reflects increasing concerns regarding the socioenvironmental impacts of business. According to Shrivastava (1994), shifting customer needs and trends towards green marketing will demand fundamental changes to the management paradigm, which underpins marketing and other business functions. This chapter aims to compare current and former studies of green marketing in the cosmetics industry, thereby examining the evolution of the green agenda. There is historical evidence from global brands in the world crises period that sustainable concepts in marketing were discovered.

Background

To date, no definition has been provided for green marketing. This is because it refers not only to a product's specific ingredients, but also to a broad range of production factors—for example, packaging, advertising, distribution, people, and the organisation as whole. Therefore, defining green marketing is neither easy nor straightforward. However, Peattie and Charter (2003) proposed that identifying, anticipating, and satisfying the needs of consumers and society in a profitable and sustainable way is through holistic management process; in other words, the need to consider environmental issues within the whole organisation, rather than only the marketing department. Furthermore, green marketing is a long-term branding issue and not a tactical concern; however, developing countries had complained that the West (particularly in Europe) was using these issues to place anticompetitive constraint on emerging economies (Johri & Sahasakmontri, 1998).

Green marketing in the cosmetics industry is emerging and gathering importance. Moreover, its history can be traced back to the wave of environmental concern in the 1970s, which emphasised the concept of 'ecological marketing' (Hennison & Kinnear, 1976). However, the serious discussion on sustainability in marketing and its physical implications was raised in the 1990s (Van Dam & Apeldoorn, 1996, Obermiller, 1995). In addition, there are factors that affect consumers in terms of green purchasing behaviour (Kaufmann, Panni & Orphanidou, 2012), thereby raising the opportunity for green marketing in the cosmetics industry where there is an industrial commitment to green and sustainable chemistry using renewable materials and developing ecofriendly processes and ingredients in cosmetics (Philippe, Didillon & Gilbert, 2012). These can be observed through the transitions in the cosmetics trend alongside the evolution of cosmetics products by gigantic brands such as L'Oréal, Estee Lauder, Avon, and others between 1990s and the present. During this period, anti-aging products, whitening products, blemish base creams (BB creams), beauty serum, and antiwrinkle products have become phenomenal in the industry.

There are several issues accompanying this trend, and there is an encouraging increase in the literature on green marketing in the cosmetics industry. However, two issues to be discussed in this chapter include (1) the relevance of green marketing in the cosmetics industry; and (2) consumers' behaviour and awareness when buying cosmetics products.

Relevance of Green Marketing in the Cosmetics Industry

According to Simon (1992), the government policies regarding consumer preferences and company strategies are being reshaped to be more ecofriendly. In addition, many firms now view environmental orientation as a long-term issue rather than a way of making short-term gains (Lee & Barrett, 1996). This is because many business opportunities are currently emerging for technologies, goods, and services that address environmental problems, or at least make less of a contribution towards them (Peattie & Charter, 2003). In contrast, there is a misspecification of green products in relation to consumers' needs and barriers to the perception of green products' environmental impact and consumers' freewill due to individual self-interest (Wong, Turner & Stoneman, 1996).

In the cosmetic industry context, Manko (2001) exposes that the sector established a 'recession-proof' image when sales of inexpensive cosmetics outsold midpriced food items and clothing in the 1930s. Interestingly, Kumar (2005) stated that the cosmetics industry also did well during the recessions of the 1960s and 1980s; however, during that of the early 1990s, new challenges arose whereby counterfeit products sold at low prices mushroomed. Furthermore, Pitman (2010) reported that, in 2009, most of the leading cosmetics brands saw declining sales due to big falls in consumer sales in the developed markets of North America and Europe. However, Elizabeth Arden and Estee Lauder experienced modest sales growth due to the restructuring of sustainability efforts that reduced carbon footprints and also Badische Anilin und Soda Fabrik (BASF). This point towards a sustainability measure resulting in cost saving as means of recovery and securing future growth.

The trend of the cosmetics industry is consistently seen as 'recession-proof,' surviving a series of economic depressions from the 1930s to the present. Behind this consistency, sustainable cosmetics, also known as green cosmetics, play some significant roles in the industry, which still has limited discussion and undisclosed historical evidence. This became one of the biggest problems with green marketing where there has been little attempt to academically examine environmental or green marketing, especially in the cosmetics industry. However, some literature exists on environmental advertising (Carlson, Grove & Kangun, 1993), strategies for environmental advertising (Davis, 1993), green marketing as a strategic approach (Polonsky & Rosenberger, 2001) and, more recently, the expression of green marketing as a concept of corporate social responsibility (Banyte, Brazioniene & Gadeikiene, 2015).

In terms of competitive impact and the performance of green marketing on cosmetics brands, the environmental concern creates increased demand for new products, which are redesigned, reformulated, and produced differently (Peattie & Charter, 2003). This variation reveals another channel in the product line that focuses particularly on natural or green-based products, with considerable knowledge of the overall process. However, other premium and mainstream cosmetics brands are not only discovering new product lines based on the green or natural concept, but also have mergers and acquisitions with existing brands; for example, Origin and Aveda are part of Estee Lauder, and The Body Shop is a subsidiary of L'Oréal. This is also part of the business strategies trend implemented by cosmetics firms in the present.

Thus, this chapter will present historical and current evidence of the relevance of green marketing within the cosmetics industry, which could offer new prospects for the industry.

Consumers' Behaviour and Awareness of Buying Cosmetics Products

The growth of the cosmetics industry has become important as consumers are increasingly becoming aware of appearance, beauty, grooming, and the choice of personal care products. Interestingly, these factors not only influence the consumers, but also their behaviour and awareness of buying green products has risen steadily. This can be seen from a market report published by Transparency Market Research, cited by Penning (2013), entitled 'Organic Personal Care Products Market for Skin Care, Hair Care, Oral Care and Cosmetics – Global Industry Analysis, Size, Share, Growth, Trends, and Forecast, 2012-2018.' It reports that the global demand for organic personal care product was over USD$7.6 billion in 2012 and is expected to reach USD$13.2 billion by 2018. This figure shows that consumer behaviour in terms of buying green products and their awareness are increasing and also shows some promising lines of business to cosmetics brands in the future. Moreover, widening distribution channels and new product development are other factors that contribute to market growth. In the present, there are various channels to purchase cosmetics products, such as at the counter in a shopping mall, pharmacy, airport duty-free shop, mobile shop, phone call, through the cosmetics brand's representatives, online shopping through the website, social media like Facebook, and others. Thus, the distribution channels of the products and promotion of cosmetics brands have become more accessible and reliable compared to the past. Further, due to advances in technology, knowledge and product information can be delivered easily straight to consumers.

In contrast, consumers' behaviour and awareness of buying cosmetics products in the past was limited. Knowledge, and product information was delivered through advertisements, television, radio, and even word-of-mouth among customers. Further, to buy the cosmetics products, customers had to get them at the pharmacy or from the brand's representative, and luxury brands were available at prestige malls. There was almost none of the awareness of green or natural cosmetics at that time aside from those who relied on traditional beauty (for example traditional methods, packaging, impact to environment) in their routine. However, there were also some cosmetics in that day that used natural extracts, such as Avon and Helena Rubinstein, who experimented with lavender, pine bark, and water lilies.

The comparison between the past and present consumers' behaviour and awareness of buying green products has changed over time. From the early 1900s to the present, the cosmetics industry changed due to innovation, technology, and globalisation (Jones, 2011). Further, the innovation in this industry relies on branding and marketing knowledge rather than technology (Lopes, 2002). This is because the role of brands and marketing knowledge provided fundamental elements of the growth strategies of cosmetics firms, which later expanded in the foreign market and reflected their evolution as a whole in the industry, where they become well known to customers. In the present, innovation in technology could add value and make it necessary for the industry to expand and grow fast, but the fundamental innovation in this industry still relies on branding and marketing knowledge as a whole.

MAIN FOCUS OF THE CHAPTER

This section discusses the history of cosmetics, emerging trends in the cosmetics industry, some case analysis, related issues, and a proposed concept of green marketing in the cosmetics industry. Although green marketing is an emerging phenomenon and aims to reduce production costs and to support the environmental campaign, there are still several issues, controversies, and problems occurring today.

History of Green Marketing in the Cosmetics Industry

Cosmetics have been used since the beginning of human civilisation. Ancient cultures were as preoccupied with the aesthetics of appearance as individuals are today. Many rituals for religious purposes insist on the use of various scents or essences and natural colours from plant extracts. Traditions from ancient civilisations like the Egyptians, the Romans, the Byzantine, the Ottoman, the Chinese, and others are evidence of resourceful peoples of various cultures who knew the usefulness of natural cosmetic ingredients.

As early as 10,000 BC, men and women rouged their lips and cheeks, stained their nails with henna, and lined their eyes and eyebrows heavily with kohl. Kohl was a dark-coloured powder made of crushed antimony, burnt almonds, lead, oxidised copper, ochre, ash, malachite, chrysocolla (a blue-green copper ore), or any combination thereof (Cohen, 1999). Today, kohl is used by the laity for inflamed lids and thin eyelashes because it is deemed of high quality when it causes a burning sensation in an application where it is mixed with other constituents such as aloe, myrrh, nutmeg, and cane sugar (Sweha, 1982).

Evidence from ancient Egypt revealed many items of a cosmetic interest in tombs and also drawings on the walls of Egyptians applying makeup. Furthermore, in ancient Rome, olive oil was applied with a strigil to exfoliate dirt from skin. In addition, egg whites were used to help to hide wrinkles, and homegrown face creams could be made from the herbs found in home gardens in the 16th and 17th centuries. However, the compounds and chemicals used in cosmetics also could be purchased from an apothecary (Mark & Rous). Thus, historical evidence shows that both natural and chemicals ingredients have been used widely in different eras.

However, do the green cosmetics that appeared in the late 1980s, still be used and become the main ingredient for some cosmetics in the present?

Polonsky (1994) defines green marketing as "set of all the activities designed to generate and facilitate any exchange intended to satisfy human needs or wants, such that the satisfaction of these needs and wants occurs, with minimal detrimental impact on the natural environment" (p. 2). Although, in the past, natural ingredients were discovered and used for generations, the issue to be dealt with here includes the awareness and needs and wants of the consumers. Further, natural or green resources were there, but with the lack of knowledge of environmental issues—including the fact that the knowledge was not spread well—the demand for such green or natural products was minimal.

However, according to the historian, when the rise of more complex societies brought an ever-increasing demand for cosmetics, perfumers, cosmetologists, barbers, and gentlewomen became pioneers, undertaking and developing the cosmetics practices that have evolved through the ages (Blanco-Dávila, 2000). The evolution of cosmetics also relied on these factors when globalisation led to exposure to different beauty routines and techniques, traditional practices, and myths about beauty from particular countries. Table 1 presents the evolution of cosmetics products.

During the Second World War for instance, British women used some natural ingredients as a substitute in cosmetics when essential ingredients, like petroleum for lipstick, were rationed. During the war, some supply ships were sunk, factories bombed, and ingredients redeployed as armaments production slowed to a trickle and people started to run out of things. Because lipstick was necessary to maintain the morale of the women who worked in munition factories or in other war work (Ogilvie & Ryan, 2011) and petroleum was rationed, beetroot was a favourite lip stain and relatively harmless; in addition, the bright colour was a boost to women's morale (Lawrence, 2015). This demonstrated that women during this era were also aware the benefit and existence of natural ingredients like beetroot but preferred multi-coloured lipsticks that were made from petroleum.

Cosmetics industry is a quite interesting industry to examine, especially in terms of consumer behaviours and preferences. Historically many natural and green cosmetics have been used as makeup, in traditions, and for health and beauty rou-

Table 1. Evolution of Some Cosmetics Products

Year	Event
10,000 BC	Men and women in Egypt use scented oils and ointments to clean and soften their skin and mask body odor.
3,000 BC	Chinese people began to stain their fingernails with gum Arabic, gelatine, beeswax, and egg.
2,000 BC	In Iraq, women use perfumes and pigments for their eyes and lips.
1,500 BC	Chinese and Japanese commonly use rice powder to make their face white.
1,200 BC	Egyptians use black eyeliner and green pigment for their eyebrows.
100 AD	Romans rub themselves with olive oil. People put barley flour and butter on their pimples.
300-400 AD	Henna is used in India as hair dye.
1250	Women use vegetable dye to color their faces and nails.
1580	White lead is used to get a pale complexion.
1860	Women use lampblack as eye shadow.
1901	First facelift is performed
1913	Mascara is invented
1915	Lipstick is first sold in push up sticks
1932	Modern lip gloss goes on sale

Source: A Timeline of Cosmetics and Make Up by Tim Lambert, Retrived from: localhistories.org/

tines in various civilisations across the centuries. However, why is it only now that natural beauty and green cosmetics is booming and emerging in the industry? It is partly, of course, that there is much more awareness of the need for environmental sustainability. However, the other part could be the business opportunity to be had by venturing more into this growing niche market and at the same time providing solutions and campaigning directly to societies. In this case, the industry also can contribute to educating and spreading awareness of the importance of green marketing, and at the same time, opening new opportunities in the industry.

Trend of Green Marketing in the Cosmetics Industry

The trend of green marketing in the cosmetics industry is emerging worldwide due to a high awareness of environmental sustainability through globalisation and rapid technological change. It is clear that green marketing in the cosmetics industry has arrived by evidence of the many environmental sustainability-based cosmetics brands like The Body Shop, Lush, Aveda, Bare Minerals, Origins, and many others. Mainstream cosmetics brands such as Avon, Estee Lauder, L'Oréal, P&G, Chanel, and few more have gradually shifted to green marketing and sustainability concerns, and their annual reports reported positive changes in their businesses, particularly in product packaging, promotion, and ingredients.

Consumers' demand for environmentally friendly products caused the cosmetics firms to invest heavily in green marketing. This is a new prospect for the cosmetics industry because those consumers live by new values and are looking for products that meet their expectations, are harmless health-wise, and at the same time do not harm or pose risk to the environment, animals, and fair trade. These particular consumers are similar to those who identify as vegan, or *halal*. This can be seen from the Organic Monitor report recently that the market in the natural cosmetics business is booming and growing by 15% in the East. However, many cosmetics brands from the West that concentrate on natural and organic cosmetics have withdrawn from the Chinese market due to the animal testing that they claimed was used there.

East Asia continues to dominate the cosmetics industry, with Hong Kong leading with the highest number of green cosmetics retailers for cosmetics brands such as Aveda, Apivita, Jurlique, Melvita, and Comvita. However, Japan is still the world's centre for cosmetics, and South Korea is emerging as the big market in the industry. Interestingly, Southeast Asia is reported to be a growing market for natural cosmetics products, especially in Singapore, Malaysia, and Thailand. In addition, Malaysia is one of the biggest *halal* hubs in several areas—including in cosmetics—should play it roles to widely venture the opportunity in natural and green cosmetics, other than their *halal* cosmetics. This is because the non-animal based products are in a high demand particularly for natural and green cosmetics as well as niche market like halal cosmetics. Figure 1 illustrates the total beauty sales and forecast based on sustainability between 2007 and 2017 by Euromonitor.

The figure shows that Asia is consistently rising from 36% to 40% over 10 years, similarly to the South America market, which saw a 5% increase in total beauty sales. In contrast, the Western market seems to decrease in total beauty sales and the 10-year forecast, with Europe dropping from 32% to 25%, and North America from 18% to 16%. This is consistent with the Organic Monitor report mentioned earlier.

Based on these reports, cosmetics firms are learning they need to invest more on their green marketing target because consumers expect their products to work as well as other cosmetics, but also have a special concern for the "environment." Hence, a great deal of research and development has been done, particularly in the use of natural ingredients, innovation in green packaging, and promotion, of which L'Oréal is an example. Due to the high awareness of consumers of environmental concerns, many cosmetics brands include detailed information on environmental and sustainability factors in their annual reports, including as Estee Lauder, Avon, L'Oréal, and others.

Today, the trend of green marketing in the cosmetic industry at large is becoming greener, and new customers are continuing to increase. Thus, this affects the entire cosmetics market in general in terms of competition. Interestingly, those cosmetics brands that were well established could have an advantage because they already have their customers. New product innovation requires having already strong brands. Further, in marketing, it is not only the product that matters, but also the brand,

Figure 1. Total beauty sales and forecast between 2007 and 2017
Source: Euromonitor, 2014

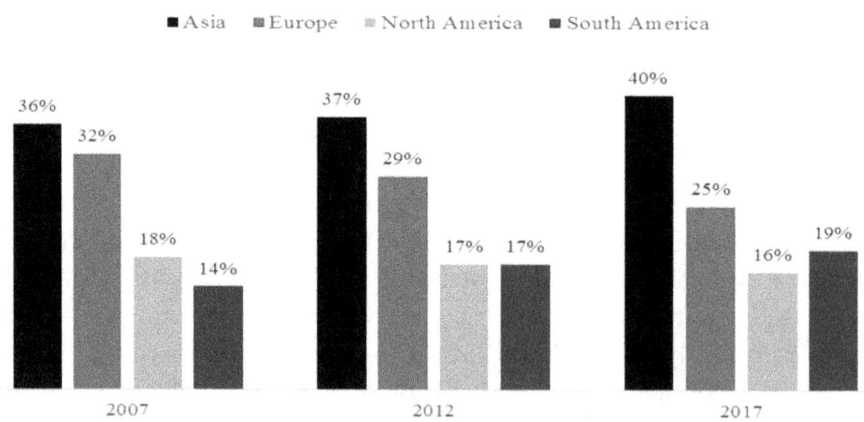

which carries and introduces the product. However, for those new entrants (such as entrepreneurs in small to medium enterprises) in the market, they can establish their green marketing identity from the beginning, but need to work harder on promotion to differentiate themselves from the competition.

The Importance of Green Cosmetics to Consumers

The marketing discipline has long argued that innovation must consider an intimate understanding of the customers. However, in this industry, innovation relies on branding and marketing strategies rather than on technology (Lopes, 2007). Therefore, it is the job of innovation to shift the awareness of consumers in explaining the importance of green cosmetics. This can be accomplished through brands, advertising, and the organisation's capabilities.

Green marketing as a concept and a demand in the cosmetics industry is emerging. However, in order to establish and align understanding of green marketing between the cosmetics manufacturer and the customers, the objective of concept must be satisfied, such as improved environmental quality and customer satisfaction, which historically has been misunderstood (Ottman, J. A., Stafford & Hartman, 2006). Consumers need to change their buying behaviours from *to fulfilling their wants and needs* to something beyond their preferences, such as considering how important their action is to the environment.

Cosmetics includes not just skincare, lipsticks, makeup, or other traditionally feminine products, but also shampoos, baby products, shower gels, shaving cream, and others. Therefore, the green concept and awareness in the cosmetics industry is responsible to all, including the buyers and sellers.

Interestingly, the rising consumer environmental concern is positive in the present (Bird & Sumner, 2010) and it shapes a trend called environmental or green consumerism, which is defined as consumers looking to protect themselves in the world through the power of their buying decisions and by scrutinising products for environmental safety when making purchases (Ottman, J. A., 1992).

There are many possible ways to educate consumers on the importance of green cosmetics. According to Matthes, Wonneberger, and Schmuck (2014), emotional ads can be a powerful marketing tool to reach out to consumers, regardless their green-purchaser background, as their empirical study shows that emotional appeals can serve to target people with no explicit attachment to environmental issues. As a result, consumers could be encouraged to tolerate and nurture their environmentally friendly consumption habits and buying behaviours.

Advertising is an enormous influence on consumers today, as they can access a wide variety of communication for products, including cosmetics. However, brands also influence consumers' purchasing behaviours; for example, a brand could represent a consumer to some extent, extending trust, a feeling of ownership, and attitudes. In a recent study of 75 brands in various industries between 2009 and 2012, it was found that the introduction of new green products can improve brand attitude, which also revealed that the brand's and category's positioning influence the introduction of such products (Olsen, Slotegraaf & Chandukala, 2014). This explains why both manufacturers and consumers need each other to achieve the objective of green marketing.

On the other hand, consumers are willing to accept green cosmetics when their main needs of performance, quality, convenience, and accessibility are met (Ottman, J., 2011). The important part of this is how they can understand their roles in helping to solve—or at least decrease—the environmental problems. As previously discussed, government, academic, industry, business people, and consumers have their own roles, which need to run strategies in parallel in order to see an obvious implication to the environment.

In this context, consumers must understand why they need to purchase and support green products, including cosmetics. The government entity or business manufacturer needs to communicate sustainability in an effective way (Ottman, J., 2011) and help consumers to envisage their behaviour if they buy green products and explain their action in terms of the environment, such as reducing the greenhouse effect, natural disasters, unfair low labour wages in developing countries, preventing illegal logging, and several others. Also, a particular awareness campaign can demonstrate to consumers on television, advertisements, the Internet, and others that the product they purchased is also affects their body. For example, almost all cosmetics products contain chemicals; however, through awareness campaigns, consumers can have an option to consider other cosmetics made by natural or organic ingredients, or at least to understand the chemical being applied to their skin.

In summary, the importance of green cosmetics to consumers is crucial because it helps save the environment, energy, and, the most important, consumer attitude. Understanding the effect and implication of their buying behaviour, particularly in green cosmetics, is the beginning of demand forecast in the future to the industry. The growth of the green marketing concept in the cosmetics industry will be discussed in the following case analysis.

Case Analysis

This section analyses some cosmetics brands in terms of sustainability and the green marketing that supports the previous discussion. Further, some reports mentioned that cosmetics could contribute to pollution; however, according to Wheeler (1993) the company is not a major polluter, nor a major user of energy and raw material. In contrast, many cosmetics firms today are aware of government laws and regulations, and also the local authority's policies to operate the businesses. The following are six case analyses from the global cosmetics brands in response to this claim.

The Body Shop

The Body Shop is one of the leading British brands in sustainable cosmetics. For more than 30 years, the five main core values still remain to activate self-esteem, to remain against animal testing, to defend human rights, to protect our planet, and to support community fair trade. Furthermore, The Body Shop has a long history of campaigning against animal testing, which it believes is unethical. Also, all of their products are advertised as cruelty free and suitable for vegetarians. In terms of ingredients, The Body Shop has a Community Fair Trade program where it could best help marginalised communities to improve their lives and decrease poverty—for example, by assisting the communities by providing a fair and stable income, building schools and healthcare centres, bringing clean water, and offering education scholarships. In relation to this, The Body Shop buys the finest ingredients and handicrafts directly from small-scale producers around the world, and in exchange, the firm offers good trading practices and fair pricing. Moreover, The Body Shop developed an ethical trade strategy by defending human rights from processes to people in the organisation. The Body Shop was among the early pioneers in green, ethical business and still has strong environmental credentials backing up its reputation. Like any other mainstream cosmetics brand, The Body Shop also has invested in environmental issues, such as setting up 800 Pulse stores worldwide through the Forestry Stewardship Council (FSC)–sourced shop where they only use FSC-certified sources, thereby ensuring the wood is from sustainably managed and harvested forests. Also, for business operation and workplace, there is an example for sustainable flooring with non-PVC flooring but trailing a bespoke flooring product made from natural minerals sourced from Scandinavia utilise efficient lighting by using fewer lamps, LED strip lights, and energy-efficient ceiling lights.

Lush

Lush is a prominent British cosmetics brand with chains worldwide. Environmental issues are the primary concern for the firm, and the brand was created as a creative solution to make a positive impact on the environment. Lush is concerned with six aspects to support the environment, such as through packaging, raw materials, waste and recycling, energy, water, and communication. Lush produced about half of its products with no packaging and saved nearly 6 million plastic bottles globally by selling shampoo bars alone. If packaging is unavoidable, recycled materials are used, and the brand with 90% by weight of its packaging material is recycled, and the aim is to have 100% recyclable and compostable packaging. Further, Lush prefers to use ingredients that are produced in sustainable ways and avoid those that are not and also prefers products that are biodegradable. In terms of waste and recycling, all Lush packaging contains about 89% recycled content. Further, in making the production processes more energy efficient, Lush has gotten its staff to switch off any equipment or machine when not use in production or in the office, replacing less efficient equipment, generating some of its own energy on-site, and increasing insulation. Lush created and sold shampoo bars globally that helped avoid using an incredible amount of water: 450,000 litres a year. Communication is an essential medium to execute the objective of green marketing, as well as green cosmetics, and so, too, for Lush. Further, Lush shares its report on environmental performance on a yearly basis and maintains green issues from the entire organisation and also through the campaign with the consumers to bring important topics to light.

L'Oreal

L'Oreal commenced its revolutionary development of ingredients by adopting green chemistry in 2007, an ecofriendly synthesis process achieved through the development of Pro-Xylane, a new anti-aging molecule. Further, L'Oreal also discovered the botanical biotechnologies area by representing it as an incredible source of innovation for beauty, in addition to or with the original active ingredients. According to L'Oreal, one of the remarkable characteristics of plants is their capacity to regenerate after various types of aggression, where the capacity is related to the existence of stem cells in the leaves, roots, and buds—for example, pruning roses in the fall. Also, from the stem cell cultures of a unique species of Delbard rose, the L'Oreal teams managed to obtain an extract that acts on skin regeneration, where the test shows an increase in the thickness of the epidermis, the secretion of growth factor, and regeneration of tissues. Further, to satisfy consumers' demand in terms of green cosmetics expectations, L'Oreal and other manufacturers do not hesitate to integrate an environmental dimension into their strategy. For instance, by creating sustainable partnerships with local producers or by growing their ingredients, brands like Sanaflore, Natura, Chanel, and Yves Rocher can guarantee to their consumers the origin and the quality of their raw materials.

Avon Products

Avon has a longstanding commitment to managing the environment. Its response to green marketing is not limited to only ingredients or the processes to produce the cosmetics products, but includes much more than that. The green action and effort by Avon cover the selection of natural ingredients to minimise the use of chemicals for its products, green buildings, emissions reduction and energy conservation, water conservation, and distribution. Avon supports sustainable building practices as part of its efforts to mitigate and reduce environmental impacts, which required it to design and build new facilities, as well as making renovations to existing facilities in accordance with the U.S. Green Building Council's Leadership in Energy and Environmental Design (LEED) Green Building Rating System certification standards. Furthermore, Avon became one of the first beauty firms to prioritise the reduction of greenhouse gas (GHG) emissions from its operations due to the awareness of climate change that resulted from fossil fuel use and the burning and clearing of tropical forests. Avon's efforts on this continue to focus on reducing its GHG emissions and energy consumption, as well as increasing the use of on-site renewable energy to reduce its carbon footprint. Also, Avon also continues to take steps to use water wisely and conserve the source to implement products to achieve zero water waste discharge in water-scarce countries where the business operates, especially in India, China, and Brazil. Moreover, terms of distribution, Avon has put forth effort to minimise fuel consumption and to focus on sourcing fuel with the lowest environmental impacts and embedded carbon footprint, which by doing so, it can increase fuel efficiency, decrease transport miles, and decrease related emissions and reduce costs.

Estee Lauder

According to Estee Lauder, green chemistry is a scientific framework that seeks to reduce the negative environmental impacts of chemical products and processes. Similar to L'Oreal, Estee Lauder supports the principles and has analysed their raw materials in terms of environmental impacts, ecotoxicity, persistence, and bioaccumulation. Therefore, the brand's chemists have to select ingredients stored in the green chemistry database according to the sustainability criteria. In terms of packaging, Estee Lauder—an early member of the Sustainable Packaging Coalition and the Sustainable Packaging Cosmetic Roundtable—supports the use of sustainable materials in its packaging and promotes responsible production practices. For example, Estee Lauder continued to encourage its suppliers to identify sustainable, renewable, and recycled materials, such as post-consumer recyclable (PCR) plastics, glass, metal, and paper. Also, Estee Lauder worked with its supplier to test the use of resins made from plant-based biopolymers for product packaging. Plant-based resins such as those derived from sugar cane, produce fewer greenhouse gas emissions than plastics made from fossil fuels.

Chanel

According to Nagasawa and Kizu (2012), green action is an important brand strategy to Chanel. It strongly emphasised the innovativeness of the material, technology, and the effects on the skin when they produced Sublimage Essential Revitalizing Concentrate in 2010 and distributed the public booklet to the media about their approach to the conservation of nature. For example, two products by Chanel are good examples of green cosmetics: "N°5" and Sublimage Essential Revitalizing Concentrate. Chanel created "N°5" from ingredients such as jasmine and Rose de Mai that was planted in its field in Grasse located in Southern France. In addition, Sublimage, as one of Chanel's skin care lines, has an active extract from vanilla panifolia in Madagascar, which was achieved through an inventive process. Further, Chanel used golden champa, grown in the Himalayas, for this skin care line. Finally, the firm entered into a partnership with Ladakh Society for Traditional Medicines (LSTM), a nongovernmental organisation (NGO) in the Himalayas, for natural resources and traditional knowledge and constructed a network for communication among the Amchi to support women and children in the area.

The cosmetics brands that support green marketing and sustainability are not limited to those globally known or mainstream brands only, but also those known to consumers with green preferences, as listed in Table 2.

Table 2 shows the emerging natural and green cosmetics brands in the industry. These brands are evidence that natural and green ingredients come from around the world; for example, the botanical products used in Juara come from Indonesia, and those for Le Couvent des Minimes from France. This is another positive response from the industry to consumer demands for natural and green cosmetics throughout the world.

The cosmetics industry is a promising industry that should not be abandoned in the evolution of green marketing. According to the previous cases, the trend for green chemistry in the cosmetics industry is emerging, particularly when the mainstream and premium cosmetics brands participated in the environment campaigns. Therefore, this trend shows some positive forecast over the next few years in this industry. By looking back at the Top 500 Most Valuable Global Brands in 2012, 16 cosmetics brands were listed, which consists of 3.2% out of 500 brands in various industries. This means that cosmetics still play significant and major roles in business and society after this industry was designated as 'recession-proof' in a series of articles by many scholars over time.

Table 2. Emerging natural and green cosmetics brands in the industry

Brands	Description
RMS Beauty	Natural products contain the absolute bare minimum ingredients.
Tracie Martyn	All of Martyn's products are free of dyes, petrochemicals, artificial fragrances, and extra fillers, leaving only super-strength skincare behind.
Seventh Generation	Natural ingredients like jojoba oil, oat extract, and tea tree oil for rejuvenation.
J.R. Watkins	Brand is known for its all-natural apothecary remedies and cooking extracts.
100% Pure	This line of carefully formulated skin care and fruit-pigmented cosmetics aims to create products using only pure, organic, and safe ingredients.
Sircuit	The products in this green beauty brand are cold-processed and formulated in small batches to ensure optimum freshness and efficacy.
Balanced Guru	Using certified organic ingredients, sustainable packaging, and aromatherapy, this brand covers all the basics of natural and green beauty needs.
Suki	Familiar ingredients like sugar, lemongrass, and coconut oil throughout its roster of products.
Tata Harper	Harper is committed to chemical-free products that make use of natural, bio-active ingredients in her skin care line.
ESPA	The company is dedicated to removing chemical "extras" from its skin care products and using natural ingredients as much as possible.
Votre Vu	Those looking for simple, effective formulas will appreciate the small-batch, botanically driven products. The Nouveau Glow Bilberry Bergamot Peel, for example, uses tomato, lemon, grapefruit, bilberry, paprika, bergamot, papaya, and little else to smooth skin naturally.
Kora Organics	The brand sticks to certified-organic ingredients and avoids any toxic or synthetic ones.
Juara	Using natural Indonesian ingredients (inspired by the founder's roots in Bali), this skin and body brand is known for bringing candlenut oil to the United States.
Antonym Cosmetics	This natural makeup line is fully certified organic by Ecocert, ensuring the highest quality and level of safety. The products make use of mineral pigments, and there are no animal-derived ingredients or synthetic components on the label. Even the eyeliner is enriched with maruba and jojoba oils, making this a great line for sensitive skin.
Le Couvent des Minimes	Using natural ingredients like rosehip oil (to protect skin), damask rosewater (to soften), and rose oil (to purify).

Source: 16 Natural and Organic Beauty Brands to Consider by Marissa Gold. Retrieved from glamour.com

Genuineness of Green Marketing in the Cosmetics Industry

First, the cosmetics industry could not be 100% purely green at the moment because it is impossible to produce cosmetics with 100% natural or organic-based products, which runs the gamut from the first process of ingredient selection to the finished product displayed at counters for consumers. Further, the direction of sustainability and green marketing is still ongoing, with various efforts from the cosmetics firms. The main key point is both academic and industry needs to define or, at least have some categories to elaborate, with the industry that having the effort to the green direction rather than generalise the definition as a whole. The scope of green as a concept is broad and complex because it can relate to issues such as ecological concerns, conservation (flora and fauna), corporate social responsibility (CSR), humanitarian concerns, fair trade, clean water, animal welfare, equality, and sustainability (Saha & Darnton, 2005). As a result, consumers remain confused regarding which brands are truly 'green' and how they can trust them. This is because most cosmetics or personal care products labelled "natural" contain some synthetic fragrances, petroleum by-product, or, at least, antimicrobial and antifungal properties. Therefore, the definition and understanding of green marketing in general and in terms of green cosmetics in particular must be defined by a certain composition.

Second, limited studies are being conducted, especially in the business and management field, that being natural or green is truly environmentally friendly in business. This is because the supply chain in production may have difficulties justifying itself as truly environmentally friendly because the quantity of plants needed to produce a tiny amount of certain ingredients for cosmetics would require large areas that need to be cultivated. However, in the West, many firms and corporations face social and legal pressure to adopt environmentally friendly business strategies (Csorba & Boglea, 2011). In contrast, chemistry scholars explain that the term 'green' implies the use of environmentally friendly material such as nontoxic and reusable reagents and solvents in the processes or the development of active catalysts and technologies consuming less energy (Cann & Connelly, 2000, Ryan & Tinnesand, 2000). The contrast of green or natural cosmetics concept to environmentally friendly among specialised fields is also an issue to resolve so that the understanding of green or natural in promoting the environmentally friendly goal will be aligned and standardised.

Furthermore, consumers nowadays are more knowledgeable and demanding—not only for natural ingredients to protect themselves from chemical usage and long-term damage, but also for ecofriendly packaging, where their buying behaviour could make a positive impact on the environment and others. According to Ramli (2015), cosmetics brands such as Avon started to focus on recycling and minimising material use as they strive to reduce waste along the production cycle, and Estee Lauder chemists selected the ingredients of products according to green chemistry sustainability criteria. These brands demonstrate some gradual changes to sustainability in cosmetics due to consumers' awareness of the goal of becoming environmentally friendly.

Communication Problem

Green marketing is an ongoing evolution, from resources to producing products, processes, supply chain management, marketing and distribution, and increasing consumers' awareness through communication. According to Duber-Smith's study (as cited in Nichol, 2010) misleading communication and exaggerated product claims are more likely to deter consumers from buying a company's products and open a business up to scrutiny. Therefore, it is important to have clear communication and transparency, which could be the key to a successful green marketing strategy in today's world, where it can help consumers increase their awareness, loyalty, and trust in products, especially in consumer products like cosmetics and personal care. For example, the firms' marketing departments need to communicate with consumers about the importance of green marketing in cosmetics and how their buying behaviour can affect the environment. This will give the perception to the consumers that the cosmetics brands that apply green marketing to their products are responsible brands, and product price may no longer be a major issue.

In the present, the sophisticated medium such as the internet platform and mobile to spread knowledge, awareness, and information is not fully utilised. The industry, through cosmetics firms as well as the governments and NGOs, can play their roles through advertisements, TV shows, and campaigns. They can start from a basic understanding of the green concept and later move to how they can contribute to realising the mission for green marketing in this industry. Many campaigns or existing advertisements are promoting the green campaign, but forgot to define the concept in the first place, which is very crucial to consumers, and not all consumers have the same level of understanding.

Clearer Product Labelling

In relation to their awareness and clear communication, consumers' nowadays rely heavily on the product label, claims, and marketing before deciding to purchase. This is because consumers are very particular about certain issues, such as animal testing (Adler et al., 2011), child labour (Omokhodion, Omokhodion & Odusote, 2006), religious restrictions for *halal* cosmetics (Ramli, 2015), environmental concerns (Alsmadi, 2007), and other ingredients identified as causing potential health concerns and skin allergies (Pauwels & Rogiers, 2010). Hence, consumers have the right to know the ingredients of the products before purchasing. Therefore, in order for the consumers to be well informed and trust the products, especially cosmetics and personal care items, the firms must be responsible for disclosing on the label the natural or green ingredients with percentages; some also claim to support sustainability by using a fair trade logo or an against animal testing logo, which is part of the green marketing for their brands.

The changing economic and demographic environment is creating an enormous market for the cosmetics industry. In addition to the ingredients and results from using the products, consumers are concerned about packaging. Some say that sustainable packaging could be interesting to add in their campaign to support green marketing, and some say it is not necessary. Furthermore, it is not among the top influencers of purchasing decisions by the consumers because what matters is the quality of the products and usage of the resource to produce the product. However, it is not that consumers are opposed to the notion of sustainable packaging, but that they are not willing to sacrifice in terms of pricing, performance, and convenience. Due to these factors, the Lush cosmetics brand, for instance, is selling naked products (no packaging) for its solid products like soaps, shampoos, and bath bar.

Consumers Will Not Pay High Prices

In marketing, the four core marketing factors, such as product, price, promotion, and place (distribution), play a crucial role in the business. This is what happened to green marketing in the cosmetics industry. Today, consumers are aware of the impact of supporting environmentally friendly products that not only benefit them, but also help the environment and support campaigns against animal testing, fair trade, democracy, and other issues. The problem for consumers when purchasing environmentally friendly products is the higher price than those that are considered less environmentally friendly. To some extent, this is related to the sustainable packaging mentioned before, which is costly. Moreover, this issue was raised recently by Jean-Paul Agon, the L'Oreal Group chairman and CEO, during the COP21 Summit in Paris, as cited by Bloomberg (2015). He discussed the challenge to provide green products, deliver them at a competitive price, and the view of progress on global sustainability, where he noted that the consumer wants greener products but refuses to pay extra for them. Therefore, the industry needs to reduce cost, especially in packaging, and at the same time support green marketing to save the environment.

Proposed Concept of Green Marketing in the Cosmetics Industry

In a broad context, green marketing could apply to various industries such automobile, consumer goods, finance and banking, beverages, engineering and information technology, healthcare, and others. However, to critically apply green marketing in an industry—for instance, the cosmetics industry—a specific concept of green marketing needs to be introduced because different industries have different customers' needs, natures, demands, capital structures, characteristics, and histories. Therefore, this chapter proposes a concept of green marketing in the cosmetics industry that will encourage an extension for further research in the future. Figure 2 demonstrates a proposed concept of green marketing in the cosmetics industry.

The proposed concept shows that green marketing in the cosmetics industry needs to consider four broad aspects, such as (1) environmental concerns, (2) management decision, (3) ethical and social concerns, and (4) new prospects (for consumers). Although the industry is moving forward to implement green marketing, the history of the industry (including its business) must not be ignored. As discussed earlier in this chapter, the history of cosmetics and the crucial role business plays in maintaining this industry must be part of management's consideration for their future products and businesses. With regard to this, the history of the cosmetics industry is embedded between green marketing and each of the four broad aspects. The significance of the business history in this proposed concept for green marketing in the cosmetics industry is that it could offer room for the cosmetics firms to look at and exploit the resources over time, which they can learn from particular periods—for example, the trends and how the cosmetics industry responded during the First World War, the Great Depression, Second World War, and the recent series of recessions. These periods of crises illustrate to some extent important strategies to the industry, and also they can learn the history of cosmetics consumers in terms of demand, trends, and awareness of quality products, which in this case refers to a

Figure 2. A proposed concept of green marketing for cosmetics industry

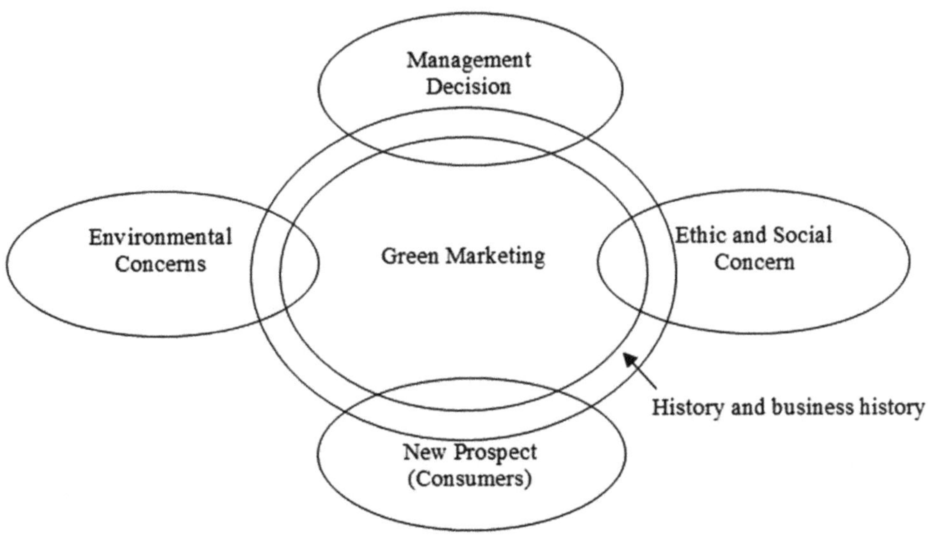

product that will not harm them or that can decrease environmental problems. The four broad areas to take under consideration are described in the following sections.

1. **Environmental Concerns:** Cosmetics firms today are focusing on the various green concepts in their processes and departments, other than green formulations, resource efficiency, and packaging, to reduce environmental impacts. Therefore, they could learn a lesson from the past, such as those crisis periods mentioned earlier. During those periods, some resources were rationed or very limited, but they were replaced by natural alternatives like burnt cork for mascara, cochineal or beetroot juice for lipstick, soda bicarbonate for deodorant, and a few more. Also, some cosmetics firms worked for the war effort; for example, Revlon factories made first-aid kits and dye markers for the U.S. Navy. Therefore, previously it was the crises that made the industry shift to use alternative resources.
2. **Management Decisions:** The management sectors of cosmetics firm that wanted to venture into green marketing also needs to revise the firm's and industry's history and how the businesses have performed over time. For example, a cosmetics firm that was created in the 1900s and still exists in the present needs to document and research its business history before making a decision to use only a business measurement tool like strengths, weaknesses, opportunities, and threats (SWOT) analysis. The significance of considering the history of cosmetics and the business history in the past could give a broad hint of how the industry performs over time particularly during a recession, and consumers' reaction when a new trend appears. Further, this will also give a unique corporate image for the firms, where the cosmetics firms will not only heavily depend on the current market and forecast, but also on learning from the past to improve their business. Moreover, this demonstrates that the heritage and origin of the firm are well preserved.
3. **Ethics and Social Concerns:** Green marketing is always associated with ethics and social concerns. This is due to the various definitions of green marketing. In the past, for example, during the Second World War when lipstick was less available due to the rationing of petroleum, women protested the War Production Board's plan to ration, arguing that it was good for the morale of the nation. Thus, what ethics and social concerns can learn from the past is customers' wants and needs, which is how green marketing emerged in the present cosmetic industry. Although investment in cosmetics firms appears slightly higher than usual, the demand and return profit can be positive and continuous due to the high awareness of consumers through global and technological advancement.
4. **New Prospects (Consumers):** The cosmetics industry always offers something new, trendy, ongoing, and sometimes phenomenal—for example, the global

boom of anti-aging cream and whitening cream in Asia. This is similar to green marketing in the cosmetics industry, where the sustainability trend and growing preference for green and natural cosmetics are regarded as recent driving forces. Estee Lauder was a pioneer of the 'gift with purchase' concept, and Avon Products (formerly known as California Perfume Company) was a pioneer of direct selling. Both became role models for other cosmetics brands, and their business models continue to be adopted and inherited by other brands. Therefore, green marketing in the cosmetics industry could be another new cycle of the phenomenon in the industry based on the history, current trend, and the forecast that were discussed in this chapter, which are expected to bring billions of more dollars in the future. Green marketing in the cosmetics industry could offer new prospects in the future, where strong cosmetics brands can lead this direction and open more opportunities to new entrants (entrepreneurs in small to medium enterprises) in the industry, similarly to what Estee Lauder and Avon had done in the industry. Although green and natural cosmetics can be considered a niche market, with the demand and awareness of consumers and the role of cosmetics brands, this niche market can become a mass market in the future.

In sum, the proposed concept of green marketing in the cosmetics industry is useful. The relevance of considering the history of cosmetics and the business history of the industry in each of the four aspects is that the outcome of the past could prompt the firms' decision to execute the implementation of green marketing for their cosmetics brands.

SOLUTIONS AND RECOMMENDATIONS

There are significant solutions and recommendations for green marketing in the cosmetics industry as it offers a new prospect in the future based on the historical cycle in the industry and trends.

First, the borderless world becomes an open market for every product worldwide, and this encourages healthy competition among manufacturers, making them more innovative, intensive, and concerned cosmetics brands among consumers. For example, gigantic brand names in the industry are gradually starting to venture into the green cosmetics market. The shifting to this niche market in the industry experienced at least two waves of natural products: first by botanicals formulae in the early and mid-1970s; and the second wave with the similar trend on fruit-based formulae but stronger phenomenon and demand that began in the mid-1980s and continues today

(Csorba & Boglea, 2011). Thus, this is evidence that green marketing is occurring sooner or later, starting with green formulae and raw resources.

Second, the Internet and communication technology have changed consumers' preferences due to their behaviours. The technology and innovation had encouraged consumers to be well informed and updated through smartphones and gadgets other than a common laptop, desktop, magazines, and newspapers on current issues such as environmental campaigns and against animal testing and recommendations for brands that support such matters in the market. Further, to survive in a continuously changing environment, understanding and adapting to changes in consumers' behaviour is an important key aspect (Song, kyeong Kim & Kim, 2001). Therefore, cosmetics brands should utilise the maximum potential of this medium to spread awareness of green products, also known as digital marketing and mobile communications. Mobile communications have a profound impact on consumer behaviour. Consumers are now more educated and informed than at any other time in history, raising their expectations of cosmetics products. Cosmetics are also associated with digital marketing, where, for example, mobile applications can be used to assess the safety of cosmetics products by the consumers. The potential of digital marketing and booming social media can help the online retailer share their experiences in selling directly to consumers. This has been a contrast to Swidi et al.'s (2010) findings that consumers' preferences have changed due to cultural changes. It is not cultural changes, but the trend in consumer behaviour that can encourage prospects for green marketing in the cosmetics industry.

Third, public engagement through educational events like public seminars and dialogues, workshops, campaigns, hands-on activities, and others can offer another source of new prospects in the cosmetics and personal care industry to promote green marketing and why it matters to them. This means that the promotion in the future could be more sustainable ways to live and consume. The green marketing must satisfy two objectives: (1) improved environmental quality and (2) customer satisfaction (Ottman, J. A., Stafford & Hartman, 2006). Therefore, through public engagement, the effort and objectives of green marketing can be satisfied because the awareness of its importance could reach consumers and they might respond positively, which could affect their buying behaviour and improve environmental quality. However, it is not easy to start with the consumer because consumers have different wants, needs, attitudes, beliefs, and knowledge. Although an interesting challenge in the green marketing agenda is to start with the consumers, more broadly in terms of researching the needs of the firm's other stakeholders and considering future generations of consumers also need to consider and pay attention (Dennis et al., 2005). In addition, the lack of awareness in parts of the world is the major constraint on the implementation of green marketing taking place worldwide. Launching a strong awareness of the environmental concern with the help of academicians, government bodies, NGOs, and corporate entities can actually help overcome this challenge. With regard to this, the strict government laws and regulations for the firms and consumers can enforce an eco-friendly norm and generate green society.

Finally, the role of strong cosmetics brands in the industry could make a significant impact on the consumers and the environment. This is because strong brands can offer a range of strategic marketing benefits, the product from a strong brand might be the premium brand, associated with perceived quality, a recognisable image, market leadership, and a differentiated position (Michell, King & Reast, 2001). Therefore, with the power of a strong brand name, those premium and mainstream cosmetics brands could lead and venture the green marketing in their product line. Although the premium brands charge higher prices than the other cosmetics brands, customers have a strong belief in the cost and value of these brands after making some comparisons and evaluations (Keller, 2003). The role of cosmetics firms should not consider a marketing mix only like products, price, promotion, and place (distribution), where they need to implement the green concept in, but also another aspect like through corporate social responsibility (CSR). This is because the firms are the backbone of the cosmetics brands, where consumers are aware of what are their people do and how they respond to the community and environmental issues. Hence, the influence of brand knowledge on consumers' buying behaviour could also be facilitated by brand attitude.

FUTURE RESEARCH DIRECTIONS

This chapter is an open door for future research of green marketing in the cosmetics industry. Some issues have been discussed, but can be researched in greater detail in the future—for example; building a sustainable brand in cosmetics by considering a differentiation of the products' attributes; applying the values of social responsibility in corporate branding; and core values in the green concept that influence continuity, consistency, and credibility in building these brands.

Further, a rethinking of green marketing in the cosmetics industry as a business strategy also requires a change in corporate cultures from the organisational aspect, management, people, aim, and others. These open up new opportunities to reassess other aspects of the business to compete within the industry, giving a 'win-win' outcome to businesses, partners, communities, and the environment. Green marketing as a business strategy can be risky because of some the issues discussed in this chapter, such as the definition of the green concept, the genuineness of green marketing in the cosmetics industry, communication problems, clearer product labelling, and consumers will not pay higher amounts for the green product. However, the cosmetics firms could take an alternative way as a stepping stone for this strategy through mergers and acquisitions like Estee Lauder and L'Oréal that created their natural or green product line from existing cosmetics brands. Moreover, this could be another future research direction for green marketing in the cosmetics industry as a business strategy.

Green marketing in the cosmetics industry can offer a new prospect and opportunities to existing firms for their brands and encourage new entrants (entrepreneurs in small to medium enterprises) to venture into a niche market that promises steady profit. However, besides the external environmental issues of waste and pollution, consumer awareness and demand, and extensive cultivation of raw material to produce green cosmetics, there are other issues that need to be addressed. These include animal testing, treatment of women and minority groups, belief system sensitivity, worker welfare, democracy at the workplace, public rights and accountability, and the impacts for populations from the decision of green marketing in the cosmetics industry. The consideration of these issues should not be separate entities as new business strategies can be considered within the green marketing concept to conduct business ethically.

CONCLUSION

In conclusion, the key concept of green marketing in the cosmetics industry relies on the cosmetics' brands philosophy of business. The green marketing agenda is still new in this industry, but is steadily going forward based on multiple industry reports, companies' historical records, and other evidence such as cosmetics magazines, newspapers, and consumer surveys. Therefore, the effort undertaken by the cosmetics industry to slowly shift to green marketing should not be underestimated because the return on investment (Mung & Lacroix, 2003) from this industry is huge, as proven by historical records. Furthermore, the newborn cosmetics brands, which were created particularly for natural and green cosmetics, should not be abandoned because they could give a challenge to those premium brands. Otherwise, those gigantic cosmetics brands will not take over or acquire those brands specialising in this area. However, many of the issues discussed will necessarily challenge the very foundations of the green marketing concept in the cosmetics industry, which often seem light and easy.

The current business environment demonstrates that the investment of green marketing in the cosmetics industry is a promising prospect and feasible for the following reasons. First, the increasing number of consumers with green and natural preferences due to growing concern over issues like climate change. Second, cosmetics consumers are seeking natural and safe products, thereby explaining why green cosmetics or cosmetics with green marketing have boomed in recent years. Third, the new generations are becoming more knowledgeable and highly educated; thus, they demand safe products that are in line with globalisation and technological advances. Finally, natural and green cosmetics present excellent business opportunities; particularly in Asia, where demand is high and sustainable resources are available.

REFERENCES

Adler, S., Basketter, D., Creton, S., Pelkonen, O., van Benthem, J., Zuang, V., & Zaldivar, J.-M. et al. (2011). Alternative (non-animal) methods for cosmetics testing: Current status and future prospects—2010. *Archives of Toxicology*, *85*(5), 367–485. doi:10.1007/s00204-011-0693-2 PMID:21533817

Alsmadi, S. (2007). Green marketing and the concern over the environment: Measuring environmental consciousness of Jordanian consumers. *Journal of Promotion Management*, *13*(3-4), 339–361. doi:10.1080/10496490802306905

Banyte, J., Brazioniene, L. & Gadeikiene, A. (2015). Expression of green marketing developing the conception of corporate social responsibility. *Engineering Economics, 21*(5).

Bird, L., & Sumner, J. (2010). *Green power marketing in the United States: a status report (2009 data).* Retrieved from: http://www.nrel.gov/docs/fy11osti/49403.pdf

Blanco-Dávila, F. (2000). Beauty and the body: The origins of cosmetics. *Plastic and Reconstructive Surgery*, *105*(3), 1196–1204. doi:10.1097/00006534-200003000-00058 PMID:10724281

Bloomberg, L. P. (2015). *L'Oreal CEO: Commitment to Make Every Product Green.* Retrieved December 10, 2015, from http://www.bloomberg.com/news/videos/2015-12-04/l-oreal-ceo-commitment-to-make-every-product-green

Cann, M. C., & Connelly, M. E. (2000). *Real-world cases in green chemistry.* Washington, DC: American Chemical Society.

Carlson, L., Grove, S. J., & Kangun, N. (1993). A content analysis of environmental advertising claims: A matrix method approach. *Journal of Advertising*, *22*(3), 27–39. doi:10.1080/00913367.1993.10673409

Cohen, M. (1999). *Cosmetics and perfumes, Egypt, 10,000 BCE.* Retrieved November 13, 2015, from http://www.smith.edu/hsc/museum/ancient_inventions/hsc01b.htm

Csorba, L. M. & Boglea, V. A. (2011). Sustainable cosmetics: A major instrument in protecting the consumer's interest. *Regional and Business Studies, 3*(1).

Davis, J. J. (1993). Strategies for environmental advertising. *Journal of Consumer Marketing, 10*(2), 19–36. doi:10.1108/07363769310039102

Hennison, K., & Kinnear, T. (1976). *Ecological marketing*. Englewood Cliffs, NJ: Prentice Hall.

Johri, L. M., & Sahasakmontri, K. (1998). Green marketing of cosmetics and toiletries in Thailand. *Journal of Consumer Marketing, 15*(3), 265–281. doi:10.1108/07363769810219134

Jones, G. (2011). Globalization and beauty: A historical and firm perspective. *Ou Mei yan Jiu* [Eur America], *41*, 885-916.

Kaufmann, H. R., Panni, M., & Orphanidou, Y. (2012). Factors affecting consumers' green purchasing behavior: An integrated conceptual framework. *Amfiteatru Economic, 15*(31), 50–69.

Keller, K. L. (2003). Brand synthesis: The multidimensionality of brand knowledge. *The Journal of Consumer Research, 29*(4), 595–600. doi:10.1086/346254

Kumar, S. (2005). Exploratory analysis of global cosmetic industry: Major players, technology and market trends. *Technovation, 25*(11), 1263–1272. doi:10.1016/j.technovation.2004.07.003

Lawrence, S. (2015). *Beetroot and boot polish: How Britain's women faced World War 2 without make-up*. Retrieved November 20, 2015, from http://www.telegraph.co.uk/women/womens-life/11393852/Beauty-in-World-War-2-How-Britains-women-stayed-glamorous.html

Lee, J., & Barrett, P. (1996). *Body in need of reshaping*. Marketing, UK.

Lopes, T. D. S. (2002). Brands and the evolution of multinationals in alcoholic beverages. *Business History, 44*(3), 1–30. doi:10.1080/713999275

Lopes, T. D. S. (2007). *Global brands: The evolution of multinationals in alcoholic beverages*. Cambridge University Press. doi:10.1017/CBO9780511550911

Manko, K. L. (2001). A depression-proof business strategy: The California Perfume Company's motivational literature. *Beauty and Business*, 142-168.

Mark, S. H., & Rous, S. I. (2014). *A brief history of cosmetics by Baroness Anastasia Alexandrovna Andreeva (OL)*. Retrieved online on November 14, 2015,from http://www.florilegium.org

Matthes, J., Wonneberger, A., & Schmuck, D. (2014). Consumers green involvement and the persuasive effects of emotional versus functional ads. *Journal of Business Research, 67*(9), 1885–1893. doi:10.1016/j.jbusres.2013.11.054

Michell, P., King, J., & Reast, J. (2001). Brand values related to industrial products. *Industrial Marketing Management, 30*(5), 415–425. doi:10.1016/S0019-8501(99)00097-8

Mung, E., & Lacroix, T. (2003). *France: the narrow path. In Immigrant Entrepreneurs. Venturing Abroad in the Age of Globalisation* (pp. 173–194). Oxford, UK: Berg.

Nagasawa, S., & Kizu, Y. (2012). Green action as a luxury strategy in the field of cosmetics. *Waseda Business and Economics Studies Departmental Bulletin Paper, 48*, 1–17.

Nichol, K. (2010), *Sustainable Cosmetics Summit to explore green marketing challenges*. Retrieved October 9, 2015, from http://www.cosmeticsdesign.com/Market-Trends/Sustainable-Cosmetics-Summit-to-explore-green-marketing-challenges

Obermiller, C. (1995). The baby is sick/the baby is well: A test of environmental communication appeals. *Journal of Advertising, 24*(2), 55–70. doi:10.1080/00913367.1995.10673476

Ogilvie, M., & Ryan, M. (2011). Lipstick: More than a fashion trend. *Research Journal of Social Science and Management, 1*(6), 117–128.

Olsen, M. C., Slotegraaf, R. J., & Chandukala, S. R. (2014). Green claims and message frames: How green new products change brand attitude. *Journal of Marketing, 78*(5), 119–137. doi:10.1509/jm.13.0387

Omokhodion, F., Omokhodion, S., & Odusote, T. (2006). Perceptions of child labour among working children in Ibadan, Nigeria. *Child: Care, Health and Development, 32*(3), 281–286. doi:10.1111/j.1365-2214.2006.00585.x PMID:16634973

Ottman, J. (2011). *The new rules of green marketing: Strategies, tools, and inspiration for sustainable branding*. San Francisco: Berrett-Koehler Publishers.

Ottman, J. A. (1992). Industrys response to green consumerism. *The Journal of Business Strategy, 13*(4), 3–7. doi:10.1108/eb039498 PMID:10120307

Ottman, J. A., Stafford, E. R., & Hartman, C. L. (2006). Avoiding green marketing myopia: Ways to improve consumer appeal for environmentally preferable products. *Environment: Science and Policy for Sustainable Development, 48*(5), 22–36. doi:10.3200/ENVT.48.5.22-36

Pauwels, M., & Rogiers, V. (2010). Human health safety evaluation of cosmetics in the EU: A legally imposed challenge to science. *Toxicology and Applied Pharmacology, 243*(2), 260–274. doi:10.1016/j.taap.2009.12.007 PMID:20006634

Peattie, K., & Charter, M. (2003). Green marketing. *The Marketing Book, 5*, 726–755.

Peattie, K., & Crane, A. (2005). Green marketing: Legend, myth, farce or prophesy? *Qualitative Market Research: An International Journal, 8*(4), 357–370. doi:10.1108/13522750510619733

Penning, A. (2013). *Demand for organic beauty to grow over $13 billion by 2018, report says*. Retrieved October 25, 2015, from http://www.cosmeticsandtoiletries.com/formulating/category/natural/Demand-for-Organic-Beauty-to-Grow-to-Over-13-Billion-by-2018-Report-Says-213160491.html

Philippe, M., Didillon, B., & Gilbert, L. (2012). Industrial commitment to green and sustainable chemistry: Using renewable materials & developing eco-friendly processes and ingredients in cosmetics. *Green Chemistry, 14*(4), 952–956. doi:10.1039/c2gc16341a

Pitman, S. (2010). *Key cosmetics players to sustainability as way out of recession*. Retrieved November 7, 2015, from http://www.cosmeticsdesign-europe.com/Business-Financial/Key-cosmetics-players-point-to-sustainability-as-way-out-of-recession

Polonsky, M. J. (1994). An introduction to green marketing. *Electronic Green Journal, 1*(2), 1–10.

Polonsky, M. J., & Rosenberger, P. J. III. (2001). Reevaluating green marketing: A strategic approach. *Business Horizons, 44*(5), 21–30. doi:10.1016/S0007-6813(01)80057-4

Ramli, N. S. (2015). Immigrant entrepreneurs on the worlds successful global brands in the cosmetic industry. *Procedia: Social and Behavioral Sciences, 195*, 113–122. doi:10.1016/j.sbspro.2015.06.417

Ryan, M. A., & Tinnesand, M. (2000). *Introduction to green chemistry*. Washington, DC: American Chemical Society.

Saha, M., & Darnton, G. (2005). Green companies or green con-panies: Are companies really green, or are they pretending to be? *Business and Society Review, 110*(2), 117–157. doi:10.1111/j.0045-3609.2005.00007.x

Shrivastava, P. (1994). Castrated environment: Greening organizational studies. *Organization Studies, 15*(5), 705–726. doi:10.1177/017084069401500504

Simon, F. L. (1992). Marketing green products in the triad. *The Columbia Journal of World Business, 27*(3-4), 268–285.

Song, H. S., Kyeong Kim, J., & Kim, S. H. (2001). Mining the change of customer behavior in an Internet shopping mall. *Expert Systems with Applications, 21*(3), 157–168. doi:10.1016/S0957-4174(01)00037-9

Sweha, F. (1982). Kohl along history in medicine and cosmetics. *Histoire des Sciences Medicales, 17*(2), 182–183. PMID:11612287

Swidi, A., Cheng, W., Hassan, M. G., Al-Hosam, A., & Mohd Kassim, A. W. (2010). The mainstream cosmetics industry in Malaysia and the emergence, growth, and prospects of halal cosmetics.*The Third International Conference on International Studies.*

Van Dam, Y. K., & Apeldoorn, P. A. (1996). Sustainable marketing. *Journal of Macromarketing, 16*(2), 45–56. doi:10.1177/027614679601600204

Wheeler, D. (1993). Auditing for sustainability: Philosophy and practice of The Body Shop International. *Eco-Management and Auditing, 1*(1), 10–16. doi:10.1002/ema.170

Wong, V., Turner, W., & Stoneman, P. (1996). Marketing strategies and market prospects for environmentally-friendly consumer products. *British Journal of Management, 7*(3), 263–281. doi:10.1111/j.1467-8551.1996.tb00119.x

KEY TERMS AND DEFINITIONS

Aesthetic: Appreciative of, responsive to, relating to, or dealing with; zealous about the beautiful, pleasing in appearance, art in cosmetics.

Exfoliate: To remove the top layer of skin.

Halal: Anything that is lawful in Islamic law; prohibits the consumption of alcohol, pork, or pork by-products and by-products of animals that aren't slaughtered according to Islamic law. Products that do not conform are known as '*haram*' (prohibited).

Mainstream Cosmetics Brands: Refers to cosmetics that are readily available to and appealing to the general public.

Natural Cosmetics: Cosmetics whose ingredients are derived from nature without inclusion or interference of synthesis chemicals.

Organic Cosmetics: Cosmetics with components that are obtained through a predefined, strict, and regulated farming process.

Premium Cosmetics Brands: Refers to less ostentatious, more accessible, more rational products; the best within the industry according to customer satisfaction and precision in fabrication.

Pro-Xylane: A sugar-protein derived from xylose (a natural sugar) found in beech trees, a key ingredient of antiwrinkle skincare products.

Chapter 8
Green Airport Investments to Mitigate Externalities:
Procedural and Technological Strategies

Maria Nadia Postorino
University Mediterranea of Reggio Calabria, Italy

Luca Mantecchini
University of Bologna, Italy

Filippo Paganelli
University of Bologna, Italy

ABSTRACT

Transport systems are important pollution sources, mainly in terms of greenhouse gases, noise and land consumption. To mitigate the problem and safeguard airport development at the same time, the involved stakeholders are fixing goals, priorities and duties in order to promote the sustainable development of the air transport industry at global level and the wellness of local communities as well. It is desirable to estimate airport noise and carbon impacts in order to suitably manage them and identify strategies in line with the concept of green economy. In this chapter, a general framework to identify optimal procedures and methods to evaluate the effectiveness of policies addressed to reduce airport impacts on the airport surroundings is proposed. The case study of the airport of Bologna is presented as an example of Transport Company that effectively operates to minimize its noise and carbon impacts. According to the proposed general framework, impacts and estimated costs to achieve the status of green company have been computed.

DOI: 10.4018/978-1-5225-2075-7.ch008

INTRODUCTION

Transport activities allow displacement of both people and goods – which are variously located in time and space – to fulfil activities and production needs. Transport systems have always had an important role for the development and control of a territorial system. Since the Roman Age, roads and bridges have followed military conquests in order to guarantee supplies to troops first, and then a widespread transport network for trading and territory development. The road network was the connective tissue linking the ancient Rome to the distant provinces with a total length of about 100.000 Km at the Roman Empire's maximum extent. The availability of well-established roads, as the renowned Silk Route, was the premise to start trading relationships among distant areas, encourage the alliance of civilisations, and explore new lands. In the ancient times, a crucial role in perishable and raw materials restocking as well as export of finished products was played mainly by harbours, which made it possible also the exploration of distant and unknown lands. After the discovery of the New World, further inventions and evolutions of transport means led to the development of mass transit systems, which made available travels to a large percentage of population. Later on, and in particular after World War II, more and more significant traffic volumes developed along routes. Airports took the role of harbours in being strategic nodes of the worldwide transport network for both passengers and freight. Routes have linked first cities and countries where the economic activities were more important, then all countries all over the world. Such network has established relationships among distant areas and has had undeniable advantages for the several actors involved in the production, management and supply of the air transport.

Despite their important role, however transport systems are important pollution sources, mainly in terms of greenhouse gases (GHG), noise and land consumption. According to some recent figures (Fulton et al., 2009), transport systems account for 22% of the total amount of GHG emissions and at European level this percentage increases to 25% (EEA, 2012). Atmospheric pollution and induced climate changes are then some of the most important externalities taken into consideration to measure the performances of transport companies. Nevertheless, in specific contexts such as airports located in the neighbouring of densely urbanised areas, noise as well might be a relevant impact. Infrastructure interventions within airport boundaries – for example - might aim at both enhancing capacity and driving airborne traffic over different areas to reduce noise emission – e.g., new runways. However, it requires relevant monetary investments as well as the availability of large areas and then is considered only at large hub airports. Airport infrastructures can be examined under several points of view. From a managerial point of view, traditionally there has been a split between public and private airport facilities management, while the assets are commonly public owned. From the infrastructure point of view, key topics have been airport location and development plans within and outside airport boundaries. All those decisions entail consequences on the territory, airport managers' policies and, finally, on the relationships between airport and territory.

As nodes of a wide transport network – which includes also the surface transport networks linking airports to the main cities they serve – the airport location is not trivial. Particularly, there is a dualism between airport proximity to or distance from the relevant built-up areas. From one side, proximity strengthens the relationships with the territory, particularly by benefitting from road and rail networks to enhance the airport catchment area. From the other side, distant airports are preferred to protect the territory and its communities from the detrimental effects caused by the airport presence. Such protection is counterbalanced by the need to realize a suitable surface access network, which is a relevant land-consuming and potentially polluting activity – particularly if a wide-ranging modal split is expected. Moreover, features such as itineraries, frequencies, travel times, intermediate stops play a key role in defining the overall travel cost perceived by airport users, and as far as the relative distance between cities and airport increases the attractiveness of this latter could decrease, particularly if the offered air services are not relevant.

This chapter investigates technical and organisational solutions addressed to reduce Landing/Take Off induced GHG and noise emissions through green investments and projects in a context of existing interactions between airport and territory. To achieve sustainability, the EU has recently proposed many long-term policy actions to create a common framework among Member States to deal with climate changes (European Commission, 2011). Particularly, transport companies generate local impacts that can be grouped into two macro-classes: impacts produced by the infrastructure itself and impacts produced by the transport function. As for the second class – which will be analysed in the following – airports with intensive movements produce several environmental impacts that reduce the wellness degree of the surrounding communities. To mitigate the problem and safeguard airport development opportunities at the same time, the main involved associations and governmental bodies are in charge of setting goals, priorities and duties in order to promote the sustainable development of the air transport industry within a common framework at the global level and the balanced wellness of local communities as well. In details, several accreditation rules have been established to reward airport companies that realize effective actions addressed to reduce impacts stemming from their transport function.

The most relevant airport impacts so far are noise and GHG emissions. As for noise, although technological improvements in aircraft design and more severe regulations have resulted in a softening of the issue in absolute terms, however the increasing traffic level makes the problem still relevant due to the cumulative effects of "noise events" during the day. Airport operators failing in managing properly their noise impacts might incur in traffic restrictions with the side effect of reducing their transport offer as well as their revenues.

As for GHG emissions, the concept of "carbon footprint" developed in the last decades refers to the total amount of greenhouse gases – in particular carbon dioxide, CO_2 – produced to support directly and indirectly human activities. Thus, airport operators should identify their "carbon footprint" – due not only to aircraft-related operations but also to landside and airside on-ground operations (e.g., handling) and ground access transport modes – to achieve sustainability and ultimately international accreditation.

It is desirable to estimate airport noise and carbon emissions, in order to manage suitably these impacts and identify strategies and actions coping with the concept of green companies and economy. Apart from rules and goals set by external Authorities, the identification of "green" strategies to reduce air transport impacts – among them the use of solar plants to produce energy or electric handling vehicles instead of fuel engine ones – is under the airport competence. The implementation of such strategies generally requires financial efforts to comply with the concept of green companies.

In this light, methodological approaches able to identify not only the whole impacts – noise or carbon – but also the main sources and/or elements responsible for the highest shares of the total emission help to evaluate the effectiveness of transport-related policies and investments addressed to reduce the airport impacts.

Some accreditation procedures are in place to reward airport companies that realize effective actions to gain environmental sustainability. However, investments made by airports to achieve a green status have to be financially sustainable too, i.e. the expected reduction of environmental impacts should be compared with the financial sustainability of the implemented measures.

Starting from the above overview, in this chapter a general framework to identify optimal procedures/actions to evaluate the effectiveness of transport related policies to reduce airport impacts on the airport surrounding areas is proposed. In particular, the actions implemented by Bologna Airport Company to reduce both noise levels and carbon footprint due to the transport function are here presented as a case study, with a specific reference to the required financial efforts and attained environmental benefits.

In this authors' opinion, the topic and the proposed framework are of utmost importance as far as airport infrastructure development and relationship with the territory are concerned. Literature and evidence from real case studies show that a well-connected airport – both in terms of air services and surface transport networks – is a key driver for the development of the territory. However, side-effects such as polluting emissions and noise can harm this win-win relationship. Airport managements are requested to look for the smoothest and seamless opportunities to realize satisfactory trip experiences for passengers and, at the same time, seek for close cooperation with local bodies to integrate positively the airport in the territorial context as far as the wellness of living communities is concerned. Involved players should ensure reliable services by pursuing green attitudes, without losing the focus on investment and users' quality of service and security.

BACKGROUND: IMPACTS DUE TO THE AIRPORT TRANSPORT FUNCTION

As briefly described in the introduction, the main environmental effects produced by the airport transport function are noise and GHG emissions.

Noise effects due to the use of jet engines are known since 1950s. Noise is associated to aircraft operations (flyovers, landings, take-offs), although in different ways and at different spatial levels depending on the activity (Schipper et al., 2001; Postorino & Mantecchini, 2016). Over time, the focus has switched from the single event to the cumulative effects and many authors (Yu et al., 2004; Schürmann et al., 2007; Unal et al., 2005; Lu & Morrell, 2006) have studied social and monetary impacts of noise. Scientific literature extensively agrees in linking aircraft induced noise with detrimental effects on human health such as annoyance (Miedema & Vos, 1998; WHO, 2011), cardiovascular or psychological diseases (Smith, 2002; Franssen et al., 2004) and sleep disturbance (Wijnen & Visser, 2003). In addition, airport noise has also a detrimental effect on property values (Uyeno et al., 1993; Espey & Lopez, 2000; Nelson, 2004; McMillen, 2004; Lu & Morrell, 2006; Cohen & Coughlin, 2008).

The ICAO Committee on Aviation Environmental Protection – dealing with air traffic noise problems – has introduced in 2008 the "balanced approach" based on four main areas where actions can be implemented to mitigate aviation noise negative effects:

- Noise decrease at source, i.e. revision of existing technological standards related to aircraft noise;
- Regulation and land-use planning and management, i.e. detailed policy guidelines concerning land-use around airports;
- Noise Abatement Procedures (NAPs), i.e. operational flight procedures designed to minimize the noise footprint generated by aircraft operations;
- Air traffic operational restrictions, introduced to reduce or limit air traffic in noise-sensitive airports, particularly during night and evening periods.

As for the first area, technological improvements and better understanding of aerodynamics principles led to the introduction of thrusters, improved aircraft design and more detailed aircraft classification (Annex 16 ICAO). At the same time, older aircraft were progressively phased out, thus inducing a reduction of the equivalent noise level under 65dB (Nelson, 2004). On the other hand, some on ground measures have been adopted, such as the use of barriers – sheds or banks - to hamper sound diffusion (Upham et al., 2003). The second area of actions deals with avoiding annoyance on future enlargement of urban districts. In this case, governmental bodies are in charge of planning a suitable use of airport neighbouring to avoid urban development plans and mainly the construction of buildings such as schools and hospitals. The third area refers to variations of standard Instrumental Flight Rules (IFR) during landing/take-offs. The goal is to direct aircraft over unpopulated or less built-up areas. The most common NAP measures, which have been largely applied mainly at large airports in EU, are tailored trajectories, thrust cutbacks under/over a given threshold and distance from the runway (FAA, 1993; Filippone, 2014), the use of fixed – usually steeper – climb/descent ratios. While technical and infrastructural improvements generally take many years, NAPs provide an immediate reduction of noise and a conservation or improvement of air transport capacity, by maintaining at the same time high levels of safety even under strict environmental constraints. Heterogeneous national regulatory frameworks and concern at local level, coupled with inobservance of local conditions (i.e. perceived noise and amount of involved population) have been the main drawbacks to the effectiveness of NAPs (Postorino & Mantecchini, 2016; Erkelens, 2000; Hebly & Visser, 2008; Girvin, 2009; Bentes et al., 2011, 2013). Finally, the forth area, concerning operational restrictions such as a capping of the number of movements during given periods of the day – following the EU Directive 2002/49/EC (Upham et al., 2003) – should be applied only as extreme measure, after a careful analysis of the benefits attainable from other solutions (ICAO, 2008).

Given the importance of noise effects on the involved population, several other documents exist that deal with mitigation measures and monitoring actions. The ICAO Annex 16 defines criteria for noise monitoring around the airport and rules on the implementation of noise reduction operational procedures. This document is also supported by several international documents and regulatory acts dealing with air traffic noise issued by many regulatory bodies (for example 2002/30/EC and 2002/49/EC). In addition, the "Noise Charge Scheme" refers to measures addressed to reduce noise impacts through aeronautical charge modulation, i.e. by penalising night and evening movements. The idea to apply environmental charges in air transport came out thirty years ago in the context of OECD (Pearce, 1976) by the introduction of a charge proportional to the number of people suffering from airport noise. Finally, the "Polluter Pays Principle" claims that the amount of environmental damages and disturbance caused by transport activities is paid by the polluter (Turner et al., 1994) as an "addition" or a "deduction" to the normal amount of taxes paid, or as a real "environmental tax" (noise tax).

Over time, the concern on airport-induced impacts has switched from noise to noxious GHG emissions due to aircraft, handling vehicles and vehicles used by passengers to reach the airport from the catchment area. Impacts caused by noxious emissions are mainly due to carbon dioxide (CO_2) with smaller contributions of sulphur oxide (SOx), nitrogen (NOx) and particulate (PMx) depending on the fuel characteristics as well as engine performances. Nowadays, airports all over the world are doing great efforts towards sustainable development, which can be defined as "the use of resources to guarantee needs while preserving the environment". In this context, the estimation of the carbon emissions due to the airport transport function has become particularly relevant (Lu & Morrell, 2006; Schürmann et al., 2007; Daley & Preston, 2009; Miyoshi & Mason, 2013; Ryley et al. 2013). The total amount of GHG produced to support both directly and indirectly human activities has been labelled in the scientific literature as "Carbon Footprint" and it can be derived for whichever entity (individual, city, nations) and site (house, industry, transport node). ICAO recognized the importance of the airport carbon footprint since 2007, when the report "Carbon emission calculator" – successfully launched in 2008 – started and was then followed by other reports (e.g. ICAO, 2010, 2011). It is desirable that the overall impacts produced by airport nodes – particularly CO_2 – are estimated and suitably managed (Graham, 2003). Guidelines specifically dealing with airport GHG reduction have been published by both ACI and ACRP in 2009. A comprehensive approach able to identify the "Airport Carbon Footprint" due not only to aircraft-related operations but also to land airport activities (e.g., handling) and surface connecting transport modes has been proposed by Postorino (2010) and Postorino and Mantecchini (2014).

Given the importance of the issue, the Airport Carbon Accreditation programme launched in 2009 by ACI Europe has the aim to reduce airport carbon emissions and, ultimately, neutralize the carbon footprint. The aim of the programme is to push and enable airports to implement best practice for carbon and energy management processes and to gain public recognition for their achievements. It involves also the improvement of surface accessibility by public transport and new business opportunities through the "triple helix" cooperation involving airport stakeholders, research institutes and public authorities. The Airport Region Conference (ARC) showed that actions involving both airport operations and surface access modes (Budd et al., 2011) have greater impacts than single actions. Several European airports gained such certification: currently, 92 airports are involved in this programme, covering 63.9% of EU air passenger traffic (ACI Europe, 2015). In addition, 20 airports have reached carbon neutrality status for the activities within their direct control (10 airports in Sweden, 2 in Norway, 2 in Netherlands, 4 in Italy and 2 in Turkey). Airports undergo a four-step certification process with acknowledgement of improvements at each stage: level 1 (Mapping), requires airports to produce an externally verified carbon footprint estimation (stemming from several sources) along with evidence of a publically available environmental / carbon policy endorsed at the highest level of airport management. The carbon footprint serves as basis for developing carbon management and engagement plans (level 2 Reduction and level 3 Optimisation) through which airports commit themselves to reduce carbon footprint on yearly basis. Airports may then achieve CO_2 neutrality by offsetting their residual emissions (level 3+: Neutrality).

In recent years, the Decarbonizing Airport Regions project (dAIR, http://www.dairproject.eu/) has been put in place at EU level to assess policies addressed to reduce carbon impacts due to airport activities and airport surface access modes. Particularly, the project has defined emission standards and procedures to obtain a reduction of airport operation CO_2 emissions (handling operations, airside traffic and power/heating/cooling sources within terminals).

Figure 1 summarizes noise and carbon impacts that depend on two main transport variables: movements and passengers. In fact, the number of movements – and then aircraft – depends on the air demand level (passenger) in the catchment area. Aircraft in turn require handling vehicles for all the operations in the airside (such as refuelling, passenger boarding/disembarkation, cleaning, pushback). Aircraft then generate direct and indirect noise and carbon impacts – the indirect ones due to handling vehicles required for each movement. On the other hand, passengers use several surface transport modes to reach the airport from the catchment area. Among those, cars generate the most relevant carbon impacts.

Figure 1. Main sources of airport environmental impacts

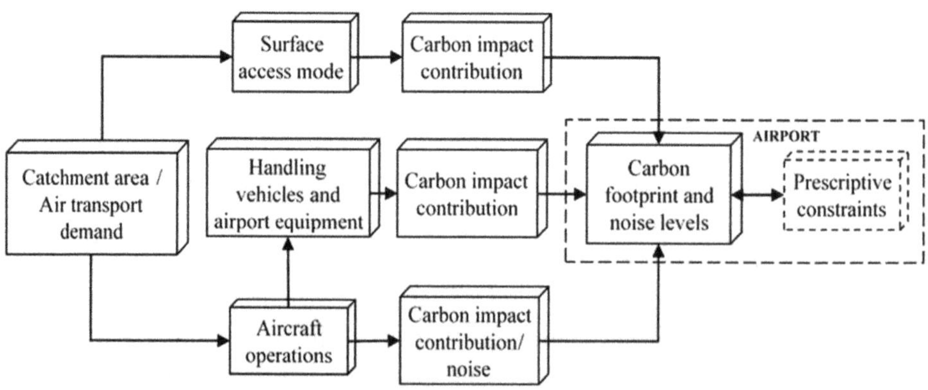

Starting from this framework, the following sections describe the methodological approach to quantify noise and carbon effects starting from the transport relevant variables (passengers and movements).

THE GENERAL FRAMEWORK TO ASSESS THE EFFECTS OF ACTIONS

Airport development projects have been recently accompanied by actions addressed to improve their environmental sustainability, such as NAPs to reduce noise impacts on the surrounding communities or the already described Airport Carbon Accreditation Scheme to achieve carbon neutrality.

As for noise, it is a relevant hurdle between air traffic expansion and welfare of local communities around airports. The noise impact generated by an airport is identified by using noise contours. A noise contour is defined as a line on a geographical map representing equal levels of noise exposure (typically 65, 70, and 75 dBA, ranging from moderate to significant). Starting from airport operational characteristics – such as number of movements and their day-evening-night distribution, aircraft type and approaching path – the noise contours identifying noise levels imposed by regulatory frameworks are drawn by using noise simulation models such as INM (FAA, 2007). The number of movements during a given time interval, the aircraft type and the distribution of movements during the day depend on airline schedule at the airport. On the other hand, the percentage of runway heads utilization – and then the effects of noise on the territory linked to the resulting approaching path – depends on navigation systems, visibility, congestion along the route defining the trajectories to be followed during landing and take-off.

Sound level is the most used metric to evaluate human long-term exposure to noise. To deal with noise variability, magnitude and frequency, regulations concerning noise annoyance are based on the equivalent sound level (Leq), which depends on the duration of the event T and on the variation of sound pressure over time with reference to a standard pressure value (see ISO 1996 and ISO 3891). The Italian reference legislation (DM 14/11/1997 and DM 31/10/1997) defines the equivalent sound level for airports as the Airport Noise Evaluation Index (L_{VA}) with reference to a 21 days period (chosen within the following periods: October 1st - January 31th, February 1st - May 31th and June 1st - September 30th). The daily noise value (both daytime and night-time components, the evening or night-time event weighting 5 or 10 times more than a daytime event), the number of operations and the equivalent sound level compressed in 1 second (SEL) are the most important parameters to compute L_{VA}.

On the other hand, noise actual impact depends on activities and population's level of annoyance. Generally, high noise levels in densely populated areas are more relevant than the same levels in uninhabited areas. The equal loudness contour area alone does not give information about the impact on the affected population unless it is connected to the land-use characteristics. In this light, Geographic Information Systems helps identifying the number of living people and dwellings, type of buildings and other human-related features in the geographical area interested by noise.

Noise contours and territory features are the factors required to measure the effectiveness of actions addressed to reduce noise impacts.

Figure 2 depicts the methodological approach proposed to assess the effects of airport noise on the territory surrounding the airport itself. The Noise and Territory Overlap (NTO) index – which is the parameter proposed by Postorino and Mantecchini (2016) – synthesizes the impacts of airport noise on the territory, enables comparisons among airports and/or land use characteristics and measures the effectiveness of potential actions. The index is defined as:

$$NTO = [(\alpha E+\beta R)/S_{CCL}] \quad (1)$$

where

- S_{CCL} is the area bounded by the equal loudness contour – for the identified critical level – projected on the earth surface;
- E is the number of involved people – also identified by their activities, such as commercial, health, education activities – within S_{CCL};
- R is the number of residents within S_{CCL};
- α and β are parameters weighting the relative importance of E and R.

The variable E introduces information on the building use in terms of categories, more in detail the several categories could be weighted according to the following expression:

$$E = \Sigma\, a_i X_i \quad (2)$$

where X_i is the number of people – actual or potential – of category *i* within S_{CCL} while a_i is the weight. The number of involved people is identified by number of employees, hospital beds, students and similar depending on the categories.

The comparison among NTO values for the same equal loudness noise contour on several scenarios provides a measure of the effectiveness of the adopted strategies. Although all the variables defining the airport and territory systems could be modified, in already built-up areas the most usual strategies are variations in landing/

take-off approaching and glide path or variations in building destination depending on the context. Furthermore, only transport features are directly dependent – and in some cases to just some extent – on the airport company, which will consider the financial sustainability of potential actions other than the attained benefits.

Besides noise, the other relevant impact is due to carbon dioxide. As depicted in Figure 1, the main sources of carbon dioxide emissions are surface access modes, handling vehicles and airport terminal equipment as well as aircraft operations. These latter are at the same time the main source of noise emissions.

In Postorino and Mantecchini (2014) a methodological approach is proposed to assess the contribution of each carbon emission main source in order to evaluate the effectiveness of transport-related policies addressed to reduce the airport carbon impact – and ultimately, to estimate the airport carbon footprint due to the airport transport function. Particularly, carbon emissions are attributed to two relevant transport variables – passenger demand and number of aircraft movements within the same time interval – and the related relevant sources due to direct and indirect consumptions (for these latter, energy required to move ground vehicles and aircraft, energy required for passenger terminal functions). For each source, the Unit Carbon Footprint (UCF) related to the transport variable is computed in order to define a reference unit indicator to measure both the polluting contribution to the whole airport carbon impact and – when actions are put in place - the expected reduction. In some cases, the expected reduction due to the implementation of technological and procedural strategies could not be as relevant as required and then some mitigation actions could be needed. In both cases, financial investments are

Figure 2. Noise assessment for actual and testing scenarios

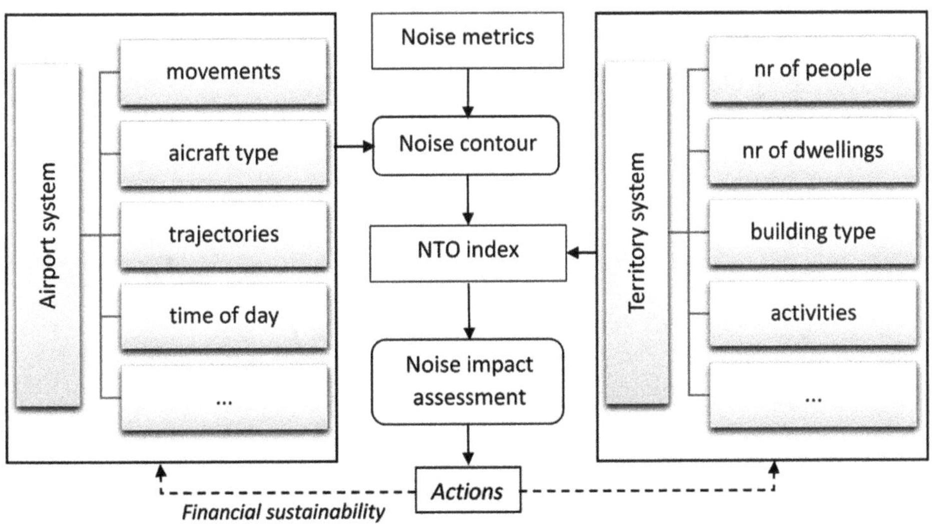

required, whose sustainability has to be verified and compared with the expected environmental benefits.

As depicted in Figure 3 – which further enhances the methodology proposed by Postorino and Mantecchini (2014) –passenger demand and number of aircraft movements are not long-lasting features of the airport. In fact, passenger demand depends on the catchment area – i.e., passengers' socio-economic characteristics and airport accessibility by land transport modes. The number of movements is linked to airline schedule at the airport and depends on frequency and aircraft type. Passengers and movements are linked by the load factor – i.e., depending on the expected demand and the average load factor, the number of movements can be estimated. Each aircraft movement is defined by a LTO cycle, made of landing, taxiing, take-off other than turnaround. During turnaround, several handling vehicles are involved depending on aircraft type, size and offered service (low cost/charter versus full service and short vs medium/long range). Given the average number of movements of each

Figure 3. Assessment procedure to evaluate the effects of action to reduce airport carbon impacts

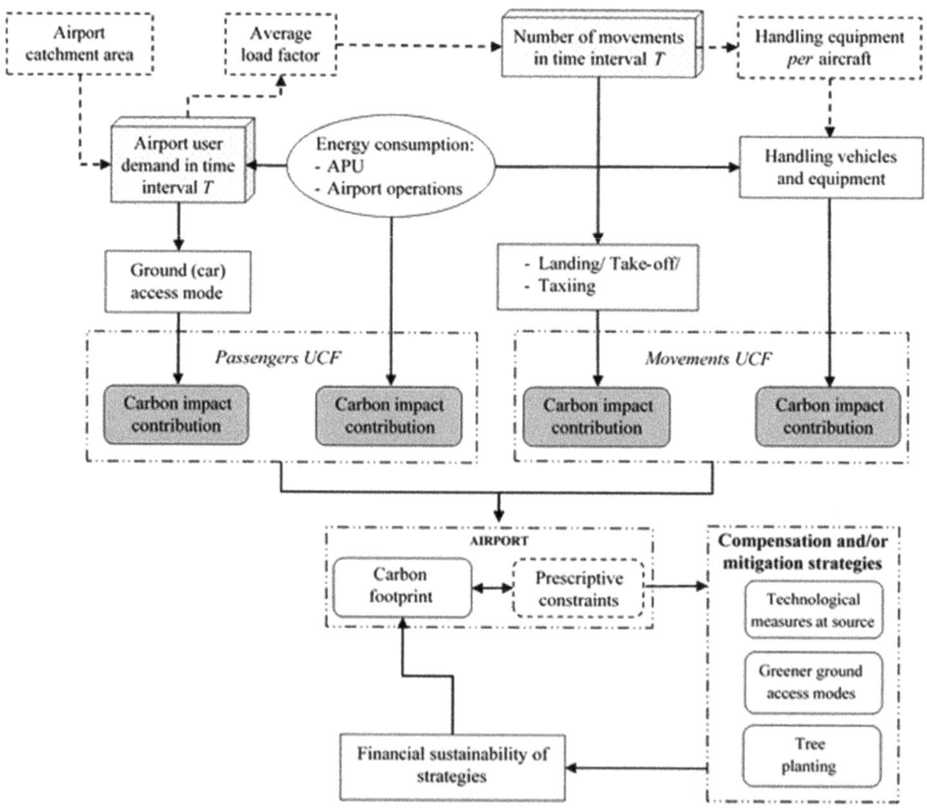

aircraft type and the average number of handling vehicles needed by each aircraft, the handling requirement in the time interval is estimated.

Then, the Carbon Dioxide Emission depends on four main sources (MS): ground access modes; airport terminal plants feeding terminal activities (check-in, security, boarding, advertisement and merchandising); aircraft and handling vehicles contribution during LTO cycles (Figure 3). The contribution of each source during the time interval, which in turn depends on the relevant transport variables (RV) – passengers and movements – is labelled as Unit Carbon Footprint (UCF)

$$UCF_{RV\text{-}MS} = TA_{MS} / RV \qquad (3)$$

Passenger UCF (PUCF) stems from ground access modes and terminal activities, while Movement UCF (MUCF) stems from LTO cycle and handling. Airport Transport Carbon Footprint (TCF) is derived by multiplying PUCF by the number of passengers and MUCF by the number of movements within the same time interval. Airport TCF value is used to decide on compensation/mitigation measures to reduce carbon dioxide polluting effects stemming from transport activities at airports or environmental sustainability restrictions for the next future. The second action requires an operational reduction, which in turn means less financial contributions, and then airport operators generally avoid it. On the contrary, there could be several compensation/mitigation measures ranging from technological to management actions. Technological measures at the source require investments in heating/cooling, lighting, photovoltaic plants and rising of building energetic efficiency through insulation. Management actions are mainly addressed to encourage the use of greener ground access alternatives such as green-powered taxi, light rail and transit services, biofuel and electric cars and similar. Finally, other actions are directly addressed to the environment, such as tree plantings.

The financial sustainability and the amount of time needed to achieve the first results are an important part of the procedure in order to identify the best actions at the best Benefit-Cost Ratio (BCR).

THE CASE OF BOLOGNA AIRPORT

Airport investments are twofold: traditional investments in infrastructures to improve operative parameters such as capacity, level of service or safety and "green investments" in order to achieve the status of "green company" according to EU policies.

In this section, the test case of Bologna International Airport is described, which represents a good example of an airport company investing to achieve its green status.

The measures adopted by the airport have been evaluated within the methodological framework discussed in the previous sections.

International Bologna Airport is located in Northern Italy in a key position at the crossing of several road and rail transport corridors. Its catchment area refers to a region of about 10 million inhabitants. The airside (Figure 4) is characterized by a single runway (RWY 12/30 NW-SE oriented; length 2803m and width 45m; ICAO CODE 4), 11 taxiways and 2 apron areas accounting for 34 aircraft stands. Both runway heads are equipped with ILS (head 12: CAT IIIB ILS; head 30: CAT I ILS), which enables a mixed-operation capacity of up to 26 movements/h.

As for air services, Bologna airport is connected with 99 national and international destinations, served by 48 airlines with 6,500,000 passengers and 67,257 movements in 2014 (SAB 2014 data). Mid-size aircraft – mainly Boeing 737 series (31%), Airbus series A-319 and A-320 (26%), Embraer 190-195 (18%) – characterizes the operating fleet mix. The traffic is almost equally split between full (45%) and low-cost carriers (52%) within a point-to-point network. The remaining 3% is made of charter traffic towards some long haul destinations.

Communities living in the neighbourhoods of an airport are generally more concerned with noise effects due to the heavy impacts they could experiment on their daily life. For this reason, during the last years airports were forced to find strategies of noise management addressed to improve the welfare of the exposed local communities. As described in section 3, airport and territory measures could be implemented to reduce noise effects. The effectiveness and sustainability of noise abatement procedures have been tested on the case study of Bologna Airport, where

Figure 4. Bologna airport layout

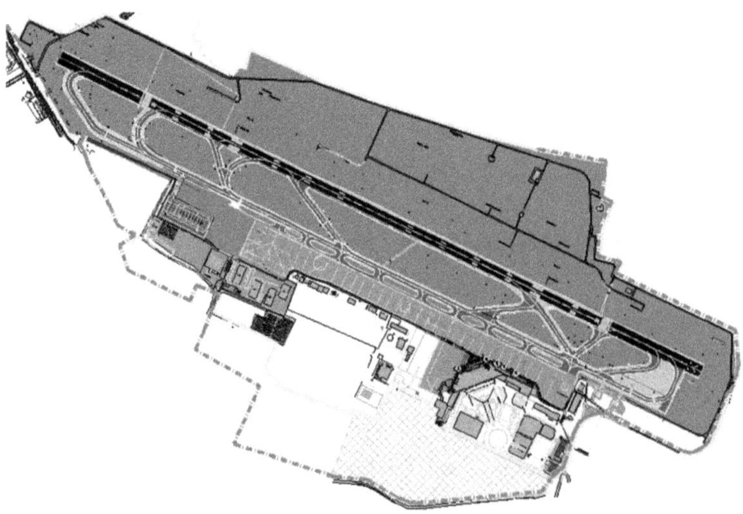

the significant traffic growth since 2008, the proximity to the city centre and densely populated residential and industrial zones represent a potential limit to the traffic sustainability in the future.

Since 1996, the airport management in cooperation with the national air navigation service provider (ENAV) has implemented a standard flight path for take-offs and a limit of operations over inhabited areas during night-time, thus reducing both the number of people and buildings affected by airport noise. As described in Figure 2, the shape and size of the equal loudness contours have been evaluated by using the equivalent sound level L_{VA} adopted by the Italian legislation to assess airport noise. Similarly, the number of buildings and residents exposed to critical noise levels – i.e., those included within the equal loudness contours projected on the earth surface – have been evaluated starting from census data. Figure 5 depicts the noise contours for two scenarios (before and current, dashed and continuous line respectively). These two scenarios correspond to the flight procedures respectively used until 2012 (before) and the new flight procedures started in 2013 (current). These latter modified the equal loudness curves, which are now closer to the runway threshold and bound for North towards less densely populated areas.

As reported in Table 1 in terms of L_{VA} noise indicator, the current-scenario has significantly reduced the amount of people, buildings and areas exposed to noise. Although before and current equal loudness contours are in some cases similar,

Figure 5. Comparison between the before scenario (dashed lines) and the current scenario (continuous lines)

however differences in dwellings and people exposed highlight a different impact on the territory, as the NTO index shows. Average take-off routes overflying less populated areas now account for about 70% vs about 45% in the before scenario.

It is important to notice that this action does not require financial investments and then it has not direct impact on the airport. Nevertheless, further analysis could be performed in order to evaluate the effect of such measures on airlines, in particular in terms of fuel burned and, finally, atmospheric emissions.

Although population is more concerned with noise, however polluting emissions could be a heavier burden. For this reason, in these latter years airports are dealing with polluting emissions other than noise impacts. As a partner of the dAIR project, recently Bologna Airport has implemented some actions to mitigate its environmental impacts due to the transport function. Despite the increase of about 40% in passenger traffic since 2008, the airport company has succeeded in reducing its CO_2 emissions as shown in Figure 6 – about 30% from 2010 to 2013.

This result is due to the Airport Decarbonization Plan undertaken by the airport management together with local shareholders (Chamber of Commerce, public institutions and private investors) and local transport authorities. Several actions are included in this plan, whose time-frame spans from short to long terms. The attainable reduction of CO_2 emission can be estimated by using the procedural framework described in section 3. However, the topic requires careful attention due to its complexity. As an example, the internalization of external costs (including noise, local pollution and congestion) is a relevant subject in the agenda to recover wear and tear costs. Similarly, the simple provision of incentives to green alternatives may generate market distortions.

As already discussed, CO_2 emissions originating from surface access modes account for an important share of the total CO_2 emissions. Airports are more and more

Table 1. Comparison between the before and current scenarios

L_{VA} [dB(A)]	Population	Buildings	Equal loudness contour area (m²)			NTO		
	Diff (%)	Diff (%)	2013	2012	Diff (m²)	2013	2012	Diff (%)
50 - 55	- 9720 (-40)	- 814 (-36)	38206	39887	-1681	0.35	0.89	-61.15
55 - 60	- 1447 (-19)	- 66 (-8)	16162	16754	-592	0.29	0.66	-56.78
60 - 65	- 633 (-18)	- 62 (-18)	6455	6856	-401	0.51	0.54	-5.73
65 - 70	0	0	2333	2477	-144	0.007	0.008	-4.44
70 - 75	0	0	1	1038	-1037	0.00	0.00	
> 75	0	0	0,5	0,5	0	0.00	0.00	
Total	-11800(-33)	- 942 (-28)			-3.855			

Figure 6. CO_2 emission and passenger evolution at Bologna Airport (source: Bologna Airport)

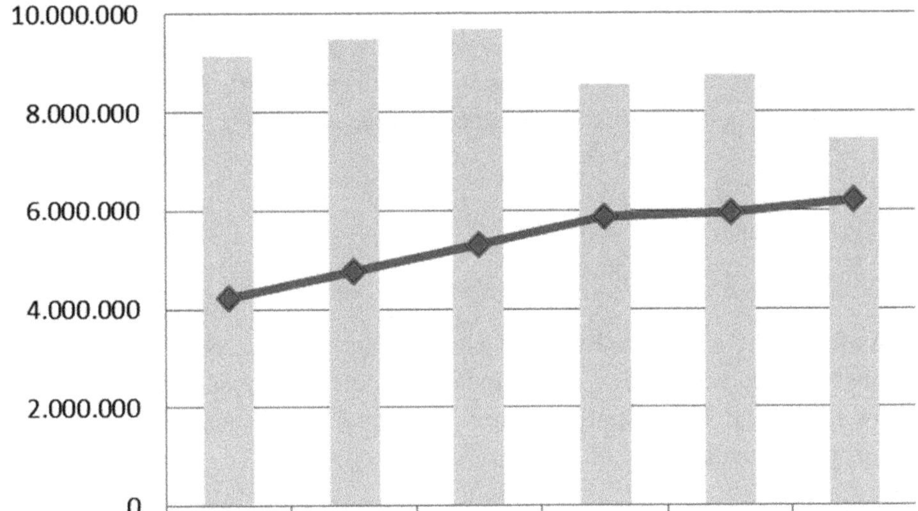

	2008	2009	2010	2011	2012	2013
CO2 [kg]	9.145.385	9.492.112	9.677.688	8.554.601	8.754.641	7.437.810
PAX	4.223.509	4.774.697	5.306.106	5.876.213	5.958.648	6.193.783

devoting efforts on decarbonization programs not only to face the environmental issues but also to grant themselves additional transport capacity and business opportunities in the next future. In this light, a focus on "green" airport accessibility and transport plans to/from airports might result financially profitable in the long term. Furthermore, the involvement of local transport stakeholders in the program could lead to better achievements.

A first group of actions discussed by the airport management refers to organizational or information measures:

- Permanent round-table to manage the airport de-carbonization plan
- Mobility manager in airport surroundings to study staff travel planning
- Information campaign on sustainable transport alternatives to access the airport and smart accessibility solutions.

Particularly, the mobility manager figure is intended to promote the use of sustainable transport modes by encouraging travellers to change their attitude towards transportation issues. Promotion is realized by measures such as advertising campaigns, panels, coordination between partners and stakeholders as well as permanent roundtables to supervise the obtained progresses. Such measures require lower investments than infrastructure-oriented ones and could ensure higher Benefit - Cost Ratio.

A second group of actions – which potentially generate a direct effect on CO_2 emissions – refers to transport variables, in particular to the surface transport systems to access the airport. They can be grouped in three sets:

1. Public transport
2. Private transport
3. Non-motorized transport

As for public transport, Bologna Airport management has envisaged several actions with the cooperation of the local transport agency and local authorities (municipality and administrative region) to improve the transport service to/from the airport, particularly:

- Monorail system to link the airport and the central railway station by 2018
- Airport rail station within urban light-rail system by 2018
- Enhancement of public shuttle buses between the central railway station and the airport

The monorail system – which will link the airport to the main central station located less than 6 km away – will replace the current bus transit system and will connect the two transport terminals in about 7.5 min. In the meantime, measures to raise efficiency of shuttle bus services between the Central Railway Station and the Airport Terminal will be taken; among those, on-line seat purchase, fast tracks, renewal of the fleet with greener vehicles up to capacity enhancement. The local transport agency has committed itself to refurbish bus stops within the city, while Bologna Airport management will devote areas to signage, information points and ticket vendor machines in and outside the terminal.

As for private transport alternatives, apart from usual actions concerning different fees based on several criteria (e.g., distance to terminal, number of available car parks), the airport management plans to adopt further measures in the next future to promote and encourage the use of greener cars:

- Discounted and reserved parking areas, use of sustainable fleet for car-hire services and installation of charging points – without fees during the stopover at the airport parking – for electric cars for both passengers and staff
- Car-pooling, discounted transport to the airport by coach for airport staff

- Introduction of low emission shuttle buses to carry passengers from the airport terminal to the airport car parking
- Contractual benefits for car sharing agencies adopting hybrid/electric fleets
- Connect the airport with local cycle path networks

On the other hand, setting higher car parking fees for polluting vehicles might encourage passengers and staff to use public transport wherever possible. As for the widely used "Kiss & Fly" practice, generally free of charge for a certain period, it generates twice the number of car journeys if compared to those of passengers who use an airport car park. The emission rate is even higher than the one stemming from private car parking at airports and then several airports are considering the idea of removing or pushing away the facility.

As for non-motorized transport, bike could represent a good alternative to private and mass transport mainly for those staff living suitably close to the airport. This transport alternative could be encouraged by bike lanes and bike sharing stations in the neighborhoods of the airport. A study for a bike path – linking the existing urban road and cycle networks to the airport – has been realized together with local authorities.

A third group of measures related to airport energy consumption and efficiency is addressed to raise energetic efficiency of airport buildings (e.g., replacement of gasoline power plants, non-LED lights, adoption of photovoltaic plants on rooftops).

Finally, to compensate the emission of CO_2, which remains rather high, the airport company has engaged to realize a green belt north of the runway able to compensate, through photosynthesis induced by sunlight, 25% of the total CO_2 emission stemming from airport activities on a yearly basis. In addition, it will improve the landscape and system of green areas at local level. The main drawback linked to green belts close to runways is the risk of bird-strikes. To avoid this, the neighbourhoods of the runway (in Figure 7) are going to be filled with grass and rushes only, while in remoter area (depicted in intense green or in green stripes) trees will be planted. Within the orange area, vegetable gardens for residents will be installed. The red/orange lines show future cycle paths that will link the airport area to the existing urban and touristic cycle network. The area sums up around 90 ha of whom 38 will host around 20.000 trees in total and 43 ha rushes, gardens and bio-agricultural cultures. The area as a whole is estimated to redeem 23.000 CO_2 t/century plus 30.000 t/20 years stemming from rush areas, which makes more than 1.800 t/year (about 25% of the total CO_2 average emission).

In Table 2, the expected CO_2 reduction for each measure previously introduced is defined. In particular, the measures have been grouped separately for each emission main source, in accordance with the proposed methodology.

Figure 7. Green belt

Table 2. Expected CO_2 reduction after the adoption of the described measures

Main source	Measure	Expected CO_2 reduction
Ground access mode	Monorail system to link the airport and the central railway station	3,000 tons/year
	Airport rail station within urban light-rail system	600 tons/year
	Enhancement of public shuttle buses	50 tons/year
	Introduction of low emission shuttle buses	10 tons/year
	Car-pooling, discounted transport to the airport by coach, reserved parking areas for electric cars/cycles for airport staff	150 tons/year
	Connect the airport with local cycle path networks	40 tons/year
Energy consumption	Raising energetic efficiency of airport buildings	1,250 tons/year
	Green belt	1,850 tons/year

Table 3 summarizes the expected costs for the realization of the measures envisaged in the next future by the Bologna Airport management, with reference to their time frame. The realization of the green belt as well as the interventions addressed to increase building energy efficiency are the most relevant from a financial point of view but also can provide relevant outcomes. Some measures (i.e. promotional campaign or monitoring system) have not a direct effect on CO_2 emission/compensation but generate a direct financial impact. Some other measures related to ground access transport systems (monorail system, airport light rail station and enhance-

Table 3. Expected costs and time-span of the described measures

Main source	Measure	Total cost (€)	Time-span
Ground access mode	Monorail system to link the airport and the central railway station	Contribution by the airport to be defined	2016-2018
	Airport rail station within urban light-rail system		2016-2018
	Enhancement of public shuttle buses		2016
	Introduction of low emission shuttle buses		2016-2018
	Car-pooling, discounted transport to the airport by coach, reserved parking areas for electric cars/ cycles and recharging points	60,000	2016-2018
	Connect the airport with local cycle path networks	1,500,000	2016-2022
Energy consumption	Raising energetic efficiency of airport buildings (photovoltaic system, high performing UTA engines, heat pump, new lighting systems)	1,520,000	2016-2019
	Green belt	5,000,000	2016-2023
	Promotional campaign, round table, air quality monitoring	340,000	2016-2023

ment of public shuttle buses) are not under direct financial responsibility of the airport company. Nevertheless, a financial contribution to these projects – that will have a wide effect on public transport system not only related to the airport – is under evaluation by the airport management.

MAIN FINDINGS

The methodological approach applied to the test case of Bologna airport has shown its potentialities to assess the effects of actions addressed to reduce negative impacts due to the airport transport function.

As for noise, the application of the NTO index has allowed an immediate comparison between the before and current scenarios. The two considered scenarios have been simulated by using statistical data, although both have been already realized at Bologna airport, in order to assess the potentialities of the method. The "before" scenario refers to the flight path scheme in force until 2012, which was ineffective and noisier for the involved population. The "current" scenario refers to the changes adopted in the flight path in order to reduce noise impacts. In terms of NTO values, significant noise impact reductions have been quantified for critical noise levels ranging from 50 to 70 dB(A). According to its definition, the NTO index provides a combined evaluation of the involved area sizes and features of the exposed territory (see table 1). Moreover, it provides a measure of the effectiveness of the actions potentially implemented by comparing more than one scenario. Such approach helps airport management to evaluate the feasibility of solutions, even from the economic point of view if needed, before actually implementing them. The simulation of potential actions and the evaluation of their effects is appealing because implementation of wrong measures – and then unnecessary financial investments – can be avoided.

As for carbon impacts, the proposed carbon footprint approach allows identifying UCF linked to relevant transport variables to compute the unit contribution of the identified main emission sources to the total amount of CO_2. Bologna airport has planned a wide range of actions to reduce its airport carbon footprint or to compensate the effects of carbon emissions on the local population. By using the estimated UCF for the relevant transport variables, together with transport models and statistical data, both the environmental and financial effects of such actions have been estimated by using the proposed methodological approach. As reported in tables 2 and 3, some actions can contribute better to the reduction of the airport carbon footprint with lower financial costs (e.g., car-pooling vs. cycle path network). In some cases, the same financial effort results in significant differences in terms of saved emissions (e.g., efficiency of airport buildings vs. cycle path network). Again, the proposed procedure makes it possible to evaluate the effects of actions before implementing them. Particularly, according to the estimated UCF some actions produce more relevant emission cuts with the same or even lower financial effort. As generally there are budget constraints, this quantitative analysis allows airports to choose the best solution within the budget limits.

To summarize, airports are requested to make investments and financial efforts in order to become more sustainable and "green". As for the environment, greenhouse gases and noise are two of the most relevant sources of pollution generated by an airport. Here, a general framework to evaluate the effectiveness of measures to reduce both airport noise impacts and carbon footprint has been proposed. In particular, the focus of the proposed framework is, at a first stage, on the link between the transport function and the impacts, and at a second stage on the evaluation of the balance among attained impacts reduction and estimated costs of adopted measures. The analysis of the regulatory framework and the scientific background has confirmed that the reduction of airport carbon contribution and noise impact in the surrounding territory is a strategic goal for both planners and airport operators. The application of the proposed methodology to the test case of Bologna airport, in Italy, has shown that synergic actions and planning policies developed in close cooperation with Local Authorities and transport companies in a private-public partnership can be adopted to reduce impacts due to the airport transport function by keeping a financially sustainable approach.

REFERENCES

Air Transport Action Group. (n.d.). Retrieved from www.atag.org

Airport Cooperative Research Program (ACRP) Report 11. (2009). *Guidebook on Preparing Greenhouse Gas Emissions Inventories*. Transportation Research Board.

Airports Council International (ACI). (2009). *Guidance Manual: Airport Greenhouse Gas Emissions Management*. ACI.

Bentes, F. M., Heleno, T. A., & Slama, J. G. (2013). Analysis of airport noise exposure around Viracopos International Airport using geographic information systems. *Journal of Air Transport Management, 31*, 15–17. doi:10.1016/j.jairtraman.2012.11.001

Bentes, F. M., & Slama, J. G. (2011). Sensitivity analysis of airport noise using computer simulation. *Journal of Aerospace Technology and Management, 3*(3), 295–300. doi:10.5028/jatm.2011.03033011

Budd, T., Ison, S., & Ryley, T. (2011). Airport surface access in the UK: A management perspective. *Research in Transportation Business & Management, 1*(1), 109–117. doi:10.1016/j.rtbm.2011.05.003

Cohen, J. P., & Coughlin, C. C. (2008). Spatial hedonic models of airport noise. proximity. and housing prices. *Journal of Regional Science, 48*(5), 859–878. doi:10.1111/j.1467-9787.2008.00569.x

Daley, B., & Preston, H. (2009). Aviation and Climate Change: Assessment of Policy Options. In S. Gössling & P. Upham (Eds.), *Climate change and aviation. Issues, challenges and solutions* (pp. 347–372). London: Sterling.

Directive 2002/49/EC of the European Parliament and the Council of 25 June 2002 relating to the assessment and management of environmental noise.

DM 14/11/97 Determination of the limits of sound sources.

DM 31/10/97 Airport noise methodology of measurement.

Emissions and Dispersion Modeling System (EDMS). (2009). *Technical Manual, version 5, FAA-AEE-07-07 (Rev. 1 – 04/08/09)*. Washington, DC: CSSI, Inc.

Erkelens, L. J. J. (2000). Research into New Noise Abatement Procedures for the 21st Century. In *AIAA Guidance,Navigation and Control Conference*. AIAA.

Espey, M., & Lopez, H. (2000). The impact of airport noise and proximity on residential property values. *Growth and Change*, *31*(3), 408–419. doi:10.1111/0017-4815.00135

European Commission. (2011). A Roadmap for moving to a competitive low carbon economy in 2050. COM(2011) 112 final. Brussels: Author.

Federal Aviation Administration (FAA). (1993). *Noise Abatement Departure Procedures*. FAA.

Federal Aviation Administration (FAA), Office of Environment and Energy. (2007). Integrated Noise Model (INM), Version 7.0, User's guide. FAA.

Filippone, A. (2014). Aircraft noise prediction. *Progress in Aerospace Sciences*, *68*, 27–63. doi:10.1016/j.paerosci.2014.02.001

Franssen, E. A. M. et al.. (2004). Aircraft noise around a large international airport and its impact on general health and medication use. *Occupational and Environmental Medicine*, *61*(5), 405–413. doi:10.1136/oem.2002.005488 PMID:15090660

Fulton, L., Cazzola, P., Cuenot, F. O., Kojima, K., Onoda, T., Staub, J., & Taylor, M. (2009). *Transport, energy and CO_2: Moving toward sustainability*. Paris, France: International Energy Agency.

Girvin, R. (2009). Aircraft Noise Abatement and Mitigation Strategies. *Journal of Air Transport Management*, *15*(1), 14–22. doi:10.1016/j.jairtraman.2008.09.012

Graham, A. (2003). *Managing the Airports: an International Prospective* (2nd ed.). Elsevier.

Hebly, S. J., & Visser, H. G. (2008). *Advanced noise abatement departure procedures: Custom optimized departure profiles*. AIAA Guidance, Navigation and Control Conference, Honolulu. HI. doi:10.2514/6.2008-7405

International Civil Aviation Organization (ICAO). (1993). *Environmental Protection, Annex 16* (Vol. 1). Montreal: Aircraft Noise.

International Civil Aviation Organization (ICAO). (2002). Amendment 7 to international standards and recommended practices. Annex 16 to the Convention on International Civil Aviation: Environmental Protection.

International Civil Aviation Organization (ICAO). (2008). *Guidance on the balanced approach to aircraft noise management. Doc 9829*. ICAO.

International Civil Aviation Organization (ICAO). (2010). *Environmental Report*. Retrieved from http://www.icao.int/environmental-protection/Pages/EnvReport10.aspx

International Civil Aviation Organization (ICAO). (2011). *Airport air quality guidance manual, Doc 9889*. Retrieved from http://www.icao.int/environmental-protection/Documents/Publications/FINAL.Doc 9889.1st Edition.alltext.en.pdf

Lu, C., & Morrell, P. (2006). Determination and Application of environmental costs at different sized airports – aircraft noise and engine emissions. *Transportation*, *33*(1), 45–61. doi:10.1007/s11116-005-2300-y

McMillen, D. P. (2004). Airport expansions and property values: The case of Chicago OHare Airport. *Journal of Urban Economics*, *55*(3), 627–640. doi:10.1016/j.jue.2004.01.001

Miedema, H. M. E., & Vos, H. (1998). Exposure-response relationships for transportation noise. *The Journal of the Acoustical Society of America*, *104*(6), 3432–3445. doi:10.1121/1.423927 PMID:9857505

Miyoshi, C., & Mason, K. J. (2013). The damage cost of carbon dioxide emissions produced by passengers on airport surface access: The case of Manchester Airport. *Journal of Transport Geography*, *28*, 137–143. doi:10.1016/j.jtrangeo.2012.12.003

Nelson, J. P. (2004). Meta-Analysis of Airport Noise and Hedonic Property Values. *Journal of Transport Economics and Policy*, *38*(1), 1–27.

Pearce, D. W. (1976). *Charging for Noise*. Paris: OECD.

Postorino, M. N. (2010). Environmental effects of airport nodes: A methodological approach. *International Journal of Sustainable Development and Planning*, *5*(2), 192–204. doi:10.2495/SDP-V5-N2-192-204

Postorino, M. N., & Mantecchini, L. (2014). A transport carbon footprint methodology to assess airport carbon emissions. *Journal of Air Transport Management*, *37*, 76–86. doi:10.1016/j.jairtraman.2014.03.001

Postorino, M. N., & Mantecchini, L. (2016). A systematic approach to assess the effectiveness of airport noise mitigation strategies. *Journal of Air Transport Management*, *50*, 71–82. doi:10.1016/j.jairtraman.2015.10.004

Schipper, Y., Rietveld, P., & Nijkamp, P. (2001). Environmental externalities in air transport markets. *Journal of Air Transport Management*, *7*(3), 169–179. doi:10.1016/S0969-6997(01)00002-3

Schürmann, G., Schäfer, K., Jahn, C., Hoffmann, H., Bauerfeind, M., Fleuti, E., & Rappenglück, B. (2007). The impact of NO_x, CO and VOC emissions on the air quality of Zurich airport. *Atmospheric Environment*, *41*(1), 103–118. doi:10.1016/j.atmosenv.2006.07.030

Smith, A., Nutt, D., & Wilson, S. (2002). Noise and insomnia: a study of community noise exposure. sleep disturbance. noise sensitivity and subjective reports on health. Centres for Occupational and Health Psychology, Cardiff University; Psychopharmacology Unit, University of Bristol.

Turner, R. K., Pearce, D., & Bateman, I. (1994). *Environmental economics: an elementary introduction*. Harvester Wheatsheaf.

Unal, A., Hu, Y., Chang, M. E., Odman, M. T., & Russell, A. G. (2005). Airport related emissions and impacts on air quality: Application to the Atlanta International Airport. *Atmospheric Environment*, *39*(32), 5787–5798. doi:10.1016/j.atmosenv.2005.05.051

Upham, P., Thomas, C., Gillingwater, D., & Raper, D. (2003). Environmental capacity and airport operations: Current issues and future prospects. *Journal of Air Transport Management*, *9*(3), 145–151. doi:10.1016/S0969-6997(02)00078-9

Uyeno, D., Hamilton, S. W., & Biggs, A. J. (1993). Density of residential land use and the impact of airport noise. *Journal of Transport Economics and Policy*, *27*(1), 3–18.

Wijnen, R. A. A., & Visser, H. G. (2003). Optimal departure trajectories with respect to sleep disturbance. *Aerospace Science and Technology*, *7*(1), 81–91. doi:10.1016/S1270-9638(02)01183-5

World Health Organization (WHO). (2011). *Burden of disease from environmental noise. Regional Office for Europe JRC*, European Commission.

Yu, K. N., Cheung, Y. P., Cheung, T., & Henry, R. C. (2004). Identifying the impact of large urban airports on local air quality by nonparametric regression. *Atmospheric Environment*, *38*(27), 4501–4507. doi:10.1016/j.atmosenv.2004.05.034

Chapter 9
Cover Crops:
Achievement of Sustainability in the Ecological Systems of Agriculture

Vladan Ugrenović
Institute "Tamiš" Pančevo, Serbia

Vladimir Filipović
Institute for Medicinal Plants Research "Dr Josif Pančić", Serbia

ABSTRACT

The use of cover crops is widespread practice in organic farming systems. Cover crops can be defined as crops that are usually not grown commercially, and can have a multiple role in crop rotations. The benefit of cover crops has been known since long. Legumes are used as biological fixer of nitrogen for the next crop, and are established during periods when the soil is without major crops in order to reduce erosion. In recent years, the role of cover crops has been extended to the biocontrol of weeds, pests and diseases, as well as to the overall improvement of soil quality by increasing organic matter, encouraging the circulation of nutrients and reducing soil compaction. At the same time, their use tends to reduce costs and even create new sources of income on the farm.

DOI: 10.4018/978-1-5225-2075-7.ch009

INTRODUCTION

Multiple environmental and economic benefits are achieved by the application of environmentally sustainable agritechnical measures (Filipović et al., 2011). Climate change, energy costs and available nitrogen will have an increasing impact on agricultural production in the coming years. Cover crops are possible solution to some of these issues. Cover crops can favourably affect yield increase, reduce the costs of nitrogen and pesticide application, reduce the use of machinery, and increase profits. However, cover crops can bring a number of other agronomic benefits, such as: (1) soil health enhancement / the enhancement of soil health (Wang et al., 2011), (2) the reduction in / soil erosion reduction (Mazzoncini et al., 2011), (3) water quality protection / the protection of water quality (Malone et al., 2014) and (4) biodiversity (Castro et al., 2014), all of which can hardly be measured financially. As stated by Filipović and & Ugrenović (2010), biological diversity can be achieved by switching from monoculture systems to crop rotation, which would include cover crops. The introduction of cover crops in agricultural practices could significantly increase the sustainability of agricultural production systems.

ROLE OF COVER CROPS AND THEIR EFFECTS

The role of cover crops in crop production is almost always manifold. In order to facilitate coherence, it is divided into 7 subsections relating to individual positive effects that the implementation of this bioagritechnical measure brings along, and they are as follows: (1) erosion control, (2) the increase in organic matter content, (3) the enhancement of soil structure, (4) the fixation of atmospheric nitrogen, (5) the protection of water quality, (6) the management of soil moisture, and (7) the control of weeds and pests.

SOIL EROSION CONTROL

Throughout the year, agricultural areas in Serbia are affected by wind and water erosion (Ličina et al., 2011). The highest intensity of wind erosion in the northern and northeastern regions is during autumn, winter and spring, whereas the effects of water erosion are the greatest on slopes and along rivers (Djukić & Petković, 2009). Establishing cover crops with high biomass production can effectively protect soil against erosion, especially in the part of the season when the soil is bare. Plant cover crops splice soil particles with their roots, while the above-ground biomass prevents prevents fine particles of soil surface from being flushed away by water or carried off by wind. Dense perennial crops improve the retention and absorption of water by the soil, and reduce runoff, whereas the above-ground parts of the plants reduce the impact of raindrops (Parlak & Ozaslan Parlak, 2010). After the destruction of the cover crops, the dry above-ground biomass forms mulch on the soil surface, which also provides the protection against soil erosion (Zdravković et al., 2012). Grasses and grass mixtures provide the best protection against erosion, and winter grains or winter brassicas are suitable for covering the soil during the winter (Kruidhof et al., 2008).

INCREASING THE ORGANIC MATTER CONTENT

Cover crops leave plant residues thus causing the increase of organic matter in the soil (Santos et al., 2011). The increase depends on the amount of the biomass formed in a cover crop and the ratio of carbon between nitrogen in plant residues (C:N ratio). This ratio depend on by plant species and the time of the year when the cover crops are destroyed (Restovich et al., 2012). Tosti et al. (2012) explain that cover crop residues with a low ratio of C:N – legumes (*Fabaceae*), are decomposed faster than those with a high ratio – grasses (*Poaceae*). After the destruction of grass cover crops, crop residue on on a certain area of the soil is left with a high C:N ratio, which causes a very slow decomposition, and a long-term impact on the soil organic matter increase (Diekow et al. 2005). For the degradation of plant residues in which the C:N ratio is above 30, the microorganisms consume additional nitrogen (nitrogen immobilisation), creating a shortage of this element for the next crop, which then must be compensated by the addition of nitrogen nutrients (Muhammad et al., 2011). The pairing of different plant species from different families (grasses and legumes) in cover crops can reduce the C:N ratio, and thus accelerate the decomposition of the total biomass produced (Fageria et al. 2005). Knowing the individual characteristics of the species in cover crops, the processes in the soil can be directed towards the set goal, whether we need organic matter or available nitrogen for the next crop.

Thanks to their powerful roots, plants from the grass family accumulate nutrients, especially nitrogen, that remain in the soil after the harvest, which, according to Popović (2010), accumulates more than 70 kg N ha^{-1} during a three months period. However, these nutrients become available to plants rather slowly, so that grass cover crops have more effect on the increase of organic matter in the soil. On the other hand, plant residues of legumes are rapidly degraded in the soil due to their lower C:N ratio, therefore less increasing the content of organic matter in the soil (Fageria et al., 2005).

ENHANCEMENT OF SOIL STRUCTURE

Cover crops can help to maintain or enhance soil structure, because they protect the soil from adverse climatic influences (Hartwig & Ammon, 2002). Plant roots in cover crops bind soil particles, during their decomposition in the soil, organic molecules are released, and, also, fungal networks are formed (Gosling et al., 2006).

The best effects to enhance soil structure are achieved by the establishment of cover crops that form a strong hairy root system, such as grass species (Liu et al., 2005; Snapp et al., 2005). The roots of these species bind soil, and can also penetrate compact soils (Chen & Weil, 2010). Species with spindly, turnip-like root (brassicas) penetrate into deeper layers of the soil, thus making it possible for the following crop roots to easily penetrate into those deeper layers, where they make use of water and nutrients (Gregory, 2008).

Plant species with strong root systems can also be used in mitigating soil compaction. It was noted that crops such as corn, sorghum, Sudan grass, common millet relieve the effects of compaction (Chen and Weil, 2010). Cover crops that grow in the winter are suitable for breaking compact layers in the soil, because they can penetrate through those layers when they are softened with plenty of water during this period (which is less likely in the summer).

In the course of decomposition, cover crops with a low C:N ratio will release large amounts of organic molecules, such as polysaccharides, which enhance soil structure (Downie, 2010). That is the reason why the soil is soft in the spring after a crop of legumes. This effect is expected to last only as long as there are biodegradable residues. Cover crops with a high C:N ratio will have a slower release of polysaccharides, which brings about slower soil structure enhancement than in cover crops with a low C:N ratio.

In a symbiotic relationship with the majority of grown plant species (excluding brassicas) live mycorrhizal fungi (Himmelbauer et al., 2005; Plenchette et al., 2005). The plants provide these fungi with energy, and the fungi extend the zone of the root system, can help the absorption of water and nutrients such as phosphorus (Parniske, 2008). Mycorrhizas settle the cells of root tops, so, as the root is growing, they are dying, on which occasion, glomalin is being released (Wu et al., 2012). It is this rejected glycoprotein that contributes to a better soil structure. The practices that stimulate the creation of mycorrhizas, and hence, the creation of glomalin itself, include: (1) the implementation of conservation cultivation, (2) continuous occupation of soil with the living root systems where mycorrhizas can settle, as well as (3) the avoidance of excessive phosphorus fertilisation (Parniske, 2008). Therefore, the establishment of cover crops at the time of the year when soil is without the main crop positively affects the formation of mycorrhiza populations.

FIXATION OF ATMOSPHERIC NITROGEN

It is well known that a large number of plant species live in different symbiotic relationships with microorganisms (Fuhrmann et al., 2005). This group of plants belongs to all annual and perennial legumes, as well as many other species (mostly grains), with nitrogen fixing microorganisms (bacteria or fungi) developed on the roots. As explained by Popović et al. (2012), soil nitrogen fixing bacteria (*Rhizobiaceae*) are located on the roots of legumes (*Fabaceae*), which bind atmospheric nitrogen into compounds available to plants, hence reducing the need for additional nutrition of crops with mineral nitrogen nutrients. The intensity of nitrogen fixation depends on the agro-ecological and soil conditions. In the soils with low nitrogen content, nitrogen fixation is significantly higher (Fuhrmann et al., 2005). To ensure the fixation of nitrogen, plant seeds are treated with biological products containing micro-organism cultures in order to start symbiotic processes quickly (Đukić et al. 2010). These symbiotic communities are particularly useful in a cover crop. The three years' research by Hanson et al. (1993) indicated that hairy vetch, from early March onwards, secured 2 kg of nitrogen per day, and was proved to increase the yield of corn to such an extent that it justified the use of cover crops. Winter peas, vetch and alfalfa in a cover crop can provide up to 100% of nitrogen for the next crop of potato (Stark, 1995). In intercrops, legumes transfer significant amounts of nitrogen to the main crop (Felipe Alfonso Cortes at. al., 2010), and according to Fustec et al., (2010), these values range from 30 to 50% of the total fixation. Also the adoption of cover crops can reduce losses of nitrogen in the soil and thus preserve it for the next crop (Robertson et al., 1991). As legume plant residues decompose quickly in the soil and release large amounts of nitrogen, in wet springs, it can cause its leaching into the deeper layers of the ground. This should be considered in the management of such cover crops. These occurrences can be prevented by establishing cover crops with mixed legumes and grasses, which allows a slower decomposition of plant remains (Sarrantonio, 2007).

WATER QUALITY PROTECTION

By slowing down the process of erosion and preventing the surface water run-off, cover crops reduce the possibility of water pollution and the accumulation of agricultural chemicals. In the areas with mismanaged pollutants (nitrates, pesticides, heavy metals and others), some cover crops (rye, wheat, barley, rye grass and *Miscanthus*) are used for soil and groundwater remediation (Didier et al., 2012; Malone et al., 2014). The roots of some species can adopt these matters, reduce their concentration, and thus prevent their flushing into the groundwater. Djordjević-Miloradović et al. (2002) reported that canola can completely clean lead from the soil in the zone of its root system growth.

The excessive use of nitrogenous nutrients leads to the accumulation of nitrate in the soil, which gets rinsed and pollutes ground water in rainy periods (Kaspar et al., 2007). This phenomenon is also negative for farmers because it represents the loss of nutrients for crops. Cover crops adopt soil nitrogen preventing its leaching and the pollution of groundwater, thus preserving it for the next crop (Malone et al., 2014). Rye cover crops adopt 35 to 60% of residual nitrogen from the previous production of the main crops (Kaspar et al., 2007). Cover crops whose harvest residue C:N ratio is above 30 (rye full maturity, corn stalks), need additional nitrogen for their decomposition by microorganisms (Larsen et al., 2011), and this phenomenon can be used to manage nitrates in the soil (Ugrenović et al., 2015).

SOIL MOISTURE MANAGEMENT

Cover crops consume water, and after the destruction of these plants, their residues prevent water evaporation from the soil (Gava et al., 2013). Also, biomass of the plants and the shredded plant residues prevent surface water run-off and improve its absorption into the soil (Adekalu et al 2007). These positive effects of the utilisation of cover crops are expressed fully only if crop residues are left on the soil surface as mulch, while the effect is minor when the crop residues are incorporated in the soil (Gava et al., 2013). In mulched carrot production, the demand for water is reduced by 30%, due to lower water evaporation (Filipovic et al., 2012). Mulch is particularly needed in the main crops if the previous crop has not left any residues (corn silage). Cover crop stubble may retain the snow, especially if it is left in different altitudinal zones (Zhang et al., 2007).

To avoid most of the problems with the lack of water in the spring, cover crops should be destroyed at least two weeks before planting the main crop, which will prevent water loss (Celette et al., 2008). On the other hand on flooded soils, the mulch formed from cover crops residues prevent soil from drying and makes the establishment of the main crop difficult. In such situations, the destruction of the cover crop should be delayed, as living cover crops consume water, and may result in the decrease of moisture excess in the soil. The optimal way to solve the issue of flooded soil after the destruction of cover crops is strip cropping, i.e. strip-tillage, which makes it possible for the soil to dry out in the area of sowing, and, on the other hand, the mulch formed between the rows shows positive effects (Ugrenović et al., 2015).

Good examples of cover crops are: (1) grass cover crops, (2) rye, which increases organic matter and conserve moisture, (3) sorghum and Sudan grass, whose roots penetrate deeply into the ground and favourably affect the physical properties of the soil, as well as (4) ryegrass, which, in the case of overwet soil, stabilises inter-row space in crops, perennial plantations, on the headlands of agricultural lots and non-agricultural areas (Snapp et al., 2005; Kaspar et al., 2007). Fodder radish forms a large root, and thus allows the easy infiltration of water into the soil (Lawley et al., 2011). Xerophyte leguminous plants, yellow lentils and alfalfa utilise water efficiently, and, in cover crops, they conserve soil moisture better than on bare uncultivated soil (Sormunen-Cristian et al., 2008).

CONTROL OF WEEDS AND HARMFUL ORGANISMS

Cover crops help weed control (Steinmaus et al., 2008), as well as the reduction of damage from diseases, insects and nematodes (Hooks et al., 2010) with different mechanisms. Cover crops suppress weeds physicaly or due to their allelopathic effect. The physical activity is about competitive relations which can manifest (1) as plant shading, resulting in a change in light frequency crops (Steinmaus et al., 2008), which prevents weed seeds from germinating, or (2) as a mechanical suppression of weed by high-coverage crops (Drazić, 1999), such as the crops of small grains, buckwheat and brassicas (Kruidhof et al., 2008). According to the research of Farooq et al. (2011), allelopathic effect is linked with root secretions, which may have a natural herbicidal effect on the weeds. These natural processes can have a negative effect on the main crop (rye, corn), which can be exceeded by timely destruction of cover crops and a proper nutrition of the main crop.

The introduction of bioactive plants - "plant friends" - can be successfully performed in the biocontrol of cropping systems (Ugrenović et al., 2012). They can repel harmful insects (pyrethrum, yarrow), or attract beneficial predators and parasitoids (fennel, cumin, dill, mint, buckwheat), and, in this way, the number of insect pests can be reduced below a certain level (Ugrenović et al., 2011; 2012). Cover crops can create a negative environment for diseases, especially those based on mustard or phacelia which are capable of producing compounds that reduce pest populations of nematodes (Kokalis-Burel & Rodriguez-Kabana, 2006; Henderson et al., 2009).

SELECTION AND MANAGEMENT OF COVER CROPS

The reasons for and goals of cover crop establishment must be set carefully prior to the establishment. According to Clark (2008), the manifestation of the use of cover crops and the strength of their effects depends on the site and the season, but a properly set cover crop will almost always achieve at least two or three positive effects (Snapp et al., 2005; Fageria et al., 2005). To start with the advantages the advantages which certain cover crops allow, the goals should be reduced to one or two primary and several secondary ones goals. Goals could be: to provide nitrogen, to manage organic matter, to enhance soil structure, to reduce soil erosion, to conserve soil moisture, to provide weed control, to establish biocontrol of harmful organisms and others.

Apart from their benefits, cover crops bear some potential disadvantages (increased seed costs, the increase in the amount of labor, the competition with main crops for soil moisture and nutrients, potential attraction to certain harmful organisms, etc.), which further limits their applicability. When choosing and setting up a cover crop management plan, one should start from setting crop rotations for a longer term, and, for each lot, possible rotational crops should be pointed out, as well as the terms of the sowing and the harvesting of the main crop. It is also necessary to take into consideration some issues such as: local agroecological conditions (for example: the amount of rainfall, the occurrence of early autumn and late spring frosts ect.), main crop needs, system of production (organic or integral, irrigation or no irrigation, conservation or classic processing etc.). In the scope of the above mentioned facts, it is necessary to find time and space for the establishment of cover crops, determine the needed plant species, as well as the technological model that will meet the objectives.

In keeping with to sowing terms, cover crops can be established as inter-cover crops (subsequent, stubble, winter), and, in wide-row crops, they can be sowed in inter-row space as intercrops (Fageria et al., 2005; Kruidhof et al., 2008). Cover crops can be established as annual or perennial crops (Snapp et al., 2005).

COVER CROPS AS SUBSEQUENT OR PRECROP

Cover crops should be established during the period between two main crops, in order to cover the soil surface with biomass throughout the year (Pictures 1and 2).

After the harvest of the main crop early in the summer, fast-growing plant species (buckwheat, sorghum, Sudan grass, etc.) are usually used for cover crop establishment to prevent erosion, provide weed control and manage organic matter (Filipović et al., 2005; Popović et al., 2013). Sikora et al. (2013) state that in subsequent cropping with irrigation, millet can provide higher yields in comparison with regular sowing. Sowing in summer in conditions without irrigation may cause a problem with the lack of moisture for germination of cover crops, and the sowing

Figure 1. Buckwheat: spatially isolated cover crops, established by direct sowing in the experimental field of the "Tamiš" Institute
(photograph by (Ugrenović, 2014).

Figure 2. Buckwheat: with the cover of predominantly adult crops, grown in the experimental field of the "Tamiš" Institute
(photograph by Ugrenović, 2014).

must be done just before the rain, and small seeds species (alfalfa) should be chosen for they do not require much moisture for germination.

When sowing cover crops in late summer and early autumn, when the soil is not occupied with main crops, varieties of winter plants are used. These belong to the grass family, legumes or brassicas and they are used for their resistance to low temperatures. Before the planting of the main crop, cover crop plants form roots and a significant amount of above-ground biomass. The advantages of such crops are reflected in the enhancement of the soil structure, protecting it from erosion during the winter, reducing nitrate leaching and adding organic matter. A destruction of cover crops is performed two to three weeks before the planting the main crop, using a roller crimper for cover crops, as well as wood chippers or herbicides. The delayed destruction during dry springs leads to the risk of cover crop plants consuming the most of the soil moisture planned for the next crop (Duiker, 2013).

The destruction of cover crops forms a layer of crop residue on the soil surface (mulch), which preserves soil moisture and increases water infiltration from precipitation, thus creating favourable conditions for the establishment of the main crop. In such circumstances, the implementation of direct drilling (no till) or partial treatment (strip till) and planting, creates the base of the main crop and the mulch, which will be formed later to prevent weeds and keep soil moisture (Ugrenović et al., 2015), as seen in Picture 3.

Figure 3. Strip till farming on the experimental field of the "Tamiš" Institute (photograph by Ugrenović, 2014).

COVER CROPS IN INTERCROPPING

Intercropping represents the growing of two or more crops together in which plant species have a positive competitive ratio (facilitation), and the goal of this kind of soil treatment is the increase in productivity per unit area. In intercropping, crop yields are often individually slightly lower than when there is one main crop, but their total combined yield is higher (Tsubo et al., 2005). Also, the combination of small grains with legumes provides a higher yield of protein when there is one crop of small grains (Kadžiulienė et al., 2011).

In addition to their productive and protective functions with a certain group of plants, intercrops also affect the environment (Walker et al., 2011), and thus perform the function of cover crops. In intercrops, land cover is increased, and therefore, we get the impact on erosion reduction. If the combined species have complementary needs, i.e. they equally efficiently use resources (light, water, nutrients), then, there is less of it left for weeds to use there is less of it left for weeds to use. As Ugrinović et al. (2014) observe, legumes can provide nitrogen for other plant species in intercrops. Stems in two parallel crops have a more balanced nutrient composition than in single crops – more favourable C:N. In intercrops, problems with pests are reduced because the pests have difficulties locating and navigating through the crop (Martin et al., 1989). In addition to these beneficial effects, intercropping leads to an increase in farm production diversity, as well as an increase in production safety, because adverse conditions will always affect one crop more than the other, so the one that is less endangered will provide the desired yield (Kovačević, 2003).

In intercrops, the crops that are usually combined are generically related to one another (cereals with legumes or grains with broadleaf crops), which leads to greater manifestation of beneficial effects (Martin et al., 1991). For that purpose, plant species tolerant to shade are frequently used, such as white clover, one-ryegrass, rye, hairy vetch, crimson clover, red clover, sweet clover and others (Sarrantonio, 2007).

A cover-cropping combination of two or more plant species (mixed intercropping) is often more effective than single cover crops based on only one plant species. By using the differences in biological and morphological characteristics of various plant species, for example, by combining the advantages of grasses and legumes, the objectives set with the establishment of cover crops can be achieved. Legumes in a cover crop with grasses receive a support which allows them to get more sunlight and higher nitrogen fixation.

Intercrops can be grown in alternate rows (e. g. Canola and barley, corn and soybeans), with the same or different spacing. One way is growing intercrops in alternating bands (strip-intercropping) with customised width for mechanical cultivation, which allows sowing, cultivating and harvesting every single crop separately (Vandermeer, 1989).

As noted by Sullivan (1999), the intercropping with cover crops may be performed by subsequent undersowing of a second crop with the existing one. Vandermeer (1989) lists delayed sowing of a second crop with the existing one as an example of the so-called delayed intercropping (relay intercropping). Red clover or alfalfa can be sown together with winter grains during the spring, and grass species with perennial legume crops in the autumn, which enhances coverage area and provides nitrogen.

PERENNIAL COVER CROPS

Perennial plant species of legume and grass family and mixtures of these are suitable to improve fertility and increase organic matter content in the soil. In several years, soil quality can be improved significantly. One of the characteristics of previously mentioned cover crops is that the aboveground biomass forms a living mulch, in which main crop is sown in strips. If it consists of legumes, nitrogen can be transferred to the main crop, and provided for a future one.

The practice of cover cropping imposes certain problems, such as: labor intensification, the best time to destroy one crop is not the best for another, the selection of herbicides is difficult, unwanted amounts of plant residues. The advantages of the use of intercropped cover crops usually outweigh the shortcomings, but it takes careful management to prevent problems.

EVALUATION OF COVER CROP PLANT SPECIES

Cover crops can be based on plant species from different families. The most commonly used are grasses, legumes, brassicas, as well as others.

Grass species – which are utilized as cover crops – are small grains, winter and spring ones, sorghum, Sudan grass, ryegrasses and buckwheat (Table 1). They are most commonly used for the adoption of the nutrient surplus from the soil, erosion control, the increase in organic matter content in the soil and weed control.

The sowing of small winter grains should be performed prior to the recommended optimal terms (late August, early September), so that the plants form a sufficient amount of biomass until the planting of the main crop, and thereby ensure the performance of the functions of the cover crop. Due to its pronounced resistance to low temperatures, winter rye is most commonly used. The other small winter grains (wheat, triticale and barley) are less resistant to low temperatures than rye, thus this characteristic is even more pronounced when they make cover crops, in case of which, they are sown earlier. By the length of vegetation period, rye is the first to yield, followed by barley and triticale and, finally, wheat. Rye grows particularly

Table 1. The plant varieties most commonly used in cover crops (a source with multiple authors)

Family	Variety	Impact within a Cover Crop
Grass (Poaceae)	Barley (*Hordeum vulgare*) Rye (*Secale cereale*) Oats (*Avena sativa*) Triticale Wheat (*Triticum sp*)	- Erosion prevention - Nutrient adoption from the soil - Increase in organic matter content in the soil - Weed control - Allelopathic action
	Sorghum (*Sorghum bicolor* sp)	- Erosion prevention - Nutrient adoption from the soil - Increase in organic matter content in the soil - Weed and nematode control
	Annual Ryegrass (*Lolium multiflorum*)	- Erosion prevention - Soil structure and drainage improvement - Increase in organic matter content in the soil - Weed control
Buckwheat (Polygonaceae)	Buckwheat (*Fagopyrum esculentum* Moench.)	- Weed control - Stimulation of biocontrol - Allelopathic action - Attraction of beneficial insects - Soil structure improvement
Legumes (*Fabaceae*)	Hairy vetch (*Vicia villosa* Roth) Woollypod vetch (*Vicia villosa* ssp. dasycarpa) Field peas (*Pisum sativum* subsp. arvense) Lupinus (*Lupinus sp*) Crimson Clover (*Trifolium incarnatum* L) Cowpeas (*Vigna unguiculata*)	- Fixation of atmospheric nitrogen - Soil structure improvement - Weed suppression
	Medics (*Medicago sp.*) Red Clover (*Trifolium pretense*) White clover (*Trifolium repens*) Subterranean clovers (*Trifolium subterraneum*) Berseem clover (*Trifolium alexandrinum*) Yellow sweetclover (*Melilotus officinalis*)	- Fixation of atmospheric nitrogen - Soil structure improvement - Weed suppression - Erosion prevention - Beneficial insect habitat
Brassicas (*Brassicaceae*)	White mustard (*Sinapsis alba* L) Rapeseed (*Brassica napus* L. em. Metzg. var. napus)	- Nutrient adoption from the soil - Increase in organic matter content in the soil - Soil structure improvement - Erosion prevention - Biocontrol of soil pests - Weed control
	Rapini (*Brassica rapa rapifera*) Fodder beet (*Beta vulgaris* L. *ssp. vulgaris convar. crassa* Alef) Cultivated radish (*Raphanus sativus* L) Rauola (*Raphanus sativus* var. oleiformis)	- Nutrient adoption from the soil - Increase in organic matter content in the soil - Improvement of the physical characteristics of the soil - Biocontrol of soil pests

rapidly in the spring, when it forms a large biomass, and some old varieties of reach stem height of up to 2 m. Barley and wheat have a slower growth, form a smaller biomass and a lower stem, and therefore, can be expected to bring fewer benefits to a cover crop than rye. After the destruction of a rye cover crop, the plant residues have a high C:N ratio, which causes a very slow decomposition, and brings about a short-term lack of nitrogen for the main crop, but, in the long run, it affects the increase in organic matter content in the soil. Grass cover crops acquire significant amounts of nutrients, nitrogen in particular, so, they are successfully used for the management of nitrates in the soil.

Unlike winter grains, oats does not have to go through the process of vernalisation, so if it is sown early enough, i.e., in July or August, it forms stems until winter, and sometimes even ears, so, it can produce more biomass until the winter than winter grains themselves. However, in that case, because of the sensitivity to low temperatures during the winter, oats plants freeze, so, the overall production of organic matter is still higher in winter cereals. Plant residues of ripe oats slowly degrade due a the high C:N ratio.

Legumes are highly valued for their establishment of cover crops, and both their annual and their perennial varieties are used (Table 1). On the roots of the plants from this family, bumps are formed with nitrogen-fixing bacteria, which synthesis a certain amount of nitrogen compounds, by which they fulfill their needs, but also, the needs of the crop to follow. Therefore, in a cover crop, legumes adopt less nitrogen surplus from the soil than grass species.

Legume plant residues quickly decompose in the soil because they have lower C:N ratio, and thereby, enrich it with biogenic ingredients. Biomass, at the time of overblooming, is especially rich in easily soluble compounds. As plant residues rapidly decompose after the destruction of cover crops with legumes, their effect on the prevention of erosion, the suppression of weeds, as well as the increase in organic matter content in the soil is smaller than that of grass cover crops.

Winter legumes produce the largest part of their biomass and nitrogen in the spring. The most commonly used are: hairy vetch, crimson clover, red clover and pea. When handling such cover crops, it is of utmost importance to determine the time of sowing, so as to allow plant overwintering on the one hand, and, on the other, to form a greater amount of biomass and tie up more atmospheric nitrogen. Hairy vetch is very resistant to low temperatures, and, in the autumn, it forms a small amount of biomass, so it should be sown earlier, i.e. in late August. A larger biomass provides more fixed nitrogen. The destruction of a legume cover crop for the purpose of the establishment of the main crop is performed when the first pods occur. This legume in a cover crop can provide for the needs of corn for nitrogen (Hanson et al., 1993). Crimson clover is also very resistant to low temperatures, so it overwinters well even when it is sown earlier, in late August. Its contribution in providing nitrogen through fixation is slightly lower than that of hairy vetch. The suitable species for the establishment of cover crops in the spring and the summer are: red clover, white clover, spring peas, and the great importance of several species of annual lupines should be particularly emphasized. In more arid areas (which is most of the Republic of Serbia), the most appropriate one is white lupine, because it endures drought better. Another good choice is red clover in case it is established before the summer heat. One way is after sowing in a crop of the wheat or barley (pairing) after the winter. In those conditions, a crop of red clover grows intensively only after the harvest. Winter pea is also used in cover, and its use takes place as part of the autumn sowing, and after the crops of small grains.

Perennial legumes in cover crops can bring the same benefits as annual ones can. But what makes them particularly suitable is the formation of "living mulch", as well as the fact that, after the destruction of aboveground biomass, nitrogen fixers on the roots of living plants continue to adopt atmospheric nitrogen. Suitable perennial legumes are: alfalfa, clovers and common bird's-foot trefoil.

Brassicas are known for their rapid growth, high biomass production, and the adoption of large amounts of nutrients. They can provide more than 80% of soil coverage when they are established as winter cover crops (Haramoto and Gallandt, 2004). Thus they stop erosion and stifle weeds. By the powerful spindle root, they deeply penetrate into the soil, spread it, consequently favourably affecting its physical properties. Brassicas acquire nutrients from deeper soil layers, making them available for the next crop through the plant establishment in the cover crop. Also, the effects of the creation of the acidic reaction of the soil around the roots stimulate the adoption of phosphorus, for which reason brassicas are more suitable for the use as green manure. What particularly singles brassicas out from other families whose plant species are commonly used as cover crops is the fact that most of them release the chemical compounds of glucosinolates, which are toxic to soil pathogens, harmful nematodes and some weeds. In cover crops, the most frequently used brassicas are: rapeseed, white mustard, as well as oilseed and fodder radish (Table 1).

The sowing of winter brassicas for the establishment of cover crops should be done as early as possible. Premature sowing, however, can adversely affect the overwintering, but, on the other hand, a delay in sowing reduces the effect a cover crop. It is recommended that the seeding should be done 4 weeks prior to early autumn frosts. If the plants reach rosette stage (6 to 8 leaves) before the first frosts, most brassicas overwinters well. In this phase, rapeseed withstands temperatures as low as -12°C (Rife and Zeinalib, 2003). This plant species is particularly suitable for the establishment within cover crops because it adopts as much as 95 kg of residual nitrogen per hectare, and, very soon, forms a large amount of biomass as much as 19 t ha^{-1}, after 45 days of vegetation period (Smith et al., 2005). Sowing brassicas in the spring delivers lower results, and it should also be done earlier, and so, low soil temperatures occur as a problem.

Brassicas can be sown on stubbles in the early summer for biomass production and the biocontrol of pests and weeds. Mustard is often used as biofumigant, as its biomass contains a large concentration of glucosinolates, whose products in the soil reduce the abundance of microsclerotia pathogenic fungus and harmful nematodes, and they also prevent the germination of some weeds.

In addition to the benefits that they provide us with in cover crops, brassicas may lead to the emergence of diseases, insect pests and weed seed germination in the following crop, so, attention should be paid to cover crop seeds. In the flowering stage, rapeseed often falls ill from white tree rot, especially in rainy years, so it should not be grown as a cover crop for seed if the crop to follow susceptible to the disease (beans, sunflower).

Grown in cover crop intercropping, brassicas exhibit high competitiveness and may suppress other species in a crop (oats, rye, clover). The ratio of seed quantity must be balanced so as to ensure unhindered growth of all components in intercropping. Because of the small seeds of brassicas, the intercropping with large seeded species is performed by the sowing in alternating rows: two rows of oats – one row of fodder radish. Rye can be successfully intercropped with fodder radish, which freezes during the winter, but it suppresses winter weeds. The required quantities of seed for this mixture is in ratio of 120 kg ha^{-1} of rye and 15 kg ha^{-1} of forage radish.

In order to prepare the soil for the sowing of the main crop, brassica cover crops are destroyed in the spring in the flowering stage with herbicides or with a cover crop roller. It is difficult to destroy rapeseed with herbicides at an advanced stage of development, and thus, it is necessary to use higher herbicide concentrations, because sprouts in incompletely destroyed crops can bring about weed the succeeding crop. The destruction can also be performed with a mulcher when the processing is performed in strips (strip-till), or the plant residues are ploughed. The plant residues of brassicas improve the structure and fertility of the soil, because they have a more favourable C:N ratio than cereals.

CONCLUSION

A large number of scientists all over the world have worked on cover crops application, whereas in Serbia, there is little knowledge of this technology to be used in practice. Crop production is seasonal, with significant impact of agro-ecological conditions, hence intensive research is needed to find a model for the introduction of cover crops in agricultural practice of different regions in Serbia. Some cases of the cover crops introduction have been registered and the results were modest. They were achieved in some scientific research institutions and in several, mostly organic farms, where the costs, the use of machinery, nitrogen and pesticides were reduced, and therefore, yields and profit were increased. However, cover crops can bring a number of other agronomic benefits such as: soil health enhancement, the prevention of erosion, water quality protection, the protection of biodiversity, which could hardly be measured financially. Thus, biological diversity can be achieved by switching from monoculture to crop rotation systems which would include cover crops. The introduction of cover crop in the broader production practices could significantly affect the increase in viability of the existing agricultural production systems.

ACKNOWLEDGMENT

This paper is part of the project research 46006 "Sustainable agriculture and rural development in the function of the Republic of Serbia strategic goals achievement within the Danube region", financed by the Ministry of Education, Science and Technological Development of the Republic of Serbia.

REFERENCES

Adekalu, K. O., Olorunfemi, I. A., & Osunbitan, J. A. (2007). Grass mulching effect on infiltration, surface runoff and soil loss of three agricultural soils in Nigeria. *Bioresource Technology*, *98*(4), 912–917. doi:10.1016/j.biortech.2006.02.044 PMID:16678407

Castro, J., Gomez, J. A., & Tortosa, F. S. (2014). *The role of cover crop and hedges in intensive olive orchards: Preventing soil erosion and promoting biodiversity*. The Earth Living Skin: Soil, Life and Climate Changes, *SSS Conference*, Bari, Italy.

Celette, F., Gaudin, R., & Gary, C. (2008). Spatial and temporal changes to the water regime of a Mediterranean vineyard due to the adoption of cover cropping. *European Journal of Agronomy*, *29*(4), 153–162. doi:10.1016/j.eja.2008.04.007

Didier, T., Philippe, L. G., Sonia, H., Amar, B., Claudia, M. C., Marielle, D. I., & Jairo, F. (2012). Prospects of Miscanthus x giganteus for PAH phytoremediation: A microcosm study. *Industrial Crops and Products*, *36*(1), 276–281. doi:10.1016/j.indcrop.2011.10.030

Diekow, J., Mielniczuk, J., Knicker, H., Bayer, C., Dick, D. P., & Kogel-Knabner, I. (2005). Soil C and N stocks as affected by cropping systems and nitrogen fertilization in a southern Brazil Acrisol managed under no-tillage for 17 years. *Soil & Tillage Research*, *81*(1), 87–95. doi:10.1016/j.still.2004.05.003

Dražić, D. (1999). Plodoredi u ratarstvu. In U I. Molnar (Ed.), Plodoredi u ratarstvu. Naučni institute zaratarstvoipovrtarstvo, Novi Sad.

Duiker, S. W. (2013). *The Agronomy Guide 2013-2014*. Penn State.

Đukić, V., Đorđević, V., Popović, V., Balešević-Tubić, S., Petrović, K., Jakšić, S., & Dozet, G. (2010). Effect of nitrogen and Nitragin application on soybean yield and protein content. *Ratarstvoipovrtarstvo*, *47*(1), 187–192.

Đukić, V., & Petković, S. (2009). Review of soil erosion and sediment transport models in river basins. *Vodoprivreda*, *41*(4-6), 117–125.

Fageria, N. K., Baligar, V. C., & Bailey, B. A. (2005). Role of cover crops in improving soil and row crop productivity. *Communications in Soil Science and Plant Analysis*, *36*(19-20), 2733–2757. doi:10.1080/00103620500303939

Farooq, M., Jabran, K., Cheema, Z. A., Wahid, A., & Siddique, K. H. (2011). The role of allelopathy in agricultural pest management. *Pest Management Science*, *67*(5), 493–506. doi:10.1002/ps.2091 PMID:21254327

Filipović, V., Glamočlija, Đ., Kajgana, M., & Jevđović, R. (2005). The Application of Eco – fertilisers in the buckwheat crop (*F. esculentum* Moench.).*XL Croatian Symposium on Agriculture with International Participation*. University of Zagreb, Faculty of Agriculture.

Filipović, V., Glamočlija, Đ., Popović, V., Jaćimović, G., Dimitrijević, S., Marković, T., & Radanović, D. (2013). Yarrow (*Achillea millefolium* L.) as a plant in perennial "eco-corridors".*VI Symposium with International Participation Innovations in Crop and Vegetable Production*. Faculty of Agriculture, Belgrade – Zemun.

Filipović, V., Jevđović, R., Dimitrijević, S., Marković, T., & Grbić, J. (2012). Uticaj primene organskih malčeva na agrofizičke osobine i prinos korena mrkve. Institut za proučavanje lekovitog bilja ″Dr Josif Pančić″, Beograd.

Filipović, V., Radivojević, S., Ugrenović, V., Jaćimović, G., Lazić, B., & Subić, J. (2011). *The Eco – corridor in Organic Agricultural Production. 22. Međunarodni simpozijum "Proizvodnja zdravstveno bezbedne hrane"*. 22nd International symposium "Safe food production", Trebinje, Bosnia and Herzegovina.

Filipović, V., & Ugrenović, V. (2010). *Biološka raznolikost organske proizvodnje u funkciji očuvanja biodiverziteta. Četvrti forum o organskoj proizvodnji*. Centar za organsku proizvodnju, Selenča.

Fuhrmann, J. J., Hartel, P., & Zuberer, D. A. (2005). *Principles and applications of soil microbiology*. Pearson Prentice Hall.

Fustec, J., Lesuffleur, F., Mahieu, S., & Cliquet, J. B. (2010). Nitrogen rhizodeposition of legumes. *Agron. Sustain. Dev.*, *30*(1), 57–66. doi:10.1051/agro/2009003

Gava, R., de Freitas, P. S., de Faria, R. T., Rezende, R., & Frizzone, J. A. (2013). Soil water evaporation under densities of coverage with vegetable residue. *Engenharia Agrícola*, *33*(1), 89–98. doi:10.1590/S0100-69162013000100010

Hanson, J. C., Lichtenberg, E., Decker, A. M., & Clark, A. J. (1993). Profitabilityofno-tillage corn following ahairy vetch cover crop. *Journal of Production Agriculture*, *6*(3), 432–436. doi:10.2134/jpa1993.0432

Haramoto, E. R., & Gallandt, E. R. (2004). Brassica cover cropping for weed management: A review. *Renewable Agriculture and Food Systems*, *19*(04), 187–198. doi:10.1079/RAFS200490

Henderson, D. R., Riga, E., Ramirez, R. A., Wilson, J., & Snyder, W. E. (2009). Mustard biofumigation disrupts biological control by Steinernemaspp. nematodes in the soil. *Biological Control*, *48*(3), 316–322. doi:10.1016/j.biocontrol.2008.12.004

Hooks, C. R., Wang, K. H., Ploeg, A., & McSorley, R. (2010). Using marigold (*Tagetes spp.*) as a cover crop to protect crops from plant-parasitic nematodes. *Applied Soil Ecology*, *46*(3), 307–320. doi:10.1016/j.apsoil.2010.09.005

Kadžiulienė, Ž., Šarūnaitė, L., & Deveikytė, I. (2011). Effect of Pea and Spring Cereals Intercropping on Grain Yield and Crude Protein Content. *Field and Vegetable Crops Research*, *48*, 183–188.

Kaspar, T. C., Jaynes, D. B., Parkin, T. B., & Moorman, T. B. (2007). Rye Cover Crop and Gamagrass Strip Effects on NO Concentration and Load in Tile Drainage. *Journal of Environmental Quality*, *36*(5), 1503–1511. doi:10.2134/jeq2006.0468 PMID:17766830

Kokalis-Burelle, N., & Rodriguez-Kabana, R. (2006). Allelochemicals as biopesticides for management of plant-parasitic nematodes. In *Allelochemicals: Biological control of plant pathogens and diseases* (pp. 15-29). doi:10.1007/1-4020-4447-X_2

Kovačević, D. (2003). Opšte ratarstvo. Univerzitet u Beogradu, Poljoprivredni fakultet, Beograd.

Kruidhof, H. M., Bastiaans, L., & Kropff, M. J. (2008). Ecological weed management by cover cropping: Effects on weed growth in autumn and weed establishment in spring. *Weed Research*, *48*(6), 492–502. doi:10.1111/j.1365-3180.2008.00665.x

Larsen, K. S., Andresen, L. C., Beier, C., Jonasson, S., Albert, K. R., Ambus, P., & Stevnbak, K. et al. (2011). Reduced N cycling in response to elevated CO2, warming, and drought in a Danish heathland: Synthesizing results of the CLIMAITE project after two years of treatments. *Global Change Biology*, *17*(5), 1884–1899. doi:10.1111/j.1365-2486.2010.02351.x

Lawley, Y. E., Weil, R. R., & Teasdale, J. R. (2011). Forage radish cover crop suppresses winter annual weeds in fall and before corn planting. *Agronomy Journal*, *103*(1), 137–144. doi:10.2134/agronj2010.0187

Ličina, V., Nešić, L., Belić, M., Hadžić, V., Sekulić, P., Vasin, J. & Ninkov, J. (2011). The soils of Serbia and their degradation. *Ratarstvo i povrtarstvo, 48*(2), 285-290.

Malone, R. W., Jaynes, D. B., Kaspar, T. C., Thorp, K. R., Kladivko, E., Ma, L., & Searchinger, T. et al. (2014). Cover crops in the upper midwestern United States: Simulated effect on nitrate leaching with artificial drainage. *Journal of Soil and Water Conservation*, *69*(4), 292–305. doi:10.2489/jswc.69.4.292

Martin, R. C., Arnason, J. T., Lambert, J. D. H., Isabelle, P., Voldeng, H. D., & Smith, D. L. (1989). Reduction of European Corn Born (Lepidoptera: Pyrolidae) damage by intercropping sorn with soybean. *Journal of Economic Entomology*, *82*(5), 1455–1459. doi:10.1093/jee/82.5.1455

Martin, R. C., Voldeng, H. D., & Smith, D. L. (1991). Nitrogen transfer from nodulating soybean to maize to nonnodulating soybean in intercrops: The 15N diltion method. *Plant and Soil*, *132*(1), 53–63. doi:10.1007/BF00011012

Mazzoncini, M., Sapkota, T. B., Barberi, P., Antichi, D., & Risaliti, R. (2011). Long-term effect of tillage, nitrogen fertilization and cover crops on soil organic carbon and total nitrogen content. *Soil & Tillage Research*, *114*(2), 165–174. doi:10.1016/j.still.2011.05.001

Muhammad, W., Vaughan, S. M., Dalal, R. C., & Menzies, N. W. (2011). Crop residues and fertilizer nitrogen influence residue decomposition and nitrous oxide emission from a Vertisol. *Biology and Fertility of Soils*, *47*(1), 15–23. doi:10.1007/s00374-010-0497-1

Parlak, M. & Ozaslan Parlak, A. (2010): Measurement of splash erosion in different cover crops. *Turkish Journal of Field Crops, 15*(2), 169-173.

Popović, V. (2010). Agrotehnički i agroekološki uticaji na proizvodnju semena pšenice, kukuruza i soje. Doktorska disertacija, Univerzitet u Beogradu, Poljoprivredni fakultet, Beograd.

Popović, V., Sikora, V., Glamočlija, Đ., Ikanović, J., Filipović, V., Tabaković, M., & Simić, D. (2013). Influence of agro-ecological conditions and foliar fertilization on yield and yield components of buckwheat in conventional and organic cropping system. Biotechnology in Animal Husbandry. Institute for Animal Husbandry. *Belgrade-Zemun, 29*(3), 537–546.

Popović, V., Vidić, M., Tatić, M., Zdjelar, G., Glamočlija, Đ., & Kostić, M. (2012): Uticaj folijarne ishrane na prinos i kvalitet soje proizvedene u organskoj proizvodnji. Zbornik radova Instituta PKB Agroekonomik, Beograd.

Restovich, S. B., Andriulo, A. E., & Portela, S. I. (2012). Introduction of cover crops in a maize–soybean rotation of the Humid Pampas: Effect on nitrogen and water dynamics. *Field Crops Research, 128*, 62–70. doi:10.1016/j.fcr.2011.12.012

Rife, C. L., & Zeinalib, H. (2003). Cold tolerance in oilseed rape over varying acclimation durations. *Crop Science, 43*(1), 96–100. doi:10.2135/cropsci2003.9600

Robertson, T. (1991). *Long-run impacts of cover crops on yield, farm income, and nitrogen recycling. Cover Crops for Clean Water*. Ankeny, IA: Soil and Water Conservation Society.

Santos, N. Z. D., Dieckow, J., Bayer, C., Molin, R., Favaretto, N., Pauletti, V., & Piva, J. T. (2011). Forages, cover crops and related shoot and root additions in no-till rotations to C sequestration in a subtropical Ferralsol. *Soil & Tillage Research, 111*(2), 208–218. doi:10.1016/j.still.2010.10.006

Sarrantonio, M. (2007). Selecting the Best Cover Crops for Your Farm. Managing Cover Crops Profitably. SARE, National Institute of Food and Agriculture, U.S. Department of Agriculture.

Sikora, V., Filipović, V., Berenji, J., & Popović, V. (2013). Agro-biological Traits of Common Millet (Panicum miliaceum L.) Genotypes in Regular and Stubble Crop. Ratarstvo i povrtarstvo / Field and Vegetable Crops research. Institute of Field and Vegetable Crops, Novi Sad.

Smith, R. F. (2005). *Mustard cover crops to optimize crop rotations for lettuce production*. California Lettuce Research Board.

Snapp, S. S., Swinton, S. M., Labarta, R., Mutch, D., Black, J. R., Leep, R., & O'Neil, K. et al. (2005). Evaluating cover crops for benefits, costs and performance within cropping system niches. *Agronomy Journal*, *97*(1), 322–332.

Sormunen-Cristian, R., Taponen, S., & Saastamoinen, I. (2008). Yellow-flowered lucerne: Properties and influence on performance and reproduction of ewes. *Agricultural and Food Science*, *7*(4), 437–446.

Stark, J. C. (1995). *Development of sustainable potato production systems for the Pacific NW*. SARE Project report #LW91-029. Western Region SARE. Retrieved from www.sare.org/projects

Steinmaus, S., Elmore, C. L., Smith, R. J., Donaldson, D., Weber, E. A., Roncoroni, J. A., & Miller, P. R. M. (2008). Mulched cover crops as an alternative to conventional weed management systems in vineyards. *Weed Research*, *48*(3), 273–281. doi:10.1111/j.1365-3180.2008.00626.x

Sullivan, P. (1999). Intercropping Principies and Production Practices. Agronomy Systems Guide. Appropriate Technology Transfer for Rural Areas. Fayetteville, AR: ATTRA. Retrieved from http://www.attra.org/attra-pub/intercrop.html

Tosti, G., Benincasa, P., Farneselli, M., Pace, R., Tei, F., Guiducci, M., & Thorup-Kristensen, K. (2012). Green manuring effect of pure and mixed barley–hairy vetch winter cover crops on maize and processing tomato N nutrition. *European Journal of Agronomy*, *43*, 136–146. doi:10.1016/j.eja.2012.06.004

Tsubo, M., Walker, S., & Ogindo, H. O. (2005). A simulation model of cereal–legume intercropping systems for semi-arid regions I. Model development. *Field Crops Research*, *93*(1), 10–22. doi:10.1016/j.fcr.2004.09.002

Ugrenović, V. (2015). *Pokrovni usevi u organskoj proizvodnji. In Alternativne ratarske biljke u konvencionalnom i organskom sistemu gajenja. Monografija, Institut za primenu nauke u poljoprivredi* (pp. 176–185). Beograd: Srbija.

Ugrenović, V., Bačić, B., Filipović, V., & Vučković, J. (2011). Buvač (Pyrethrum cinerariaefolium Trev.) korisna biljka u sistemu organske proizvodnje. XI Savetovanje o zaštiti bilja, Zlatibor, 158-159.

Ugrenović, V. & Filipović, V, (2012). *Značaj eko koridora u organskoj proizvodnji*. V naučno-stručni simpozijum iz selekcije i semenarstva Društva selekcionara i semenara Srbije, Vršac, Srbija.

Ugrenović, V., Filipović, V., Glamočlija, Đ., Subić, J., Kostić M. & Jevđović R. (2012). *Pogodnost korišćenja morača za izolaciju u organskoj proizvodnji.* Ratarstvo i povrtarstvo / Field and Vegetable Crops Research, Novi Sad.

Ugrinović, M., Girek, Z., Zdravković, J., Đorđević, M., Oljača, S., Brdar-Jokanović, M., & Zečević, B. (2014). Postrni usev rotkve u organskom sistemu gajenja. *Zbornik naučnik radova Instituta PKB Agroekonomik, 20*(1-4), 129-138.

Vandermeer, J. H. (1989). The Ecology of Intercropping. Cambridge University Press. doi:10.1017/CBO9780511623523

Wang, K. H., Hooks, C. R. R., & Marahatta, S. P. (2011). Can using a strip-tilled cover cropping system followed by surface mulch practice enhance organisms higher up in the soil food web hierarchy? *Applied Soil Ecology, 49*, 107–117. doi:10.1016/j.apsoil.2011.06.008

Zdravković, J., Mijatović, M., Pavlović, N., Ugrinović, M., & Adžić, S. (2012): Prvi koraci ka organskoj proizvodnji povrća. Institut za povrtarstvo, Smederevska Palanka i Ministarstvo poljoprivrede, šumarstva i vodoprivrede Republike Srbije, Beograd.

Zhang, G., Chan, K., Li, G., & Huang, G. (2011). The effects of stubble retention and tillage practices on surface soil structure and hydraulic conductivity of a loess soil. *Acta Ecologica Sinica, 31*(6), 298–302. doi:10.1016/j.chnaes.2011.07.006

ADDITIONAL READING

Dabneya, S. M., Delgadob, J. A., & Reevesc, D. W. (2001). Using winter cover crops to improve soil and water quality. *Communications in Soil Science and Plant Analysis, 32*(7-8), 1221–1250. doi:10.1081/CSS-100104110

Glamočlija, Đ., Janković, S., Popović, V., Filipović, V., Kuzevski, J., & Ugrenović, V. (2015). *Alternative crop plants in conventional and organic cropping system. Monograph, Institute for Science Application in Agriculture*. Belgrade: Serbia.

Hartwig, N. L., & Ammon, H. U. (2002, November). Cover crops and living mulches. *Weed Science, 50*(6), 688–699. doi:10.1614/0043-1745(2002)050[0688:AIACCA]2.0.CO;2

Holland, J. M. (2004). The environmental consequences of adopting conservation tillage in Europe: Reviewing the evidence. *Agriculture, Ecosystems & Environment, 103*(1), 1–25. doi:10.1016/j.agee.2003.12.018

Liebman, M., & Dyck, E. (1993). Crop Rotation and Intercropping Strategies for Weed Management. *Ecological Applications*, *3*(1), 92–122. doi:10.2307/1941795 PMID:27759234

Teasdale, J. R. (1996). Contribution of Cover Crops to Weed Management in Sustainable Agricultural Systems. *Journal of Production Agriculture*, *9*(4), 475–479. doi:10.2134/jpa1996.0475

Zhang, F., & Long, L. (2003). Using competitive and facilitative interactions in intercropping systems enhances crop productivity and nutrient-use efficiency. *Plant and Soil*, *248*(1), 305–312. doi:10.1023/A:1022352229863

KEY TERMS AND DEFINITIONS

Biodiversity: The definition of biodiversity refers to the amount of diversity between different plants, animals and other species in a given habitat at a particular time.

Biological Nitrogen Fixation: Can include conversion to nitrogen dioxide. All biological nitrogen fixation is done by way of nitrogenase metalloenzymes which contain iron, molybdenum, or vanadium. Microorganisms that can fix nitrogen are prokaryotes (both bacteria and archaea, distributed throughout their respective kingdoms) called diazotrophs. Some higher plants, and some animals (termites), have formed associations (symbiosis) with diazotrophs.

Cover Crops: Can be defined as crops that are usually not grown commercially, and can have a multiple role in crop rotations.

Crop Rotation: A pre-defined shift of cultivated plants in time and space. It is seen as an important phytosanitary measure that reduces the incidence of diseases, pests and weeds. In all biological farming systems, solid-seeded crop rotations are applied with a significant share of annual and perennial legumes and their mixtures with grasses to enrich the soil with nitrogen and provide enough roughage for livestock on a farm.

Erosion: In geomorphology and geology, erosion is the action of exogenic processes (such as water flow or wind) which remove soil and rock from one location on the Earth's crust, then transport it to another location where it is deposited.

Organic Agriculture: A production management system that promotes the recovery of ecosystems, including biodiversity, biological cycles and emphasizes the use of methods that largely excludes the use of off-farm inputs (FAO).

Soil Fertility: Refers to the ability of a soil related to plants its ease of tillage, fitness of seedbed, and impedance to seedling emergence and root penetration by providing nutrients and suitable soil structure to support the plants/trees growth.

Compilation of References

A.A. V.V. (1998). *Atti del Convegno Nazionale AIDEA - Lecce 1997*. Bologna: Clueb.

Adams, C. A. (2004). The ethical, social and environmental reporting-performance portrayal gap. *Accounting, Auditing & Accountability Journal, 17*(5), 731–757. doi:10.1108/09513570410567791

Adams, W. M. (2001). *Green Development: environment and sustainability in the third world*. London: Routledge.

Adekalu, K. O., Olorunfemi, I. A., & Osunbitan, J. A. (2007). Grass mulching effect on infiltration, surface runoff and soil loss of three agricultural soils in Nigeria. *Bioresource Technology, 98*(4), 912–917. doi:10.1016/j.biortech.2006.02.044 PMID:16678407

Adler, S., Basketter, D., Creton, S., Pelkonen, O., van Benthem, J., Zuang, V., & Zaldivar, J.-M. et al. (2011). Alternative (non-animal) methods for cosmetics testing: Current status and future prospects—2010. *Archives of Toxicology, 85*(5), 367–485. doi:10.1007/s00204-011-0693-2 PMID:21533817

Adner, R., & Kapoor, R. (2010). Value creation in innovation ecosystems: How the structure of technological interdependence affects firm performance in new technology generations. *Strategic Management Journal, 31*(3), 306–333. doi:10.1002/smj.821

AdnKronos. (2015). Ecco il 'muscolo di grano', la carne vegetale nata per amore. *Focus*. Retrieved April 9, 2015, from http://www.focus.it/ambiente/ecologia/ecco-il-muscolo-di-grano-la-carne-vegetale-nata-per-amore

Agreste, S., Carfì, D., & Ricciardello, A. (2012). An algorithm for payoff space in C^1 parametric games. *Applied Sciences, 14*, 1-14. Retrieved from http://www.mathem.pub.ro/apps/v14/A14-ag.pdf

Air Transport Action Group. (n.d.). Retrieved from www.atag.org

Airport Cooperative Research Program (ACRP) Report 11. (2009). *Guidebook on Preparing Greenhouse Gas Emissions Inventories*. Transportation Research Board.

Airports Council International (ACI). (2009). *Guidance Manual: Airport Greenhouse Gas Emissions Management*. ACI.

Albanesi, R. (2013). *Muscolo di grano*. Retrieved from http://www.albanesi.it/alimentazione/cibi/muscolo.htm

Albert, S. (1999). E-commerce Revitalizes Co-opetition. *Computerworld*, *33*(15), 36.

Aldrich, H. E. (1999). *Organizations evolving*. London: Sage Publications.

Aldrich, H. E. (2001). Who wants to be an evolutionary theorist: Remarks on the occasion of the Year 2000 OMT Distinguished Scholarly Career Award Presentation. *Journal of Management Inquiry*, *10*(2), 115–127. doi:10.1177/1056492601102004

Alexander, S. S. (1949). The effects of size of Manufacturing Corporation on the Distribution of Rate of Return. *The Review of Economics and Statistics*, *31*(3), 229–235. doi:10.2307/1927749

Al-Najjar, B., & Anfimiadou, A. (2012). Environmental policies and firm value. *Business Strategy and the Environment*, *21*(1), 49–59. doi:10.1002/bse.713

Alsmadi, S. (2007). Green marketing and the concern over the environment: Measuring environmental consciousness of Jordanian consumers. *Journal of Promotion Management*, *13*(3-4), 339–361. doi:10.1080/10496490802306905

Alvarez, S. A., & Barney, J. B. (2001). How Entrepreneurial Firms Can Benefit from Alliances with Large Partners. *The Academy of Management Executive*, *15*(1), 139–148. doi:10.5465/AME.2001.4251563

Ambec, S., & Lanoie, P. (2008). Does it pay to be green? A systematic overview. *The Academy of Management Perspectives*, *22*(4), 45–62. doi:10.5465/AMP.2008.35590353

Amendola, C. (2006). *La gestione ambientale e i suoi strumenti – Il bilancio ambientale per la rilevazione dei costi*. Roma: Aracne.

AMP. (n.d.). *Veganism*. Retrieved from http://www.abbotsmillproject.co.uk/what-we-do/veganism/

Anand, S., & Sen, A. (2000). Human Development and Economic Sustainability. *World Development*, *28*(12), 2029–2049. doi:10.1016/S0305-750X(00)00071-1

Anderson, D. R., & Anderson, K. E. (2009). Sustainability risk management. *Risk Management & Insurance Review*, *12*(1), 25–38. doi:10.1111/j.1540-6296.2009.01152.x

Anderson-Gough, F., Grey, C., & Robson, K. (2001). Tests of time: Organizational time-reckoning and the making of accountants in two multi-national accounting firms. *Accounting, Organizations and Society*, *26*(2), 99–122. doi:10.1016/S0361-3682(00)00019-2

Andrei, P., & Pesci, C. (2009). L'area di riferimento del bilancio socio-ambientale nei gruppi aziendali: spunti critici di riflessione emergenti da un'indagine empirica. *Financial Reporting*, (2), 45-70.

Andreopoulou, Z., Stiakakis, E., & Vlachopoulou, M. (2013). *E-Innovation for Sustainable Development of Rural Resources During Global Economic Crisis (Practice, Progress, and Proficiency in Sustainability)*. New York: IGI Global.

Andronic, B. C. (2000). *Performanţa firmei. Abordare transdisciplinară în analiza microeconomică*. Iaşi: Ed. Polirom.

Animalvibe. (2015). *Muscolo di grano*. Retrieved September 23, 2015, from http://animalvibe.org/2015/09/muscolo-di-grano/

Aragon-Correa, J. A., & Sharma, S. (2003). A contingent resource based view of proactive corporate environmental strategy. *Academy of Management Review*, *28*(1), 71–88.

Artene, A.E., Sabău, C., & Domil, A. (2009). Analiza performanţelor companiilor şi standardizarea situaţiilor financiare, Analele Seria Ştiinţe Economice. *Timişoara*, (15), 715-719.

Arthanari, T., Carfì, D., & Musolino, F. (2015). Game Theoretic Modeling of Horizontal Supply Chain Coopetition among Growers. *International Game Theory Review, 17*(2). doi:.10.1142/S0219198915400137

Asch, S. E. (1952). *Social Psycology*. Englewood Cliffs, NJ: Prentice Hall. doi:10.1037/10025-000

Ashford, N. A., & Hall, P. R. (2011). The Importance of Regulation-Induced Innovation for Sustainable Development. *Sustainability*, *3*(1), 270–292. doi:10.3390/su3010270

Aubin, J. P. (1998). Optima and Equilibria. Springer Verlag. doi:10.1007/978-3-662-03539-9

Aubin, J. P. (1997). *Mathematical Methods of Game and Economic Theory* (Revised Edition). North-Holland.

Australian Bureau of Statistics Business Register (ABSBR). (n.d.). *Counts of Australian Businesses, including Entries and Exit, Jun 2009 toJun2013*. Retrieved from http://www.abs.gov.au/AUSSTATS/abs@.nsf/Lookup/8165.0Main+Features1Jun%202009%20to%20Jun%20 2013?OpenDocument

Avare, P., Ravary, L., Legros, G., & Lemonnier, P. (2000). Gestiune şi analiză financiară. Ed. Economică, Bucureşti.

Baglieri, D., Carfì, D., & Dagnino, G. (2010). Profiting from Asymmetric R&D Alliances: Coopetitive Games and Firms' Strategies. In *Proceedings of 4th Workshop on Coopetition Strategy "Coopetition and Innovation"*. doi:10.13140/RG.2.1.2072.9043

Baglieri, D., Carfì, D., & Dagnino, G. (2016a). *A Coopetitive Game Model for Asymmetric R&D Alliances within a generalized "Reverse Deal"*. Aracne editrice.

Baglieri, D., Carfì, D., & Dagnino, G. B. (2012a). Asymmetric R&D Alliances and Coopetitive Games. In *Advances in Computational Intelligence: 14th International Conference on Information Processing and Management of Uncertainty in Knowledge-Based Systems, IPMU 2012, Proceedings, Part IV*. Springer-Verlag. doi:10.1007/978-3-642-31724-8_64

Baglieri, D., Carfì, D., & Dagnino, G. (2016b). Asymmetric R&D Alliances in the Biopharmaceutical Industry. *International Studies of Management & Organization*, *46*(2(3)), 179–201. doi:10.1080/00208825.2016.1112154

Bamadio, B., & Lebedev, K. A. (2015). Development of Altman Five-Factor Model of Assessing the Creditworthiness of an Enterprise. *Modern Economy*, *6*(07), 797–807. doi:10.4236/me.2015.67075

Bansal, P. (2005). Evolving sustainably: A longitudinal study of corporate sustainable development. *Strategic Management Journal*, *26*(3), 197–218. doi:10.1002/smj.441

Banyte, J., Brazioniene, L. & Gadeikiene, A. (2015). Expression of green marketing developing the conception of corporate social responsibility. *Engineering Economics, 21*(5).

Baum, J. A. C., Calabrese, T., & Silverman, B. S. (2000). Dont Go It Alone: Alliance Network Composition and Startups Performance in Canadian Biotechnology. *Strategic Management Journal*, *21*(3), 267–294. doi:10.1002/(SICI)1097-0266(200003)21:3<267::AID-SMJ89>3.0.CO;2-8

Bayyurt, N. (2007). İşletmelerde Performans Değerlendirmenin Önemi ve Performans Göstergeleri Arasındaki İlişkiler. *Sosyal Siyaset Konferansları Dergisi*, *53*, 577–592.

Bazerman, M., & Hoffman, A. (1999). Sources of Environmentally Destructive Behavior: Individual, Organizational, and Institutional Perspectives. *Research in Organizational Behavior*, *21*, 39–79.

Beal, A. (2010). The Role of the Business Analyst in Green ICT. In B. Unhelkar (Ed.), *Handbook of Research on Green ICT: Technology, Business and Social Perspectives* (pp. 42–50). New York: IGI Global.

Becker-Blease, J. R., Kaen, F. R., Etebari, A., & Baumann, H. (2010). Employees, firm size and profitability in U.S. manufacturing industries. *Investment Management and Financial Innovations*, *7*(2), 7–23.

Bell, J. (2010). Student business plan competitions: who really does have access?*Small Business Institute National Conference Proceedings*, *34*(1), 18-25.

Beloglazov, A., Abawajy, J., & Buyya, R. (2012). Energy-aware resource allocation heuristics for efficient management of data centers for Cloud computing. *Future Generation Computer Systems*, *28*(5), 755–768. doi:10.1016/j.future.2011.04.017

Bengtsson, M., & Kock, S. (2014). Coopetition-Quo Vadis? Past Accomplishments and Future Challenges. *Industrial Marketing Management*, *43*(2), 180–188. doi:10.1016/j.indmarman.2014.02.015

Bentes, F. M., Heleno, T. A., & Slama, J. G. (2013). Analysis of airport noise exposure around Viracopos International Airport using geographic information systems. *Journal of Air Transport Management*, *31*, 15–17. doi:10.1016/j.jairtraman.2012.11.001

Bentes, F. M., & Slama, J. G. (2011). Sensitivity analysis of airport noise using computer simulation. *Journal of Aerospace Technology and Management*, *3*(3), 295–300. doi:10.5028/jatm.2011.03033011

Bertoncelj, A., & Kovac, D. (2008). The influence of management capital on enterprise performance. *International Journal of Management and Enterprise Development*, *5*(4), 444–461. doi:10.1504/IJMED.2008.018761

Biggadike, R. C. (1976). *Corporate diversification: entry, strategy and performance*. Cambridge, MA: Harvard University Press.

Bilkey, W. J., & Tesar, G. (1977). Export behavior of smaller-sized Wisconsin manufacturing firms. *Journal of International Business Studies*, *8*(1), 93–98. doi:10.1057/palgrave.jibs.8490783

Biondi, Y., & Giannoccolo, P. (2012). Complementarities and Coopetition in Presence of Intangible Resources: Industrial Economic and Regulatory Implications. *Journal of Strategy and Management*, *5*(4), 437–449. doi:10.1108/17554251211276399

Bird, L., & Sumner, J. (2010). *Green power marketing in the United States: a status report (2009 data)*. Retrieved from: http://www.nrel.gov/docs/fy11osti/49403.pdf

Bird, B. J. (1993). Demographic approaches to entrepreneurship: The role of experience and background. *Advances in Entrepreneurship, Firm Emergence, and Growth*, *1*, 11–48.

Birley, S. (1989). Female entrepreneurs: Are they really different? *Journal of Small Business Management*, *27*(1), 32–37.

Blanco-Dávila, F. (2000). Beauty and the body: The origins of cosmetics. *Plastic and Reconstructive Surgery*, *105*(3), 1196–1204. doi:10.1097/00006534-200003000-00058 PMID:10724281

Bloomberg, L. P. (2015). *L'Oreal CEO: Commitment to Make Every Product Green*. Retrieved December 10, 2015, from http://www.bloomberg.com/news/videos/2015-12-04/l-oreal-ceo-commitment-to-make-every-product-green

Boiral, O. (2009). Greening the corporation through organizational citizenship behaviors. *Journal of Business Ethics*, *87*(2), 221–236. doi:10.1007/s10551-008-9881-2

Boiral, O., & Paille, P. (2012). Organizational citizenship behavior for the environment: Measurement and validation. *Journal of Business Ethics*, *109*(4), 431–445. doi:10.1007/s10551-011-1138-9

Böll-Stiftung, H. (2014). Meat Atlas. Fact and figures about the animals we eat. *Friends of the Earth Europe*. Retrieved January 9, 2014, from https://www.foeeurope.org/sites/default/files/publications/foee_hbf_meatatlas_jan2014.pdf

Bonaccorsi, A. (1992, December). (199). On the relationship between firm size and export intensity. *Journal of International Business Studies*, *23*(4), 605–636. doi:10.1057/palgrave.jibs.8490280

Borlea, S. N., & Achim, M. V. (2014). Assessing bankruptcy risk for Romanian metallurgical companies. *Metalurgija*, *53*(2), 279–282.

Boston University. (n.d.). *Vegetarian Society*. Retrieved from http://www.bu.edu/sustainability/what-you-can-do/join-a-club/vegetarian-society/

Boudreau, M. C., Chen, A. J., & Huber, M. (2007). Green IS: Building Sustainable Business Practices. In R. T. Watson (Ed.), *Information Systems*. Athens, GA: Global Text Project.

Boulding, K. (1996). The economics of the coming Spaceship Earth. In H. Jarrett (Ed.), *Environmental quality in a growing economy* (pp. 3–14). Baltimore, MD: Johns Hopkins University Press.

Brandenburger, A. M., & Nalebuff, B. J. (1995). The Right Game: Use Game Theory to Shape Strategy. *Harvard Business Review*, *64*, 57–71.

Brandenburger, A., & Stuart, H. (2007). Biform Games. *Management Science*, *53*(4), 537–549. doi:10.1287/mnsc.1060.0591

Branderburger, A. M., & Nalebuff, B. J. (1996). *Coopetition*. New York: Currency Doubleday.

Brockhaus, R. H. (1980). Risk taking propensity of entrepreneurs. *Academy of Management Journal*, *23*(3), 509–520. doi:10.2307/255515

Brockhaus, R. H., & Horwitz, P. S. (1986). The psicology of the entrepreneur. In D. L. Sexton & R. W. Smilor (Eds.), *The Art and the Science of Entrepreneurship* (pp. 25–48). Cambridge, MA: Ballinger.

Brooks, S., Wang, X., & Sarker, S. (2012), Unpacking Green IS: A Review of the Existing Literature and Directions for the Future. In Green Business Process Management. Springer Berlin Heidelberg.

Brown, H. S. (2011). Global Reporting Initiative. In Handbook of Transnational Governance. Cambridge, UK: Polity Press.

Brown, H. S., de Jong, M., & Lessidrenska, T. (2009). The rise of the Global Reporting Initiative: A case of institutional entrepreneurship. *Environmental Politics*, *18*(2), 182–200. doi:10.1080/09644010802682551

Brundtland, G. H. (1987). *Our Common Future*. Report of the World Commission on Environment and Development. Retrieved from: http://www.un-documents.net/our-common-future.pdf

Brunnert, A., & Krcmar, H. (2015). Continuous performance evaluation and capacity planning using resource profiles for enterprise applications. *Journal of Systems and Software*.

Brush, C. G. (1992). Research of women business owners: Past trends, a new perspective and future directions. *Entrepreneurship: Theory and Practice*, *16*(4), 5–30.

Budd, T., Ison, S., & Ryley, T. (2011). Airport surface access in the UK: A management perspective. *Research in Transportation Business & Management*, *1*(1), 109–117. doi:10.1016/j.rtbm.2011.05.003

Burlton, R. T. (2015). Delivering business strategy through process management. In *Handbook on Business Process Management 2* (pp. 45–78). Springer Berlin Heidelberg.

Burton, F. N., & Schlegelmilch. (1987). Profile analyses of non-exporters versus exporters grouped by export involvement. *Management International Review*, *27*, 38–49.

Busco, C., Frigo, M. L., Riccaboni, A., & Quattrone, P. (Eds.). (2003). Integrated Reporting Concepts and Cases that Redefine Corporate Accountability. Springer.

Bush, M., Lederer, L. A., Li, X., Palmisano, J., & Rao, S. (2009). The alignment of information systems with organizational objectives and strategies in health care. *International Journal of Medical Informatics*, *78*(7), 446–456. doi:10.1016/j.ijmedinf.2009.02.004 PMID:19307148

Buttà, C. (1995). *La genesi dell'impresa*. Milano: Franco Angeli.

Buttà, C. (2003). Elementi per una concettualizzazione del processo genetico. *Sinergie*, *61-62*, 71–95.

Bygrave, W. D. (1989). The entrepreneurship paradigm (II): Chaos and catastrophes among quantum jump. *Entrepreneurship: Theory and Practice*, *14*(2), 7–30.

Calero, C., & Piattini, M. (Eds.). (2015). *Green in Software Engineering*. Springer International Publishing Switzerland. doi:10.1007/978-3-319-08581-4

Campbell, M., & Carfì, D. (2015). Bounded Rational Speculative and Hedging Interaction Model in Oil and U.S. Dollar Markets. *Journal of Mathematical Economics and Finance*, *1*(1), 4–28. Retrieved from http://asers.eu/journals/jmef.html

Cannice, M. V. (2004). *Getting In on the University Business Plan Competition Circuit*. October 19. http://www.entrepreneur.com/article/73208

Cann, M. C., & Connelly, M. E. (2000). *Real-world cases in green chemistry*. Washington, DC: American Chemical Society.

Carayannis, E. G., & Alexander, J. (1999). Winning by Co-opeting in Strategic Government University-industry R&D Partnerships: The Power of Complex, Dynamic Knowledge Networks. *The Journal of Technology Transfer*, *24*(2-3), 197–210. doi:10.1023/A:1007855422405

Carfì, D. (2004). S-bases and applications to Physics and Economics. Annals of Economic Faculty, University of Messina, 165-190.

Carfì, D. (2004). S-linear operators in quantum Mechanics and in Economics. *Applied Sciences, 6*(1), 7-20. Retrieved from http://www.mathem.pub.ro/apps/v06/A06.htm

Carfì, D. (2006). S-convexity in the space of Schwartz distributions and applications. *Rendiconti del Circolo Matematico di Palermo, 77*.

Carfì, D. (2007). Dyson formulas for Financial and Physical evolutions in S'n. *Communications to SIMAI Congress, 2*, 1-10. doi:10.1685/CSC06156

Carfì, D. (2007). S-Linear Algebra in Economics and Physics. *Applied Sciences, 9*, 48-66. Retrieved from http://www.mathem.pub.ro/apps/v09/A09-CA.pdf

Carfì, D. (2008). Superpositions in Prigogine's approach to irreversibility for Physical and Financial applications. *Physical, Mathematical, and Natural Sciences, 86*(S1), 1-13. doi:10.1478/C1S0801005

Carfì, D. (2009). Decision-Form Games. In *Communications to SIMAI Congress - Proceedings of the 9th Congress of SIMAI, the Italian Society of Industrial and Applied Mathematics*. doi:10.1685/CSC09307

Carfì, D. (2009). Differentiable Game Complete Analysis for Tourism Firm Decisions. *Proceedings of the 2009 International Conference on Tourism and Workshop on Sustainable Tourism within High Risk Areas of Environmental Crisis*. Retrieved from http://mpra.ub.uni-muenchen.de/29193/

Carfì, D. (2009). Fibrations of financial events. *Proceedings of the International Geometry Center - Prooceding of the International Conference "Geometry in Odessa 2009*. Retrieved as MPRA Paper 31307 from http://mpra.ub.uni-muenchen.de/31307/

Carfì, D. (2009). Payoff space in C^1-games. *Applied Sciences, 11*, 35-47. Retrieved from http://www.mathem.pub.ro/apps/v11/A11-ca.pdf

Carfì, D. (2009). Globalization and Differentiable General Sum Games. *Proceedings of the 3rd International Symposium "Globalization and convergence in economic thought"*. Bucaresti: Editura ASE. doi:10.13140/RG.2.1.2215.8801

Carfì, D. (2010). *A model for Coopetitive Games*. MPRA Paper 59633. Retrieved from http://mpra.ub.uni-muenchen.de/59633/Carf

Carfì, D. (2010). *Topics in Game Theory*. Il Gabbiano; doi:10.13140/RG.2.1.4203.9766

Carfì, D. (2011). Financial Lie groups. *Proceedings of the International Conference RIGA 2011*. Bucharest University. Retrieved as MPRA Paper 31303 from http://mpra.ub.uni-muenchen.de/31303/

Carfì, D. (2011). Financial Lie groups. Cornell University Library. Retrieved from http://arxiv.org/abs/1106.0562

Carfì, D. (2011). Fibrations of financial events. Cornell University Library. Retrieved from http://arxiv.org/abs/1106.1774

Carfì, D. (2011). Reactivity in Decision-form Games. Cornell University Library. Retrieved from http://arxiv.org/abs/1103.0841

Carfì, D. (2012). Coopetitive Games and Applications. In Advances and Applications in Game Theory. doi:10.13140/RG.2.1.3526.6005

Carfì, D., & Cvetko Vah, K. (2011). Skew lattice structures on the financial events plane. *Applied Sciences, 13*, 9-20. Retrieved from http://www.mathem.pub.ro/apps/v13/A13-ca.pdf

Carfì, D., & Fici, C. (2012). The government-taxpayer game. *Theoretical and Practical Research in Economic Fields, 3*(1), 13-26. Retrieved from http://www.asers.eu/journals/tpref/tpref-past-issues.html

Carfì, D., & Gambarelli, G. (2015). Balancing Bilinearly Interfering Elements. *Decision Making in Manufacturing and Services, 9*(1), 27-49. Retrieved from https://journals.agh.edu.pl/dmms/article/view/1676/1410

Carfì, D., & Lanzafame, F. (2013). A Quantitative Model of Speculative Attack: Game Complete Analysis and Possible Normative Defenses. In M. Bahmani-Oskooee & S. Bahmani (Eds.), Financial Markets: Recent Developments, Emerging Practices and Future Prospects. Nova Science. Retrieved from https://www.novapublishers.com/catalog/product_info.php?products_id=46483

Carfì, D., & Magaudda, M. (2009). Complete study of linear infinite games. *Proceedings of the International Geometry Center - Prooceding of the International Conference "Geometry in Odessa 2009"*. Retrieved from http://d-omega.org/category/books-and- papers/

Carfì, D., & Musolino, F. (2011). Game Complete Analysis for Financial Markets Stabilization. In Proceedings of the 1st International On-line Conference on Global Trends in Finance (pp. 14–42). ASERS. Retrieved from http://www.asers.eu/asers_files/conferences/GTF/GTF_eProceedings_last.pdf

Carfì, D., & Musolino, F. (2012). A coopetitive approach to financial markets stabilization and risk management. In *Advances in Computational Intelligence, Part IV. 14th International Conference on Information Processing and Management of Uncertainty in Knowledge-Based Systems, IPMU 2012*. doi:10.1007/978-3-642-31724-8_62

Carfì, D., & Musolino, F. (2012). Game Theory and Speculation on Government Bonds. *Economic Modelling, 29*(6), 2417-2426. doi:10.1016/j.econmod.2012.06.037

Carfì, D., & Musolino, F. (2012). *Game Theory Models for Derivative Contracts: Financial Markets Stabilization and Credit Crunch, Complete Analysis and Coopetitive Solution*. Lambert Academic Publishing. Retrieved from https://www.lap-publishing.com/catalog/details//store/gb/book/978-3-659-13050-2/game-theory-models-for-derivative-contracts

Carfì, D., & Musolino, F. (2012). A game theory model for currency markets stabilization. University Library of Munich. Retrieved from https://mpra.ub.uni-muenchen.de/39240/

Carfì, D., & Musolino, F. (2012). Game theory model for European government bonds market stabilization: a saving-State proposal. University Library of Munich. Retrieved from https://mpra.ub.uni-muenchen.de/39742/

Carfì, D., & Musolino, F. (2013). Credit Crunch in the Euro Area: A Coopetitive Multi-agent Solution. In Multicriteria and Multiagent Decision Making with Applications to Economic and Social Sciences: Studies in Fuzziness and Soft Computing, 305, 27-48. doi:10.1007/978-3-642-35635-3_3

Carfì, D., & Musolino, F. (2013). Game Theory Appication of Monti's Proposal for European Government Bonds Stabilization. *Applied Sciences, 15*, 43-70. Retrieved from http://www.mathem.pub.ro/apps/v15/A15-ca.pdf

Carfì, D., & Musolino, F. (2014). Dynamical Stabilization of Currency Market with Fractal-like Trajectories. *Scientific Bulletin of the Politehnica University of Bucharest, Series A-Applied Mathematics and Physics, 76*(4), 115-126. Retrieved from http://www.scientificbulletin.upb.ro/rev_docs_arhiva/rezc3a_239636.pdf

Carfì, D., & Okura, M. (2014). Coopetition and Game Theory. *Journal of Applied Economic Sciences, 9*, 457-468. Retrieved from http://cesmaa.eu/journals/jaes/files/JAES_2014_Fall.pdf#page=123

Carfì, D., & Perrone, E. (2011). Asymmetric Bertrand Duopoly: Game Complete Analysis by Algebra System Maxima. In *Mathematical Models in Economics*, (pp. 44-66). ASERS Publishing House. Retrieved from http://mpra.ub.uni-muenchen.de/35417/

Carfì, D., & Perrone, E. (2011). Game Complete Analysis of Bertrand Duopoly. *Theoretical and Practical Research in Economic Fields, 2*. Retrieved from http://mpra.ub.uni-muenchen.de/31302/

Carfì, D., & Perrone, E. (2011). Game Complete Analysis of Bertrand Duopoly. In *Mathematical Models in Economics*, (pp. 22-43). ASERS Publishing House. Retrieved from http://mpra.ub.uni-muenchen.de/31302/

Carfì, D., & Perrone, E. (2012). Game complete analysis of symmetric Cournout duopoly. University Library of Munich. Retrieved from http://mpra.ub.uni-muenchen.de/ 35930/

Carfì, D., & Perrone, E. (2012). *Game Complete Analysis of Classic Economic Duopolies*. Lambert Academic Publishing. Retrieved from https://www.lap-publishing.com/catalog/details//store/ru/book/978-3-8484-2099-5/game-complete-analysis-of-classic-economic-duopolies

Carfì, D., & Pintaudi, A. (2012). Optimal Participation in Illegitimate Market Activities: Complete Analysis of 2 Dimimensional Cases. *Journal of Advanced Research in Law and Economics, 3*, 10-25. Retrieved as MPRA Paper from at https://mpra.ub.uni-muenchen.de/37822/

Carfì, D., & Ricciardello, A. (2011). Mixed extensions of decision-form games. Cornell University Library. Retrieved from http://arxiv.org/abs/1103.0568

Carfì, D., & Ricciardello, A. (2012). Algorithms for Payoff Trajectories in C1 Parametric Games. In *Advances in Computational Intelligence: 14th International Conference on Information Processing and Management of Uncertainty in Knowledge-Based Systems*. Springer-Verlag. doi:10.1007/978-3-642-31724-8_67

Carfì, D., & Ricciardello, A. (2012). *Topics in Game Theory*. Balkan Society of Geometers. Retrieved from http://www.mathem.pub.ro/apps/mono/A-09-Car.pdf

Carfì, D., & Ricciardello, A. (2013). An Algorithm for Dynamical Games with Fractal-Like Trajectories. In *Fractal Geometry and Dynamical Systems in Pure and Applied Mathematics II: Fractals in Applied Mathematics. PISRS 2011 International Conference on Analysis, Fractal Geometry, Dynamical Systems and Economics*. doi:10.1090/conm/601/11961

Carfì, D., & Ricciardello, A. (2013). Computational representation of payoff scenarios in C^1 families of normal-form games. *Uzbek Mathematical Journal, 1*, 38-52. Retrieved from https://www.researchgate.net/publication/259105575_Computational_representation_of_payoff_scenarios_in_C1-families_of_normal-form_games

Carfì, D., & Schilirò, D. (2011). Coopetitive Games and Global Green Economy. In *Moving from the Crisis to Sustainability: Emerging Issues in the International Context*. Retrieved as MPRA Paper from http://mpra.ub.uni-muenchen.de/32035/

Carfì, D., & Schilirò, D. (2011). Crisis in the Euro Area: Coopetitive Game Solutions as New Policy Tools. *Theoretical and Practical Research in Economic Fields, 2*(1), 23-36. Retrieved as MPRA Paper from http://mpra.ub.uni-muenchen.de/27138/

Carfì, D., & Schilirò, D. (2011). Crisis in the Euro Area: Co-opetitive Game Solutions as New Policy Tools. In *Mathematical Models in Economics*, (pp. 67-86). ASERS. Retrieved from http://www.asers.eu/asers-publishing/collections.html

Carfì, D., & Schilirò, D. (2011). A model of coopetitive games and the Greek crisis. Cornell University Library. Retrieved from http://arxiv.org/abs/1106.3543

Carfì, D., & Schilirò, D. (2012). A coopetitive Model for the Green Economy. *Economic Modelling, 29*(4), 1215-1219. doi:10.1016/j.econmod.2012.04.005

Carfì, D., & Schilirò, D. (2012). A Model of Coopetitive Game for the Environmental Sustainability of a Global Green Economy. *Journal of Environmental Management and Tourism, 3*(1), 5-17. Retrieved as MPRA Paper from https://mpra.ub.uni-muenchen.de/38508/

Carfì, D., & Schilirò, D. (2012). Global Green Economy and Environmental Sustainability: A Coopetitive Model. In *Advances in Computational Intelligence, 14th International Conference on Information Processing and Management of Uncertainty in Knowledge-Based Systems, IPMU 2012*. Springer Berlin Heidelberg. doi:10.1007/978-3-642-31724-8_63

Carfì, D., & Schilirò, D. (2012). Global Green Economy and Environmental Sustainability: A Coopetitive Model. Cornell University Library. Retrieved from http://arxiv.org/abs/1205.2872

Carfì, D., & Schilirò, D. (2013). A Model of Coopetitive Games and the Greek Crisis. In *Contributions to Game Theory and Management*. Saint Petersburg State University. Retrieved from http://www.gsom.spbu.ru/files/upload/gtm/sbornik2012_27_05_2013.pdf

Carfì, D., & Schilirò, D. (2014a). Coopetitive Game Solutions for the Greek Crisis. In *Design a Pattern of Sustainable Growth, Innovation, Education, Energy and Environment*. Retrieved from http://mpra.ub.uni-muenchen.de/54765/Carfì

Carfì, D., & Trunfio, A. (2011). A Non-linear Coopetitive Game for Global Green Economy. In *Moving from the Crisis to Sustainability: Emerging Issues in the International Context*, (pp. 421-428). Franco Angeli. Retrieved as MPRA Paper from http://mpra.ub.uni-muenchen.de/32036/

Carfì, D., Gambarelli, G., & Uristani, A. (2013). Balancing pairs of interfering elements. *Zeszyty Naukowe Uniwersytetu Szczecińskiego 760*, 435-442.

Carfì, D., Magaudda, M., & Schilirò, D. (2010). Coopetitive Game Solutions for the eurozone economy. Retrieved as MPRA Paper from http://mpra.ub.uni-muenchen.de/26541/1/MPRA_paper_26541.pdf

Carfì, D., Musolino, F., Ricciardello, A., & Schilirò, D. (2012). Preface: Introducing PISRS. *AAPP | Physical, Mathematical, and Natural Sciences, 90*. doi:10.1478/AAPP.90S1E1

Carfì, D., Musolino, F., Schilirò, D., & Strati, F. (2013). Preface: Introducing PISRS (Part II). *AAPP | Physical, Mathematical, and Natural Sciences, 91*. doi:.91S2E1 doi:10.1478/AAPP

Carfì, D., Patanè, G., & Pellegrino, S. (2011). Coopetitive Games and Sustainability in Project Financing. In *Moving from the Crisis to Sustainability: Emerging Issues in the International Context*, (pp. 175-182). Franco Angeli. Retrieved from http://www.francoangeli.it/Ricerca/Scheda_libro.aspx?CodiceLibro=365.906

Carfì, D. (2004). Geometric aspects of a financial evolution. *Atti della Reale Accademia della Scienze di Torino*, *138*, 143–151.

Carfì, D. (2004). The family of operators associated with a capitalization law. *Physical, Mathematical, and Natural Sciences*, *81-82*, 1–10. doi:10.1478/C1A0401002

Carfì, D. (2006). An S-Linear State Preference Model. *Communications to SIMAI*, *1*, 1–4. doi:10.1685/CSC06037

Carfì, D. (2008). Optimal Boundaries for Decisions. *Physical, Mathematical, and Natural Sciences*, *86*(1), 1–11. doi:10.1478/C1A0801002

Carfì, D. (2008). Structures on the space of financial events. *AAPP | Physical. Mathematical, and Natural Sciences*, *86*(2), 1–13. doi:10.1478/C1A0802007

Carfì, D. (2010). *Decision-Form Games*. Il Gabbiano. doi:10.13140/RG.2.1.1320.3927

Carfì, D. (2015). A model for coopetitive games. *Journal of Mathematical Economics and Finance*, *1*(1), 46–75. Retrieved from http://asers.eu/journals/jmef.html

Carfì, D., & Caristi, G. (2008). Financial dynamical systems. *Differential Geometry - Dynamical Systems*, *10*, 71–85. Retrieved from http://www.mathem.pub.ro/dgds/v10/D10-CA.pdf

Carfì, D., Caterino, A., & Ceppitelli, R. (2015). *State preference models and jointly continuous utilities*. doi:10.13140/RG.2.1.3689.0966

Carfì, D., & Donato, A. (in press). A critical analytic survey of an Asymmetric R&D Alliance in Pharmaceutical industry: Bi-parametric study case. *Journal of Mathematical Economics and Finance*.

Carfì, D., & Musolino, F. (2011). Fair Redistribution in Financial Markets: A Game Theory Complete Analysis. *Journal of Advanced Studies in Finance*, *2*(2(4)), 74–100.

Carfì, D., & Musolino, F. (2013). Model of Possible Cooperation in Financial Markets in Presence of Tax on Speculative Transactions. *Physical, Mathematical, and Natural Sciences*, *91*(1), 1–26. doi:10.1478/AAPP.911A3

Carfì, D., & Musolino, F. (2014). Speculative and Hedging Interaction Model in Oil and U.S. Dollar Markets with Financial Transaction Taxes. *Economic Modelling*, *37*, 306–319. doi:10.1016/j.econmod.2013.11.003

Carfì, D., & Musolino, F. (2015). A Coopetitive-Dynamical Game Model for Currency Markets Stabilization. *Physical, Mathematical, and Natural Sciences*, *93*(1), 1–29. doi:10.1478/AAPP.931C1

Carfì, D., & Musolino, F. (2015). Tax Evasion: A Game Countermeasure. *AAPP | Physical. Mathematical, and Natural Sciences*, *93*(1), 1–17. doi:10.1478/AAPP.931C2

Carfì, D., & Perrone, E. (2013). Asymmetric Cournot Duopoly: A Game Complete Analysis. *Journal of Reviews on Global Economics*, *2*, 194–202. doi:10.6000/1929-7092.2013.02.16

Carfì, D., & Ricciardello, A. (2009). Non-reactive strategies in decision-form games. *Physical, Mathematical, and Natural Sciences*, *87*(2), 1–12. doi:10.1478/C1A0902002

Carfì, D., & Ricciardello, A. (2010). An algorithm for payoff space in C^1 Games. *Physical, Mathematical, and Natural Sciences*, *88*(1), 1–19. doi:10.1478/C1A1001003

Carfì, D., & Romeo, A. (2015). Improving Welfare in Congo: Italian National Hydrocarbons Authority Strategies and its Possible Coopetitive Alliances with Green Energy Producers. *Journal of Applied Economic Sciences*, *10*(4), 571–592. Retrieved from http://cesmaa.eu/journals/jaes/files/JAES_summer%204(34)_online.pdf

Carfì, D., & Schilirò, D. (2012). A Framework of coopetitive games: Applications to the Greek crisis. *Physical, Mathematical, and Natural Sciences*, *90*(1), 1–32. doi:10.1478/AAPP.901A1

Carfi, D., & Schilirò, D. (2014). Improving Competitiveness and Trade Balance of Greek Economy: A Coopetitive Strategy Model. *Journal of Applied Economic Sciences*, *9*(2), 211–220. Retrieved from http://www.ceeol.com/aspx/issuedetails.aspx?issueid=583d6083-2bbf-4d8c-af1f-3b5786c6e087&articleId=8c9be4cb-86d9-43f1-b555-58b8cb28bbeb

Carland, J. W., Hoy, F., Boulton, W. R., & Carland, J. A. (1984). Differentiating entrepreneurs from small business owners: A conceptualization. *Academy of Management Review*, *9*(2), 354–359.

Carlson, L., Grove, S. J., & Kangun, N. (1993). A content analysis of environmental advertising claims: A matrix method approach. *Journal of Advertising*, *22*(3), 27–39. doi:10.1080/00913367.1993.10673409

Carroll, A. B. (1991). The Pyramid of Corporate Social Responsibility: Toward the Moral Management of Organizational Stakeholders. *Business Horizons*, *34*(July-August), 39–48. doi:10.1016/0007-6813(91)90005-G

Carroll, A. B. (1998). The Four Faces of Corporate Citizenship. *Business and Society Review*, *100/101*(1), 1–7. doi:10.1111/0045-3609.00008

Carroll, A. B. (2000). Ethical Challenges for Business in the New Millennium: Corporate Social Responsibility and Models of Management Morality. *Business Ethics Quarterly*, *10*(1), 33–42. doi:10.2307/3857692

Carter, N., Gartner, B., & Reynolds, P. (1996). Exploring Start-up Event Sequences. *Journal of Business Venturing*, *11*(3), 151–166. doi:10.1016/0883-9026(95)00129-8

Castro, J., Gomez, J. A., & Tortosa, F. S. (2014). *The role of cover crop and hedges in intensive olive orchards: Preventing soil erosion and promoting biodiversity*. The Earth Living Skin: Soil, Life and Climate Changes, *SSS Conference*, Bari, Italy.

Catturi, G. (1990). *Produrre e consumare, ma come? Verso l'ecologia aziendale*. Padova: Cedam.

Cavusgil, S. T., & John, R. N. (1981). Internal determinants of export marketing behavior: An empirical investigation. *JMR, Journal of Marketing Research*, *23*(February), 114–119. doi:10.2307/3151322

Cavusgil, S., & Naor, J. (1987). Finn and management characteristics as discriminators for export behavior. *Journal of Business Research*, *15*(3), 221–235. doi:10.1016/0148-2963(87)90025-7

CBS. (n.d.). *Statistical Abstract of Israel, 1014. Central Bureau of Statistics, Business Demography, A Collection of Statistical Data from the Business Register, 2003 – 2011*. Retrieved from http://www1.cbs.gov.il/webpub/pub/text_page_eng.html?publ=63andCYear=2011andCMonth=1

Celette, F., Gaudin, R., & Gary, C. (2008). Spatial and temporal changes to the water regime of a Mediterranean vineyard due to the adoption of cover cropping. *European Journal of Agronomy*, *29*(4), 153–162. doi:10.1016/j.eja.2008.04.007

Cerin, P., & Dobers, P. (2001). What does the performance of the Dow Jones Sustainability Group Index tell us? *Eco-Management and Auditing*, *8*(3), 123–133. doi:10.1002/ema.159

Chandler, G. N., & Hanks, S. H. (1994). Founder Competence, the environment and venture performance. *Entrepreneurship: Theory and Practice*, *18*(3), 77–90.

ChartsBin. (2009). *Current Worldwide Annual Meat Consumption per capita*. Retrieved from http://chartsbin.com/view/12730

Chen, A. J., Watson, R. T., Boudreau, M. C., & Karahanna, E. (2009). Organizational Adoption of Green Is & It: An Institutional Perspective. In ICIS 2009 Proceedings.

Chen, A. J. W., Boudreau, M. C., & Watson, R. T. (2008). Information systems and ecological sustainability. *Journal of Systems and Information Technology*, *10*(3), 186–201. doi:10.1108/13287260810916907

Chen, M., & Hambrick, D. C. (1995). Speed, Stealth, and Selective Attack: How Small Firms Differ from Large Firms in Competitive Behavior. *Academy of Management Journal*, *38*(2), 453–482. doi:10.2307/256688

Child, J. (1972). Organization structure, environment and performance: The role of strategic choice. *Sociology*, *6*(1), 2–22. doi:10.1177/003803857200600101

Chou, C. D. (2013). „Risk identification in Green IT practice. *Computer Standards & Interfaces*, *35*(2), 231–237. doi:10.1016/j.csi.2012.10.001

Ciora, C. (2013). *Analiza performanţei prin creare de valoare*. Bucureşti: Ed. Economică.

Clarke-Hill, C., Li, H., & Davies, B. (2003). The Paradox of Co-operation and Competition in Strategic Alliances: Towards a Multi-Paradigm Approach. *Management Research News*, *26*(1), 1–20. doi:10.1108/01409170310783376

Claver-Cortés, E., Molina-Azorín, J. F., & Pereira-Moliner, J. (2006). Strategic groups in the hospitality industry: Intergroup and intragroup performance differences in Alicante, Spain. *Tourism Management*, *27*(6), 1101–1116. doi:10.1016/j.tourman.2005.11.006

Coda, V. (1983). L'analisi delle relazioni di causa-effetto nel governo delle aziende. *Finanza Marketing e Produzione, 3*.

Cohen, M. (1999). *Cosmetics and perfumes, Egypt, 10,000 BCE*. Retrieved November 13, 2015, from http://www.smith.edu/hsc/museum/ancient_inventions/hsc01b.htm

Cohen, J. P., & Coughlin, C. C. (2008). Spatial hedonic models of airport noise. proximity. and housing prices. *Journal of Regional Science*, *48*(5), 859–878. doi:10.1111/j.1467-9787.2008.00569.x

Collins, C., Steg, L., & Koning, M. (2007). Customers Values, Beliefs on Sustainable Corporate Performance, and Buying Behavior. *Psychology and Marketing*, *24*(6), 555–577. doi:10.1002/mar.20173

Commission of the European Communities. (2001). Green Paper: Promoting a European framework for Corporate Social Responsibility. Brussels: Author.

Cooper, A. C. (1993). Challenges in predicting new firm performance. *Journal of Business Venturing*, *8*(3), 241–254. doi:10.1016/0883-9026(93)90030-9

Cooper, A. C., Willard, G. E., & Woo, C. Y. (1986). Strategies of high-performing new and small firms: A reexamination of the niche concept. *Journal of Business Venturing*, *1*(3), 247–260. doi:10.1016/0883-9026(86)90003-0

Corbett, C. J., & Kirsch, D. A. (2001). International Diffusion of ISO 14000 Certification. *Production and Operations Management*, *10*(3), 327–342. doi:10.1111/j.1937-5956.2001.tb00378.x

Craig, W. G. (2009). Health effects of vegan diets. *The American Journal of Clinical Nutrition*, *89*(5), 1627S–1633S. doi:10.3945/ajcn.2009.26736N PMID:19279075

Criste, A., Mosneanu, E. A., & Glod, A. G. (2008). O abordare a conceptului de competitivitate naţională[Financial Studies]. *Studii Financiare*, *12*(4), 51–59.

Crowther, D., & Aras, G. (2008). *Corporate Social Responsibility*. BookBoon.

Crowther, D., & Aras, G. (2009). *The Durable Corporation: Strategies for Sustainable Development*. Gower.

Csorba, L. M. & Boglea, V. A. (2011). Sustainable cosmetics: A major instrument in protecting the consumer's interest. *Regional and Business Studies*, *3*(1).

Dahlsrud, A. (2008). How corporate social responsibility is defined: An analysis of 37 definitions. *Corporate Social Responsibility and Environmental Management*, *15*(1), 1–13. doi:10.1002/csr.132

Daily, B. F., Bishop, J. W., & Govindarajulu, N. (2009). A conceptual model for organizational citizenship behavior directed toward the environment. *Business & Society*, *48*(2), 243–256. doi:10.1177/0007650308315439

Daley, B., & Preston, H. (2009). Aviation and Climate Change: Assessment of Policy Options. In S. Gössling & P. Upham (Eds.), *Climate change and aviation. Issues, challenges and solutions* (pp. 347–372). London: Sterling.

D'Amato, A. (2008). Rifiuti, mercati del riciclo ed efficienza economica. *Economia dei Servizi*, *3*(3), 423–440.

Damodaran, A. (2009). *Valuing young start-up and growth companies estimation issues and valuation challenges*. Stern School of Business, New York University.

Daniele, V., & Malanina, P. (2007). Il prodotto delle regioni e il divario Nord-Sud in Italia (1861-2004). *Rivista di Politica Economica*, 1–49.

Dao, V., Langella, I., & Carbo, J. (2011). From green to sustainability: Information Technology and an integrated sustainability framework. *The Journal of Strategic Information Systems*, *20*(1), 63–79. doi:10.1016/j.jsis.2011.01.002

Davis, A., & Olson, E. M. (2008). Critical competitive strategy issues every entrepreneur should consider before going into business. *Business Horizons*, *51*(3), 211–221. doi:10.1016/j.bushor.2008.01.010

Davis, J. J. (1993). Strategies for environmental advertising. *Journal of Consumer Marketing*, *10*(2), 19–36. doi:10.1108/07363769310039102

Dawkins, J., & Lewis, S. (2003). CSR in Stakeholder Expectations: And Their Implication for Company Strategy. *Journal of Business Ethics*, *44*(2), 185–193. doi:10.1023/A:1023399732720

Dedrick, J. (2010). Green IS: Concepts and Issues for Information Systems Research. *Communications of the Association for Information Systems*, *27*(11), 174–184.

Delmar, F., & Shane, S. (2002). What firm founders do: A longitudinal study of the startup process. In W. D. Bygrave, C. G. Brush, P. Davidsson, & J. Fiet (Eds.), *Frontier of Entrepreneurship Research*. Babson College.

Di Giandomenico, M. E. (2008). *Il bilancio sociale e il modulo aziendale etico*. Milano: Giuffrè.

Didier, T., Philippe, L. G., Sonia, H., Amar, B., Claudia, M. C., Marielle, D. I., & Jairo, F. (2012). Prospects of Miscanthus x giganteus for PAH phytoremediation: A microcosm study. *Industrial Crops and Products*, *36*(1), 276–281. doi:10.1016/j.indcrop.2011.10.030

Diekow, J., Mielniczuk, J., Knicker, H., Bayer, C., Dick, D. P., & Kogel-Knabner, I. (2005). Soil C and N stocks as affected by cropping systems and nitrogen fertilization in a southern Brazil Acrisol managed under no-tillage for 17 years. *Soil & Tillage Research*, *81*(1), 87–95. doi:10.1016/j.still.2004.05.003

Dinu, E. (2004). *Rentabilitatea firmei în practică* (C. H. Beck, Ed.). Bucureşti.

Directive 2002/49/EC of the European Parliament and the Council of 25 June 2002 relating to the assessment and management of environmental noise.

DM 14/11/97 Determination of the limits of sound sources.

DM 31/10/97 Airport noise methodology of measurement.

Dobler, M., Lajili, K., & Zèghal, D. (2014). Environmental performance, environmental risk and risk management. *Business Strategy and the Environment*, *23*(1), 1–17. doi:10.1002/bse.1754

Dogan, M. (2013). Does Firm Size Affect the Firm Profitability? Evidence from Turkey. *Research Journal of Finance and Accounting*, *4*(4), 53–59.

Dražić, D. (1999). Plodoredi u ratarstvu. In U I. Molnar (Ed.), Plodoredi u ratarstvu. Naučni institute zaratarstvoipovrtarstvo, Novi Sad.

Drolc, T. (2013). Education for sustainable development. *EFnews*. Retrieved January 10, 2013, from http://efnet.si/en/2013/01/10/education-for-sustainable-development/

Drucker, P. F. (1986). *Innovazione e imprenditorialità, Etas, Milano.* Eurostat. Business Demography in Europe Statistics. Retrieved from http://ec.europa.eu/eurostat/web/structural-business-statistics/entrepreneurship/business-demograpy

Dubini, P., & Schillaci, C. E. (1988). L'influsso delle variabili ambientali nella decisione di avviare una nuova impresa. In G. Lorenzoni & A. Zenoni (Eds.), *Gli studi sull'imprenditorialità in Italia* (pp. 80–110). Roma: Bulzoni.

Duiker, S. W. (2013). *The Agronomy Guide 2013-2014.* Penn State.

Đukić, V., Đorđević, V., Popović, V., Balešević-Tubić, S., Petrović, K., Jakšić, S., & Dozet, G. (2010). Effect of nitrogen and Nitragin application on soybean yield and protein content. *Ratarstvoipovrtarstvo, 47*(1), 187–192.

Đukić, V., & Petković, S. (2009). Review of soil erosion and sediment transport models in river basins. *Vodoprivreda, 41*(4-6), 117–125.

Dutto, A. (2015). Muscolo di grano: la "carne" vegan inventata in Calabria sta conquistando l'Italia. *La cucina italiana.* Retrieved October 28, 2015, from http://www.lacucinaitaliana.it/news/trend/muscolo-di-grano-carne-vegetale/

Du, W., Pan, S. L., & Zuo, M. (2013). How to balance sustainability and profitability in technology organizations: an ambidextrous perspective. In *Proceedings of IEEE Trans Eng Manag* (vol. 60, pp. 366–385). doi:10.1109/TEM.2012.2206113

Elgelany, A., & Nada, N. (2013). Energy Efficiency for Data Center and Cloud Computing: A Literature Review. *International Journal of Engineering and Innovative Technology, 3*(4).

Emissions and Dispersion Modeling System (EDMS). (2009). *Technical Manual, version 5, FAA-AEE-07-07 (Rev. 1 – 04/08/09).* Washington, DC: CSSI, Inc.

Erkelens, L. J. J. (2000). Research into New Noise Abatement Procedures for the 21st Century. In *AIAA Guidance,Navigation and Control Conference.* AIAA.

Esfahani, M. D., Rahman, A. A., & Zakaria, N. H. (2015). Green IT/IS Adoption as Corporate Ecological Responsiveness: An Academic Literature Review. *Journal of Software Computing and Decision Support Systems, 2*(1), 35–43.

Espey, M., & Lopez, H. (2000). The impact of airport noise and proximity on residential property values. *Growth and Change, 31*(3), 408–419. doi:10.1111/0017-4815.00135

Estrin, S., & Bevan, A. (2003). Determinants of Russian enterprise performance: Conclusions from the symposium. *Comparative Economic Studies, 45*(2), 192–203. doi:10.1057/palgrave.ces.8100010

Esty, D. C., & Winston, A. S. (2006). *Green to Gold: How Smart Companies use Environmental Strategy to Innovate, Create Value, and Build Competitive Advantage.* John Wiley & Sons Publishers.

Etica Vegana. (2016). *Muscolo di grano*. Retrieved from http://eticavegana.it/index.php?route=product/category&path=59

European Commission. (2011). A Roadmap for moving to a competitive low carbon economy in 2050. COM(2011) 112 final. Brussels: Author.

European Parliament and Council. (2003). *DIRECTIVE 2003/51/EC amending Directives 78/660/EEC, 83/349/EEC, 86/635/EEC and 91/674/EEC on the annual and consolidated accounts of certain types of companies, banks and other financial institutions and insurance undertakings*. Author.

Fageria, N. K., Baligar, V. C., & Bailey, B. A. (2005). Role of cover crops in improving soil and row crop productivity. *Communications in Soil Science and Plant Analysis*, *36*(19-20), 2733–2757. doi:10.1080/00103620500303939

FAO - Food and Agriculture Organization of the United Nations. (n.d.). *Sustainable food consumption and production*. Retrieved from http://www.fao.org/ag/ags/sustainable-food-consumption-and-production/en/

Farooq, M., Jabran, K., Cheema, Z. A., Wahid, A., & Siddique, K. H. (2011). The role of allelopathy in agricultural pest management. *Pest Management Science*, *67*(5), 493–506. doi:10.1002/ps.2091 PMID:21254327

Federal Aviation Administration (FAA), Office of Environment and Energy. (2007). Integrated Noise Model (INM), Version 7.0, User's guide. FAA.

Federal Aviation Administration (FAA). (1993). *Noise Abatement Departure Procedures*. FAA.

Fédération des Experts-comptables Européens. (2011). *Integrated Reporting. Debates and developments around the concept of integrated reporting are growing in importance*. Author.

Ferrara, G. (1998). L'etica ambientale nella economia delle imprese tra conflitti e condivisioni. *Rivista italiana di ragioneria e economia aziendale*, 7-8.

Fiala, N. (2008). Meeting the demand: An estimation of potential future greenhouse gas emissions from meat production. *Ecological Economics*, *67*(3), 412–419. doi:10.1016/j.ecolecon.2007.12.021

Fiegenbaum, A., & Karnani, A. (1991). Output Flexibility–A Competitive Advantage for Small Firms. *Strategic Management Journal*, *12*(2), 101–114. doi:10.1002/smj.4250120203

Figge, F., & Hahn, T. (2004). Sustainable Value Added – measuring corporate contributions to sustainability beyond eco-efficiency. *Ecological Economics*, *48*(2), 173–187. doi:10.1016/j.ecolecon.2003.08.005

Filipović, V., & Ugrenović, V. (2010). *Biološka raznolikost organske proizvodnje u funkciji očuvanja biodiverziteta. Četvrti forum o organskoj proizvodnji*. Centar za organsku proizvodnju, Selenča.

Filipović, V., Jevđović, R., Dimitrijević, S., Marković, T., & Grbić, J. (2012). Uticaj primene organskih malčeva na agrofizičke osobine i prinos korena mrkve. Institut za proučavanje lekovitog bilja "Dr Josif Pančić", Beograd.

Filipović, V., Radivojević, S., Ugrenović, V., Jaćimović, G., Lazić, B., & Subić, J. (2011). *The Eco – corridor in Organic Agricultural Production. 22. Međunarodni simpozijum "Proizvodnja zdravstveno bezbedne hrane"*. 22nd International symposium "Safe food production", Trebinje, Bosnia and Herzegovina.

Filipović, V., Glamočlija, Đ., Kajgana, M., & Jevđović, R. (2005). The Application of Eco – fertilisers in the buckwheat crop (*F. esculentum* Moench.).*XL Croatian Symposium on Agriculture with International Participation*. University of Zagreb, Faculty of Agriculture.

Filipović, V., Glamočlija, Đ., Popović, V., Jaćimović, G., Dimitrijević, S., Marković, T., & Radanović, D. (2013). Yarrow (*Achillea millefolium* L.) as a plant in perennial "eco-corridors". *VI Symposium with International Participation Innovations in Crop and Vegetable Production*. Faculty of Agriculture, Belgrade – Zemun.

Filippone, A. (2014). Aircraft noise prediction. *Progress in Aerospace Sciences*, *68*, 27–63. doi:10.1016/j.paerosci.2014.02.001

Fiori, G., Di Donato, F., & Izzo, M. F. (2007). *Corporate Social Responsibility and Firms Performance. An Analysis on Italian Listed Companies*. Retrieved from http://ssrn.com/abstract=1032851

Folan, P., & Browne, J. (2005). A review of performance measurement: Towards performance management. *Computers in Industry*, *56*(7), 663–680. doi:10.1016/j.compind.2005.03.001

Folan, P., Higgins, P., & Browne, J. (2006). A communications framework for extended enterprise performance measurement. *International Journal of Computer Integrated Manufacturing*, *19*(4), 301–314. doi:10.1080/09511920500340858

Fondazione sviluppo sostenibile. (2014). *L'Italia del riciclo 2014*. Retrieved from http://www.fondazionesvilupposostenibile.org/f/Documenti/2014/Italia+Riciclo/04_parte_uno-italia_del_riciclo_2014.pdf

Franceschelli, V. (2010). *Diritto Privato*. Milano: Giuffrè.

Franssen, E. A. M. et al.. (2004). Aircraft noise around a large international airport and its impact on general health and medication use. *Occupational and Environmental Medicine*, *61*(5), 405–413. doi:10.1136/oem.2002.005488 PMID:15090660

Freeman, R. E. (1984). *Strategic management: A stakeholder approach*. London: Pitman.

Freeman, R. E., & Evan, W. (1988). A stakeholder theory of the modern corporation: Kantian capitalism. In T. L. Beauchamp & N. E. Bowie (Eds.), *Ethical theory and business*. Englewood Cliffs, NJ: Prentice Hall.

Friedman, M. (1962). *Capitalism and Freedom*. Chicago: University of Chicago Press.

FSNC - Four Seasons Natura e Cultura. (n.d.). Retrieved from http://www.viagginaturaecultura.it

Fuhrmann, J. J., Hartel, P., & Zuberer, D. A. (2005). *Principles and applications of soil microbiology*. Pearson Prentice Hall.

Fulton, L., Cazzola, P., Cuenot, F. O., Kojima, K., Onoda, T., Staub, J., & Taylor, M. (2009). *Transport, energy and CO_2: Moving toward sustainability*. Paris, France: International Energy Agency.

Fulton, M., Kahn, B. M., & Sharples, C. (2012). *Sustainable Investing: Establishing Long-Term Value and Performance. In Climate Change Investment Research*. Deutsche Bank Group.

Fustec, J., Lesuffleur, F., Mahieu, S., & Cliquet, J. B. (2010). Nitrogen rhizodeposition of legumes. *Agron. Sustain. Dev.*, *30*(1), 57–66. doi:10.1051/agro/2009003

Gabrovec Mei, O. (1990). *Il linguaggio contabile – Itinerario storico e metodologico*. Torino: Giappichelli.

Gamble, G. O., Hsu, K., Jackson, C., & Tollerson, C. D. (1996). Environmental disclosures in annual reports: An international perspective. *The International Journal of Accounting*, *31*(3), 293–331. doi:10.1016/S0020-7063(96)90022-9

Gartner, W. B. (1985). A conceptual framework for describing the phenomenon of new venture creation. *Academy of Management Review*, *10*(4), 696–706.

Gartner, W. B. (1988). "Who is an entrepreneur?" is the wrong question. *American Journal of Small Business*, *12*(4), 11–32.

Garzella, S., Fiorentino, R., & D'Antonio, C. (2011). Le strategie ambientali ed il green management nel sistema della comunicazione ambientale.*Financial Reporting Workshop*.

Gatewood, J., Shaver, K. S., & Gartner, W. B. (1995). A longitudinal cognitive factors influencing start-up behaviors and success at venture creation. *Journal of Business Venturing*, *10*(5), 371–391. doi:10.1016/0883-9026(95)00035-7

Gava, R., de Freitas, P. S., de Faria, R. T., Rezende, R., & Frizzone, J. A. (2013). Soil water evaporation under densities of coverage with vegetable residue. *Engenharia Agrícola*, *33*(1), 89–98. doi:10.1590/S0100-69162013000100010

Gavin, M. L. (2014). Vegan Food Guide. *TeensHealth*. Retrieved March 2014, from http://kidshealth.org/teen/food_fitness/nutrition/vegan.html

George, J. A., & Rodger, J. A. (2010). *Smart data: enterprise performance optimization strategy* (Vol. 71). John Wiley & Sons. doi:10.1002/9780470583067

Georgescu, N., & Robu, V. (2001). *Analiza economico-financiară*. Bucuresti: Ed.ASE.

Ghobadi, S., & D'Ambra, J. (2011). Coopetitive Knowledge Sharing: An Analytical Review of Literature. *Electronic Journal of Knowledge Management*, *9*(4), 307–317.

Giambarrresi, F. (2013). *La dieta vegana è per tutti? Pro e contro*. Retrieved from http://www.greenstyle.it/la-dieta-vegana-e-per-tutti-pro-e-contro-50271.html

Girvin, R. (2009). Aircraft Noise Abatement and Mitigation Strategies. *Journal of Air Transport Management*, *15*(1), 14–22. doi:10.1016/j.jairtraman.2008.09.012

Gladwin, T. N., Kennelly, J. J., & Krause, T. S. (1995). Shifting Paradigms for Sustainable Development: Implications for Management Theory and Research. *Academy of Management Review*, *20*(4), 874–907.

Global Reporting Initiative. (2015). *G4 Sustainability Reporting Guidelines. Reporting Principles and Standard Disclosure*. Amsterdam: GRI.

Gnyawali, D. R., & Park, B. J. R. (2009). *C*o-opetition and Technological Innovation in Small and Medium-Sized Enterprises: A Multilevel Conceptual Model. *Journal of Small Business Management*, *47*(3), 308–330. doi:10.1111/j.1540-627X.2009.00273.x

Gomes-Cassares, B. (1997). Alliance Strategies of Small Firms. *Small Business Economics*, *9*(1), 33–44. doi:10.1023/A:1007947629435

Gordon, L. A., Loeb, M. P., & Tseng, C. Y. (2009). Enterprise risk management and firm performance: A contingency perspective. *Journal of Accounting and Public Policy*, *28*(4), 301–327. doi:10.1016/j.jaccpubpol.2009.06.006

Gouldson, A. (2004). Risk, regulation and the right to know: Exploring the impacts of access to information on the governance of environmental risk. *Sustainable Development*, *12*(3), 136–149. doi:10.1002/sd.237

Gourmandelle. (2015). *Vegetarian on a Budget | How Much Does a Vegetarian Diet Really Cost?* Retrieved September 19, 2015, from http://gourmandelle.com/vegetarian-on-a-budget-cost-diet/

Government of Canada. (n.d.). *The state of entrepreneurship in Canada*. OECD-SDBS Business Demography Indicator. Retrieved from http://www.ic.gc.ca/eic/site/061.nsf/eng/rd02473.html

Grace, M. F., Leverty, J. T., Phillips, R. D., & Shimpi, P. (2015). The Value of Investing in Enterprise Risk Management. *The Journal of Risk and Insurance*, *82*(2), 289–316. doi:10.1111/jori.12022

Graham, A. (2003). *Managing the Airports: an International Prospective* (2nd ed.). Elsevier.

Gray, L. (1914). Rent under the Assumption of Exhaustibility. *The Quarterly Journal of Economics*, *22*, 432–440.

Gray, R., Owen, D., & Adams, C. (1996). *Accounting & accountability: Changes and challenges in corporate social and environmental reporting*. London: Prentice Hall.

Gray, R., Owen, D., & Maunders, K. (1988). Corporate Social Reporting: Emerging Trends in Accountability and the Social Contract. *Accounting, Auditing & Accountability Journal, 1*(1), 6–20. doi:10.1108/EUM0000000004617

Greenwald, C. (2015). *Focus on Financial Materiality. Measuring Intangibles. In ROBECOSAM's Corporate Sustainability Assessment Methodology*. Zurich: RobecoSAM AG.

Group, F. C. A. (2014). Sustainability Report 2014. Fiat Chrysler Automobile NV.

Group, B. M. W. (2014). *Sustainable Value Report 2014*. Bayerische Motoren Werke AG.

Grove, R. H. (1996). Green Imperialism: Colonial Expansion, Tropical Island Edens, and the Origins of Environmentalism 1600-1860. Cambridge University Press.

Grove, R. H. (1995). *A Historical review of institutional and conservationist responses to fears of artificially induced global climate change: The Deforestation-Desiccation Discourse in Europe and the Clonial Context 1500-1940. In Le sciences hors d'occident au XX siècle, Orstom èditions* (Vol. 3, pp. 155–174). Nature et Environment.

Gulati, R., & Higgins, M. C. (2003). Which Ties Matter When? The Contingent Effects of Interorganizational Partnerships on IPO Success. *Strategic Management Journal, 24*(2), 127–144. doi:10.1002/smj.287

Gunasekaran, A., Williams, H. J., & McGaughey, R. E. (2005). Performance measurement and costing system in new enterprise. *Technovation, 25*(5), 523–533. doi:10.1016/S0166-4972(03)00176-7

Guthrie, J., & Yongvanich, K. (2006). An extended performance reporting framework for social and environmental accounting. *Business Strategy and the Environment, 15*(5), 309–321.

Hack, S., & Berg, C. (2014). The Potential of IT for Corporate Sustainability. *Sustainability, 7*(6), 4163–4180. doi:10.3390/su6074163

Hagedoorn, J., Carayannis, E., & Alexander, J. (2001). Strange Bedfellows in the Personal Computer Industry: Technology Alliances between IBM and Apple. *Research Policy, 30*(5), 837–849. doi:10.1016/S0048-7333(00)00125-6

Hagel, J. III, & Brown, J. S. (2005). Productive Friction: How Difficult Business Partnership Can Accelerate Innovation. *Harvard Business Review, 83*(2), 82–91. PMID:15724576

Hair, J. F. Jr, Black, W. C., Babin, B., Anderson, R., & Tatham, R. (2005). *Multivariate Data Analysis* (5th ed.). Upper Saddle River, NJ: Prentice-Hall.

Hall, M., & Weiss, L. (1967). Firms Size and Profitability. *The Review of Economics and Statistics, 49*(3), 319–331. doi:10.2307/1926642

Hanson, J. C., Lichtenberg, E., Decker, A. M., & Clark, A. J. (1993). Profitabilityofno-tillage corn following ahairy vetch cover crop. *Journal of Production Agriculture*, *6*(3), 432–436. doi:10.2134/jpa1993.0432

Haramoto, E. R., & Gallandt, E. R. (2004). Brassica cover cropping for weed management: A review. *Renewable Agriculture and Food Systems*, *19*(04), 187–198. doi:10.1079/RAFS200490

Harte, G., & Owen, D. (1991). Environmental Disclosure in the Annual Reports of British Companies: A Research Note. *Accounting, Auditing & Accountability Journal*, *4*(3), 09513579110144442. doi:10.1108/09513579110144442

Hart, L. S. (1997). Beyond Greening: Strategies for a Sustainable World. *Harvard Business Review*, (January-February), 67–79.

Haţegan, C. D., & Imbrescu, C. M. (2011). Contabilitatea şi performanţa economico-financiară. *Studia Universitatis Vasile Goldiş, Arad-Seria Ştiinţe Economice*, (1-2), 38-45.

Hebly, S. J., & Visser, H. G. (2008). *Advanced noise abatement departure procedures: Custom optimized departure profiles*. AIAA Guidance, Navigation and Control Conference, Honolulu. HI. doi:10.2514/6.2008-7405

Hedberg, C. J., & von Malmborg, F. (2003). The Global Reporting Initiative and corporate sustainability reporting in Swedish companies. *Corporate Social Responsibility and Environmental Management*, *10*(3), 153–164. doi:10.1002/csr.38

Helfat, C., Finkelstein, S., Mitchell, W., Peteraf, M. A., Singh, H., Teece, D. J., & Winter, S. G. (2007). *Dynamic Capabilities: Understanding Strategic Change in Organizations*. Oxford, UK: Blackwell.

Helfert, E. (2006). *Tehnici de analiză financiară. Ghidpentru crearea valorii*. B. M. T. Publishing.

Henderson, D. R., Riga, E., Ramirez, R. A., Wilson, J., & Snyder, W. E. (2009). Mustard biofumigation disrupts biological control by Steinernemaspp. nematodes in the soil. *Biological Control*, *48*(3), 316–322. doi:10.1016/j.biocontrol.2008.12.004

Hennison, K., & Kinnear, T. (1976). *Ecological marketing*. Englewood Cliffs, NJ: Prentice Hall.

Hinna, L. (2005). *Come gestire la responsabilità sociale dell'impresa. Processi, strumenti e modelli*. Milano: Il Sole 24 Ore.

Holzmuller, H. H., & Kasper, H. (1991). On a theory of export performance. *Management International Review*, *31*, 45–70.

Hooks, C. R., Wang, K. H., Ploeg, A., & McSorley, R. (2010). Using marigold (*Tagetes spp.*) as a cover crop to protect crops from plant-parasitic nematodes. *Applied Soil Ecology*, *46*(3), 307–320. doi:10.1016/j.apsoil.2010.09.005

Hopwood, B., Mellor, M., & OBrien, G. (2005). Sustainable development: Mapping different approaches. *Sustainable Development, 13*(1), 38–52. doi:10.1002/sd.244

Hotelling, H. (1931). The Economics of Exhaustible Resources. *Journal of Political Economy, 39*(2), 137–175. doi:10.1086/254195

Hu, Y., Song, F., & Zhang, J. (2004). *Competition, ownership, corporate governance and enterprise performance: Evidence from China.* Hong Kong Institute of Economics and Business Strategy Working paper, 1111.

Hussey, D. M., Kirsop, P. L., & Meissen, R. E. (2001). Global Reporting Initiative Guidelines: An Evaluation of Sustainable Development Metrics for Industry. *Environmental Quality Management, 11*(1), 1–20. doi:10.1002/tqem.1200

Iacovoiu, V. B., Străoanu, B. M., & Teodorescu, C. D. (2011). Instrumente şi tehnici de analiză a stării economico-financiare a firmei. Ed. Karta Graphic, Ploieşti.

Idowu, S. (Ed.). (2012). Encyclopedia of CSR. Springer.

Imbrescu, I., Băbăiţă, I., Spiridon, C.A. (2010). Performanţa–o abordare macroeconomică, Studia Universitatis Vasile Goldiş. *Arad-Seria Ştiinţe Economice*, (1), 370-380.

International Civil Aviation Organization (ICAO). (1993). *Environmental Protection, Annex 16* (Vol. 1). Montreal: Aircraft Noise.

International Civil Aviation Organization (ICAO). (2002). Amendment 7 to international standards and recommended practices. Annex 16 to the Convention on International Civil Aviation: Environmental Protection.

International Civil Aviation Organization (ICAO). (2008). *Guidance on the balanced approach to aircraft noise management. Doc 9829.* ICAO.

International Civil Aviation Organization (ICAO). (2010). *Environmental Report.* Retrieved from http://www.icao.int/environmental-protection/Pages/EnvReport10.aspx

International Civil Aviation Organization (ICAO). (2011). *Airport air quality guidance manual, Doc 9889.* Retrieved from http://www.icao.int/environmental-protection/Documents/Publications/FINAL.Doc 9889.1st Edition.alltext.en.pdf

Isaias, P., & Issa, T. (2015). *High Level Models and Methodologies for Information Systems.* Springer Science+Business Media New York.

Işfănescu, A., Hristea, A. M., & Vasilescu, C. (2003). *Analiză economico-financiară.* Bucuresti: Ed. ASE.

Isfanescu, A., Robu, V., Hristea, A. M., & Vasilescu, C. (2002). *Analiza economico-financiara.* Bucuresti: Ed. ASE.

Israeli, A. A. (2002). Star rating and corporate affiliation: Their influence on room price and performance of hotels in Israel. *International Journal of Hospitality Management*, *21*(4), 405–424. doi:10.1016/S0278-4319(02)00037-3

iVegan. (n.d.). Retrieved from http://shop.ivegan.it/28-muscolo-grano

Jan, A., & Marimuthu, M. (2015). Altman Model and Bankruptcy Profile of Islamic Banking Industry: A Comparative Analysis on Financial Performance. *International Journal of Business and Management*, *10*(7), 110. doi:10.5539/ijbm.v10n7p110

Jenkin, A. T., Webster, J., & McShane, L. (2011). An agenda for Green information technology and systems research. *Information and Organization*, *21*(1), 17–40. doi:10.1016/j.infoandorg.2010.09.003

Johann, T., Dick, M., Naumann, S., & Kern, E. (2012). How to Measure Energy-Efficiency of Software: Metrics and Measurement Results. In *Proceedings of the First International Workshop on Green and Sustainable Software (GREENS)*. doi:10.1109/GREENS.2012.6224256

Johri, L. M., & Sahasakmontri, K. (1998). Green marketing of cosmetics and toiletries in Thailand. *Journal of Consumer Marketing*, *15*(3), 265–281. doi:10.1108/07363769810219134

Jones, G. (2011). Globalization and beauty: A historical and firm perspective. *Ou Mei yan Jiu* [Eur America], *41*, 885-916.

Jónsson, B. (2007). Does the Size Matter? The Relationship between Size and Profitability of Icelandic Firms. Bifröst. *Journal of Social Sciences*, *1*, 43–55.

Jorde, T. M., & Teece, D. J. (1990). Innovation and Cooperation: Implications for Competition and Antitrust. *The Journal of Economic Perspectives*, *4*(3), 75–96. doi:10.1257/jep.4.3.75

Kadžiulienė, Ž., Šarūnaitė, L., & Deveikytė, I. (2011). Effect of Pea and Spring Cereals Intercropping on Grain Yield and Crude Protein Content. *Field and Vegetable Crops Research*, *48*, 183–188.

Kaplan, R. S., & Norton, D. P. (1996). *The Balanced Scorecard - translating strategy into action*. Boston: Harvard Business School Press.

Kaspar, T. C., Jaynes, D. B., Parkin, T. B., & Moorman, T. B. (2007). Rye Cover Crop and Gamagrass Strip Effects on NO Concentration and Load in Tile Drainage. *Journal of Environmental Quality*, *36*(5), 1503–1511. doi:10.2134/jeq2006.0468 PMID:17766830

Kato, T., & Long, C. (2006). CEO turnover, firm performance, and enterprise reform in China: Evidence from micro data. *Journal of Comparative Economics*, *34*(4), 796–817. doi:10.1016/j.jce.2006.08.002

Katz, J. A., & Gartner, W. B. (1988). Properties of emerging organization. *Academy of Management Review*, *13*(3), 429–441.

Kaufmann, H. R., Panni, M., & Orphanidou, Y. (2012). Factors affecting consumers' green purchasing behavior: An integrated conceptual framework. *Amfiteatru Economic*, *15*(31), 50–69.

Kaynak, E., & Kothari, V. (1984). Export behavior of small and medium sized manufacturers. *Management International Review*, *24*, 61–69.

Keller, K. L. (2003). Brand synthesis: The multidimensionality of brand knowledge. *The Journal of Consumer Research*, *29*(4), 595–600. doi:10.1086/346254

Key, T. J., Appleby, P. N., & Rosell, M. S. (2008). Health effects of vegetarian and vegan diets. *The Proceedings of the Nutrition Society*, *65*(1), 35–41. doi:10.1079/PNS2005481 PMID:16441942

Khemakhem, S., & Boujelbènea, Y. (2015). Credit risk prediction: A comparative study between discriminant analysis and the neural network approach. *Journal of Accounting and Management Information Systems*, *14*(1), 60–78.

King, A. A., & Lenox, M. J. (2001). Lean and Green? An Empirical Examination of the Relationship between Lean Production and Environmental Performance. *Production and Operations Management*, *10*(3), 244–256. doi:10.1111/j.1937-5956.2001.tb00373.x

Kirzner, I. M. (1979). *Percepition opportunity and profit*. Chicago: University of Chicago Press.

Kjaernes, U. (2010). Sustainable Food Consumption. Some contemporary European issues. *Sustainable Consumption Research Exchange*. Retrieved from http://www.sifo.no/files/file76709_prosjektnotat_nr.1-2010-web.pdf

Knaup, A. E. (2005). Survival and longevity in the Business Employment Dynamics data. *Monthly Labor Review*, 50–56.

Knaup, A. E., & Piazza, M. C. (2007). Business Employment Dynamics Data: Survival and Longevity. *Monthly Labor Review*, 3–10.

Knoepfel, I. (2001). Dow Jones Sustainability Group Index: A Global Benchmark for Corporate Sustainability. *Corporate Environmental Strategy*, *8*(1), 6–15. doi:10.1016/S1066-7938(00)00089-0

Knutson, P. (n.d.). Let's Uncover the Truth Behind The Vegan Food Pyramid. *Vegan Coach*. Retrieved from http://www.vegancoach.com/vegan-food-pyramid.html

Kokalis-Burelle, N., & Rodriguez-Kabana, R. (2006). Allelochemicals as biopesticides for management of plant-parasitic nematodes. In Allelochemicals: Biological control of plant pathogens and diseases (pp. 15-29). doi:10.1007/1-4020-4447-X_2

Kovačević, D. (2003). Opšte ratarstvo. Univerzitet u Beogradu, Poljoprivredni fakultet, Beograd.

Krosinsky, C., & Robins, N. (2008). *Sustainable Investing: The Art of Long-Term Performance*. London: Heartscan.

Kruidhof, H. M., Bastiaans, L., & Kropff, M. J. (2008). Ecological weed management by cover cropping: Effects on weed growth in autumn and weed establishment in spring. *Weed Research*, *48*(6), 492–502. doi:10.1111/j.1365-3180.2008.00665.x

Krut, R., & Moretz, A. (2000). The state of global environmental reporting: Lessons from the global 100. *Corporate Environmental Strategy*, *7*(1), 85–91. doi:10.1016/S1066-7938(00)80117-7

Kumar Garg, S., & Buyya, R. (2012). Green Cloud Computing and Environmental Sustainability. In S. Murugesan & G. R. Gangadharan (Eds.), *Harnessing Green IT: Principles and Practices* (pp. 76–87). Wiley-IEEE Press. doi:10.1002/9781118305393.ch16

Kumar, S. (2005). Exploratory analysis of global cosmetic industry: Major players, technology and market trends. *Technovation*, *25*(11), 1263–1272. doi:10.1016/j.technovation.2004.07.003

Lado, A. A., Boyd, N. G., & Hanlon, S. C. (1997). Competition, Cooperation, and the Search from Economic Rents: A Syncretic Model. *Academy of Management Review*, *22*(1), 110–141.

Laine, A. (2002). *Hand in Hand with the Enemy: Defining a Competitor from a New Perspective*. Paper Presented at the EURAM Conference: Innovative Research in Management, Stockholm, Sweden.

Larsen, K. S., Andresen, L. C., Beier, C., Jonasson, S., Albert, K. R., Ambus, P., & Stevnbak, K. et al. (2011). Reduced N cycling in response to elevated CO2, warming, and drought in a Danish heathland: Synthesizing results of the CLIMAITE project after two years of treatments. *Global Change Biology*, *17*(5), 1884–1899. doi:10.1111/j.1365-2486.2010.02351.x

Lawley, Y. E., Weil, R. R., & Teasdale, J. R. (2011). Forage radish cover crop suppresses winter annual weeds in fall and before corn planting. *Agronomy Journal*, *103*(1), 137–144. doi:10.2134/agronj2010.0187

Lawrence, S. (2015). *Beetroot and boot polish: How Britain's women faced World War 2 without make-up*. Retrieved November 20, 2015, from http://www.telegraph.co.uk/women/womens-life/11393852/Beauty-in-World-War-2-How-Britains-women-stayed-glamorous.html

Lee, J., & Barrett, P. (1996). *Body in need of reshaping*. Marketing, UK.

Lehman, G. (1995). A Legitimate Concern for Environmental Accounting. *Critical Perspectives on Accounting*, *6*(5), 393–412. doi:10.1006/cpac.1995.1037

Leitzmann, C. (2003). Nutrition ecology: the contribution of vegetarian diets. *The American Journal of Clinical Nutrition*. Retrieved from http://ajcn.nutrition.org/content/78/3/657S.long

Leitzmann, C. (2014). Vegetarian nutrition: past, present, future. *The American Journal of Clinical Nutrition*. Retrieved from http://ajcn.nutrition.org/content/early/2014/06/04/ajcn.113.071365

LePine, J. A., Erez, A., & Johnson, D. E. (2002). The nature and dimensionality of organizational citizenship behavior: A critical review and metaanalysis. *The Journal of Applied Psychology*, *87*(1), 52–65. doi:10.1037/0021-9010.87.1.52 PMID:11916216

Levy, D. L., Brown, H. S., & de Jong, M. (2010). The Contested Politics of Corporate Governance The Case of the Global Reporting Initiative. *Business & Society*, *49*(1), 88–115. doi:10.1177/0007650309345420

Liao, J., Welsch, H., & Wee-Liang, T. (2005). Venture gestation paths of nascent entrepreneurs: Exploring the temporal patterns. *The Journal of High Technology Management Research*, *16*(1), 1–22. doi:10.1016/j.hitech.2005.06.001

Ličina, V., Nešić, L., Belić, M., Hadžić, V., Sekulić, P., Vasin, J. & Ninkov, J. (2011). The soils of Serbia and their degradation. *Ratarstvo i povrtarstvo*, *48*(2), 285-290.

Li, J. H., Tian, B. G., Liu, T. Z., Liu, H., Wen, X., & Honda, S. (2006). Status quo of e-waste management in mainland China. *J. Mater. Cycles Waste Manag*, *8*(1), 13–20. doi:10.1007/s10163-005-0144-3

Lionzo, A. (2012). *Gli studi di financial accounting di matrice nordamericana. Fondamenti epistemologici e percorsi scientifici*. Milano: Franco Angeli.

Lipari, C., & Costa, M. (2005). Istituzionalismi di imprese e di bilancio tra passato, presente e futuro. Atti dell'VIII Convegno Nazionale della Società Italiana di Storia della Ragioneria. Teramo.

Loeser, F., Erek, K., & Zarnekow, R. (2012). Towards a Typology of Green IS Strategies: Insights from Case Study Research.*Proceedings Thirty Third International Conference on Information Systems*.

Longsworth, E. K. (1991). *The Anatomy of a Start-Up*. Boston: Inc. Publishing.

Loock, C. M., Staake, T., & Thiesse, F. (2013). Motivating Energy Efficient Behavior with Green IS: An Investigation of Goal Setting and the Role of Defaults. *Management Information Systems Quarterly*, *37*, 4.

Loos, P., Nebel, W., Gómez, J. M., Hasan, H., Watson, R. T., vom Brocke, J., & Recker, J. et al. (2011). Green IT: A Matter of Business and Information Systems Engineering? *Business & Information Systems Engineering*, *3*(4), 245–252. doi:10.1007/s12599-011-0165-5

Lopes, T. D. S. (2002). Brands and the evolution of multinationals in alcoholic beverages. *Business History*, *44*(3), 1–30. doi:10.1080/713999275

Lopes, T. D. S. (2007). *Global brands: The evolution of multinationals in alcoholic beverages*. Cambridge University Press. doi:10.1017/CBO9780511550911

Lopez-Lopez, J. C., Sissa, G., & Natvig, L. (2011). Green ICT: The Information Society's Commitment for Environmental Sustainability. *The European Journal for the Informatics Professional*, *12*(4).

López, M. V., Garcia, A., & Rodriguez, L. (2007). Sustainable Development and Corporate Performance: A Study Based on the Dow Jones Sustainability Index. *Journal of Business Ethics*, *75*(3), 285–300. doi:10.1007/s10551-006-9253-8

Löser, F. (2015). *Strategic Information Systems Management for Environmental Sustainability. Enhancing Firm Competitiveness with Green IS*. Universitätsverlag der TU Berlin.

Lounsbury, M., Ventresca, M., & Hirsch, P. M. (2003). Social movements, field frames and industry emergence: A cultural-political perspective on US recycling. *Socio-economic Review*, *1*(1), 71–104. doi:10.1093/soceco/1.1.71

Lu, C., & Morrell, P. (2006). Determination and Application of environmental costs at different sized airports – aircraft noise and engine emissions. *Transportation*, *33*(1), 45–61. doi:10.1007/s11116-005-2300-y

Lugano, M. (2012). Gli ingredienti della cucina naturale: muscolo di grano. *TuttoGreen*. Retrieved July 12, 2012, from http://www.tuttogreen.it/gli-ingredienti-della-cucina-naturale-muscolo-di-grano/

Lusk, J. L., & Bailey Norwood, F. (2007). *Some Economic Benefits and Costs of Vegetarianism*. Retrieved October 16, 2007, from http://citeseerx.ist.psu.edu/viewdoc/download?doi=10.1.1.549.1689&rep=rep1&type=pdf

Lyon, T., & Maxwell, J. (2007). Environmental Public Voluntary Programs Reconsidered. *Policy Studies Journal: the Journal of the Policy Studies Organization*, *35*(4), 723–750. doi:10.1111/j.1541-0072.2007.00245.x

Maclean, D., Akoh, B., & Egede-Nissen, B. (2010). ICTs, sustainability and the green economy. *Reconect Review*, *2*(3), 161–165.

MacMillan, A. (n.d.). 14 Best Vegan and Vegetarian Protein Sources. *Health Magazine*. Retrieved from http://www.health.com/health/gallery/0,20718479,00.html

Mahmoud, S. S., & Ahmad, I. A. (2013). Green Model for Sustainable Software Engineering. *International Journal of Software Engineering and Its Applications*, *7*(4).

Malone, R. W., Jaynes, D. B., Kaspar, T. C., Thorp, K. R., Kladivko, E., Ma, L., & Searchinger, T. et al. (2014). Cover crops in the upper midwestern United States: Simulated effect on nitrate leaching with artificial drainage. *Journal of Soil and Water Conservation*, *69*(4), 292–305. doi:10.2489/jswc.69.4.292

Malthus, T. (1798). *An Essay on the Principle of Population*. London: Macmillan.

Mandelbrot, B. (2004). *The (Mis)Behavior of Markets: A Fractal View of Risk, Ruin, and Reward*. Basic Books.

Manko, K. L. (2001). A depression-proof business strategy: The California Perfume Company's motivational literature. *Beauty and Business*, 142-168.

Marett, K., Otondo, R. F., & Taylor, G. S. (2013). Assessing the Effects of Benefits and Institutional Influences on the Continued Use of Environmentally Munificent Bypass System in Long-Haul Trucking. *Management Information Systems Quarterly*, *37*(4).

Margolis, J. D., & Walsh, J. P. (2003). Misery Loves Companies: Whither Social Initiatives by Business. *Administrative Science Quarterly*, *48*(2), 268–305. doi:10.2307/3556659

Mărgulescu, D., Mărgulescu, S. (2011). Cauzalitate şi determinism în trinomul: productivitate--cost--profit şi utilizare în analiza economico--financiară a firmei. *Internal Auditing & Risk Management*, *6*(1).

Marimon, F., del Mar Alonso-Almeida, M., del Pilar Rodríguez, M., & Alejandro, K. A. C. (2012). The worldwide diffusion of the global reporting initiative: What is the point? *Journal of Cleaner Production*, *33*, 132–144. doi:10.1016/j.jclepro.2012.04.017

Mark, S. H., & Rous, S. I. (2014). *A brief history of cosmetics by Baroness Anastasia Alexandrovna Andreeva (OL)*. Retrieved online on November 14, 2015,from http://www.florilegium.org

Marshal, R. S., & Brown, D. (2003). The strategy of sustainability: A Systems perspective on environmental initiatives. *California Management Review*, *46*(1), 101–126. doi:10.2307/41166234

Martin, R. C., Arnason, J. T., Lambert, J. D. H., Isabelle, P., Voldeng, H. D., & Smith, D. L. (1989). Reduction of European Corn Born (Lepidoptera: Pyrolidae) damage by intercropping sorn with soybean. *Journal of Economic Entomology*, *82*(5), 1455–1459. doi:10.1093/jee/82.5.1455

Martin, R. C., Voldeng, H. D., & Smith, D. L. (1991). Nitrogen transfer from nodulating soybean to maize to nonnodulating soybean in intercrops: The 15N diltion method. *Plant and Soil*, *132*(1), 53–63. doi:10.1007/BF00011012

Marzetti, L. (2001). *Manuale di diritto ambientale*. Padova: CEDAM.

Masini, C. (1970). *Lavoro e risparmio*. Torino: Utet.

Mass, S., Schuster, T., & Hartmann, E. (2014). Pollution prevention and service Stewardship strategies in the Third-part logistics industry: Effects on firm differentiation and moderating role of environmental communication. *Business Strategy and the Environment*, *23*(1), 38–55. doi:10.1002/bse.1759

Matacena, A. (1984). *Impresa e ambiente. Il bilancio sociale*. Bologna: Clueb.

Matthes, J., Wonneberger, A., & Schmuck, D. (2014). Consumers green involvement and the persuasive effects of emotional versus functional ads. *Journal of Business Research*, *67*(9), 1885–1893. doi:10.1016/j.jbusres.2013.11.054

Mazzoncini, M., Sapkota, T. B., Barberi, P., Antichi, D., & Risaliti, R. (2011). Long-term effect of tillage, nitrogen fertilization and cover crops on soil organic carbon and total nitrogen content. *Soil & Tillage Research*, *114*(2), 165–174. doi:10.1016/j.still.2011.05.001

McAfee, A. (2002). The impact of enterprise information technology adoption on operational performance: An empirical investigation. *Production and Operations Management*, *11*(1), 33–53. doi:10.1111/j.1937-5956.2002.tb00183.x

McDougall, P., Robinson, R. Jr, & DeNisi, A. (1992). Modeling new venture performance: An analysis of new venture strategy, industry structure, and venture origin. *Journal of Business Venturing*, *7*(4), 267–289. doi:10.1016/0883-9026(92)90002-9

McKinsey & Company. (2011). *The moment Is Now. Successful Pharmaceutical Alliances in Japan*. Retrieved from http://www.mckinsey.com/global_locations/asia/japan/en/latest_thinking

McMillen, D. P. (2004). Airport expansions and property values: The case of Chicago OHare Airport. *Journal of Urban Economics*, *55*(3), 627–640. doi:10.1016/j.jue.2004.01.001

McWilliams, A., & Siegel, D. (2000). Corporate social responsibility and financial performance: Correlation or misspecification? *Strategic Management Journal*, *21*(5), 603–609. doi:10.1002/(SICI)1097-0266(200005)21:5<603::AID-SMJ101>3.0.CO;2-3

Melville, P. N. (2010). Information Systems Innovation for Environmental Sustainability. *Management Information Systems Quarterly*, *34*(1), 1–21.

Messina, G. (2010). The high cost of ethical eating. *The Vegan RD*. Retrieved January, 20, 2010, from http://www.theveganrd.com/2010/01/the-high-cost-of-ethical-eating.html

Michell, P., King, J., & Reast, J. (2001). Brand values related to industrial products. *Industrial Marketing Management*, *30*(5), 415–425. doi:10.1016/S0019-8501(99)00097-8

Midgley, G., & Reynolds, M. (2004). Systems/operational research and sustainable development: Towards a new agenda. *Sustainable Development*, *12*(1), 56–64. doi:10.1002/sd.218

Miedema, H. M. E., & Vos, H. (1998). Exposure-response relationships for transportation noise. *The Journal of the Acoustical Society of America*, *104*(6), 3432–3445. doi:10.1121/1.423927 PMID:9857505

Miles, R. E., Snow, C. C., Meyer, A. D., & Coleman, H. Jr. (1988). Organizational strategy, strutture and process. In *The strategy process*. Englewood Cliffs, NJ: Prentice-Hall Inc.

Miller, A., & Camp, B. (1985). Exploring determinants of success in corporate ventures. *Journal of Business Venturing*, *1*(1), 87–105. doi:10.1016/0883-9026(85)90009-6

Milne, M. J., & Gray, R. (2013). W(h)ither Ecology? The Triple Bottom Line, the Global Reporting Initiative, and Corporate Sustainability Reporting. *Journal of Business Ethics*, *118*(1), 13–29. doi:10.1007/s10551-012-1543-8

Mingolia, S. (2015). *A Expo 2015, il "muscolo vegetale" made in Italy*. Retrieved from http://www.econewsweb.it/it/2015/05/05/muscolo-di-grano/#.VpqaLFKR4dU

Mintz, S. (Ed.). (2014). Accounting for the Public Interest – Perspectives on Accountability, Professionalism and Role in Society. Springer.

Mintzberg, H. (1973). *The nature of managerial work*. New York: Harper & Row.

Miolo Vitali, P. (1978). *Problemi ecologici nella gestione delle aziende*. Milano: Giuffrè.

Mission 2015. (n.d.). *Problems With Current Meat Production*. Retrieved from http://web.mit.edu/12.000/www/m2015/2015/meat_production.html

Mithas, S., Khuntia, J., & Roy, P. K. (2010). Green information technology, energy efficiency, and profits: Evidence from an emerging economy. In ICIS 2010 Proceedings.

Miyoshi, C., & Mason, K. J. (2013). The damage cost of carbon dioxide emissions produced by passengers on airport surface access: The case of Manchester Airport. *Journal of Transport Geography*, *28*, 137–143. doi:10.1016/j.jtrangeo.2012.12.003

Moir, L. (2001). What do we mean by corporate social responsibility?. *Corporate Governance: The International Journal of Business in Society*, *1*(2), 16 – 22.

Molla, A. (2009). Organizational Motivations for Green IT: Exploring Green IT Matrix and Motivation Models. *PACIS 2009 Proceedings*.

Molla, A. (2013). Identifying IT sustainability performance drivers: Instrument development and validation. *Information Systems Frontiers*, *15*(5), 705–723. doi:10.1007/s10796-013-9415-z

Molla, A., & Abareshi, A. (2011). Green IT Adoption: A Motivational Perspective.*Proceedings of the 15th Pacific Asia Conference on Information Systems* (PACIS), (pp. 1-14).

Molla, A., Cooper, V., & Pittayachawan, S. (2011). The Green IT Readiness (G-Readiness) of Organizations: An Exploratory Analysis of a Construct and Instrument. *Communications of the Association for Information Systems*, *29*(1), 4.

Moore, J. F. (2006). Business ecosystems and the view from the firm. *The Antitrust Bullettin*, *51*(1), 31–75.

Morin, E. (1993). *Introduzione al pensiero complesso*. Milano: Sperling & Kupfer.

Moss, K. R. (2012). Can America compete? Strategies for economic revival. *Harvard Magazine*. Retrieved from http://harvardmagazine.com/2012/09/the-business-ecosystem

Mouritsen, J., & Bekke, A. (1999). A space for time: Accounting and time based management in a high tecnology company. *Management Accounting Research*, *10*(2), 159–180. doi:10.1006/mare.1998.0092

Mraihi, F. (2015). Distressed Company Prediction using Logistic Regression: Tunisians Case. *Global Journal of Management and Business Research*, *15*(3).

Mugler, J., & Miesenbock, J. (1986). Determinants of increasing export involvement of small firms. *Proceedings, International Council of Small Business,World Conference*, (pp. 189-205).

Muhammad, W., Vaughan, S. M., Dalal, R. C., & Menzies, N. W. (2011). Crop residues and fertilizer nitrogen influence residue decomposition and nitrous oxide emission from a Vertisol. *Biology and Fertility of Soils*, *47*(1), 15–23. doi:10.1007/s00374-010-0497-1

Mung, E., & Lacroix, T. (2003). *France: the narrow path. In Immigrant Entrepreneurs. Venturing Abroad in the Age of Globalisation* (pp. 173–194). Oxford, UK: Berg.

Murugesan, S. (2008). *Harnessing Green IT: Principles and Practices*. IEEE IT Professional.

Muscle of Wheat. (n.d.). Retrieved from http://www.muscolodigrano.com/#!page3/cee5

Muscolo di Grano. (n.d.). Retrieved from https://www.facebook.com/muscolo.digrano/photos_stream

Musolino, F. (2012). Game theory for speculative derivatives: a possible stabilizing regulatory model. *Physical, Mathematical, and Natural Sciences, 90*(S1), 1-19. doi:10.1478/AAPP.90S1C1

Myers, R. (1990). *Classical and modern regression with applications* (2nd ed.). Boston, MA: Duxbury.

Nagasawa, S., & Kizu, Y. (2012). Green action as a luxury strategy in the field of cosmetics. *Waseda Business and Economics Studies Departmental Bulletin Paper, 48*, 1–17.

Nandhakumar, J., & Jones, M. (2001). Accounting for time: Managing time in project-based teamworking. *Accounting, Organizations and Society, 26*(3), 193–214. doi:10.1016/S0361-3682(99)00051-3

Napolitano, U. (2015). Muscolo di Grano, la carne vegetale del futuro, trionfa a Expo Milano quale unico prodotto alimentare veramente innovativo. *Famiglie d'Italia*. Retrieved September 27, 2015, from https://famiglieditalia.wordpress.com/2015/10/04/muscolo-di-grano-la-carne-vegetale-del-futuro-trionfa-a-expo-milano-quale-unico-prodotto-alimentare-veramente-innovativo/

National Sustainable Sales. (n.d.). *What is Vegan/Vegetarian?* Retrieved from http://www.nationalsustainablesales.com/vegan-vegetarian

Naumann, S., Dick, M., Kern, E., & Johann, T. (2011). The GREENSOFT model: A reference model for green and sustainable software and its engineering. *Sustain Comput Informat Syst, 1*(4), 294–304. doi:10.1016/j.suscom.2011.06.004

Nelson, J. P. (2004). Meta-Analysis of Airport Noise and Hedonic Property Values. *Journal of Transport Economics and Policy, 38*(1), 1–27.

Ngo, D. D., & Okura, M. (2008). Coopetition in a Mixed Duopoly Market. *Economic Bulletin, 12*(20), 1–9.

Nguyen, T. L. T., Hermansen, J. E., & Mogensen, L. (n.d.). *Environmental costs of meat production: The case of typical EU pork production*. Retrieved from http://www.researchgate.net/publication/251624206

Nichol, K. (2010), *Sustainable Cosmetics Summit to explore green marketing challenges*. Retrieved October 9, 2015, from http://www.cosmeticsdesign.com/Market-Trends/Sustainable-Cosmetics-Summit-to-explore-green-marketing-challenges

Nicolaou, A. I. (2004). Firm performance effects in relation to the implementation and use of enterprise resource planning systems. *Journal of Information Systems, 18*(2), 79-105.

Nicolò, D. (2001). Il bilancio sociale come strumento di governo delle relazioni con gli stakeholder. In Atti del Seminario Internazionale: Nuovi strumenti di comunicazione aziendale. Confronto di esperienze in tema di bilancio sociale (pp. 431-447).

Nicolò, D. (2015), Towards a theory on corporate reputation and survival of young firms. *Procedia Economics and Finance.*

Nicolò, D., & Ferrara, N. (2015). Corporate reputation, business plan and start-up sustainability. In Startups and Start-up Ecosystems: Theories, Models and Successful Cases in the Mediterranean Area. ASERS Publishing, University of Craiova Printing House.

Nicolò. (2013). Monitoraggio delle sequenze e risultati aziendali *Management Control*, F. *Angeli, Milano, 3*, 35–50.

Nicolò, D. (2000). Il bilancio sociale come strumento di governo delle relazioni con gli stakeholder. In F. Vermiglio (Ed.), *Nuovi strumenti di comunicazione aziendale. Confronto di esperienze in tema di bilancio sociale*. Torino: Giappichelli.

Nicolò, D. (2001). *La transizione al vertice delle imprese familiari minori*. Torino: Giappichelli.

Nicolò, D. (2009). *Il reporting per segmenti e l'informativa settoriale secondo l'IFRS 8*. Milano: Giuffrè.

Nicolò, D. (2011). *Caratteristiche generali delle imprese e del vertice imprenditoriale, grado di evoluzione del sistema informativo e dissesto: evidenze di un'indagine empirica. In L'accertamento del passivo. Procedimento di verifica dei crediti, giudizi di impugnazione e questioni critiche: i risultati di una ricerca sui fallimenti italiani*. Milano: IPSOA, Gruppo Wolters Kluvers.

Nicolò, D. (2015). Towards a theory on corporate reputation and survival of young firms. *Procedia Economics and Finance, 22*, 296–303. doi:10.1016/S2212-5671(15)00289-0

Nissan Motor Corporation. (2015). *Sustainability Report 2015*. Nissan Motor Co Ltd.

Noci, G. (2000). Environmental reporting in Italy: Current practice and future developments. *Business Strategy and the Environment, 9*(4), 211–223. doi:10.1002/1099-0836(200007/08)9:4<211::AID-BSE248>3.0.CO;2-9

Non solo Vegan. (2014). *Alimentazione vegana e sostenibilità ambientale*. Retrieved November 30, 2014, from http://www.nonsolovegan.it/alimentazione-vegana-e-sostenibilita-ambientale/

Normann, R. (1977). *Management for Growth*. New York: Wiley-Interscience.

Obermiller, C. (1995). The baby is sick/the baby is well: A test of environmental communication appeals. *Journal of Advertising, 24*(2), 55–70. doi:10.1080/00913367.1995.10673476

Ogilvie, M., & Ryan, M. (2011). Lipstick: More than a fashion trend. *Research Journal of Social Science and Management*, *1*(6), 117–128.

Ohkita, K., & Okura, M. (2014). Coopetition and Coordinated Investment: Protecting Japanese Video Games Intellectual Property Rights. *International Journal of Business Environment*, *6*(1), 92–105. doi:10.1504/IJBE.2014.058025

Okura, M. (2009). Coopetitive Strategies to Limit the Insurance Fraud Problem in Japan. In Coopetition Strategy: Theory, Experiments and Cases (pp. 240-257). Routledge.

Okura, M. (2012). An Economic Analysis of Coopetitive Training Investments for Insurance Agents. In *Advances in Computational Intelligence: 14th International Conference on Information Processing and Management of Uncertainty in Knowledge-Based Systems, IPMU 2012*. Springer-Verlag. doi:10.1007/978-3-642-31724-8_61

Okura, M. (2007). Coopetitive Strategies of Japanese Insurance Firms: A Game-Theory Approach. *International Studies of Management & Organization*, *37*(2), 53–69. doi:10.2753/IMO0020-8825370203

Okura, M. (2008). Why Isnt the Accident Information Shared? A Coopetition Perspective. *Management Research*, *6*(3), 219–225. doi:10.2753/JMR1536-5433060305

Olsen, M. C., Slotegraaf, R. J., & Chandukala, S. R. (2014). Green claims and message frames: How green new products change brand attitude. *Journal of Marketing*, *78*(5), 119–137. doi:10.1509/jm.13.0387

Omokhodion, F., Omokhodion, S., & Odusote, T. (2006). Perceptions of child labour among working children in Ibadan, Nigeria. *Child: Care, Health and Development*, *32*(3), 281–286. doi:10.1111/j.1365-2214.2006.00585.x PMID:16634973

One Green Planet. (n.d.). Retrieved from http://www.onegreenplanet.org/channel/vegan-food/

Organ, D. W. (1988). *Organizational citizenship behavior: The good soldier syndrome*. Lexington, MA: Lexington Books.

Oscar Green. (2015). *Oscar Green 2015 WeGreen a Muscolo di Grano*. Retrieved October 2, 2015, from http://www.oscargreen.it/notizie/oscar-green-2015-a-muscolo-di-grano-per-wegreen/

Ottman, J. (2011). *The new rules of green marketing: Strategies, tools, and inspiration for sustainable branding*. San Francisco: Berrett-Koehler Publishers.

Ottman, J. A. (1992). Industrys response to green consumerism. *The Journal of Business Strategy*, *13*(4), 3–7. doi:10.1108/eb039498 PMID:10120307

Ottman, J. A., Stafford, E. R., & Hartman, C. L. (2006). Avoiding green marketing myopia: Ways to improve consumer appeal for environmentally preferable products. *Environment: Science and Policy for Sustainable Development*, *48*(5), 22–36. doi:10.3200/ENVT.48.5.22-36

Padula, G., & Dagnino, G. B. (2007). Untangling the Rise of Coopetition: The Intrusion of Competition in a Cooperative Game Structure. *International Studies of Management & Organization, 37*(2), 32–53. doi:10.2753/IMO0020-8825370202

Parlak, M. & Ozaslan Parlak, A. (2010): Measurement of splash erosion in different cover crops. *Turkish Journal of Field Crops, 15*(2), 169-173.

Patten, D. N. (1990). The market reaction to social responsibility disclosures: The case of the Sullivan principles signings. *Accounting, Organizations and Society, 15*(6), 575–587. doi:10.1016/0361-3682(90)90035-S

Pauwels, M., & Rogiers, V. (2010). Human health safety evaluation of cosmetics in the EU: A legally imposed challenge to science. *Toxicology and Applied Pharmacology, 243*(2), 260–274. doi:10.1016/j.taap.2009.12.007 PMID:20006634

Pearce, D. W. (1976). *Charging for Noise*. Paris: OECD.

Peattie, K., & Charter, M. (2003). Green marketing. *The Marketing Book, 5*, 726–755.

Peattie, K., & Crane, A. (2005). Green marketing: Legend, myth, farce or prophesy? *Qualitative Market Research: An International Journal, 8*(4), 357–370. doi:10.1108/13522750510619733

Penning, A. (2013). *Demand for organic beauty to grow over $13 billion by 2018, report says*. Retrieved October 25, 2015, from http://www.cosmeticsandtoiletries.com/formulating/category/natural/Demand-for-Organic-Beauty-to-Grow-to-Over-13-Billion-by-2018-Report-Says-213160491.html

Pesamaa, O., & Eriksson, P. E. (2010). Coopetition among Nature-based Tourism Firms: Competition at Local Level and Cooperation at Destination Level. In Coopetition: Winning Strategies for the 21st Century. Edward Elgar Publishing.

Petcu, M. (2003). *Analiza economico-financiară a întreprinderii*. Bucureşti: Ed. Economică.

Petroff, A. (2015). Processed meat causes cancer, says WHO. *CNNMoney (London)*. Retrieved October 26, 2015, from http://money.cnn.com/2015/10/26/news/red-meat-processed-cancer-world-health-organization/

Peugeot, S. A.Group. (2014). *CSR Report 2014*. PSA Peugeot Citroën.

Pfeffer, J., & Salancik, G. R. (1978). *The External Control of Organizations: A Resource Dependence Perspective*. New York: Harper & Row.

Philippe, M., Didillon, B., & Gilbert, L. (2012). Industrial commitment to green and sustainable chemistry: Using renewable materials & developing eco-friendly processes and ingredients in cosmetics. *Green Chemistry, 14*(4), 952–956. doi:10.1039/c2gc16341a

Pigou, A. C. (1920). *The economics of Welfare*. London: Macmillan.

Pimentel, D., & Pimentel, M. (2003). Sustainability of meat-based and plant-based diets and the environment. *The American Journal of Clinical Nutrition, 78*, 660S–663S. Retrieved from http://ajcn.nutrition.org/content/78/3/660S.full PMID:12936963

Pine, R., & Phillips, P. A. (2005). Performance comparisons of hotels in China. *International Journal of Hospitality Management, 24*(1), 57–73. doi:10.1016/j.ijhm.2004.04.004

Pippo, R. (2011). *Economia dell'energia*. Bologna: Il Mulino.

Pitman, S. (2010). *Key cosmetics players to sustainability as way out of recession*. Retrieved November 7, 2015, from http://www.cosmeticsdesign-europe.com/Business-Financial/Key-cosmetics-players-point-to-sustainability-as-way-out-of-recession

Podsakoff, P. M., MacKenzie, S. B., Paine, J. B., & Bachrach, D. G. (2000). Organizational citizenship behaviors: A critical review of the theoretical and empirical literature and suggestions for future research. *Journal of Management, 26*(3), 513–563. doi:10.1177/014920630002600307

Polonsky, M. J. (1994). An introduction to green marketing. *Electronic Green Journal, 1*(2), 1–10.

Polonsky, M. J., & Rosenberger, P. J. III. (2001). Reevaluating green marketing: A strategic approach. *Business Horizons, 44*(5), 21–30. doi:10.1016/S0007-6813(01)80057-4

Poole, M. S., Van de Ven, A. H., Dooley, K., & Holmes, M. E. (2000). *Organizational Change and Innovation Process*. Oxford, UK: Oxford Univ. Press.

Popescul, D., & Georgescu, M. (2015). Social Networks Security in Universities: Challenges and Solutions. *Scientific Annals of the "Alexandru Ioan Cuza" University of Iaşi Economic Sciences, 62*(SI), 53-63.

Popović, V. (2010). Agrotehnički i agroekološki uticaji na proizvodnju semena pšenice, kukuruza i soje. Doktorska disertacija, Univerzitet u Beogradu, Poljoprivredni fakultet, Beograd.

Popović, V., Vidić, M., Tatić, M., Zdjelar, G., Glamočlija, Đ., & Kostić, M. (2012): Uticaj folijarne ishrane na prinos i kvalitet soje proizvedene u organskoj proizvodnji. Zbornik radova Instituta PKB Agroekonomik, Beograd.

Popović, V., Sikora, V., Glamočlija, Đ., Ikanović, J., Filipović, V., Tabaković, M., & Simić, D. (2013). Influence of agro-ecological conditions and foliar fertilization on yield and yield components of buckwheat in conventional and organic cropping system. Biotechnology in Animal Husbandry. Institute for Animal Husbandry. *Belgrade-Zemun, 29*(3), 537–546.

Porter, M. (1985). *Competitive Advantage. Creating and Sustaining Superior Performance*. New York: Free Press.

Porter, M. E. (2001). Strategy and the Internet. *Harvard Business Review*, (March): 62–78. PMID:11246925

Postorino, M. N. (2010). Environmental effects of airport nodes: A methodological approach. *International Journal of Sustainable Development and Planning*, *5*(2), 192–204. doi:10.2495/SDP-V5-N2-192-204

Postorino, M. N., & Mantecchini, L. (2014). A transport carbon footprint methodology to assess airport carbon emissions. *Journal of Air Transport Management*, *37*, 76–86. doi:10.1016/j.jairtraman.2014.03.001

Postorino, M. N., & Mantecchini, L. (2016). A systematic approach to assess the effectiveness of airport noise mitigation strategies. *Journal of Air Transport Management*, *50*, 71–82. doi:10.1016/j.jairtraman.2015.10.004

Puckett, J., Westerwelt, S., Gutierrez, R., & Takamiya, Y. (2005). *The Digital Dump: Exporting Re-use and Abuse to Africa*. Seattle: Basel Action Network.

Quagli, A., & Teodori, C. (2005). *L'informativa volontaria per settori di attività*. Milano: Franco Angeli.

Quintana-Garcia, C., & Benavides-Velasco, C. A. (2004). Cooperation, Competition, and Innovative Capability: A Panel Data of European Dedicated Biotechnology Firms. *Technovation*, *24*(12), 927–938. doi:10.1016/S0166-4972(03)00060-9

Radipere, S., & Dhliwayo, S. (2014). The role of age and business size on small business performance in the South African small enterprise sector. *Problems and Perspectives in Management*, *12*(4), 7–12.

Radu, L.D. (2015a, February). Investments in Technological Innovations: A Literature Review of Organization Determinants. *European Scientific Journal*.

Radu, L.D. (2015b). Green Information Systems: New Trend of Information Systems Development from the Perspective of Sustainability Improvement. *Proceedings of Globalization and Higher Education in Economics and Business Administration*.

Radu, L. D. (2014). The Ecological Behaviour Related to Green Information and Communication Technology in Romanian Organizations. *The Romanian Statistical Review*, *4*, 73–88.

Ramirez, R., Melville, N., & Lawler, E. (2010). Information Technology Infrastructure, Organizational Process Redesign, and Business Value: An Empirical Ansalysis. *Decision Support Systems*, *49*(4), 417–429. doi:10.1016/j.dss.2010.05.003

Ramli, N. S. (2015). Immigrant entrepreneurs on the worlds successful global brands in the cosmetic industry. *Procedia: Social and Behavioral Sciences*, *195*, 113–122. doi:10.1016/j.sbspro.2015.06.417

Ravenscraft, D. J., & Scherer, F. M. (1987). Life after Takeover. *The Journal of Industrial Economics*, *36*(2), 147–156. doi:10.2307/2098409

Renault, S. A.Group. (2013). *CSR Report 2013*. Groupe Renault.

Renault, S. A.Group. (2014). *Registration Document 2014*. Groupe Renault.

Restovich, S. B., Andriulo, A. E., & Portela, S. I. (2012). Introduction of cover crops in a maize–soybean rotation of the Humid Pampas: Effect on nitrogen and water dynamics. *Field Crops Research*, *128*, 62–70. doi:10.1016/j.fcr.2011.12.012

Reynolds, P., & Miller, B. (1992). New firm gestation: Conception, birth, and implications for research. *Journal of Business Venturing*, *7*(5), 405–418. doi:10.1016/0883-9026(92)90016-K

Režňáková, M., & Karas, M. (2015). The Prediction Capabilities of Bankruptcy Models in a Different Environment: An example of the Altman Model under the Conditions in the V4 Countries. *Ekonomicky Casopis*, (06): 617–633.

Rife, C. L., & Zeinalib, H. (2003). Cold tolerance in oilseed rape over varying acclimation durations. *Crop Science*, *43*(1), 96–100. doi:10.2135/cropsci2003.9600

Robeco, S. A. M. (2015). *Measuring Intangibles. ROBECOSAM's Corporate Sustainability Assessment Methodology*. Zurich: RobecoSAM AG.

Robeco, S. A. M. (2015). *The Sustainability Yearbook 2015*. Zurich: RobecoSAM AG.

Robert, K. W., Parris, T. M., & Leiserowitz, A. A. (2005). What is Sustainable Development? Goals, Indicators, Values, and Practice. *Environment: Science and Policy for Sustainable Development*, *47*(3), 8–21. doi:10.1080/00139157.2005.10524444

Roberts, C. B. (1991). Environmental Disclosures: A Note on Reporting Practices in Mainland Europe. *Accounting, Auditing & Accountability Journal*, *4*(3), 09513579110005536. doi:10.1108/09513579110005536

Robertson, T. (1991). *Long-run impacts of cover crops on yield, farm income, and nitrogen recycling. Cover Crops for Clean Water*. Ankeny, IA: Soil and Water Conservation Society.

Robinson, M., Kleffner, A., & Bertels, S. (2011). Signaling Sustainability Leadership: Empirical Evidence of the Value of DJSI Membership. *Journal of Business Ethics*, *101*(3), 493–505. doi:10.1007/s10551-011-0735-y

Robu, V., Sandu, R. (2006). Problematica analizei performanţelor–o abordare critică în contextul teoriilor informaţiei şi guvernanţei corporative. *Revista Economie Teoretică şi Aplicată*, (8), 15-28.

Rodrigues, F., Souza, V., & Leitao, J. (2011). Strategic Coopetition of Global Brands: A Game Theory Approach to Nike + iPod Sport Kit Co-branding. *International Journal of Entrepreneurial Venturing*, *3*(4), 435–455. doi:10.1504/IJEV.2011.043387

Ross, L. W., & Byrd, K. A. (2011). Business Plan Competitions: Start-up "Idols" and Their Twenty-First Century Launch Pads. *Journal of Higher Education Theory and Practice*, *11*(4), 53–64.

Ruggero, S., & D'Angella, F. (2011). Strategie e performance delle imprese alberghiere di Milano. *Economia aziendale online, 2*(2), 209-221.

Russell, R., Atchison, M., & Brooks, R. (2008). Business plan competitions in tertiary institutions: Encouraging entrepreneurship education. *Journal of Higher Education Policy and Management, 30*(2), 123–138. doi:10.1080/13600800801938739

Ryan, M. A., & Tinnesand, M. (2000). *Introduction to green chemistry*. Washington, DC: American Chemical Society.

Sacchi Hunter, E. (n.d.). Muscolo di grano. *Cure Naturali*. Retrieved from http://www.curenaturali.it/muscolo-di-grano/4188

Sacconi, L. (2004). Corporate Social Responsibility (CSR) as a Model of 'Extended' Corporate Governance: An Explanation Based on the Economic Theories of Social Contract, Reputation and Reciprocal Conformism. *LIUC, Ethics, Law and Economics*, Paper No. 142.

Saha, M., & Darnton, G. (2005). Green companies or green con-panies: Are companies really green, or are they pretending to be? *Business and Society Review, 110*(2), 117–157. doi:10.1111/j.0045-3609.2005.00007.x

Saint Louis, C. (2015). Meat and Cancer: The W.H.O. Report and What You Need to Know. *The New York Times*. Retrieved October 26, 2015, from http://www.nytimes.com/interactive/2015/10/26/health/meat-cancer-who-report.html?_r=2

Saita, M. (2012). *Economia aziendale*. Milano: Giuffrè Editore.

Saita, M. (2015). *Economia d'azienda*. Milano: Giuffrè Editore.

Sakakibara, K. (1993). R&D Cooperation among Competitors: A Case Study of the VLSI Semiconductor Research Project in Japan. *Journal of Engineering and Technology Management, 10*(4), 393–407. doi:10.1016/0923-4748(93)90030-M

Sakakibara, M. (1997). Heterogeneity of firm capabilities and cooperative research and development: An empirical examination of motives. *Strategic Management Journal, 18*(S1), 143–164. doi:10.1002/(SICI)1097-0266(199707)18:1+<143::AID-SMJ927>3.3.CO;2-P

Sandberg, W. R. (1986). *New Venture Performance: The Role of Strategy and Industry Structure*. Lexington, MA: Lexington Books.

Santoro, G. (2015). Evaluating Performance in the Hotel Industry: An Empirical Analysis of Piedmont. *Journal of Investment and Management. Special Issue: Attractiveness and Governance of Tourist Destinations, 4*, 17–22.

Santos, N. Z. D., Dieckow, J., Bayer, C., Molin, R., Favaretto, N., Pauletti, V., & Piva, J. T. (2011). Forages, cover crops and related shoot and root additions in no-till rotations to C sequestration in a subtropical Ferralsol. *Soil & Tillage Research, 111*(2), 208–218. doi:10.1016/j.still.2010.10.006

Sariannidis, N., Koskosas, I., Kartalis, N., & Konteos, G. (2009). Macroeconomic Effects on D.J.S.I. - World Returns. *International Journal of Economic Sciences and Applied Research*, *2*(2), 95–110.

Sarkis, J., Koo, C., & Watson, R. (2013). Green information systems & technologies – this generation and beyond: Introduction to the special issue. *Information Systems Frontiers*, 1–10.

Sarrantonio, M. (2007). Selecting the Best Cover Crops for Your Farm. Managing Cover Crops Profitably. SARE, National Institute of Food and Agriculture, U.S. Department of Agriculture.

Scherer, F. M. (1973). The Determinants of Plant Sizes in Six Nations. *The Review of Economics and Statistics*, *55*(2), 135–145. doi:10.2307/1926988

Schipper, Y., Rietveld, P., & Nijkamp, P. (2001). Environmental externalities in air transport markets. *Journal of Air Transport Management*, *7*(3), 169–179. doi:10.1016/S0969-6997(01)00002-3

Schmalenbach, E. (1919). Grundlagen dynamischer Bilanzlehre. Zeitschrift für handelswissenschaftliche Forschung, 13.

Schoar, A. (2002). Effects of corporate diversification on productivity. *The Journal of Finance*, *57*(6), 2379–2403. doi:10.1111/1540-6261.00500

Schürmann, G., Schäfer, K., Jahn, C., Hoffmann, H., Bauerfeind, M., Fleuti, E., & Rappenglück, B. (2007). The impact of NO_x, CO and VOC emissions on the air quality of Zurich airport. *Atmospheric Environment*, *41*(1), 103–118. doi:10.1016/j.atmosenv.2006.07.030

Sclaunich, G. (2015). La Regione Calabria punta sul muscolo di grano per Expo. *Veggo anch'io*. Retrieved April 10, 2015, from http://veggoanchio.corriere.it/2015/04/10/expo-muscolo-di-grano-regione-calabria/

Secchi, D. (2006). The Italian experience in social reporting: An empirical analysis. *Corporate Social Responsibility and Environmental Management*, *13*(3), 135–149. doi:10.1002/csr.96

Seclì, R. (2007). *VEG-ECONOMY. Fondamenti, realtà e prospettive dell'impresa "senza crudeltà"*. Retrieved from http://www.societavegetariana.org/site/uploads/570e7bd1-6289-f2b9.pdf

Shanker, D. (2015). *The US meat industry's wildly successful, 40-year crusade to keep its hold on the American diet*. Retrieved October 22, 2015 from http://qz.com/523255/the-us-meat-industrys-wildly-successful-40-year-crusade-to-keep-its-hold-on-the-american-diet/

Shannak, R. O. (2015). The Impact of Implementing an Enterprise Resource Planning System on Organizational Performance Using Balanced Scorecard. *Journal of Management Research*, *8*(1), 37–54. doi:10.5296/jmr.v8i1.8523

Sharma, S., & Vredenburg, H. (1998). Proactive corporate environmental strategy and the development of competitively valuable organizational capabilities. *Strategic Management Journal*, *19*(8), 729–753. doi:10.1002/(SICI)1097-0266(199808)19:8<729::AID-SMJ967>3.0.CO;2-4

Shaver, K., & Scott, L. (1991). Person, process, choice: The psicology of new venture creation. Entrepreneurship. *Theory into Practice*, *16*(2), 23–45.

Shenoy, S., & Earatta, R. (2011). Green Software Development Model: An Approach towards Sustainable Software Development. *Proceedings of IEEE Annual India Conference (INDICON)*. doi:10.1109/INDCON.2011.6139638

Sherringham, K., & Unhelkar, B. (2011). Strategic Business Trends in the Context of Green ICT. In B. Unhelkar (Ed.), *Handbook of research on green ICT: technology, business, and social perspectives* (pp. 66–83). New York: IGI Global. doi:10.4018/978-1-61692-834-6.ch005

Shrivastava, P. (1994). Castrated environment: Greening organizational studies. *Organization Studies*, *15*(5), 705–726. doi:10.1177/017084069401500504

Shrivastava, P. (1995). Environmental Technologies and Competitive Advantage. *Strategic Management Journal*, *16*(S1), 183–200. doi:10.1002/smj.4250160923

Shy, O. (1995). *Industrial Organization: Theory and Applications*. Cambridge, MA: The MIT Press.

Siegel, D. S. (2009). Green management matters only if it yields more green: An economic/strategic perspective. *The Academy of Management Perspectives*, *23*(3), 5–16. doi:10.5465/AMP.2009.43479260

Sikora, V., Filipović, V., Berenji, J., & Popović, V. (2013). Agro-biological Traits of Common Millet (Panicum miliaceum L.) Genotypes in Regular and Stubble Crop. Ratarstvo i povrtarstvo / Field and Vegetable Crops research. Institute of Field and Vegetable Crops, Novi Sad.

Simon, F. L. (1992). Marketing green products in the triad. *The Columbia Journal of World Business*, *27*(3-4), 268–285.

Skouloudis, A., Evangelinos, K., & Kourmousis, F. (2010). Assessing non-financial reports according to the Global Reporting Initiative guidelines: Evidence from Greece. *Journal of Cleaner Production*, *18*(5), 426–438. doi:10.1016/j.jclepro.2009.11.015

Smith, A., Nutt, D., & Wilson, S. (2002). Noise and insomnia: a study of community noise exposure. sleep disturbance. noise sensitivity and subjective reports on health. Centres for Occupational and Health Psychology, Cardiff University; Psychopharmacology Unit, University of Bristol.

Smith, R. F. (2005). *Mustard cover crops to optimize crop rotations for lettuce production*. California Lettuce Research Board.

Snapp, S. S., Swinton, S. M., Labarta, R., Mutch, D., Black, J. R., Leep, R., & O'Neil, K. et al. (2005). Evaluating cover crops for benefits, costs and performance within cropping system niches. *Agronomy Journal*, *97*(1), 322–332.

Società Scientifica di Nutrizione Vegetariana. (n.d.). Retrieved from http://www.scienzavegetariana.it/

Solomons, D. (1974). Corporate social performance: a new dimension in accounting reports? In H. Edey & B.S. Yamey (Eds.), Debits, Credits, Finance and Profits. London: Sweet & Maxwell.

Song, H. S., Kyeong Kim, J., & Kim, S. H. (2001). Mining the change of customer behavior in an Internet shopping mall. *Expert Systems with Applications*, *21*(3), 157–168. doi:10.1016/S0957-4174(01)00037-9

Sormunen-Cristian, R., Taponen, S., & Saastamoinen, I. (2008). Yellow-flowered lucerne: Properties and influence on performance and reproduction of ewes. *Agricultural and Food Science*, *7*(4), 437–446.

Spatacean, I. O. (2015). Ensuring Business Continuity Assumption for Romanian Investment Firms–An Expression of Good Governance in Financial Reporting. *Procedia Economics and Finance*, *26*, 967–974. doi:10.1016/S2212-5671(15)00917-X

Stark, J. C. (1995). *Development of sustainable potato production systems for the Pacific NW*. SARE Project report #LW91-029. Western Region SARE. Retrieved from www.sare.org/projects

Staying Vegan. (2010). *Is eating vegan more expensive than a "normal" diet?* Retrieved April 26, 2010, from http://stayingvegan.com/2010/04/is-eating-vegan-more-expensive-than-a-normal-diet/

Ştefănescu, A. (2005). *Performanţa financiară a întreprinderii între realitate şi creativitate*. Bucureşti: Ed. Economică.

Stein, H. D. (2010). Literature Overview on the Field of Co-opetition. *Verslas: Teorija ir Praktika, 11*(3), 256-265.

Steinmaus, S., Elmore, C. L., Smith, R. J., Donaldson, D., Weber, E. A., Roncoroni, J. A., & Miller, P. R. M. (2008). Mulched cover crops as an alternative to conventional weed management systems in vineyards. *Weed Research*, *48*(3), 273–281. doi:10.1111/j.1365-3180.2008.00626.x

Stekler, H. O. (1964). The Variability of Profitability with Size of Firm. *Journal of the American Statistical Association*, *59*, 1183–1193.

Steurer, R., Langer, M. E., Konrad, A., & Martinuzzi, A. (2005). Corporations, Stakeholders and Sustainable Development I: A Theoretical Exploration of Business–Society Relations. *Journal of Business Ethics*, *61*(3), 263–281. doi:10.1007/s10551-005-7054-0

Stiles, J. (2001). Strategic Alliances, in Rethinking Strategy. Sage Publications.

Storer, D. J. (1988). *Entrepreneurship and new firm*. Routledge.

Stratulat A.A.(2009). Simularea Riscului Financiar prin Metoda Altmanin, Buletinul Ştiinţific Al Universităţii Creştine "Dimitrie Cantemir". *Braşov, 10*(2), 244.

Stuart, T. E. (2000). Interorganizational Alliances and the Performance of Firms: A Study of Growth and Innovation Rates in High-technology Industry. *Strategic Management Journal*, *21*(8), 791–811. doi:10.1002/1097-0266(200008)21:8<791::AID-SMJ121>3.0.CO;2-K

Sullivan, P. (1999). Intercropping Principies and Production Practices. Agronomy Systems Guide. Appropriate Technology Transfer for Rural Areas. Fayetteville, AR: ATTRA. Retrieved from http://www.attra.org/attra-pub/intercrop.html

Sun, S., Zhang, J., & Lin, H. (2008). Evolutionary Game Analysis on the Effective Co-opetition Mechanism of Partners within High Quality Pork Supply Chain. *Service Operations and Logistics, and Informatics, 2008, IEEE/SOLI 2008. IEEE International Conference on*, (pp. 2066-2071). IEEE.

Sweha, F. (1982). Kohl along history in medicine and cosmetics. *Histoire des Sciences Medicales, 17*(2), 182–183. PMID:11612287

Swidi, A., Cheng, W., Hassan, M. G., Al-Hosam, A., & Mohd Kassim, A. W. (2010). The mainstream cosmetics industry in Malaysia and the emergence, growth, and prospects of halal cosmetics.*The Third International Conference on International Studies.*

Tabara, N., & Dicu, R. M. (2011). Indicatori de performanţă în contextul reglementărilor contabile internaţionale. *EIRP Proceedings, 2.*

Tacito, P. C. (98). *De origine et situ Germanorum.* Mondadori.

Taleby, M., & Way, T. (2009). Methods, Metrics and Motivation for a Green Computer Science Program.*Proceedings of the 40th ACM technical symposium on Computer science education*, (pp. 362-366). doi:10.1145/1508865.1508995

Teece, D. J. (2014). The foundations of enterprise performance: Dynamic and ordinary capabilities in an (economic) theory of firms. *The Academy of Management Perspectives, 28*(4), 328–352. doi:10.5465/amp.2013.0116

The Vegan Society. (n.d.). *Why go vegan?* Retrieved from https://www.vegansociety.com/try-vegan/why-go-vegan

The Vegetarian Resource Group. (n.d.). Retrieved from https://www.vrg.org/nutshell/market.htm

The World Commission on Environment and Development. (1987). *Our Common Future, New York.* Oxford University Press.

Thomas, K. (n.d.). *Dairy sustainability made me rethink being vegan.* Dairy Council of Utah & Nevada. Retrieved from http://thecowlocale.com/2014/04/22/dairy-sustainability-made-me-rethink-being-vegan/

Timmons, J. (1990). *New venture creation* (3rd ed.). Homewood, IL: R.D. Irwin.

Tinker, T. (Ed.). (1984). Social Accounting for Corporations. Private Enterprises versus Public Interest. Manchester, UK: Manchester University Press.

Ţole, M. (2000). Analiza economico-financiară a firmelor. Ed. Fundaţiei "Romania de Mâine".

Tosti, G., Benincasa, P., Farneselli, M., Pace, R., Tei, F., Guiducci, M., & Thorup-Kristensen, K. (2012). Green manuring effect of pure and mixed barley–hairy vetch winter cover crops on maize and processing tomato N nutrition. *European Journal of Agronomy*, *43*, 136–146. doi:10.1016/j.eja.2012.06.004

Troie, L., Zaharia, O., Roman, M., & Hurduzeu, M. (2003). *Analiza statistică a activității economice şi a gestiunii financiare a întreprinderii.* Bucureşti: Ed. Economică.

Tsubo, M., Walker, S., & Ogindo, H. O. (2005). A simulation model of cereal–legume intercropping systems for semi-arid regions I. Model development. *Field Crops Research*, *93*(1), 10–22. doi:10.1016/j.fcr.2004.09.002

Tu, J. C., & Huang, D. S. (2015). Analysis on the Relationship between Green Accounting and Green Design for Enterprises. *Sustainability*, *7*(5), 6264–6277. doi:10.3390/su7056264

Turnbull, S. (2015). *How to eat vegan at any restaurant (and not order salad).* Retrieved June 22, 2015, from http://itdoesnttastelikechicken.com/2015/06/22/eat-vegan-restaurant-order-salad/

Turner, P., Kane, R., & Jackson, C. (2015). Implementing performance improvement through the enterprise culture. *British Journal of Healthcare Management*, *21*(11), 523–527. doi:10.12968/bjhc.2015.21.11.523

Turner, R. K., Pearce, D. W., & Bateman, I. (1993). *Environmental Economics. An elementary introduction.* Baltimore, MD: Johns Hopkins University Press.

Turner, R. K., Pearce, D., & Bateman, I. (1994). *Environmental economics: an elementary introduction.* Harvester Wheatsheaf.

Ugrenović, V. & Filipović, V, (2012). *Značaj eko koridora u organskoj proizvodnji.* V naučno-stručni simpozijum iz selekcije i semenarstva Društva selekcionara i semenara Srbije, Vršac, Srbija.

Ugrenović, V., Bačić, B., Filipović, V., & Vučković, J. (2011). Buvač (Pyrethrum cinerariaefolium Trev.) korisna biljka u sistemu organske proizvodnje. XI Savetovanje o zaštiti bilja, Zlatibor, 158-159.

Ugrenović, V., Filipović, V., Glamočlija, Đ., Subić, J., Kostić M. & Jevđović R. (2012). *Pogodnost korišćenja morača za izolaciju u organskoj proizvodnji.* Ratarstvo i povrtarstvo / Field and Vegetable Crops Research, Novi Sad.

Ugrenović, V. (2015). *Pokrovni usevi u organskoj proizvodnji. In Alternativne ratarske biljke u konvencionalnom i organskom sistemu gajenja. Monografija, Institut za primenu nauke u poljoprivredi* (pp. 176–185). Beograd: Srbija.

Ugrinović, M., Girek, Z., Zdravković, J., Đorđević, M., Oljača, S., Brdar-Jokanović, M., & Zečević, B. (2014). Postrni usev rotkve u organskom sistemu gajenja. *Zbornik naučnik radova Instituta PKB Agroekonomik, 20*(1-4), 129-138.

Unal, A., Hu, Y., Chang, M. E., Odman, M. T., & Russell, A. G. (2005). Airport related emissions and impacts on air quality: Application to the Atlanta International Airport. *Atmospheric Environment, 39*(32), 5787–5798. doi:10.1016/j.atmosenv.2005.05.051

UNEP. (2010). *Recycling – from E-waste to Resources*. Berlin, Germany: Oktoberdruck AG.

Unerman, J. (2000). Methodological issues: Reflections on quantification in corporate social reporting content analysis. *Accounting, Auditing & Accountability Journal, 13*(5), 667–680. doi:10.1108/09513570010353756

United Nations, European Commission, International Monetary Fund, Organization for Economic Cooperation and Development, & World Bank (2003). The Handbook of National Integrated Environmental and Economic Accounting. New York: ONU.

United Nations. (1992). *Agenda 21.United Nations Conference on Environment & Development, Rio de Janerio*, Brazil.

United States Department of Labor, Bureau of Labor Statistics. (n.d.). *Business Employment Dynamics, Entrepreneurship and the U.S. Economy*. Author.

Universo Vegano. (n.d.). Retrieved from http://www.universovegano.it/

Upham, P., Thomas, C., Gillingwater, D., & Raper, D. (2003). Environmental capacity and airport operations: Current issues and future prospects. *Journal of Air Transport Management, 9*(3), 145–151. doi:10.1016/S0969-6997(02)00078-9

Uyeno, D., Hamilton, S. W., & Biggs, A. J. (1993). Density of residential land use and the impact of airport noise. *Journal of Transport Economics and Policy, 27*(1), 3–18.

Vallance, S., Perkins, H. C., & Dixon, J. E. (2011). What is social sustainability? A clarification of concepts. *Geoforum, 42*(3), 342–348. doi:10.1016/j.geoforum.2011.01.002

Van Dam, Y. K., & Apeldoorn, P. A. (1996). Sustainable marketing. *Journal of Macromarketing, 16*(2), 45–56. doi:10.1177/027614679601600204

Van de Ven, A. H. (1992). Longitudinal Methods for studying the process of entrepreneurship. In D.L. Sexton & J.D. Kasarda (Eds.), The State of the Art of Entrepreneurship. Boston: PWS-Kent Publisher.

Van de Ven, A. H., & Engleman, R. M. (2004). Event- and outcome-driven explanations of entrepreneurship. *Journal of Business Venturing, 19*(3), 343–358. doi:10.1016/S0883-9026(03)00035-1

Van de Ven, A. H., & Poole, M. S. (1995). Explaining development and change in organizations. *Academy of Management Review, 20*(3), 510–540. doi:10.2307/258786

Van Marrewijk, M. (2003). Concept and definitions of CSR and corporate sustainability: Between agency and communion. *Journal of Business Ethics, 44*(2), 95–105. doi:10.1023/A:1023331212247

Vandermeer, J. H. (1989). The Ecology of Intercropping. Cambridge University Press. doi:10.1017/CBO9780511623523

Vasilescu, G. (2002). Analiza statistică economică şi metode de evaluare a firmei. Ed.Didactică şi Pedagogică, Bucureşti.

Vegan Outreach. (2014). *What Do Vegans Eat?* Retrieved from http://veganoutreach.org/what-to-eat/

Vegan Starter Kit. (n.d.). *Eating*. Retrieved from http://vegankit.com/eat/

Veganblog. (2015). Muscolo di grano sbriciolato. *Ricette di Terra*. Retrieved December 22, 2015, from http://www.veganblog.it/2015/12/22/muscolo-di-grano-sbriciolato/

Vegans of Color. (2009). *Does being vegan cost more money?* Retrieved February, 20, 2009, from https://vegansofcolor.wordpress.com/2009/02/20/does-being-vegan-cost-more-money/

Venkataraman, S., Van de Ven, A. H., Buckeye, J., & Hudson, R. (1990). Starting up in turbulent environment: A process model of failure among firms wih high customer dependence. *Journal of Business Venturing*, *5*(5), 277–296. doi:10.1016/0883-9026(90)90006-F

Vermiglio, F. (Ed.). (2000). Nuovi strumenti di comunicazione aziendale. Confronto di esperienze in tema di bilancio sociale. Torino. Giappichelli.

Vesper, K. H. (1990). *New Venture Strategies* (2nd ed.). Englewood Cliffs, NJ: Prentice Hall.

Villalonga, B. (2004). Diversification discount or premium? New evidence from the business information tracking series. *The Journal of Finance*, *59*(2), 475–502. doi:10.1111/j.1540-6261.2004.00640.x

von Hippel, E. (1987). Cooperation between Rivals: Informal Know-how Trading. *Research Policy*, *16*(6), 291–302. doi:10.1016/0048-7333(87)90015-1

Vykoukal, J., Wolf, M., & Beck, R. (2009). Does Green It Matter? Analysis of the Relationship between Green It and Grid Technology from a Resource-Based View Perspective.*Proceedings of the Pacific Asia Conference on Information Systems*.

Walker, P., Rhubart-Berg, P., Mckenzie, S., Kelling, K., & Lawrencw, R. S. (2005). Public health implications of meat production and consumption. *Public Health Nutrition*, *8*(4), 348–356. doi:10.1079/PHN2005727 PMID:15975179

Walker, R. H., & Hanson, D. J. (1998). Green marketing and green places: A taxonomy for the destination marketer. *Journal of Marketing Management*, *14*(6), 623–639. doi:10.1362/026725798784867671

Walley, K. (2007). Coopetition: An Introduction to the Subject and an Agenda for Research. *International Studies of Management & Organization*, *37*(2), 11–31. doi:10.2753/IMO0020-8825370201

Wang, K. H., Hooks, C. R. R., & Marahatta, S. P. (2011). Can using a strip-tilled cover cropping system followed by surface mulch practice enhance organisms higher up in the soil food web hierarchy? *Applied Soil Ecology*, *49*, 107–117. doi:10.1016/j.apsoil.2011.06.008

WCED. (1987). *Our Common Future. World Commission on Environment and Development.* Oxford University Press.

Weaver, S., Ellen, P., & Mathiassen, L. (2015). Contextualist Inquiry into Organizational Citizenship: Promoting Recycling Across Heterogeneous Organizational Actors. *Journal of Business Ethics*, *129*(2), 413–428. doi:10.1007/s10551-014-2165-0

Weick, K. E. (1972). *The social Psychology of Organizing* (2nd ed.). New York: Random House.

Wen, C. T., & Chen, Y. W. (2007). The innovation process of entrepreneurial teams in dynamic business plan competition: From sense-making perspective. *International Journal of Technology Management*, *39*(3/4), 346–363. doi:10.1504/IJTM.2007.013505

Werther, W. B., & Chandler, D. (2011). Strategic Corporate Social Responsibility: Stakeholders in a Global Environment. *Sage (Atlanta, Ga.).*

Wheeler, L. (2015). Vegan diet best for planet. *The Hill*. Retrieved May 4, 2015, from http://thehill.com/regulation/237767-vegan-diet-best-for-planet-federal-report-says

Wheeler, D. (1993). Auditing for sustainability: Philosophy and practice of The Body Shop International. *Eco-Management and Auditing*, *1*(1), 10–16. doi:10.1002/ema.170

White, L., & Lee, J. G. (2009). Operational research and sustainable development: Tackling the social dimension. *European Journal of Operational Research*, *193*(3), 683–692. doi:10.1016/j.ejor.2007.06.057

WHO. (2015). *Q&A on the carcinogenicity of the consumption of red meat and processed meat.* Retrieved October, 2015, from http://www.who.int/features/qa/cancer-red-meat/en/

Whole Foods Market. (n.d.). Retrieved from http://www.wholefoodsmarket.com/healthy-eating/special-diets/vegan

Wick, A. (2011). The Conscious Case Against Veganism. *Ecosalon*. Retrieved March 17, 2011, from http://ecosalon.com/reasons-not-to-be-vegan/

Wijewardena, H., Nanayakkara, G., & De Zoysa, A. (2008). The owner/managers mentality and the financial performance of SMEs. *Journal of Small Business and Enterprise Development*, *15*(1), 150–161. doi:10.1108/14626000810850892

Wijnen, R. A. A., & Visser, H. G. (2003). Optimal departure trajectories with respect to sleep disturbance. *Aerospace Science and Technology*, *7*(1), 81–91. doi:10.1016/S1270-9638(02)01183-5

Wilkinson, I., & Young, L. (2002). On Cooperating: Firms, Relations and Networks. *Journal of Business Research*, *55*(2), 123–132. doi:10.1016/S0148-2963(00)00147-8

Williamson, D., Lynch-Wood, G., & Ramsay, J. (2006). Drivers of Environmental Behaviour in Manufacturing SMEs and the Implications for CSR. *Journal of Business Ethics*, *67*(3), 317–330. doi:10.1007/s10551-006-9187-1

Willis, A. (2003). The Role of the Global Reporting Initiatives Sustainability Reporting Guidelines in the Social Screening of Investments. *Journal of Business Ethics*, *43*(3), 233–237. doi:10.1023/A:1022958618391

Wilmshurst, T. D., & Frost, G. R. (2000). Corporate environmental reporting: A test of legitimacy theory. *Accounting, Auditing & Accountability Journal*, *13*(1), 10–26. doi:10.1108/09513570010316126

Wilson, J. S. (1858). On the general and gradual desiccation of the earth and atmosphere. *Proceedings of the British Association for the Advancement of Science.*

Wong, V., Turner, W., & Stoneman, P. (1996). Marketing strategies and market prospects for environmentally-friendly consumer products. *British Journal of Management*, *7*(3), 263–281. doi:10.1111/j.1467-8551.1996.tb00119.x

Working Group on Environmental Auditing. (2010). *Environmental Accounting: Current Status and Options for SAIs*. INTOSAI.

World Health Organization (WHO). (2011). *Burden of disease from environmental noise. Regional Office for Europe JRC*, European Commission.

Worldwatch Institute. (2004). Is Meat Sustainable? *World Watch Magazine, 17*(4). Retrieved from http://www.worldwatch.org/node/549

Yu, J., Williams, E., Ju, M., & Yang, Y. (2010). Forecasting Global Generation of Obsolete Personal Computers. *Environmental Science & Technology*, *44*(9), 3232–3237. doi:10.1021/es903350q PMID:20302363

Yu, K. N., Cheung, Y. P., Cheung, T., & Henry, R. C. (2004). Identifying the impact of large urban airports on local air quality by nonparametric regression. *Atmospheric Environment*, *38*(27), 4501–4507. doi:10.1016/j.atmosenv.2004.05.034

Zanni, M. (2013). Il Muscolo di grano: una valida e gustosa alternativa alla carne. *Saggi e Assaggi*. Retrieved January 30, 2013, from http://www.saggieassaggi.it/il-muscolo-di-grano-una-valida-e-gustosa-alternativa-alla-carne/

Zappa, G. (1937). *Il reddito d'impresa: Scritture doppie, conti e bilanci di aziende commerciali.* Milano: Giuffrè.

Zdravković, J., Mijatović, M., Pavlović, N., Ugrinović, M., & Adžić, S. (2012): Prvi koraci ka organskoj proizvodnji povrća. Institut za povrtarstvo, Smederevska Palanka i Ministarstvo poljoprivrede, šumarstva i vodoprivrede Republike Srbije, Beograd.

Zhang, G., Chan, K., Li, G., & Huang, G. (2011). The effects of stubble retention and tillage practices on surface soil structure and hydraulic conductivity of a loess soil. *Acta Ecologica Sinica*, *31*(6), 298–302. doi:10.1016/j.chnaes.2011.07.006

Zikopoulos, P., deRoos, D., Bienko, C., Andrews, M., & Buglio, R. (2014). *Big Data Beyond the Hype: A Guide to Conversations for Today's Data Center*. McGraw-Hill Professional.

About the Contributors

Andrei Jean-Vasile is Associate professor at Petroleum -Gas University of Ploiesti, Department of Business Administration. He holds a PhD in economics at National Institute of Economics Research - Romanian Academy of Sciences. He holds a B.S. degree in Administrative Sciences (2005) and in Banks and Finances (2007) from the Petroleum and Gas University of Ploiesti. He has M.A. degree in Economics, Administrative and Business Management (2007) earned at the same university. Jean Andrei is Editor-in-Chief of International Journal of Sustainable Economies Management (USA), Associate Editor of Economics of Agriculture (Ekonomika poljoprivrede) -Serbia, scientific reviewer for International Business Information Management Association Conferences – IBIMA. He is also member of scientific organizations as: The Balkan Scientific Association of Agrarian Economists, Serbia (December 2008). Particularly issues like business investments process, economic efficiency and valuing economic and human potential are among his research and scientific interests, where he has published articles (over 20), scientific books (4) and conferences presentations.

Domenico Nicolò is Prof. of Economia Aziendale (Business Economics and Management). Head Degree in Economics. Director/Scientific Coordinator of the University Lab ReTMES.

* * *

Alexandra Alecu graduated the Faculty of Economics Sciences from Petroleum-Gas University of Ploiesti (2015), Accountancy and Economic Informatics Specialization, and currently, she is perusing the MA degree in business administration field at the same faculty. She has attended and presented scientific papers at the young economist scientific conferences where she proved skills in field of business and sustainable economics. She became member of Lab ReTMES - Research Team for Mediterranean Entrepreneurship and Startups, Italy as a young researcher. She is passionate in studying the economic phenomena and its implication among economic and business structures where she proofed specific skills and earned two important prizes.

David Carfì is a Researcher, Assistant Professor and Lecturer of: Advanced Linear Algebra and Functional Analysis with Applications to Economics, Finance, Relativity and Quantum Mechanics; Game Theory and Applications to Economics, Finance, Social Sciences and Industrial Organization; Differential Geometry and Applications to Physics, Relativity, Financial Mathematics and Mathematical Finance; Decision Theories and Applications to Economics (micro and macro), Finance and Industrial Organization; Laurent Schwartz Theory of Distributions and Applications to Physics, Quantum Mechanics, Finance and Economics; Coopetition in Game Theory and Applications to Economics, Finance and Industrial Organization; Mathematics and Music, Algebraic structures in Music composition. He is a classic concert pianist and composer.

Massimo Costa is Associate Professor of Accounting at the University of Palermo, Dept. of Statistical, Business and Economic Sciences, qualified for Full Professor in Business Economics.

Alessia Donato is an engineer experienced in infrastructure and territorial defense with deep knowledge of operating systems and many software related to Engineering, such as Auto-cad, CDS, SAP, arc-view, KEN-PAVE, Civil Design and HEC-RAS. Expert in the use of Matlab, in particular on the use of genetic algorithms. Expert of TeX, of word processors and Microsoft office. She also studies and researches in theoretical engineering, probability theory, Game Theory and stochastic calculus applied to infrastructural design, Management and Economic theories.

Vladimir Filipović, PhD, a Research Associate with the Institute for Medicinal Plants Research "Dr Josif Pančić", Tadeuša Košćuška street 1, Belgrade, Serbia. At this Institute, he has been hired on several projects financed by the Ministry of Education, Science and Technical Development, as well as part of a team for creating several international, national and local studies and projects. His main fields of research cover the following issues: the enhancement of the production of industrial, medicinal, aromatic and spice plants, the maintenance of the collection of industrial, medicinal, aromatic and spice plants, introduction of less cultivated medicinal plants, seed production the processing of industrial, medicinal, aromatic and spice plants, treatment of the secondary waste produced by different processing and organic production of industrial, medicinal, aromatic and spice plants. He has published scientific research papers in national and international journals and in thematic proceeding, as well as chapters in several monographs.

Maria Vittoria Franceschelli is a PhD student in Business Administration and Management, University of Milano-Bicocca.

Luca Mantecchini received his MS in Civil Engineering from the University of Bologna (Italy) in 2000. In 2004 obtained his PhD in Transportation Engineering at the same university, where is Researcher in Transportation since 2005. His research activity is mainly focused on air transportation, sustainable transport and traffic engineering. He is involved in EU research projects on economic development of airport catchment areas, external costs of transport activities and airport de-carbonization. He is author or co-author of more than 40 scientific publications in referred journals and books.

Filippo Paganelli received his MS in Civil Engineering from the University of Bologna (Italy) in 2008 with a thesis on the sustainability of flight procedures at airports. He received PhD in Geomatics Engineering and Transport, earning further competences in competition and management of transport infrastructures and tenders, participating in numerous conferences both in Italy and abroad and collaborating in the drafting of publications and educational activities. Further experience has been gained in airport handling and freight logistic chain by road. Since 2013, he has been involved in European Projects on Economic Development of Airport Catchment Areas and External Costs of Transport Activities carried out by both Department of Architecture and Department of Civil Engineering of the University of Bologna, as well as Research Agreements with Local and National Institutions.

Dania Panuccio has a Master Degree in economics. She studies game theory applied to economics and finance. Specialized in planning legislation, she also researches in mathematical methods of economics and Social Sciences.

Maria Nadia Postorino, PhD in Transport, is Professor of Transport Engineering at the "Mediterranea" University of Reggio Calabria, representative for Equal Opportunities appointed by the Rector, component of the Scientific Committee of the Ecole Nationale des Ponts et Chaussées (Paris, France). She is reviewer for several international journals. Her research interests focus mainly on transport demand analysis, air transport systems and applications of computer science techniques to transport issues.

Laura-Diana Radu (b. September 26, 1978) received his BSc in Accounting and Information Systems (2001), M.Sc. in Business Information Systems (2003), PhD in Accounting (2006) from "Alexandru Ioan Cuza" University of Iasi. Now she is researcher in Research Department of Faculty of Economics and Business

Administration, "Alexandru Ioan Cuza" University of Iasi, Romania. Her current research interests include Digital Accounting, XBRL, Financial Auditing, Green ICT, and Business Information Systems. She has participated in over 30 international conferences in Romania and abroad (Morocco, Czech Republic, Greece, Egypt, Spain, Turkey, Malaysia, Ireland and Italy) and is the author of more than 40 scientific papers published in journals, conference proceedings or as book chapters.

Nur Suhaili Ramli is a PhD candidate in Management at the York Management School, University of York, UK who is expecting to submit her thesis in September 2016. She is a member of The Centre for Evolution of Global Business and Institutions (CEGBI), Association of Business Historians (ABH), and the European Business History Association (EBHA). She published book reviews, academic journals, and few other articles in newspapers on global brands in cosmetics, business history, marketing strategies and diaspora entrepreneurship. She was one of 20 sustainability-minded researchers for greenREACTIONS project funded by the Royal Society of Chemistry at Green Chemistry Centre of Excellence University of York. Her main research fields are in international business and marketing that particularly looking in business history, evolution of global brands, marketing strategies, and entrepreneurship.

Massimo Saita, PhD, is Professor in Business Administration and Corporate Strategy, Former Dean of the Business and Law School University of Milano-Bicocca.

Vladan Ugrenović, PhD, a Research Associate with the "Tamiš" Institute. He is currently working on several projects funded by the Ministry of Education, Science and Technological Development, and the Ministry of Agriculture and Environment of the Republic of Serbia, and has participated in a team that created several international, national and local strategies, studies and projects. His main area of research is related to ecological systems of agricultural and seed production. In 2008 he established an experimental field with the aim of conducting applied research in the field of organic production. The issues covered so far have been: agrobiodiversity, ecological corridors, cover crops, biocontrol and organic seed production. He has published several scientific papers in national and international journals, is the author of a technical solution in the field of organic production, and is editor of the collection of papers "Organic production and biodiversity".

Giuseppe Valenza is PhD student in Law and Economics, University Mediterranea of Reggio Calabria. His research activity is focused on financial accounting, accounting history, entrepreneurship and startups.

Index

G

H

I

L

M

N

O

P

R

S

T

W

www.ingramcontent.com/pod-product-compliance
Lightning Source LLC
LaVergne TN
LVHW080558300926
849162LV00005B/988